Orange County, Virginia Families

-Volume #2 -

Compiled by:
William Everett Brockman

Southern Historical Press, Inc.
Greenville, South Carolina

This volume was reproduced from
An 1957 edition located in the
Publisher's Private Library
Greenville, South Carolina

All rights reserved. No part of this publication may be reproduced,
stored in a retrieval system, transmitted in any form, posted
on to the web in any form or by any means without
the prior written permission of the publisher.

Please direct all correspondence and orders to:
www.southernhistoricalpress.com
or
SOUTHERN HISTORICAL PRESS, Inc.
PO Box 1267
Greenville, SC   29602-1267
southernhistoricalpress@gmail.com

Originally published: Minneapolis, MN, 1957
New Material Copyright 1986
    By: Southern Historical Press, Inc.
ISBN #0-89308-794-7
All rights Reserved.
Printed in the United States of America

INTRODUCTION TO SECOND EDITION OF ORANGE COUNTY
VIRGINIA FAMILIES, VOLUME II.

During the past month I have been on the go seeking confirmation of books already published and finding new data. In New York I searched for evidence of the report that the Brockmans had an interest in the land occupied by Trinity Church, but the law suit on this property was long and extended and did not give the names of the fifty litigants. Henry Brockman could well have been one of them. In Charlottesville, Virginia I had the help of Mrs. Mildred Marshall and the spouse of Eva Martin, the county clerk who is collecting all the data from law suits. The origin to the title of the 350 acres of land in Albermarle County owned by Samuel Brockman, the first, is still not solved, although he certainly acquired it when it was either a part of New Kent, Hanover or Louisa, although the Essex County deeds ran right up to this line and a conveyance could well have been made in error. Either it was bought and the deed lost or else it was inherited from former owners. This land, sold to John White in 1779 was next to Jason Bocock, who lived in the Priddy's Creek area. In 1806 Nimrod Branham, as executor of the estate of John White sold this 350 acres to Jason Bocock, adjoining the latter's property, and the tax records in the Land Book at Richmond show that Jason had 500 acres which most likely included the land bought from White's administrator.

In 1816 the Heirs of Jason Bocock sold off their father's land in a dozen transactions so that it is impossible to identify the purchaser of the Brockman land. In 1816 the Heirs sold 133 acres to Samuel Brockman (wife Ann Sims) and it is most likely that this was a part of the original plot as these old timers always went back to their ancestor's property to acquire it and die on it. Another tract was sold to Mildred Flint in 1820, and Richard Durrett's daughter, one of them married a Flint or Flynt. In 1824 another sale to Michie and in 1842 another to William Browning. The home of Samuel Brockman was apparently the old Sims homestead "Green Plains". March 2, 1798, the Commissioners of the County offered at auction, with the consent of Agatha widow of William Sims and the Heirs, the Sims homestead. Samuel Brockman bid in two-thirds of the total of 238 acres, the other one-third of 79 and three-quarters acres, was the widow's dower, that is Agatha the widow of Capt. William Sims, and this would include the homestead, Green Plains. With the consent of the widow and with a consent to the reversion, the children of William Sims gave up their interest in Green Plains to Samuel Brockman for a price. This was on November 8, 1799, and since he lived there for sometime and died and was buried there in 1807, it is obvious that this was the Green Plains property, and that Agatha the widow went to live there on her dower land with her son-in-law Samuel Brockman.

Curiosity as to the title of property of 370 acres is aroused by a deed May 2, 1775, D.B. 6, page 472, when Thomas Jones, son of Orlando Jones, who was ancestor to Martha Dandridge, and Patty his wife, Richard Durrett, and William Brockman, gave up their interest in the 370 acres to Jason Bocock for a price and it would appear that this deed reflects an inheritance of these three men. The elder Richard Durrett married Sarah Marshall, daughter of Elizabeth, a later one is said to have married a Terrill, and we don't know who were the wives of William Brockman and Thomas Jones. Were they all sisters? Thomas Jones left a Will at Orange April 28, 1788, naming two children Elizabeth and James, but wife Patty was not mentioned, therefore deceased. In 1777, Thomas Jones exchanged 57 acres in Albermarle for land owned by William Brockman in Orange. The elder Richard Durrett died and left a Will at Albermarle 1784, referred to in Wood's History of Albermarle, and this date ties in with the transfer of 370 acres in 1788. I searched the lower courts in York, James City and the files of the Virginia Gazette and found the administration of John Murre in the Isle of Wight in 1702. At Williamsburg I found evidence of the homestead of the Singletons, and the sale of the estate of Richard Singleton. There were also records of John, Daniel, who died at Orange, Anthony, Mary, John, and it is assumed because of the dates that Richard Hunt Singleton was spouse of Mary Brockman. At Bruton Church, in 1753, Sarah, Richard and Mary Singleton were baptized, which would be the right age to have been children of Mary Brockman Singleton. I saw the Bolling records at Williamsburg and John Bolling married a Brockman, and Mary Singleton's daughter married John Crittenden Webb, and they were in York, and there it was in plain print, John Brockman, buried by the Rev. Mr. Hudson from Bruton Church in 1696. Elizabeth Brockman married Anthony Street, and right there in Hanover were and are the Streets, so we now know that the Brockmans lived in the York area before moving up to King and Queen, and there was the Shurlow hundred area where Isaac Madison lived and the family moved up along with the Brockmans. Although a genealogist assured me that she had checked the records I found in plain writing that in 1737-39 Mrs. Brockman with two over 21, and John Brockman lived in the Thos Graves precinct in Orange, so that Mrs. Brockman was mother of Samuel and most likely Rebecca Salmon Brockman, and it is likely that grandson Samuel married Rebecker Salmon, and she died 1814. In the National Archives at Washington, I found that Jesse Brockman, probably son of Samuel and Mary Bell enlisted in the Revolution on Feb. 13, the same day as Major Brockman, and his death is recorded May 30-31, 1778 and that he enlisted for a year and received pay up to Feb. 16, 1779, when he was discharged. He was in the 7th Infantry under several different commanding officers. In June 1778 Major Brock is shown as having joined the 7th Infantry "since muster" and served in the 3rd., 5th., and 7th. Infantry and the war record is confused and each are called Brock and each Brockman, so it is fair to assume that there were two Major Brockmans in the Revolution and that when they were both in the 7th. one was called Brock to keep their pay separate, and the latter is shown as a waggoner. The first Major Brockman was discharged February 1779, but the second Major Brockman, this time, received pay in May 1779. To settle a long dispute, I could just say that the first Major son of John married Mary Patterson in 1779, soon after leaving the army and the second one married Nancy, daughter of John Mercer, formerly of Caroline but who left a Will at Duplin, S. C. naming daughter Nancy Brockman. Thomas Brockman of Albermarle signed his name boldly as Thomas Brockman, but poor Joseph who was stricken with palsy had to sign with an X. Thomas was 75 in 1834, and Joseph, 78 in 1721, John Brock or Brockman enlisted March 1, 1777, and died on the 18th. John Brockman (Elizabeth Burris) was appointed Lieut. 1777 and William Brockman son of John and Mary Collins Brockman was made a Lieut. Elizabeth Brockman, a daughter of William Brockman, Jr. and wife, Mary Smith, married a Harris and had children James (son Overton) Calvin, Mary Polly, who married William Mahannes. Elizabeth Harris, widow, married Samuel Mahannes May 28, 1816. Her marriage to Harris was Nov. 2, 1812. Deed Book 58, page 230, February 1859, has a deed from Heirs of Elizabeth Mahanes to Thomas Gilbert, Feb. 1859, which approximates her death. The heirs are shown as F. M., Cornelia E., Austin M., Emily A. Leake, C. P. Shepherd, and Mildred Shepherd.

October 15, 1957
Midland Bank Building,
Minneapolis, Minnesota.

W. E. Brockman

CONTENTS

Orange County Virginia Families

Volume II

	Page
Marriage Bonds	1
Importations	50
Military Commissions	57
Revolutionary Soldiers	64
Colonial Soldiers	66
Bonds and Administrations	68
Chancery Suits	73
Bonds, Beginning, 1730	74
Court Orders--Military Services	83
Military Claims	85
Brockmans of England and Virginia	87
Collins of King and Queen	105
The Gaydens	107
More About Sims	117
The Rhodes Family	118
Woolfolks of Virginia	124
The Merry's	126
Corrections to Previous Book	128
The Caves of Virginia	130
Gayden, Supplemental	133
Tithables from 1736	135

SUPPLEMENT TO VOLUME II

The Crosthwait's	148
Asa Brockman	157
Corrections	159
Terrett Family	165

Orange County, Virginia, Marriage Records

1747	Wyatt, Thom.	to	Edmonson, Sukey
1756			
Apr. 12	Crump, Benjamin	to	Price, Mary Barber
May 31	Dawson, Musgrave (clerk)	to	Waugh, Mary
Nov. 24	Robinson, John	to	Smith, Lucy
Dec. 4	Shropshire, John	to	Porter, Mary
Jan. 5	Marr, Alexander	to	Rucker, Sarah
Jan. 16	Robinson, James	to	Embry, Judy
Jan. 26	Smith, George	to	Luggett, Elizabeth
Mar. 10	Jones, Richard	to	Leonard, Grace
Oct. 3	Garnett, Thomas	to	Hawkins, Rachel
Nov. 7	Daniel, Reuben	to	Merry, Elizabeth
Nov. 24	Terrill, Edmund	to	Willis, Peggy
Dec. 15	Hyte, Jacob	to	Beale, Francis
1757			
Jan. 2	Bowen, Francis	to	Cristopher, Francis
Jan. 6	Green, Nicholas	to	Price, Elizabeth
Jan. 27	Robinson, William	to	Smith, Agnes
Jan. 21	Holland, George	to	Coleman, Mary
Apr. 5	Thomas, Roland	to	Thurston, Jane
Apr. 9	Thomas, Robert	to	Moore, Ann
1761			
Nov. 9	Moore, Francis, Jr.	to	Hawkins, Lucy
Dec. 18	Mathershed, Nathaniel	to	Minor, Mary
Dec. 28	Carr, William	to	Mallory, Mary
1770			
Feb. 10	Johnson, William	to	Barnett, Anne
Mar. 3	Hawkins, William	to	Strother, Susanna
Oct. 3	Moore, Bernard	to	Price, Catey

Marriage records from a fly leaf of a Memo book

1771	Barnett, William	to	Carrell, Elizabeth
1771-74	Barbour, Thomas	to	Thomas, Mary
Mar.3'70	Hawkins, Moses	to	Strother, Susan
1771	Herndon, Zachariah	to	Scott, Mary
Feb.10'70	Johnson, William	to	Barnett, Ann
1771-74	Sisson ——— c	to	Braham, Millie
" "	Taylor, Zachariah	to	Chew, Alice
" "	Terrill, Zachariah	to	Walker, Millie
" "	Terrell, Reuben	to	Walker, Millie
" "	Issac, George	to	Spencer, Caroline
" "	Gibbs, James	to	Johnson, Ann -widow

Recorded on back page of Deed Book 17

1772	Married Wm. Camp of Culpeper County to Francis Willis Dec. 1st
Dec. 8	Married Michael Markspile and Ann Long
1773	
Jan. 3	Peter Rucker and Jemimah Crawford
Jan. 7	Samuel Ham and Clary Wisdom
Jan. 18	John Furnace and Elizabeth Duncome
Jan. 19	Zachariah Garton and Millie Sulling
Jan. 24	Joseph Bain Johnson and Elizabeth Shopshire
Feb. 22	Lewis Perry and Mary Burrows

1773
Feb. 23	Benjamin Reynolds and Elizabeth Reynolds
Mar. 8	John Delany of Bromfield parish & Susanah Watts of St. Thomas
Mar. 9	John Gayden and Caty Collins
Mar. 29	Samuel Welsh and Jane Bruce
Apr. 2	Stephen Easting and Susanna Johnson
Apr. 6	Daniel James of St. Marks parish, Culpeper County, and Lucy Davis of St. Thomas
May 12	James Addoms and Eley Welsh
June 16	Wm. Plumer Thurston and Lucy Mary Taliaferro
June 24	Francis Lowins and Sarah Davis
July 4	Stephen Smith and Blessing Stevens
July 27	Francis Burk and Lucy Davis
Aug. 18	Joseph Wisdom and Sarah Gardener
Aug. 22	John Bawling and Mary Ballard
Sept. 2	Geo. Petty and Elizabeth McNeal
Sept. 11	Wm. Linney and Ann Bell
Sept. 12	Geo. Blows of Agusta and Katherine Keen of St. Marks parish
Sept. 23	Joseph Wm. Watts and Rachael Foster
Sept. 23	Abraham Card and Ann Archer
Sept. 24	Ambrose Darbour of Bromfield parish and Catherine Thomas of St. Thomas
Oct. 3	Sam'l Dixon and Charlotte Brown
Oct. 12	Richard Waggoner and Caty Gaines
Oct. 31	James Sleet and Ann Ford
Oct. 31	John Rogers of Fredricksville parish and Barbara Ellis of St. Thomas
Nov. ?	Robert Daniel and Frances Head Humphrys
" "	John Blair and Elizabeth Smith
" "	Jacob Arhart and Nanny Ballard
" "	Wm. Lucas and Ann Burbridge

1774
Jan. 9	George Grace and Ann Micheal
Jan. 16	Wm. Vauter and Ann Ballard
Jan. 23	John Reynolds and Hanner Darnel
Feb. 10	Joseph Reynolds and Susannah Wright
Feb. 12	Robert Chandler and Sukey Edmonson
Feb. 31	Patrick Cokrane and Winifred Spencer
June 24	Benjamin Jones and Elizabeth Foster
Aug. 4	Wm. Sebree and Hannah Kavinner
Oct. 2	Samuel Smith and Dorcas Douglas
Nov. 1	Winslow Parker and Mary Thomas
Nov. 17	Thomas Foster and Mary Sawyer
Nov. 26	John Dear and Katherine Smith
Nov. 26	John Harris and Frances Rowzee
Dec. 20	Wm. Humphries and Susannah Webb
Dec. 20	John Witherspoon and Mary Boston

1775
Jan. 5	Wm. Morton and Milly Taylor
Jan. 16	John Faulconer and Margaret Morrison
Jan. 24	Wm. Dunn and Mary Bledsoe
Jan. 29	John Temple and Mary Ann Canterbury
Feb. 21	William Sawyer and Elizabeth Wright

Feb. 21	James Donohony and Winifred Dawler	
Feb. 23	Benjamin Harvey and Sussannah Harvey	
Feb. 27	Robert Ausburn and Milly Cudden	
Mar. 14	John Goodrich and Betty Dear	
Apr. 6	Wm. Sutton and Alice Brown	
May 4	Wm. Hancock of Trinity and Jemima Brockman of St. Thomas parish	
May 26	John Warner and Ann Walker	
June 15	Thomas Hughs and Mary Davis	
June 25	Wm. Strother and Ann Kavenaugh, widow	
June 25	Ephrim Rucker and Elizabeth Randall	
June 27	Wm. Sebree and Mary Strother	
July 29	Geo. Bradley and Lucy Rice	
Aug. 11	Nehemiah Mossell and Patty Collins	
Aug. 15	Geo. Stubblefield and Sarah Morrison	
Aug. 25	Benjamin Finnell and Sarah Carter	
Sept. 14	John Smith and Jane Smith	
Sept. 21	John Morris and Linney Brown	
Sept. 22	Joseph Alkins and Milly James	
Oct. 19	Elliot Wood and Mary Conner	
Nov. 2	John Dawson and Ann Chisom	

1775

Nov. 9	James Smith and Patty Cleaveland	
Nov. 16	Charles Finnell and Nancy Saunders	
Nov. 19	Thos. Lancaster and Frances Nailley (?)	
Nov. 20	Wm. Fearney and Sarah Norton	
Dec. 10	Weir Long and Ann Sinalt (?)	
Dec. 10	Ben Zachary of Bromfield and Frankey White of St. Thomas parish	
Dec. 5	James Head of St. Thomas parish and Elizeth Finnel Kirtly of Brumfield parish	
Dec. 14	Thos. Robbins and Mary Lenox (?)	
Dec. 14	Ambrose Medly of Brumfield and Franky Burton of St. Thomas parish	
Dec. 23	Thos. Bryant and Franky Thornton	
Dec. 28	James Taylor and Delilah Stanton	

1776

Jan. 1	Lenard Davis and Susannah Burrows	
Jan. 23	Robert Cockburn and Sarah Brown	
Feb. 10	David Morris and Jemima Grunter	
Feb. 19	Thos. Fearney and Agy Lucas	
Mar. 3	John Patterson of Berkley and Peggy Cudding of St. Thomas parish	
Apr. 8	John Richard and Milly Watts	
Apr. 4	Anthony Foster and Elizabeth Price	
Apr. 10	James Alexander and Martha Townsend	
May 5	Francis and Nanny Harvey	
June 1	William Smiley and Estin Norwell	
July 21	Francis Gaines and Betsy Lewis	
July 22	John Music and Mary Berrey	
July 22	Samuel Estes and Winifred Holliday	
July 26	John Daniel and Lucy Marshall	
Aug. 8	Jonathan White of Fredricksville parish and Nancy Martin of St. Thomas	
Aug. 22	Uriah Proctor and Martha Singleton	
Aug. 23	Joseph Hoomes and Rachel Davis	
Aug. 25	Alex. Downey and Sally Bell	
Aug. 16	Wm. Collins and Patty Snell	

Sept. 11	Reuben Willis and Ann Garnett of St. Marks parish	
Sept. 29	May Burton and Sarah Head	
Oct. 21	Andrew Glassell and Elizabeth Taylor	
Dec. 2	James Cushingberry (Quinsenberry) and Jane Burrows	

1777

Feb. 4	William Alkins and Winifred Briant
Feb. 25	Thos. Foster and Frances Jones
Mar. 4	John Leatherer and Sarah White
Mar. 15	Thos. Rumsey and Patty Cope
Mar. 16	John Beedles and Elizabeth Casen
Mar. 30	Richard Lancaster and Joanna Singleton
Apr. 25	Thos. Robinson and Lucy Robinson
Apr. 20	James Alkins and Amy Pigg
May 8	William Proctor and Elizabeth Wiatt
May 22	William Reynolds and Nancy Nixon
May 29	David Harrel Stage (?) and Maryan Mooney
July 14	Gideon Lea and Ann Coffery
July 15	Robt. Smith of Spotsylvania County and Ann Conner
Aug. 28	Augustine Woolfolk and Franky Thomas
Sept. 21	Mordecai Bruce and Christina Aheart
Sept. 21	Jacob Aheart and Mary Bruce
Oct. 5	_____ Abel and Margaret Tinder
Dec. 7	John _____ and Elizabeth Middlebrook
Dec. 10	Moses Bledsoe and Ann Perry

1779

Jan. 7	John Gillock and Hannah Wolfenburger
Jan. 21	Wm. Brooking and Ann Thompson
Jan. 27	Thos. Dear and Lucy Fennell
Feb. 11	John Alkins and Ann Burrass
Jan. 30	Robert Boston and Lucy Wright
Feb. 3	Philemon Richards and Susannah Wood
Feb. 11	Henry Miller and Margaret Piglen
Feb. 17	John Mallory and Sarah Sawyer
Feb. 24	Jacob Peck and Polly Coursey
Mar. 7	David Phillips and Mary Davis
Mar. 5	John Williams and Elizabeth Rumsey
Mar. 5	Henry Hill and Susannah Jones
Apr. 7	William Thomas and Elizabeth Woolfolk
Apr. 19	Thos. Harvie and Sarah Hobbs
Apr. 19	John Moore and Lucy Estes
Mar. 8	Thos. Ballard and Elizabeth Smith
May 1	Thos. Morris and Peggy Reynolds
May 11	Thos. Gilbert and Ann Fearneyhough

Orange County, Virginia, Marriage Records

1772

Feb. 25	Davis, John	to	Jones, Mary
Apr. 27	Willis, John	to	Thomas, Sally
Apr. 5	Daniel, James	to	Davis, Lucy
May 12	Taliaferro, John	to	Stockdell, Amy (Ann?)
May 26	Duncan, Joseph	to	Stephens, Nancy
June 11	Thurston, Wm. Plumer	to	Taliaferro, Lucy Mary
June 23	Early, Joel	to	Smith, Lucy

1772

July 26	Burnley, Richard	to	Jones, Eliza Swan

Date	Groom		Bride
Sept. 24	Barkesdale, Nathaniel	to	Douglas, Ann
Oct. 9	Madison, Francis	to	Bell, Susanna
Nov. 23	Daniel, Robert	to	Humphries, Francis Head
Dec. 1	Champel, William (of Culpeper Co.)	to	Willis, Francis

1774

Date	Groom		Bride
Jan. 9	Grace, George	to	McMeal, Ann
Jan. 16	Vawter, Wm.	to	Ballard, Ann
Jan. 23	Reynolds, John	to	Darnell, Anna
Feb. 10	Reynolds, Joseph	to	Wright, Susanna
Feb. 24	Chandler, Robert	to	Robinson, Sukey
Apr. 9	Cockrane, Patrick	to	Spencer, Winifred
May 12	Jones, Benjamin	to	Foster, Elizabeth
May 31	Sebree, Wm.	to	Kavanaugh, Hannah
June 24	Smith, Samuel	to	Douglass, Dorcas
Aug. 4	Parker, Winslow	to	Thomas, Mary
Oct. 8	Foster, Thomas	to	Sawyer, Mary
Nov. 1	Dear, John	to	Smith, Catherine
Nov. 17	Harris, John	to	Rowzee, Francis
Nov. 26	Humphries, Wm.	to	Webb, Susannah

1775

Date	Groom		Bride
Jan. 5	Morton, Wm.	to	Taylor, Milly

1774

Date	Groom		Bride
Dec. 20	Witherspoon, John	to	Boston, Mary

1775

Date	Groom		Bride
Jan. 16	Faulconer, John	to	Morrison, Margaret (guardian & executor Taliaferro, Craig)
Jan. 24	Dunn, Wm.	to	Bledsoe, Mary
Jan. 29	Temple, John	to	Canterberry, Mary Ann
Feb. 21	Sawyer, Wm.	to	Wright, Elizabeth
Feb. 23	Harvey, Benjamin	to	Harvey, Susanna
Feb. 23	Dohony (?), James	to	Vawter, Winifred
Feb. 27	Ausbum, Robert	to	Cudden, Milly
Mar. 14	Goodrich, John	to	Deer, Betty
Apr. 6	Sutton, Wm.	to	Brown, Alice
May 4	Hancock, Wm.	to	Brockman, Jemima
May 26	Warner, John	to	Walker, Ann
June 8	Hughes, Thomas	to	Davis, Mary
June 11	Strother, William	to	Kavanaugh, Ann
June 25	Rucker, Ephriam	to	Randall, Elizabeth
June 27	Sebree, Wm.	to	Strother, Mary
July 29	Bradley, George	to	Rice, Lucy
Aug. 11	Russell, Nehemiah	to	Collins, Sally
Aug. 15	Stubblefield, George	to	Morrison, Sarah
Aug. 15	Reynolds, Richard, wife		Catherine Reynolds
Aug. 25	Finnell, Benjamin	to	Sleet, Sara Carter (widow)
Sept. 14	Smith, John	to	Smith, Jane
Sept. 21	Morris, John	to	Brown, Linny
Sept. 22	Atkins, Joseph	to	James, Milly
Oct. 19	Dawson, John	to	Chism, Ann
Oct. 19	Wood, Elliot	to	Conner, Mary
Nov. 9	Smith, James	to	Cleveland, Patty
Nov. 9	Fennel, Charles	to	Saunders, Nancy
Nov. 16	Lancaster, Thomas	to	Hailey, Francis

Nov. 19	Fearney, Wm.	to	Morton, Sally
Nov. 20	Long, Weir	to	Smith, Ann
Dec. 5	Head, James	to	Kirtley, Elizabeth Jannet
Dec. 12	Medley, Ambrose	to	Burton, Frankie(Bondsman, May Burton, Brumfield parish)
Dec. 10	Zachary, Benjamin	to	White, Frankie
Dec. 20	Taylor, James	to	Staunton, Deliah
Dec. 23	Bryant, Thomas	to	Thornton, Frankie
Dec. 24	Robbins, Thomas	to	Foster, Mary

1777

Feb. 4	Atkins, Wm.	to	Bryant, Wintifred
Feb. 25	Foster, Thomas	to	Jones, Francis
Mar. 4	Leatherer, John	to	White, Sarah
Mar. 15	Rumsey, Thomas	to	Cope, Patty
Mar. 16	Beedle, John	to	Cassen, Elizabeth
Mar. 30	Lancaster, Richard	to	Singleton, Johanna
Apr. 25	Robinson, Thomas	to	Robinson, Lucy-license
Apr. 29	Atkins, James	to	Pigg, Amey
May 8	Proctor, Wm.	to	Hiatt, Elizabeth
May 22	Reynolds, Wm.	to	Nixon, Nancy
May 29	Stage, David R.	to	Mooney, Maryan
July 14	Lea, Gidieon	to	Coffery, Amey
July 15	Smith, Robert	to	Conners, Ann(Spotsylvania)
Aug. 28	Woolfolk, Augustine	to	Thomas, Frankie-license
Sept. 21	Bruce, Mordecai	to	Aheart, Christiana
Sept. 21	Aheart?, Jacob	to	Bruce, Mary
Oct. 7	Page, John	to	Middlebrook, Elizabeth
Oct. 5	Abel, John	to	Tinder, Margaret
Oct. 10	Bledsoe, Moses	to	Perry, Ann

1776

Jan. 1	Davis, Leonard	to	Burrows, Susanna
Jan. 23	Cockburn, Robert	to	Brown, Sara
Feb. 18	Morris, David	to	Grunter, Jemima
Feb. 19	Fearney, Thomas	to	Lucas, Agy
Mar. 3	---Patterson, John	to	Cudding, Page
Apr. 3	Richards, John	to	Watts, Milly
Apr. 4	Foster, Anthony	to	Price, Elizabeth
Apr. 10	Alexander, James	to	Townsend, Jerusa
May 5	Williams, Francis	to	Harvey, Nanny
June 1	Smiley, Wm.	to	Norwell, Esten
July 21	Gaines, Francis	to	Lewis, Betsy
July 21	Estes, Samuel	to	Holladay, Winifred
July 22	Musick, John	to	Berry, Mary
July 26	Daniel, John	to	Marshall, Lucy
Aug. 8	White, Jonathan	to	Martin, Nanney(Fredricksburg)
Aug. 22	Proctor, Uriah	to	Singleton, Martha "
Sept. 17	Willis, Reuben	to	Garnett, Ann
Aug. 23	Noomes, Joseph	to	Davis, Rachel
Aug. 25	Dabney, Alexander	to	Bell, Sally
Sept. 16	Collins, Wm.	to	Snell, Patty
Sept. 29	Purton, May	to	Head, Sara
Oct. 21	Glassell, Andrew	to	Taylor, Elizabeth-Bondsman, James Taylor
Nov. 20	Conner, John	to	Daniel, Lucy

Date	Groom		Bride
Dec. 2	Quisenberry, James	to	Burrows, Jane
1778			
Jan. 7	Gillock, John	to	Wolfengerger, Hannah
Jan. 21	Brooking, Wm.	to	Thompson, Ann
Jan. 27	Dear, Thomas	to	Fennell, Lucy
Jan. 30	Boston, Robert	to	Wright, Lucy
Feb. 3	Richards, Philemon	to	Woods, Susanna
Feb. 5	Fennell, Wm., Jr.	to	Bourn, Jeany
Feb. 11	Miller, Henry	to	Piglen, Margaret
Feb. 11	Atkins, John	to	Burrass, Ann-bondsman Joseph Atkins -father, Edmund Burrass
Feb. 17	Mallory, John	to	Sawyer, Sarah
Feb. 24	Peck, Jacob	to	Coursey, Polly
Mar. 2	Philips, David	to	Davis, Mary -license
Mar. 5	Williams, John	to	Rumsey, Elizabeth-license
Mar. 5	Henry, Hill	to	Jones, Susanna-license
Mar. 8	Ballard, Thomas	to	Smith, Elizabeth
Apr. 7	Thomas, William	to	Woolfolk, Elizabeth Parent, Joseph Woolfolk
Apr. 19	Harvey, Thomas	to	Hobbs, Sarah
Apr. 19	Harvey, John	to	Estes, Lucy
May 1	Morris, Thomas	to	Reynolds, Peggy
May 11	Gilbert, Thomas	to	Tearneaugh-Parent,Thomas Tearnehaugh
June 4	Watts, William	to	Beazley, Elizabeth-Parents, James & Ann Beasley
Aug. 24	Reynolds, Richard	to	Roach, Ann - widow
Oct. 13	Thomson, Rhodes	to	Vivion, Sally-parent, John Vivion
1779			
Jan. 4	Stapp, Thomas	to	Barbage, Betsy
Jan. 19	Burton, James	to	White, Mary -Parent, Jeremiah White
Jan. 28	Chiles, James	to	Land, Jenny
Sept. 3	Quarles, Wm.	to	Vivion, Frances -parent, John Vivion
Nov. 8	Burnley, Garland	to	Taylor, Frances-Bondsman, Robert Taylor
Nov. 9	Brockman, Major	to	Patterson, Mary-Parents, Turner & Susanna Patterson
Dec. 27	Gibbs, Julius	to	Davis, Aggy -Parent, Joseph Davis
1780			
Jan. 25	Atkins, Edward	to	Wisdom, Frankie -Bondsman, Joseph Atkins
Mar. 1	Davis, James	to	Johnson, Mary
Apr. 14	Coleman, James	to	Taylor, Sarah
Apr. 17	Parker, Richard	to	Cave, Hannah-Parent,Wm.Cave
Apr. 27	Rucker, John	to	Tinsley,Betty - " John Tinsley
Apr. 27	Loyd, Thomas	to	Gresham, Sally -widow
May 16	Wood, Henry	to	Weatherspoon, Mary
June 20	Tomlinson, John	to	White,Mildred -Bondsman, Wm. White

Date	Groom		Bride
Aug. 21	James, Spencer	to	Davis, Frances -Bondsman, Philimon Davis
Oct. 28	Hayes, Moses	to	Petty, Sarah
Oct. 28	Hawkins, Sebree	to	Gaines, Mary -Bondsman, Joseph Hawkins
Oct. 30	Blakey, John	to	Cowherd, Sarah -Parent, Jonathan Cowherd
Nov. 2	Lancaster, Robert	to	Dear, Lucy-Parent, John Dear
Nov. 15	Garnett, Thomas	to	Brockman, Suksy -Parent, Samuel Brockman
Nov. 20	Linney, Wm.	to	Burrus, Ann (widow)
Nov. 23	Terrill, Wm.	to	Daniel, Ann
Dec. 4	Henshaw, John	to	Newman, Patty-Parent, James Newman
?	King, Azariah	to	Abel, Mary
1781			
Feb. 7	Scott, Reuben	to	Cope, Margaret
Mar. 22	Wood, Joseph	to	Bell, Margaret-Mother, MaryBell
Mar. 22	Gulley, John	to	Land, Mary-Parent, John Land
Apr. 7	Adams, Benjamin	to	Coleman, Milly
Apr. 10	Moore, Wm.	to	Grymes, Betty Johnson-Bondsman, Ludwell Grymes
Apr. 19	Herndon, John	to	Wright, Elizabeth-Parent, John Wright
Apr. 20	Willis, Moses	to	Thomas, Elizabeth -Parent, Joseph Thomas, Sr.
May 24	Collins, Edward	to	Collins, Ann
June 28	Coleman, Thomas	to	Hawkins, Susannah
Aug. 11	Mothershed, Nathaniel	to	Birt, Ruthy
Aug. 24	Olive, James	to	Minor, Susannah
Oct. 3	Lindsay, Wm.	to	Shepherd, Nancy
Oct. 25	Smith, Absolem	to	Chandler, Justine-Parent, Joseph Chandler
Oct. 31	Taliaferro, Nicholas	to	Taliaferro, Ann-Bondsman, Francis Taliaferro
Nov. 29	Young, Wm.	to	Douglass, Mildred
Dec. 18	Lee, John	to	Bell, Elizabeth -Parent, Thomas Bell
1781			
Dec. 24	Mallory, Henry	to	Long, Lucy
1782			
Jan. 23	Goodall, James	to	Harvey, Sally
Feb. 6	Gaines, Richard	to	Eastin, Elizabeth-Parent, Elizabeth Eastin
Feb. 6	Cox, John	to	Bryson, Mary
Mar. 13	Dade, Francis	to	Taliaferro, Sarah -Parent, Laurence Taliaferro
Mar. 23	Eastin, Philip	to	Henderson, Elizabeth-Parent, Alexander Henderson
May 16	Adams, James	to	Chambers, Mary(?)-Parent, Thomas Chambers
May 27	Rhodes, Robert	to	Delaney, Lissa (Albermarle)
Aug. 3	Neal, Miscajah	to	Beazley, Milly-Parent, James Beazley

Sept. 10	White, Wm.	to	Brockman, Mary-Parent, Samuel Brockman
Sept. 25	Taylor, John	to	Kavanaugh, Elizabeth
Nov. 11	Waugh, Richard	to	Brown, Margaret
Nov. 11	Porter, Charles, Jr.	to	Proctor, Betsy-Parent, George Proctor
Nov. 27	Stapp, Achilles	to	Wawter, Margaret-Parent, Mary Wawter
Dec. 5	Furnis, Jacob	to	Page, Mary-Parent, John Page
Dec. 31	Hite, Isaac, Jr.	to	Madison, Nelly-Bondsman, Ambrose Madison
Dec. 21	Taylor, John	to	Jarrell, Mary-Parent, James Jarrell
Dec. 17	Baber, Robert	to	Spradling, Nancy-Parent, David Spradling

1783

Jan. 14	Carrol, Jacob	to	Reynolds, Tabitha-Parent, Rachel Reynolds
Feb. 11	Taylor, Reuben	to	Moore, Rebecca
Feb. 20	White, Richard	to	Olliver, Caty-Parent, Tabatha Olliver
Feb. 24	Fitzhugh, Wm.	to	Taliaferro, Ann-Parent, Laurence Taliaferro
Mar. 10	Cox, Thomas	to	Olliver, Milly-Parent, Tabatha Olliver
Mar. 20	Proctor, Hezekiah	to	Young, Nancy-Parent, John Young
Mar. 27	Coates, John	to	Thompson, Sarah-Bondsman, Edw. Crates
Mar. 27	Quinn, Richard	to	Wood, Ann
Apr. 24	Davis, Thomas	to	Early, Elizabeth-Parent, Theodosia Early
May 22	Quisenberry, George	to	Daniel, Jane-Bondsman, Vivion Daniel
June 2	Smith, Wm.	to	Smith, Lucinda-Parent, Joseph Smith
June 10	Cave, Wm.	to	Christy, Frances-Parents, Julius Christy & John Cave
June 14	Martin, George	to	Jones, Elizabeth-Parent, Thos. Jones
June 19	Deering, Thomas	to	Rumsy, Mary-Bondsman, James Deering
	Permission signed by Mary Treasley		
June 19	Smith, Charles	to	Morton, Jane-Parent, Elijah Morton
July 8	Webb, Wm. Crittenden	to	Buckner, Jane
July 11	Sharmarard, Elisha	to	Powell, Elisha
July 21	Stragham	to	Sanders, Mary-Parent, Nathaniel Sanders
Aug. 18	Walker, Thomas	to	Powell, Misiniah-Parent, Mary Powell (widow)
Aug. 28	Lanton, Thomas	to	Walker, Mary
Aug. 29	Vass, Vincent	to	Manning, Elizabeth (widow)
Sept. 8	Powell, Ambrose	to	Gritt, Sally-Parent, Mary Gritt
Sept. 13	Boston, Reuben	to	Hawkins, Sara
Nov. 5	Wright, John	to	Jones, Margaret-Bondsman, John Jones
Dec. 11	Orant, John	to	Lintor, Peggy -Bondsman, Ben Hansford
Dec. 12	Ham, Joseph	to	Hearen, Sarah-Parents, Francis & Sarah Hearen
Dec. 12	E? Aheart, John	to	Pearson, Peggy-Parent, Robert Pearson
Dec. 22	Page, John, Jr.	to	Collins, Mary-Parent, Mary Collins
	(His parents, John Page, Sr. & Elizabeth, his wife)		
Dec. 24	Hiatt, Lewis	to	Allen, Barbary
Dec. 25	Riddle, Wm.	to	Riddle, Joyce. "Lewis Riddle Uncle"
Dec. 30	Hiatt, John	to	Arnold, Sarah-Bondsman, Nicholas Arnold

1784

Jan. 8	Gillock, Thomas	to	Morgan, Elisabeth-Bondsman, Joseph Thomas
Feb. 11	Breedlove, Madison	to	Buckner, Judy "Francis Bush"
Apr. 2	Herring, James	to	Cofer, Judah -Parent, James Cofer

Date	Groom		Bride
May 1	Haney, James	to	Petros, Nance-Bondsman, John Goodall, Jr.
May 27	Hiatt, Lewis	to	Connor, Mary-Parent, Rachel Connor
May 31	Helm, Wm.	to	Taliaferro, Matilda-Parent, Francis Taliaferro
June 19	Vawter, Wm.	to	Rucker, Mary-Parent, Mary Rucker
July 22	Thornton, Jesse	to	Bohon, Ann-Parents, Benjamin & Ann Bohon
July 22	Grant, Samuel	to	Craig, Lidia-Bondsman, Elijah Craig
Aug. 13	Reynolds, Aaron	to	Chambers, Caty, Bondsman, James Adams
Aug. 19	Thompson, David Bondsman, James Brockman	to	Brockman, Elizabeth-Parent, Samuel Brockman, Jr.
Aug. 21	Head, Benjamin, Jr.	to	Garr, Margaret, Parent, Lewis Garr
Oct. 25	Lamb, John	to	Lamb, Nelly-Parent, John Lamb
Nov. 23	Brockman, Wm.	to	Smith, Mary-Bondsman, George Smith
Dec. 13	Finnell, Reuben	to	Bourn, Elizabeth-Parent, Henry Bourn
Dec. 21	Leak, Robert	to	Leak, Susanna-Bondsman, Lewis Willis
1785			
Jan. 13	Webb, Wm.	to	Leathers, Sarah-Parent, John Leathers
Jan. 17	Embre, Richard	to	Payne, Judith-Bondsman, George Payne
Jan. 27	Buckhaunon, John	to	Smith, Mary-Bondsman, Henry Smith
Feb. 1	Cogwell, Ralph	to	Reynolds, Sarah-Bondsman, John Dawson
Feb. 3	Tindar, James	to	Shadrick, Molly -Parent, Jobe Shadrick
Feb. 3	Daniel, William	to	Gaines, Mary-Bondsman, Henry Childs
Feb. 7	Connor, John	to	Lancaster, Mary-Parent, Mary Lancaster
Feb. 10	Long, James	to	Reynolds, Elizabeth
Mar. 3	Lindsay, Cabel	to	Stevens, Sally-Parent, John Stevens
Mar. 3	Right, James	to	Rawson, Sarah-Bondsman, Luke Jennings
Mar. 11	Franklin, John	to	Pearson, Mary " Wm. Milligan
Mar. 15	Goodall, Wm.	to	Davis, Lucy-Parent, Jonathan Davis
Mar. 15	Alcock, Wm.	to	Bell, Caty
Mar. 24	Smith, John	to	Warren, Elizabeth-Bondsman, Thomas Bell
Apr. 3	Thompson, Wm.	to	Breeding, Acquiles-Bondsman, John Warren
Apr. 28	Eastin, John	to	Griffith, Sarah-Bondsman, David Griffith
June 13	Cook, Wm.	to	Garton, Susannah-Parent, Uriah Garton
June 17	Lee, Kendall	to	Gordon, Sarah-Bondsman, James Gordon, Jr.
July 20	Watts, John	to	Davis, Suckey-Parent, Joseph Davis
July 21	Bledsoe, Wm.	to	Morton, Sally-Parent, Elijah Morton
July 28	White, Joel	to	Rucker, Frankie-Parent, John Rucker
Aug. 1	Cowgill, Daniel	to	Martin, Betsy-Parent, Ann Bowen
Aug. 23	Neal, Charles	to	Miller, Ann-Robert Miller signs permission
Aug. 28	Davis, James	to	Modiset, Ann-Bondsman, Patrick Cockran
Sept. 4	Bragg, Benjamin	to	Twentyman, Polly (Prettyman?)
Sept. 7	Jones, John	to	Abell, Margaret
Sept. 7	Dersy, Lavay (?)	to	Wye, Ann-Bondsman, James Head
Sept. 7	Jones, James	to	Robinson, Caty-Parent, John Robeson
Sept. 14	Bibb, Thomas	to	Brockman, Sarah-Parent, Samuel Brockman, Jr.
Sept. 22	Hinshaw, Edmund	to	Newman, Macy-Parent, James Newman
Sept. 22	Sams, John	to	Bledsoe, Mary - Aaron Bledsoe signed permission
Oct. 14	Silvey, Stephen	to	Dear, Frankey-Bondsman, John Dear

Oct. 18	Gordon, Nathaniel	to	Gordon, Mary-Bondsman, David Hening
Nov. 7	Long, Henry	to	Manspoile, Lucy- " , John Song
Nov. 8	Pendleton, John	to	Taylor, Elizabeth " , James Taylor
Nov. 24	Tomlinson, George	to	White, Elizabeth-Parent, Henry White
Dec. 14	Ford, Wm.	to	Moore, Ann-Bondsman, Reuben Boston
Dec. 15	King, Sadrut	to	Wayt, Mary-Bondsman, Richard White
Dec. 19	Young, Edwin	to	Wright, Frances(widow-Bondsman, Healy
Dec. 22	Brooking, Samuel	to	Taylor, Mary-Bondsman, Chapman Taylor
Dec. 22	Watts, Julius	to	Eve, Mary-Bondsman, Prettyman Murry

Marriage records from a fly leaf of a Memo. book.
1771-74

	Barnett, William	to	Carrell, Elizabeth
	Barbour, Thomas	to	Thomas, Mary

1770

Mar. 3	Hawkins, Moses	to	Strother, Susan
Feb. 10	Johnson, William	to	Barnett, Ann

1786

Jan. 7	Coleman, Francis	to	Davis, Betty-Parents, Joseph & Elizabeth Davis
Jan. 13	Alcock, Robert	to	Bell, Mary -widow
Jan. 13	Ballard, Larkin	to	Gaines, Elizabeth-Parent, Sally Gaines
Jan. 24	Poulter, John	to	Ransdell, Patty -Bondsman, Sanford Randell
Feb. 23	Bell, Wm.	to	Johnson, Elizabeth-Parent, Ben Cave
Feb. 28	Daniel, Beverly	to	Hiatt, Jane-Bondsman, Benjamin Hiatt
Mar. 1	Atkins, Silence	to	Jennings, Frances-Parent, John Jennings
Mar. 11	Joseph, Jonathan	to	Deering, Sarah-Robt. Deering, Sr. signed permission
Mar. 20	Staunton, Beverly	to	Stanton, Jemimah -Parent, Betty Stanton
Mar. 23	Perry, Moses	to	Brockman, Susan-Bondsman, Samuel Brockman
Mar. 25	Williams, Jacob	to	Delaney, Mary -James Gordon, Jr., bro of Hannah
Mar. 30	Beale, Wm., Jr.	to	Gordon, Hannah-Bondsman, John Gordon
Aug. 24	Bray, Patrick	to	Stocks, Mary -Parent, Thomas Stocks
Aug. 26	Smith, Edward	to	Warren, Rose
Oct. 11	Watson, Abner	to	Dear, Elizabeth -Parent, Catherine Dear
Oct. 28	Broughton, Thomas	to	Kamp, Sara-Bondsman, James Newman, Jr.
Oct. 30	Balmaine, Alexander	to	Taylor, Lucy -Parent, Erasmus Taylor
Nov. 1	Campbell, Archibald	to	Arnold, Susannah -Bondsman, William Hancock
Nov. 2	Stockdell, John Jr.	to	Duvall, Sally-Bondsman, John Stockdell
Nov. 10	Stone, Henry	to	Golden, Nancy -parent, William Golding
Nov. 24	Steele, Samuel	to	McQuiddy, Mary -Bondsman, John Robinson
Nov. 16	White, Jonathan	to	Townsend, Elizabeth, " , George Brooks
Dec. 11	Tinder, Jesse	to	Abell, Aleaper(?) " Richard Abell
Dec. 20	Rucker, Joel	to	Oliver, Nancy -Parent, Tabatha Oliver
Dec. 18	Coleman, James	to	Chew, Milly

1787

Jan. 5	Veach, Lander	to	Thorpe, Peggy
Jan. 9	Atkins, Joseph	to	Atkins, Ann -Bondsman, John Atkins, Jr.
Jan. 24	Wright, Edward	to	Powell, Frankey -Parent, John Powell
Jan. 31	Turner, Thomas	to	Brown, Catey -Bondsman, James Brown
Feb. 10	Dickinson, Robert	to	Parish, Ruth -Parent, Joseph Parish
Mar. 22	Thomas, Barbour	to	Taylor, Mary -Bondsman, James Taylor
Mar. 5	Robertson, John	to	Porter, Frances - " , Joseph Thomas, Jr.
May 5	Herndon, Wm.	to	Perry, Sukey - " , Moses Bledsoe

Date	Groom		Bride / Notes
May 31	Lantor, Peter	to	Webb, Hannah –Bondsman, Maton Jones
July 3	Bell, John	to	Burnley, Judith – " Reuben Burnley
July 4	Stowers, Lewis	to	Shifflet, Joice –Parent, Elizabeth Shifflet
July 23	Michi, John	to	Earley, Francis –Parent, Theodon Earley
Aug. 7	Taylor, George	to	Stanton, Ann –Parent, Charity Stanton
Aug. 11	Wright, Wm.	to	Perry, Rachel
Aug. 13	Cowherd, Frances	to	Scott, Lucy –Parent, Johnny Scott
Sept. 23	Allen, James	to	Woolfolk, Patsy –Bondsman, Thomas Woolfolk, Jr.
Sept. 29	Rucker, Wisdom	to	Burrus, Rosanna –Parent, Mary Burrus
Sept. 30	Marshall, George	to	Boswell, Ann –Bondsman, Wm. Loyd
Nov. 12	Neal, Fielding	to	Beazley, Catherine – Parent, James Beazley
Nov. 7	Spencer, Edward	to	Woolfolk, Eleanor – Par., Cristo Brockman
Nov. 14	Fitzgarrell, Stephen	to	Bruce, Catherine –Bonds., Wm. Fitzgarrell
Nov. 15	Jones, Zachariah	to	Dean, Rebecca – Bonds., John Jones
Nov. 20	Herndon, Benjamin	to	Ehart, Catherine
Nov. 24	Cooper, Wm.	to	Quisenberry, Mary – Par. Moses Quisenberry
Nov. 26	Head, John	to	Sanford, Nancy – Par. Ann Sanford
Nov. 26	White, James	to	Wood, Lucy –Parent, James Wood
Dec. 20	Lantor, Jacob	to	Webb, Polly –Bonds., Henry Clayton
Dec. 21	Self, Samuel	to	Sheflett, Frances – Par. Elizabeth Sheflett
Dec. 22	Sims, Wm., Jr. Parent, Wm. Sims, Sr.	to	Watts, Nancy, John Douglas, father in law of Nancy
Dec. 24	Thomas, Reuben	to	Spencer, Ann – Par., Joseph Spencer Bondsman, James Brockman
Dec. 29	Scott, George	to	Wood, Nancy –Bonds., William Scott
1788			
Jan. 7	Williams, Richard	to	Rogers, Nancy –Bonds., James Earley
1789			
Feb. 24	Lee, Richard	to	Dodd, Anna – Parson, John Leland
Feb. 8	Shadrack, John	to	Sanders, Betsy
Feb. 7	Herring, Wm.	to	Shiflett, Molly –Par. William Shiflett
Feb. 14	Goodall, Parks	to	Cox, Frankey –Bonds., Thomas Cox
Feb. 21	Taylor, Francis	to	Thompson, Elizabeth –Wm. Thompson, Joel Thompson signed permission
Feb. 14	Young, John	to	Rogers, Sarah –Parent, Aaron Rogers
Mar. 11	McCoy, George	to	Nickings, Elizabeth – Par. Nathaniel Nicking
Apr. 11	Casay "or Kersey?", Wm.	to	Taylor, Agnes – Charles Taylor signed permission
Apr. 24	Robinson, Wm.	to	Adams, Frankey – Bonds., James Adams
Apr. 27	White, Thomas	to	Long, Elizabeth " Zachariah Burnley
Apr. 11	Brooking, Robert	to	Russell, Patsy " John Scott
Apr. 24	Morton, John	to	Tandy, Mary – Par. Henry Tandy and Ann Mills Tandy
May 12	Morse, Francis	to	Ward, Lucy –Wm. Lucas, Bonds., signed permission
May 25	Sheller, John	to	Cox, Ann – Bonds., Thomas Cox
May 26	Gillock, Laurence	to	Twentyman, Betsy – Bonds., John Orant
June 11	Spalding, Robertson	to	Jones, Fanny –Bonds., Elijah Jones
June 18	Graves, Thomas	to	Grady, Anna –Parent, Wm. Grady
June 30	Sanford, John	to	Ransdell, Betsy

July 4	Bridges, Wm.	to	Row, Ann - parent, Richard Row
July 28	Webster, Andrew	to	Smith, Usilla, -Bonds., James Caims
Aug. 16	Airy, Wm.	to	Stowers, Mary, " Lewis Stowers
Sept. 1	Overton, Willis	to	Bradley, Nancy " Reuben Boston
Sept. 9	Goforth, Thomas	to	Foster, Milly " John Foster
	Overton, John	to	Richards, Polly
Sept. 20	Wright, John	to	Grasty, Susanna
Oct. 1	Boling, Wm.	to	Hawkins, Pheobe -Pheobe Hawkins Pomdexter signs permission
Oct. 2	Overton, Beverly	to	Conner, Elizabeth -Bonds.Willis Overton
Oct. 24	Burrus, Samuel	to	Rucker, Caty
Oct. 24	Lucus, James	to	Henderson, Nancy
Nov. 3	Pendleton, Rice	to	Quisenberry, Elizabeth
Nov. 3	Pitcher, Jonathan	to	Mason, Betsy -Bonds.,Charles Mason
Nov. 5	Bickers, John	to	Landrum, Nancy
1788			
Nov. 11	Brown, James	to	Harrod, Nancy -Bonds.,John Harrod
Nov. 23	Atkins, Hesekiah	to	Chiles, Sally -Bonds.,James Chiles
Nov. 27	Riddell, James	to	Rhodes, Theodosia -Bonds.,Charles Neal
Dec. 2	Brockman, John	to	Long, Nancy
Dec. 11	Churning, Lorimer	to	Carter, Judith
Dec. 22	Roach, James	to	Lindsay, Betsy
Dec. 24	Hamilton, John	to	Richard, Francis -Parent, Wm. Richard
Dec. 24	Hill, Samuel	to	Tate, Nancy -Bondsman, Uriah Tate
Dec. 27	Garrell, Demey	to	Stanton, Sally -Parent, Christy Stanton
1789			
Jan. 5	Terrill, Oliver	to	Mallory, Susannah-Bonds., Wm. Mallory
Jan. 7	Shadrick, John	to	Sanders, Elizabeth
Jan. 10	Davis, John	to	Pannill, Elizabeth, Par. Wm. Panel
Mar. 9	Lucas, Thomas	to	Garnett, Sally -Bonds.,Eastham Snell
Jan. 15	Sims, Jeremiah	to	Taylor, Margaret " Zachariah Taylor
Feb. 12	Taylor, Wm.	to	Walker, Elizabeth " Zachariah Taylor
Feb. 5	Davis, Wm.	to	Easton, Nancy
Feb. 6	Sutherland,Kenneth	to	Webster,Ruth -Bonds.,Daniel Webster
Feb. 24	Lee, Richard	to	Dodd, Anna -Bonds.,Mordicai Mastin
Mar. 5	Sanford, Reuben	to	Webb, Francis -Par. Wm. Crittenden Webb & Jane Vivion Webb
Mar. 13	Brook, George	to	Taylor, Dorothy
Mar. 21	Russell, Wm.	to	Merry, Mary -Bonds.,Thomas Herndon
May 6	Rucker, Elliot	to	Smith, Nancy- " ,Samuel Smith
June 2	Deane, Wm.	to	Boston, Sarah- " ,Joseph Boston
June 9	Mallory, Reuben	to	Carter, Dorothy-Bonds.,John Bledsoe
June 29	Clarkson, Anselm	to	Jones, Milly - Bonds.,Thomas Jones
July 27	Davis, John	to	Eastin, Mary " Reuben Eastin
Aug. 3	Jones, Reuben	to	Stowers, Patty,widow -Mary Stowers signed permission
Aug. 10	Watson, Jesse	to	Ballard, Milly -Parent,Philip Ballard
Sept. 10	Pearson, John	to	Goodrich, Betsy -Bonds.,Killis Oliver
Sept. 15	Bower, Thomas	to	Landrum, Margaret " John Bickers
Sept. 25	Wright, John	to	Grasty, Susanna -Parent, Ann Grasty
Oct. 12	Webb, John	to	Jones, Judah -Bondsman,Thomas Jones
Oct. 15	Griffey(?), Joseph	to	Wisdom, Fanny- " Edmund Burrus
Nov. 10	Head, George Marshall	to	Rucker, Milly -Par. John & Mary Rucker
Dec. 1	Chisham, James	to	Raines, Catherine-Bonds.,Francis Hughes
Dec. 3	Page, James	to	Shefflet, Winny -Par.,Elizabeth Shefflet
Dec. 7	Breeding, Ephriam	to	Franklin, Molly-Parent, Edward Franklin
Dec. 8	Mothershead, John	to	Burras, Sukey-Bonds.,Joseph Griffin

Date	Groom		Bride
Dec. 19	Graves, Absolem	to	White, Felicia –Parent, John White
Dec. 22	Chandler, James	to	McNeal, Francis –Parent, Martha McNeal
Dec. 26	Taylor, James	to	Hunt, Sary –Bondsman, George Brook
Dec. 30	Dollins, Reuben	to	Hensley, Elizabeth –Parent, Wm. Hensley
1790			
Jan. 5	Wells, Wm.	to	Harvey, Mary –Bondsman, Samuel Scriviner
Jan. 8	Burrus, Roger	to	Mills, Cynthia –Parent, Nathaniel Mills
Jan. 20	Webb, John, Jr.	to	Lantor, Mildred –Bonds., Jacob Lantor
Jan. 19	Wharton, Zacheus	to	Young, Sally –Bondsman, James Tinder
Jan. 25	Webb, Jesse Bennet	to	Mason, Sarah –Bondsman, Charles Mason
Jan. 28	Twentyman, Bononia	to	Nutly, Elizabeth (widow)
Jan. 27	Donover, John	to	Gaer, Sally –Parent, Nathaniel Gaer
Jan. 30	Macon, Thomas	to	Madison, Sarah –Bonds., James Madison
Feb. 2	Crew, Jacob	to	Dollins, Martha –Bonds., Wm. Dollins
Feb. 8	Arnold, James	to	Atkins, Elizabeth –Bonds., James Atkins
Feb. 18	Simson, John	to	Dawson, Polly Stevens –Bonds.,John Dawson
Mar. 10	Cornelius, Oystin (Augustine?)	to	Terrell, Sarah – Parent, Peggy Terrell
Mar. 15	Morris, Gilson	to	Knight, Molly –Parent, Knight
Apr. 7	Rumsy, John	to	Deering, Mary –Robert Deering signed permission
May 20	Rumsy, Wm.	to	Barrett, Peggy –Bonds., Wm. Leathers
May 25	Lee, Zachariach	to	Mansfield, Sara –Par. Adam & Mary Mansfield
June 3	Gillett, Samuel	to	Pannill, Sally
June 9	Battaile, Laurence	to	Taliaferro, Ann Hay
June 28	Webb, Vivion John	to	Woodward, Lucy –Bondsman, James Taylor
July 15	Chambers, Thomas	to	Robinson, Milly –Par., Artemeus Robinson
July 29	Turner, John	to	Fitzgarrell, Sarah
July 31	Breeding, Richards	to	Franklin, Elizabeth –Par. Edward Franklin
July 31	Franklyn, Jonathan	to	Breeding, Susannah –Par. Job Breeding
Aug. 4	Hundley, Nehemiah	to	Cave, Elizabeth –Par. Benjamin Cave
Aug. 18	Doane, John	to	Mays(?), Elizabeth
Aug. 16	Hobday, John	to	Davis, Mary
Oct. 19	Dahoney, Rhodes (Mahoney?)	to	Chapman, Jinney –Par. Joseph Chapman
Nov. 4	Perry, Peter	to	Faulcowr, Lucy –Bonds. David Faulcowr
Nov. 4	Spencer, Frances	to	George, Wintifred –Prettyman, Merry signed permission
Nov. 18	Chambers, Abraham	to	Dawson, Mary –Parent, John Dawson
Dec. 6	Brockman, James	to	Bledsoe, Nancy –Bonds., Aaron Bledsoe
Dec. 6	Fortson, Benjamin	to	Head, Sally –Parent, James Head
Dec. 21	Mitchel, Wm.	to	Grinnils(?), Rebecca –Par., Sarah Grinnils
Dec. 27	Robert, Thomas	to	Henry, Frances –Parent, Wm. Henry
Dec. 28	Paul, Robert	to	Edwards, Rachel –Bonds., Charles Finnell
Dec. 28	Howard, Richard	to	Sullivan, Margaret –Bonds., Wm. Faulcowr
Dec. 31	Owens, John	to	Hambleton?Sarah(widow) –Bonds.,Wm. Richard
1791			
Jan. 4	Underwood, Gidion	to	Dohony –Bonds., R. H. Dohony
Jan. 18	Spincer, Seth	to	Thornton, Ann –Bonds., Abner Beckham
Jan. 29	Cox, Wm.	to	Estes, Betsy – Bonds., John Bell
Jan. 31	Jonathan, Valentine	to	Bennett, Nancy –Bonds., Howard Bennett
Feb. 2	Turnley, Frances	to	Watts, Susannah – Bonds., Robert Alcock
Feb. 5	Graves, Thomas	to	Burrus, Mourning – Par., Thomas Burrus
Feb. 10	Scott, Wm.	to	Shadrick, Nelly –Bonds., John Shadrick
Feb. 15	Coats, Jeremiah	to	Webster, Sally –Bonds., Francis Weatherall
Feb. 28	Perry, James	to	Tandy, Nancy – Bonds., Roger Tandy
Mar. 7	Harwood, Moses	to	Sutton, Elizabeth – Bonds., Wm. Sutton

Date	Groom		Bride / Notes
Mar. 15	Dooling, Thomas	to	Finnell, Elizabeth -Bonds., John Quinn
Mar. 17	Sebree, John	to	Johnson, Sally - Parent, Richard Sebree
Mar. 31	Bishop, Joseph	to	Clark, Ann -Parents, John & Macy Clark
Apr. 1	Rhodes, George	to	Wright, Mary -Parent, B. Bennett?
Apr. 5	Taliaferro, Hay	to	Thurston, Lucy M.(widow)-Bonds. Francis Dade
Apr. 19	Boling, John	to	Bell, Susannah -Thomas Bell signed permission
Apr. 14	Blair, James	to	Shepherd, Helen -Bonds.Alexander Shepherd
May 20	Stanton, Spencer	to	Powell, Sally -Bonds., Honorias Powell
May 20	Stubblefield, George	to	Hawkius, Ann - Bonds., Joseph Bishop
June 9	Beasley, John	to	Eaves, Sally -Parent, William Eaves " Gustin Beasley
June 28	Foushee, Thornton	to	Graves, Nancy -Parent, Richard Graves
June 28	Sampson, Thomas	to	Powell, Winney -Bonds., Thomas Walker
July 12	Barker, James	to	Mazes, Sarah, widow -Bonds., Wm. Rumsy
Aug. 2	Norman, Cuthbert	to	Jollet, Sophia -Bonds., James Jollet
Aug. 16	Bramham, Marmaduke	to	Hughes, Fanny -Bonds., Thomas Chisham Parent, Francis Hughes
Aug. 18	Finnel, James	to	Chambers, Rebecca
Aug. 22	Snell, Joseph	to	Miller, Elizabeth -Par., Robert Miller
Aug. 23	Knight, Wm.	to	Cave, Frances - Bonds., Wm. Cave
Oct. 13	Bowling, Charles	to	McKenney, Sarah -Par., Wm. McKenney
Oct. 20	Lamb, James	to	Watson, Ann -Parent, Isaac Watson
Oct. 24	Brockman, Samuel, Jr.	to	Durrett, Nancy -Bonds., Joel Durrett
Nov. 16	Philips, Thomas	to	Davis, Milly -Par., Jonathan & Milly Davis and Thomas Philips
Nov. 22	Cave, Wm.	to	Jollett, Judy -Parent, Mary Jollett
Nov. 25	Bickers, George	to	Mallory, Nance - Bonds., Thomas Dear
Dec. 17	Sweney, Daniel	to	Griffith, Mary -Par. David Griffin
Dec. 22	Thornton, Cabel	to	Ford, Patsy - Bonds., James Stett
Dec. 21	Beckham, Abner	to	Thomas, Frances - Par., Elizabeth Thomas
Dec. 26	Chandler, John	to	Terrell, Elizabeth -Par., Wm. Terrell
Dec. 29	Peaches, Reuben	to	Johnson, Sarah - Par., Nancy Johnson
1792			
Jan. 5	Wright, Bledsoe	to	Beasley, Sarah - Par. Augustine Beasley
Jan. 1	Maggard, Henry	to	Lamb, Betsy - Bonds., George Albright
Jan. 5	McCullan, Patrick	to	Walker, Sarah -Parents, John McCullan and "Theodora (Beasley)"
Jan. 17	Ford, Absolem	to	Ransdell, Molly -Bonds., Sanford Ransdell
Jan. 13	Collins, James	to	Harvie, Sarah -Parent, John Harvie
Feb. 6	Maxwell, John	to	Henry, Agatha - Bonds., Benson Henry
Mar. 5	Booth, Joseph	to	Grace, Polly -Parent, George Grace
Mar. 29	Blanton, John	to	Grady, Mary -Parent, Nathaniel Sanders
Apr. 3	Maxwell, Thomas	to	Henry, Dulley -Parent, Wm. Henry
Apr. 9	Faulconer, Richard	to	Sanders, Nancy -Parent, Nathaniel Sanders
Apr. 6	Atkins, James	to	Foe, Elizabeth, -Wit. John Smith
May 2 or Apr. 17	Fitzhugh, Henry, Jr.	to	Conway, Elizabeth - John B. Fitzhugh, guardian.
Apr. 18	Leathers, Wm.	to	Finnell, Nancy -Bonds., Roger Bell
Apr. 28	Sanford, Robert	to	Grymes, Hannah -Ludwell Grymes signed permission
Apr. 23	Carter, Joseph	to	Bell, Polly - Bonds., John Carter
May 17	Henry, Benjamin	to	Roberts, Nancy -Parent, Hugh Roberts
May 31	Crawford, Jeremiah	to	Crawford, Janey -Par., Archelan Crawford
June 2	Lancaster, Reuben	to	Conner, Betsy -Bonds., John Conner
June 14	Alexander, James	to	Ahart(E?), Franksy

(16)

Date	Groom		Bride / Details
July 25	Rixey, John	to	Sutherland, Betsy -Bonds., Joseph Sutherland
July 25	McDonald, Patrick (or McDaniel, Patrick)	to	Miller, Elizabeth, Par., Judith Miller
Aug. 17	Crosthwait, Aaron	to	Brockman, Nelly -Par., John Brockman
Aug. 20	Henshaw, John	to	Newman, Elizabeth -Par., James & Elizabeth Newman
Aug. 21	Gaer, Wm.	to	Ham, Sally -grandparent, Sam Ham
Aug. 27	Spicer, Rawser	to	Wood, Nancy -Hannah & John Hinsley, Step father
Sept. 5	Branham, Tavner	to	Sisson, Polly -Parent, Sarah Sisson
Sept. 10	Oliver, Cabel	to	White, Nancy - Parent, Thomas White
Sept. 15	Cowhill, George	to	Wait, Phoebe - Bonds., Edward Wait
Oct. 30	Beazley, Charles	to	Wait, Elizabeth -Bonds., Wm. Phillips
Nov. 6	Dade, Wm.	to	Dade, Sarah - Bonds., Townshead Dade
Nov. 7	Clarke, Wm.	to	Cook, Betsy - Bonds., Edward Pagett
Dec. 27	Roberts, George	to	Tippett, Lavinia - Bonds., James Powell Parent, Samuel Tippett
Dec. 12	Jameson, Thomas R.	to	Samuel, Polly - Bonds., Henry Samuel
Dec. 19	Taylor, Zachariah	to	Gerrell, Susanna -Bonds., Joell Cofer
Dec. 20	Powell, Benjamin	to	Pickett, Ester -Parent, Mace Pickett
Dec. 21	Ogg, John	to	Goodall, Sally -Bonds., John Goodall
Dec. 24	Collins, Lewis Dillard	to	Williams, Elizabeth -Bonds., Jacob Williams
Dec. 31	Dod, Wm., or John Dodd	to	Lee, Susanna -Bondsman, Zachariah Wood

1793

Date	Groom		Bride / Details
Jan. 1	Powell, Lewis Gorden	to	Powell, Sally -Parent, Benjamin Powell
Jan. 12	Peach, Bailey	to	Vaughn, Nancy -Bonds., James Vaughn
Jan. 16	Hubbard, Carter	to	Durrett, Betsy - " Joel Durrett
Jan. 23	Stockdell, Wm.	to	Roszell, Delphia-" George Chapman
Jan. 28	Terrell, Wm., Jr.	to	Morton, Jane - " John Morton
Feb. 9	Rhodes, Richard	to	Wright, Lucy - " George B. Wright
Feb. 13	George, William	to	Hawkins, Lucy -Thomas Coleman, guardian
Mar. 11	Howard, Charles P.	to	Taylor, Jane -Bonds., Charles Wardell
Mar. 13	Gaines, John	to	Gaines, Jenny - " Richard Collins
Mar. 15	Bryant, Edward	to	Hambleton, Polly -Edward Hambleton signed permission
Mar. 19	Waugh, Waugh	to	Boston, Elizabeth -Bonds., Pierce Sanford
Mar. 25	Ehart, Abram	to	Kirk, Judith -Bonds., George McDaniel
Mar. 27	Page, Wm.	to	Alexander, Elizabeth -Parents, James & Elizabeth Alexander
Mar. 30	Wood, Thomas	to	Porter, Rebecca -Sarah & Rebecca Porter signed permission
Apr. 2	White, Jesse	to	Martin, Elizabeth-Bonds., Robert Martin
Apr. 2	Hudson, John	to	Dedman (R?), Mary - " Francis Taylor
Apr. 6	Daniel, Cornelius O.	to	Plunkett, Peggy (widow) -Bonds., John O. Bryant
Apr. 10	Goodall, David	to	Davis, Elizabeth -Parent, Joseph Davis
Apr. 19	Foster, Wm.	to	Hawkins, Tabitha -Bonds., Richard Howard
Apr. 22	Wood, Hopewell	to	Terman, Willy -Bonds., George Bingham
Apr. 22	Henry, William	to	Warren, Elizabeth (widow) -Bonds., Thomas Roberts
Apr. 22	Brockman, Andrew	to	Brockman, Amelia -Par., William Brockman
May 7	Shepherd, Alexander	to	Burnley, Mary -Parent, Zachary Burnley
May 10	Rhodes, John	to	Pearson, Tabatha - " Robert Tabatha
May 13	Bell, Patrick	to	Quisenberry, Polly
June 13	Jarrell, James	to	Sirus, Frances -Bonds., Zachariah Taylor
June 5	Wright, Benjamin	to	Herndon, Ann -Bonds., James Herndon
June 7	Ogg, Wm.	to	Lamb, Frankey -Parent, John Lamb

Date	Groom		Bride
June 8	Faulconer, George	to	Coleman, Nancy –Parent, James Coleman
June 10	Morris, Reubin	to	Coleman, Molly – " James Coleman
June 13	Finnell, James	to	Chambers, Rebecca –Bonds., Marmaduke Branham
July 8	Martin, Brice	to	Lucus, Rachel –Bonds., Isaac Davis, Jr.
July 28	Paul, Jacob	to	Neale, Catey (widow) –Bonds., John Hause
Aug. 6	Payne, John	to	Lindsay, Sucky –Bonds., Adam Lindsay
Aug. 7	Thomas, Robert	to	Smith, Polly –Parent, Joseph Smith
Aug. 9	Hambleton, Edward	to	Rippito, Elizabeth –Par., John Rippito
Aug. 26	Collins, James	to	Burton, Lucy –Parent, May Burton, Jr.
Sept. 13	Griffey, Abell	to	Sutton, Catherine
Sept. 25	McDaniel, Derensey	to	Brooks, Susanna –Parent, Jane Brook
Sept. 29	Bishop, Joseph	to	Terrell, Jane –Bonds., Edmund Terrell
Oct. 11	Foster, John	to	Deering, Susannah –Par., Robert Deering
Oct. 30	Rothrock, George	to	Pollock, Elizabeth –Parent, Wm. Pollock
Nov. 8	Fleek, Andrew	to	Lower, Rachel – Bonds., John Coleman
Nov. 12	Loyd, John	to	Montague, Nancy – " Andrew Montague
Nov. 18	Shepherd, George	to	Porter, Ann –Bonds., Camp Porter
Nov. 25	Hennessy, Peter	to	Routt, Winney –Bonds., James Taylor
Dec. 5	Wells, James	to	Reynolds, Fennetta –Par., Joseph Reynolds
Dec. 9	Gon, John, Jr.	to	Grace, Gracey –Parent, George Grace
Dec. 6	Wells, Thomas	to	Clark, Mary –Parent, John Clark, Sr.
Dec. 23	Powell, Ptolemy	to	Lavit, Sidney (widow)
Dec. 24	Porter, John	to	Carter, Catherine –Bonds., Pierce Sanford
Dec. 23	Stevenson, John	to	Payne, Milly –Bonds., Thomas Payne
1794			
Jan. 15	Chandler, Joseph	to	Homs?, Nancy –Bonds., George Scott
Jan. 21	Cave, Benjamin, Jr.	to	White, Elizabeth –Bonds., Wm. White
Jan. 27	Finnell, George	to	Dawson, Sally –Bonds., Lawrence Gillock
Jan. 27	Roberts, John	to	White, Mary –Bonds., John White
Feb. 7	Landrum, John	to	Collins, Mary – " Thomas Landrum
Feb. 10	Collins, George	to	Mitchell, Elizabeth –Bonds., Wm. Mitchell
Mar. 8	Mitchell, Henry	to	Lucas, Molly –Parent, Wm. Lucas, Jr.
Mar. 30	Faulconer, David	to	Grady, Sarah –Parent, William Grady
Apr. 27	Collins, Francis	to	Dahoney, Peggy –Parent, Thomas Dahoney
Apr. 30	Voss (Vass?), Nicholas	to	Spotswood, Mary –Parent, T. Spotswood
May 15	Cowgill, Isaac	to	Gillock, Sally –Parent, Elizabeth Gillock
May 17	Clayton, Philip	to	Stubblefield, Elizabeth Hackley –Parent, George Stubblefield
June 3	Bickers, Wm.	to	Leathers, Sally –Bonds., Cabel Bickers
June 23	Faulconer, James	to	Sisson, Milly –Parent, Sarah Sisson
June 26	Cowherd, Reuben	to	Woolfolk, Frances –Parent, Thomas Woolfolk
July 12	Hundley, John	to	Loyd, Nancy –Bonds., Nehemiah Hundley
July 26	Lancaster, Henry	to	Wright, Mary – " George Finnell
July 28	Foster, Haskew	to	Snell, Caty – " John Williams
Aug. 21	Darnell, Thomas	to	Ehart, Elizabeth –Bonds., James Alexander
Aug. 20	Lewis, James	to	Watkins, Mary –Bonds., James Landrum Parent, Isham Watkins
Sept. 10	Terrell, John	to	Miller, Caty –Bonds., Wm. Brockman
Nov. 5	Head, Henry	to	Sanford, Elizabeth –Parent, Sanford, Ann
Nov. 5	Clark, John	to	Powell, Winney –Parent, John Powell
Nov. 16	Buckner, Baldwin	to	Burton, Fanny –Bonds., James Collins
Dec. 11	Lahoney, Daniel	to	Furney (or Finney), Fanny–Bonds., Wm. Garde
Nov. 26	Robinson, Wm.	to	Collins, Margaret– Par., Richard Collins
Dec. 24	Coleman, John	to	Bradley, Elizabeth-Par., George & Lucy Bradley

Date	Groom		Bride
Dec. 20	Graves, Joel	to	Graves, Sarah – Bonds., Isaac Graves
Dec. 21	Davis, Jickenias	to	Lowry, Babby
Dec. 25	Rucker, Wm.	to	Taliaferro, Caty T.
Dec. 26	Pollard, Edmund	to	Herndon, Sally –Bonds., Benj. Wright
Dec. 26	Tatum, Thomas	to	Evens, Nancy –Bonds., John Buckhannon

1795

Date	Groom		Bride
Jan. 13	Miller, Thomas	to	Plunkett, Sarah –Parent, Thomas Plunkett
Jan. 9	Brockman, Elijah	to	Tomlinson, Sally –Bonds., Wm. Tomlinson
Jan. 12	Stevens, James	to	Gaines, Disney –John Robinson signed permission
Jan. 18	Mallory, Henry	to	Jones, Ann –Parson, George Bingham
Jan. 18	Shifflet, Stephens	to	Hicks, Rachel
Feb. 17	Riddle, Fielding	to	Waits, Milly –Bonds., Wm. Lewis Powell
Feb. 17	Cason, Wm.	to	Thompson, Mary –Parents, John & Catherine Thompson
Feb. 26	Taylor, Elijah	to	Walker, Dilla –bonds., Jeremiah Sims
Mar. 7	Ballard, Wm.	to	Snow, Mary –Parson, George Bingham
Mar. 23	Hutchen, Wm.	to	Robinson, Siler –Parent, John Robinson
Mar. 3	Williams, Francis	to	Rogers, Sally –Bonds., Sam'l Ham
Mar. 25	Payne, Wm.	to	Foster, Nancy –Parent, Richard Payne
Mar. 31	Owens, Sturd	to	Harris, Caty –Parson, George Bingham
Mar. 31	Boswell, Charles	to	Thompson, Lucy –Bonds., Henry Wood
Apr. 7	Morris, George	to	Graves, Susannah –Parent, Richard Graves
Apr. 13	Pence, John	to	Lucas, Elizabeth –Bonds., Zachariah Lucas
May 13	Ferrell, George	to	Wolf, Polly –Parent, Lenard Wolf
June 3	Williams, James	to	Bruce, Elizabeth –Bonds., Thomas Farish
June 5	Johnson, Isaac, Jr.	to	Terrill, Elizabeth – Archibald Terrill
June 25	Shifflett, Pickott	to	Powell, Lucretia –Bonds., Francis Powell
July 21	Shadrick, Thomas	to	Sanders, Sarah –Parent, Nathaniel Sanders
July 30	Thompson, Wm. Theodocius	to	McNeal, Jane – Bonds., John Samuel
Aug. 25	Dawson, John	to	Pollard, Nancy –Bonds., Benj. Hawkins
Aug. 26	Mason, James	to	Oaks, Nancy – Bonds., Charles Mason
Sept. 10	Smoot, Cabel	to	McShamrock, Martha –Bonds., James Smoot
Sept. 14	Galasby? John	to	Goodridge, Betsy –Bonds., Richard Goodridge
Oct. 8	Taylor, John	to	Pearson, Elizabeth
Nov. 9	Walker, Benjamin	to	Sims, Polly –Bonds., Wm. Sims, Jr.
Oct. 22	Fleak? Andrew	to	Rhoads, Frankey –Par., Epaphroditus Rhoads
Oct. 20	Barbour, James	to	Johnson, Lucy (Governor of Va.)
Oct. 17	Young, John	to	Grady, Frankey –Parent, Samuel Gradey
Nov. 3	Garde, Wm.	to	Yates, Mary –Bonds., Edward Bracken
Nov. 26	Taylor, William	to	Gibson, Susannah –Bonds., James Taylor
Dec. 4	Blackerby, Thaddeus	to	Marshall, Jane –Parent, Merrineau Marshall
Dec. 7	Tandy, Rogers	to	Adams, Mary –Bonds., Thomas Adams
Dec. 17	McGlarney, Roger	to	Morris, Sarah – " Aurelius Hawkins
Dec. 21	Taylor, James, Jr.	to	Moore, Frances –" Gabriel Barbour
Dec. 21	Bell, Wm.	to	Atkins, Rhoada –Parents, John & Susannah Atkins
Dec. 24	Terry, John	to	Oaks, Lucy –Bonds., James Mason
Dec. 22	Homes, James	to	Hilman, Sally –Parent, Joseph Hilman
Dec. 22	Adams, Elisha	to	Smith, Delia –Parent, James Smith
Dec. 27	Mason, John	to	Selbree, Lucy –Parson, Hamilton Goss
Dec. 28	Bell, Thomas	to	Burnley, Sally –Bondsman, Wm. Shepherd
Dec. 30	Bridges, Mathew	to	Row, Mary –Bondsman, Edmund Row

1796

Date	Groom		Bride
Jan. 6	Martin, Benjamin	to	Knight, Mary –Parent, Ephriam Knight
Jan. 8	Roberts, John	to	Knight, Agnes –Parent, Mathew Knight

Date	Groom		Bride
Jan. 10	Gamble, Mathew	to	Bell, Nancy -Bondsman, David Holmes
Feb. 11	Miller, Jesse	to	Stevens, Ann -Parent, Joseph Stephens
Feb. 26	Amus, Benj.	to	Acre, Nancy -Bondsman, Wm. Acre
Feb. 24	Sims, Wm.	to	Walker, Tannie -Parent, Elizabeth Walker
Feb. 17	Sylva, George	to	Poe, Lucy -Bonds., Dennis Shea
Feb. 19	Manspoile, Johny	to	Wood, Sally -Parent, Katie Wood
Mar. 5	Bourne, Ambrose	to	Newman, Jane -Parent, Frances Newman
Mar. 15	Nipper, Jacob	to	Fleck, Elizabeth -Bonds., Andrew Fleck
Mar. 29	Williamson, Thomas	to	Bledsoe, Milly -Parent, Aaron Bledsoe
Mar. 7	Fox, Stephen	to	Herndon, Elizabeth -Bonds., Zachariah Herndon
Mar. 14	McMillan, James	to	Kendall, Edy -Parents, Henry & Ruth Kendall & John McMillen
Mar. 22	Barbour, Richard	to	Moore, Mary -Bonds., Thom. Barbour, Jr.
Mar. 25	Hambleton? Theophilus	to	Powell, Nutty -Bonds., John Hambleton
Apr. 2	Hause, Conrad	to	Thompson, Susannah -Bonds., Conrad Hause, Sr.
Apr. 20	Smith, John	to	Smith, Sukey -Par., Raife & Sukey Smith
Apr. 25	Crask, James	to	Hollins, Jane-Bonds., Edward Hollins
Apr. 20	Harrod, Benjamin	to	Blair, Betsy -Bonds., Absolom Tyler
Apr. 25	Brockman, Moses	to	Brockman, Nelly - " Wm. Dollins
Apr. 25	Douglas, Charles	to	Payne, Mary -Bonds., John Payne
May 11	Boston, George	to	Vaughn, Elizabeth -Bonds., Joseph Vaughn
May 16	Cook, Elijah	to	Turner, Polly -Parent, Ann Turner
May 24	Grigsby, Elisha	to	Porter, Elizabeth -Parent, Abner Porter
May 25	Taylor, Absolem	to	Smith, Frances -Par. Jeremiah & Eliz. Smith
June 3	Higdon, John	to	Ross, Mary
June 9	Flick, John	to	Kiblinger, Barbary -Bonds., Jacob Kiblinger
June 31	Sher, Robert	to	Addison, Jean -Bonds., Archilaus Rosson
June 2	Pendleton, Benj.	to	Quisenberry, Elizabeth -Parent, Wm. Quisenberry
July 18	Sewers, Christopher	to	Pierce, Sarah -Bonds., Adam Manspoile
July 7	Gillespy, John	to	White, Ann -Daughter of John White, Sr. (H.S.-1919)
Aug. 3	Stuart, Alexander	to	Reid, Ann (widow)Bonds., Robert Stuart
Aug. 16	Mason, John	to	Faulconer, Elizabeth -par. Thomas Faulconor
Aug. 10	Breedwell, Wm.	to	Blackwell, Anny(?) -Par. Thos. Breedwell
Aug. 18	Sims, Nathaniel	to	Johnson, Susannah
Aug. 22	Porter, Wm.	to	McCauley, Polly -Bonds., Charles Urquart
Aug. 27	Chisam, Benjamin	to	Beckham, Elizabeth -Par. Henry Beckham
Sept. 4	Thurman, Nathan	to	Lowry, Tabitha
Sept.13	Graves, Benjamin	to	Collins, Elizabeth -Parent, Wm. Collins
Sept. 22	Powell, Lewis	to	McMillan, Lucy -Parent, John McMillan
Sept. 19	Bell, Henry	to	Adkins, Susanna -Par. John & Nancy Adkins
Oct. 13	Limmands, Elijah	to	Sandage, Lucy
Oct. 27	Shifflet, John	to	Davis, Susanna
Nov. 1	Faulconer, Reuben	to	Faulconer, Jenny -Par., Thomas Faulconer
Nov. 15	Darby, Adam	to	Shepherd, Catherine -Par., Andrew Shepherd
Nov. 28	Tandy, Henry, Jr.	to	Adams, Betsy, -Bonds., Thomas Adams
Dec. 10	Rogers, Samuel	to	Davis, Sally
Dec. 15	Kendall, Robert	to	Garnett, Ursula -Bonds., Adam Lindsay
Dec. 15	Buck, Anthony	to	Shepherd, Mary -Bonds., Andrew Shepherd, Jr.
Dec. 22	Cave, Bartlett	to	Snow, Jenny

Date	Groom		Bride / Notes
Dec. 22	Graves, Wm.	to	Hilman, Betsy –Bonds., Uriel Hilman
Dec. 23	Gamboe, Samuel	to	Chism, Catherine –Par., John Chisam
Dec. 25	Davis, Absolom	to	Davis, Jerusha
Dec. 26	Riader, Isaac	to	McKelamy, Susannah –Bonds., Wm. Hutchinson
Dec. 26	McKinley, Hugh	to	Finnell, Anna Reita –Bonds., Wm. Finnell
Dec. 29	Long, Richard	to	Stevinson, Nancy –Bonds., Joseph Stromson
Dec. 31	Stephens, Edmund	to	Robinson, Agnes –Parent, Agnes Robinson

1797

Date	Groom		Bride / Notes
Jan. 12	Snow, Berd	to	Mayhugh, Polly – Parent, Polly Watson
Jan. 12	Perry, Elijah	to	Webb, Ann –Parent, Richard Crittenden Webb
Jan. 16	Boxley, George	to	Graves, Drucilla –Parent, Isaac Graves
Jan. 19	Lamb, Benjamin	to	Lamb, Peggy –Par., John Lamb
Jan. 26	Oliver, Killis	to	Riddell, Winney –Parent, James Riddell
Jan. 23	Hunley, James	to	Chiles, Susannah –Bonds., Benjamin Cave
Jan. 23	Webb, Wm., Jr.	to	Smith, Patsy –Bonds., Wm. Crittenden Webb
Jan. 23	Wright, John	to	Sebree, Elizabeth –Bonds., Valentine Johnson
Jan. 23	Faulconer, Wm.	to	Chistram, Betsy –Bonds., Wm. Dawson
Jan. 28	Wells, Martin	to	Marshall, Sarah – " Thomas Marshall
Jan. 30	Clark, Larkin	to	Bell, Rebecca – " Roger Bell Par., Thomas & Sally Bell
Jan. 31	Pendleton, Robert	to	Burrus, Elizabeth –Bonds., Edmund Burrus
Jan. 31	Johnson, Thomas	to	Richards, Diannah –Parent, Wm. Richards
Feb. 2	Finnell, John	to	Surry, Caty –Bondsman, James Finnell
Feb. 2	Overton, John	to	Carleton, Martha –Bonds., Willis Overton
Feb. 15	Stokes, Wm.	to	Silvey, Lucy –Bondsman, Lewis Collins
Feb. 23	Knight, Wm.	to	Oakes, Delphia –Bonds., Thomas Oaks
Feb. 25	Simmonds, Ephriam	to	Hanes, Sarah
Feb. 27	Harris, Peter	to	Estes, Mary Stanfield, –Bonds., Wm. Estes
Mar. 14	Garrel, James	to	Taylor, Sarah
Mar. 14	Taliaferro, Hay	to	Conway, Susannah –Bonds., Catlet Conway
Apr. 8	Daniel, James	to	Finnell, Alse –Bonds., James
Apr. 10	Cook, Thomas	to	Chiles, Mary –Bonds., Reuben Garlon
Apr. 12	Rippito, Wm.	to	Stow, Betsy –Parent, Zanny Aranzy
May 6	Fleck, Henry	to	Smatts, Betsy –Bonds., Peter Sekle
May 16	Mallory, Roger	to	Payne, Mary –Bonds., Thomas Payne
May 22	Waddell, James Gordon	to	Gordon, Lucy –Bonds., Nat. Gordon
May 29	Pallis?, Thomas	to	James, Polly – Bonds., James Coleman
June 7	Atkins, Mallachi	to	Montague, Sally –Bonds., Roger Bell
June 5	Bledsoe, John	to	Dear, Polly –Parents, Thomas Dear & Aaron Bledsoe
June 9	Baber, Robert	to	Spradling, Nancy –Bonds., Wm. Burton
July 11	Hilman, Uriel	to	Graves, Sally –Bonds., Thomas Graves
July 18	Perry, Abraham	to	Wharton, Polly –Parent, George Wharton
Dec. 25	Beazley, Wm.	to	Powell, Betsy –Parent, Benjamin Powell
Dec. 25	Ballad, Medley	to	Dehoney, Jane–Par. Thos & Hannah Dehoney
Dec. 25	Maupin, Jennings	to	Miller, Sally –Bonds., Thomas Miller
Dec. 27	Mason, Isam B.	to	Sebree, Lucy –Martin Johnson signs permission
Jan. 2	Williams, Richard	to	Beazley, Sarah –Mildred & John Williams, stepfather
Jan. 2	Percy, Charles	to	Lower, Elizabeth, Parent, Mical Lower
Jan. 2	Henderson, John	to	Daniel, Frankey–Bonds., Cabel Lindsay
Jan. 8	Thompson, Joel	to	Thompson, Sarah –Par., Elizabeth Thompson

Date	Groom		Bride
Jan. 9	Smith, Colby	to	Kendall, Sally -Bonds.,Robert Kindall
Jan. 9	Eaves, Wm.	to	Highlander, Nancy -Par., George Highlander
Jan. 11	Finell, John	to	Chambers, Elizabeth -Bond.,James Finnell
Jan. 15	Overton, Joshua	to	Palmer, Francis -Bonds.,Willis Overton
Jan. 18	Blakey, Wm.	to	Davis, Elizabeth - " Elijah Graves
Jan. 22	Groom, John	to	Delaney, Dise -Bonds.,Jacob Williams
Jan. 23	Moore, John	to	Smith, Elizabeth - " Wm. Loyd
Jan. 23	Rosson, Archelaus	to	Warren, Haney Ritter -Par., Elizabeth Warren
Feb. 9	Hundley, Joshua	to	Gressom, Betsy -Bonds.,James Hundley
Feb. 15	Eddins, Elijah	to	Osborn, Nancy -Parent,William Osborn
Feb. 15	Garton, Spencer	to	Hancock, Polly -Par., Wm. Hancock
Feb. 22	Terrill, Robert	to	Mallory, Ann -Par., Uriel & Hannah Cave Mallory -John & Ann Quarles Terrill

1798

Date	Groom		Bride
Jan. 27	Webb, Wm.	to	Atkins, Margaret -Bonds.,Cabel Webb
Mar. 7	Newman, Thomas	to	Barbour, Lucy -Bonds.,John Henshaw
Apr. 7	Pritchett, Benjamin	to	Herndon, Polly - " Wm. H. Stannard
Apr. 18	Amos, Joseph	to	Marr, Ann -Bonds., Alexander Marr
May 10	Spradlin, John	to	Foster, Elizabeth -Par., Lucy Foster
May 3	Golden, Richard	to	Walton, Ann - W. M. Golding?
May 14	Faulconer, Samuel	to	Burges, Sarah -Bonds.,Edmund Burges
June 5	Eastham, Edward	to	Thornton, Ann - " Wm. Rucker, Jr.
Aug. 7	Gibson, John	to	Harvey, Elizabeth-Parson,Geo.Bingham
Aug. 21	Gear, Wm.	to	Rogers, Polly -Parent, John Rogers
Aug. 23	Vaughan, Joseph	to	Turner, Nancy -Parent, Ann Turnar
Aug. 27	Ott, Michael	to	Pence, Catherine -Bonds.,Wm.Campbell
Aug. 28	Edwards, Elisha	to	Eaton, Elizabeth -Parent, Wm.Edwards
Sept. 5	Flick, Wm.	to	Lower,Catherine-Par.,Michael Lower,Sr.
Sept. 5	Bush, Edmund	to	Walker, Elizabeth
Sept. 24	Edington, Edmund	to	Gordon, Priscilla -Bonds.,Sam Gordon
Oct. 17	Mallory, Robert	to	Mallory, Nancy
Oct. 19	Alvis, Henry	to	Armstrong, Agnes
Oct. 22	Smith, John	to	Sutton, Nancy -Bonds.,Wm. Sutton
Oct. 22	Newman, Thomas	to	Morris, Patsy Oliver-Par. George Morris
Oct. 24	Anderson, Nathan D.	to	Bell, Milly, Bonds.,Thomas Bell
Nov. 1	Burnley, James	to	Parsons, Nancy -Bonds.,Andrew Shepherd, Jr.
Nov. 13	McAlister, John	to	Turner, Cary or Clary -Par., Ann Turner
Sept. 15	Shiflet, John	to	Hicks, Ann -Parson, George Bingham
Dec. 8	Simpson, Wm.	to	Thompson, Ann -Par.,George Thompson
Dec. 18	Cooper, James	to	Smith, Mildred -Par., James Smith
Dec. 19	Smith, George	to	Abell, Elizabeth -Bonds.,Cabell Abell
Dec. 23	Goodall, Jonathan	to	Russell, Patsy -Bonds., Cabel Smoot
Dec. 20	Head Tavenah	to	Plunkett, Jenny -Par., Jessy Plunkett
Dec. 21	Acre, James	to	Acre, Elizabeth -Bonds., John Morris
Dec. 27	Lamb, Wm.	to	Gear, Mary -Bonds.,John Murray
Dec. 23	Lane, John	to	Crew, Tabitha
Dec. 24	Goss, Hamilton	to	Major, Martha(widow) Bonds.,John Goss
Dec. 26	Eddins, Thomas	to	Collins, Frances -Par.,William Collins
Dec. 26	Robuks, Hugh	to	Sisk, Elizabeth -Bonds., Thomas Robuks
Dec. 27	Rogers, John	to	Knight, Elizabeth
Dec. 29	Shifflet, John (S.B.)	to	Shifflet, Rhoda

1799
Date	Groom		Bride
Jan. 1	Fillinger, Henry	to	Ferrel, Betsy
Jan. 2	Roberts, Hugh	to	Silk, Elizabeth
Jan. 18	Crutchfield, Thomas	to	Taylor, Ann Pendleton -Bonds., James Taylor, Jr.
Jan. 29	Yates, James	to	Sanford, Sally -Parent, Pierce Sanford
Jan. 29	Knight, Wm.	to	Rogers, Elizabeth -Parson, George Bingham
Jan. 31	Lucas, Zachariah	to	Wood, Nancy -Parson, Hamilton Goss
Jan. 31	Davis, Bartlett	to	Lowry, Sally - " George Bingham
Mar. 7	Hawkins, Benjamin	to	Scott, Sally -Bondsman, Reuben Scott
Mar. 21	Raines, Merry	to	Floyd, Annie - " Samuel Floyd
Mar. 21	Willet, David	to	Baughon, Polly -" Joseph Baughon
Mar. 30	Bell, Thomas, Jr.	to	Reynolds, Lucy -Par., Elizabeth Reynolds
Mar. 31	Bohannon, Thomas	to	Marquess, Lavinia -Par., John Marquess
Apr. 3	Burton, James	to	Goodridge, Betsy
Apr. 9	Stone, John	to	Burton, Elizabeth -Parent, James Burton
Apr. 16	Floyd, Samuel	to	Herring, Jane -Parent, Thomas Herring
Apr. 4	Watson, Isaac	to	Robbards, Susanna
Apr. 11	McDaniel, Stacy	to	Lamb, Sally
May 27	Taylor, James	to	Anderson, Nanna -Bonds., Thomas Roberts
May 28	Stephen, Benjamin	to	Nelson, Agnes -Bonds., Edmund Stephens
June 24	Thornton, Luke	to	Sleet, Sarah -Bondsman, James Sleet
Aug. 19	Eve, Joseph	to	Smith, Polly -Par., Raif & Patty Smith
Sept. 3	Hawkins, James	to	Coleman, Betsy -Parent, James Coleman
Aug. 21	Padgett, John	to	Beckham, Nancy -Bonds., Benjamin Chishom
Sept. 23	Robertson, Richard	to	Collins, Elizabeth -Bonds., Edward Collins
Oct. 7	Smonts?, John	to	Fleek, Polly -Bondsman, John Fleek?

1800
Date	Groom		Bride
Jan. 9	Spicer, Benjamin	to	Snell, Caty A. Parent, Robert Snall

1799
Date	Groom		Bride
Nov. 4	Hestand, John	to	Nowell, Tanlipy -Bonds., Abraham Hestand
Nov. 11	Hawkins, James	to	Rector, Elizabeth -Bonds., J. K. Richards
Oct. 16	Smith, Wm.	to	Porter, Mary C. -Bonds., Camp Porter
Oct. 18	Phits, Thomas	to	Montague, Polly -Bonds., John Montague
Oct. 21	Sleet, Weedon	to	Petty, Patsy -Parent, George Petty
Oct. 26	Bowcock, Tandy	to	Douglas, Judith -Parent, John Douglas
Oct. 25	Hunter, Pleasant	to	Harris, Jane -Parent, Lindsay Harris
Oct. 26	Wright, Larkin	to	James, Lucy -Bondsman, George James
Dec. 4	McDaniel, Jeremiah	to	Brooks, Rachel -Parent, Jane Brooks
Dec. 6	King, Gabriel	to	Biggers, Huldah -Parent, Mason Biggers
Dec. 20	Robinson, Michael	to	Williams, Polly -Bondsman, Wm. Arnett
Dec. 21	Wright, Augustine	to	Lindsay, Mary -Parent, Mary Lindsay
Dec. 22	Walton, Francis	to	Speers, Elizabeth -Parson, Geo. Bingham
Dec. 24	Hamilton, Wm.	to	Olive, Jenny -Parent, Elizabeth Olive
Dec. 23	Lee, William	to	Limeco?, Polly -Bondsman, John Simeco
Dec. 26	Eatis, John	to	Cox, Sarah -Bondsman, Joan Cox
Dec. 28	Finnell, Benjamin	to	Robinson, Elizabeth -Parents, Artemus & Pheobe Robinson
Dec. 30	Jacobs, Benjamin	to	Martin, Sarah -Parent, Henry Martin

1800
Date	Groom		Bride
Jan. 1	Grady, Benjamin	to	Adams, Catherine -Bonds., John Montague
Jan. 2	Hall, Wm.	to	Davis, Susannah -Parson, Geo. Bingham
Jan. 12	Hambleton, LeRoy	to	Blunt, Suckey -Par., Michael Blunt

Jan. 22	Sleet, John	to	Wright, Frances -Par., Wm. Wright
Jan. 22	Harvey, John	to	Felix, Elizabeth -Parent, Wm. Felix
Jan. 14	Jenkins, Thomas	to	Taylor, Elizabeth -Bonds.,Charles Taylor
Jan. 23	Taylor, Stanton	to	Stanton, Elizabeth -Par.,George Bingham
Jan. 30	Paggett, James	to	Beacon, Phillis -Elizabeth Beacon, guardian
Feb. 13	Lamb, Jeremiah	to	Jones, Ann
Feb. 24	Brightwell, Absalom	to	Pines, Winefred -Bonds.,John Montague
Mar. 4	Snow, John	to	Lower, Elizabeth -Par., Peter Lower
Mar. 5	Gaines, John	to	Sanders, Joanna -Bonds., George Mason
Mar. 27	Styers, Leonard	to	Wolf, Elizabeth -Parent, L. Wolf
Mar. 31	Meezings, Joseph	to	Clements, Polly -Bonds.,Henry Clements
Apr. 27	Hughes, Armstead	to	Chisham, Sally -Bonds., Wm. Dawson
May 3	Simpson, Daniel	to	Jones, Elizabeth -Bonds., James Jones
June 1	Moore, Nathaniel	to	Adams, Sally -Parent, John Adams
June 3	Jones, Rev. Robert	to	Herndon, Mary(widow, nee Scott)-Bonds., Hamilton Coss
June 24	Dalton, John	to	Earles, Polly -Bonds., Rodham Earles
June 27	Sampson, James	to	James, Anney
July 3	Watson, James	to	Lamb, Catey
July 7	Young, Lawrence	to	Martin, Catherine -Bonds.,John Martin
July 10	Lorrill, Thomas	to	Clee, Elizabeth -Bonds., Wm. Duke
July 12	Harvey, Wm.	to	Wood, Alley -Parent, Hopeful Wood
July 16	Taylor, Edmund	to	Thornton, Nancy -Bonds.,Willis Overton
Aug. 5	Williams, James	to	Thompson, Sally -Parent, John Thompson
Sept. 11	Merriwether, Charles	to	Minor, Ann -Bonds., Dabney Minor
Oct. 8	Graves, Jacob	to	White, Fanny -Bonds., John White
Oct. 24	Atkins, Wisdom	to	Atkins, Nancy -Bonds.,Edward Atkins
Oct. 30	Walters, George	to	Harvey, Nancy -Bonds.,John Harvey
Oct. 8	Hutcherson, James	to	Dear, Catherine -Bonds.,James Johnson
Oct. 27	Gear, Joshua	to	Watson, Jane -Parent, Isaac Watson
Oct. 28	Bailey, Wm. P.	to	Grymes, Mary Lee -Bonds.,Garnett Peyton
Nov. 3	Harris, John	to	Price, Milly(widow) " ,Thomas Bell
Nov. 10	Lee, George	to	Foster, Catey -Parent, Wm. Foster
Nov. 16	Kirtley, St.Clair	to	Panill, Ann -Parent, Wm. Pannill
Nov. 24	Graves, Roda	to	Marquess, Marian -Par., John Marquess
Dec. 4	Parsons, David	to	Clark, Elizabeth-Bonds.,John Clark
Dec. 17	Linton, Moses	to	R? Pead?, Nancy -Bonds., Joel Durrett
Dec. 21	Powell, Reuben	to	Ballard, Elizabeth -Parents, Moreman & Martha Ballard
Dec. 22	Smith, Oswald	to	Quisenberry, Joice -Par.,Wm.Quisenberry
Dec. 24	Sanford, Reuben	to	Wallace, Nancy -Par.,James Wallace, Sr.
Dec. 24	Reynolds, Richard	to	Finnel, Lucy -Parent, Simon Finnel
Dec. 25	Page, Elijah	to	Sisk, Nelly -Parent, Martin Sisk
Dec. 26	Gaines, Thomas	to	Row, Milly -Parent, Thomas Row
Dec. 31	Thornton, George	to	Webb, Nancy -Bonds.,Reuben Webb

1801

Jan. 1	Watson, Abner	to	Long, Nancy -Bonds., John Long
Jan. 7	McKinney, Travis	to	Pollard, Betsy -Bonds., Edmund Pollard
Jan. 23	Curtis, Elijah	to	Daniel, Nancy -Bonds., John D. Long
Jan. 26	Rose, Robert H.	to	Madison, Frances -Bonds.,Reynolds Chapman
Jan. 30	Humes, Francis	to	Payne, Elizabeth -Par.,Reuben Payne

(24)

Date	Groom		Bride
Jan. 31	Clark, Reuben	to	Petty, Lizzy -Par.,George Petty
Feb. 9	Stevens, Wm.	to	Mills, Margaret -Par.,Nathaniel Mills
Feb. 24	Strow, John	to	Walters,Catherine-Bonds.,Geo.Walters
Mar. 8	Powell, Fielding	to	Ballard, Susanna-Bonds.,Elijah Powell
Mar. 8	Boyer, Thomas	to	Thompson,Martha -Bonds.,James Williams
Mar. 23	Murphy, Zacharias	to	Atkins, Lucy -Par.,James Atkins, Jr.
Mar. 29	Lucas, Ezekiel	to	Ahaart(?E) Catherine -Bonds., John Furguson
May 12	York, Armistead	to	Hilman, Joanna -Bonds.,Uriel Hilman
May 18	Bradley, John	to	Hancock, Sally -Bonds.,Wm. Hancock
May 18	Johnson, James	to	Smith, Elisabeth -Par.,Absolom Smith
May 25	Rippeto, Peter	to	Taylor, Martha -Par.,William Taylor
May 27	Gambrel, Walter	to	Lee, Betsy -Bonds.,Wm. Lee
June 18	Hall, Wm. J.	to	Shepherd, Elizabeth Bell -Par,Andrew Shepherd
June 29	Stevens, Waller	to	Adams, Lucy -Par.,Thomas Adams
July 12	Taylor, James	to	Wood, Sally -Bonds.,Richard Wood
July 21	Newman, Andrew	to	Garner, Jinnette -Bonds.,James Sleet
Aug. 13	Allen, Wm.	to	Wallace, Elizabeth -Bonds.,James Wallace
Aug. 24	Lucas, Elijah	to	Brockman, Nancy -Par.Wm. Brockman
Aug. 27	Payne, John	to	Bledsoe,Elizabeth (widow)Bonds., Ambrose Richards
Aug. 3	Bruner, Peter	to	Kiblinger, Caty-Bonds.,Daniel Kiblinger
Aug. 4	Wright, John,Jr.	to	Faulconer, Caty -Bonds.,John Faulconer
Aug. 25	Hume, Benjamin	to	Taliaferro, Elizabeth (widow) (Col. Wm.Taliaferro was her 1st husband)
Aug. 27	Hamilton, John	to	Rippeto, Sara W. -Bonds.,Edward Hamilton
Aug. 29	Grady, Samuel	to	Montague, Caty -Bonds.,John Henderson
Oct. 1	Melburn, Wm.	to	Taylor, Sarah -Bonds.,Charles Taylor
Oct. 3	Turner, John		
Oct. 13	Kirtley, Johnathan	to	Anderson, Theodosia-Parson,Geo.Bingham
Oct. 15	Silvey, Wm.	to	Adkinson, Mary -Par.,John Adkinson
Oct. 20	Peacher, Edmund	to	Hilman, Lucy -Par.,Joseph Hilman
Oct. 25	Grady, Richard	to	Montague, Hannah -Bonds.,John Montague
Oct. 25	Thompson, Samuel	to	Lindsey, Sully-Bonds.,Reubin Lindsay
Nov. 5	McClary, David	to	Picker,Caty -Parson,George Bingham
Nov. 5	Brag, Moore	to	York, Jenny -Bonds.,Armistead York
Nov. 12	Sims, John	to	Beazley, Betty (widow) Sims par., Wm. Sims
Nov. 17	Henry, Zachary	to	Kirtley, Lucy -Parson,George Bingham
Nov. 16	Wright, John	to	Shavers, Polly (widow)
Nov. 18	Bailey, Lewis	to	Mallory, Lucy
Nov. 18	Gentry, Aaron	to	Ogg, Polly
Nov. 24	Wallace, James, Jr.	to	Day, Elizabeth -Bonds.,Pierce Sanford
Dec. 9	Crawford, Martin	to	Lamb, Susanna
Dec. 17	Clark, Reubin	to	Clark, Martha E.-Par.,Joseph Clark
Nov. 31	Wells, Wm.	to	Sams, Nancy -Par., John Sams
Dec. 21	Mallory, James	to	Brockman, Polly -John Brockman signs permission
Dec. 24	Alkins, Gentry	to	Chiles, Frankey -Bonds.,Widsom Alkins
Dec. 24	Blackerly, Thomas	to	Herring, Elizabeth-Par., Thomas Herring
Jan. 5	Clark, Henry	to	Grasty, Nanney -Bonds.,O. S. Grasty
Dec. 31	Ansell, Henry	to	Beazley, Nancy -Bonds.,Richard Williams

Date	Groom		Bride
Dec. 28	McHoney, James	to	Sleet, Patsy -Par., James Sleet, Jr.
Dec. 31	Robinson, Joseph	to	Snell, Philadelphia -Bonds., Robert Snell
Dec. 30	Rogers, John	to	Chishom, Mildred -Par., John Chishom
1802			
Jan. 1	Payne, John	to	Chassam, Mildred -Bonds., Samuel Gamboe
Jan. 5	Watkins, Thomas	to	Mosley, Fanny -Bonds., Leonard Mosely
Jan. 7	Keaton, Nelson	to	Davis, Edna
Jan. 13	Cave, Abner	to	Sims, Betty
Jan. 18	Bradley, Wm.	to	Marshall, Polly -Bonds., Thomas Marshall
Jan. 18	Thornton, Peter	to	Miller, Mary -Par., Robert Miller
Jan. 19	Alkinson, Thomas	to	Silby, Sally -Par., Sarah Silby
Jan. 26	Clark, Walker	to	Vawter, Elizabeth -Par., Wm. Vawter
Jan. 27	Arnold, Thomas	to	Sanford, Peggy -Bonds., Pierce Sanford
Feb. 6	Morris, Wm. Anderson	to	Quisenberry, Winifred -Par., Aaron Quisenberry
Jan. 28	Morris, Josiah	to	Shiflet, Sukey -Parson, George Bingham
Jan. 28	Fitzgerald, Easom	to	Self, Mary -Parson, George Bingham
Jan. 28	Geer, Johnathon	to	Thackwel, Sarah -Parson, George Bingham
Feb. 9	Morris, Elijah	to	Geer, Elizabeth
Feb. 13	Henry, Benfield	to	Kirtley, Elizabeth
Feb. 23	Geer, Ransom	to	Lamb, Polly -Parson, George Bingham
Feb. 25	Thomas, Joseph, Capt.	to	Beazey, Betsy -Bonds., Mack Hornsey
Mar. 16	Hawkins, Benjamin	to	Bickers, Polly -Par., Augustine Beazley
Mar. 25	Jones, Walter	to	Freeman, Sally
Mar. 22	Bush, Thomas	to	Breadwall, Liddy -Bonds., Henry Wood
Mar. 16	Harvy, Jonathan	to	Ross, Margaret -Parson, George Bingham
Apr. 1	Bott, John	to	Spotswood, Susannah C. -Bonds., Robert Spotswood
Apr. 6	True, Thomas	to	Murphy, Susanna -Bonds., Nathaniel Middlebrook
Apr. 15	Lowell, James	to	Harvy, Elizabeth -Bonds., Wm. Harvy
May 2	Wood, Hezekiah	to	Bradley, Sally -Parson, Hamilton Goss
May 6	Durrett, Killam	to	Thompson, Elizabeth -Parson Hamilton Goss
June 2	Twyman, Reubin	to	Cowherd, Drucilla -Bonds., Anthony Twyman
June 2	Brookman, Bledsoe	to	Landrum, Elizabeth -Par., Thomas Landrom
June 13	Lowry, Abner	to	Lowry, Nancy -Parson, George Bingham
June 30	Beazley, Valentine	to	Powell, Franky -Parson, Robt. Jones
July 13	Milton, James C.	to	Taylor, Mary -Bonds., James Taylor
Aug. 18	McClamock, John	to	Estes, Jenny -Par., Elisha Estes
Aug. 24	Jacob, Wm.	to	Martin, Polly -Par., Henry Martin
Aug. 26	Hunt, James	to	Darnold, Susanna -Bonds., Abraham Darnold
Sept. 22	Johnson, Wm.	to	Fitzhugh, Alice -Bonds., Henry Fitzhugh
Oct. 5	Ballard, Washing(?)	to	Thornhill, Elizabeth -Parson, Geo. Bingham
Oct. 22	Read, Wm.	to	Rumsey, Dysa -Bonds., Henry Teel
Oct. 27	Landrum, Reubin	to	Atkins, Susannah -Par., John & Susanna Atkins
Nov. 8	Croxton, Joseph	to	Turner, Delphy -Bonds., Ezekeel Turner
Nov. 16	Bradford, Alexander	to	Burton, Hannah -Par., May Burton
Nov. 17	Turner, Ezekial	to	Chissam, Sally -Par., Thomas Chissam
Nov. 25	Mahanes, Samuel	to	Brockman, Elizabeth -Par., Wm. Brockman
Nov. 27	Faulconer, Elias	to	Newman, Polly -Par., Wm. Newman, Sr.

Date	Groom		Bride
Dec. 2	Hall, Bazel	to	Maiden, Ducia –Parson,George Bingham
Dec. 16	Herndon, Henry	to	Wood, Lucinda –Par., James Wood
Dec. 19	Stowers, John	to	Herndon, Sally –Par., James Herndon & Mack Stowers
Dec. 15	Tinder, Benjamin	to	Terrill, Nancy –Bonds.,Reubin Terrill
Dec. 23	Hensley, James	to	Maiden, Elizabeth –Parson,George Bingham
Dec. 23	Beazley, John	to	Porter, Lucy –Par., Abner Porter
Dec. 22	Sleet, Reubin	to	Mallory, Frances –Par.,Henry Mallory
Dec. 22	Garnett, Larkin	to	Bell, Elizabeth –Par.,Joseph & Elizabeth Bell
Dec. 24	Landrum, Lewis	to	Atkins, Rebecca –Par.,John & Rebecca Atkins
Dec. 30	Hambleton, Elige(?)	to	Balye, Polly –Par.,John Balye(prob.Bayle?
Dec. 29	Moore, Yelly(?)	to	Brown, Elizabeth –Par., John Brown
Dec. 31	Kirtley, Willis	to	Presley, Mary –George Thornton signed permission

1803

Date	Groom		Bride
Jan. 3	Cox, Joab	to	Estes, Lucy –Bonds., Wm. Estes
Jan. 4	Collins, John	to	Kirtley, Elizabeth
Jan. 8	Cave, Abner	to	Sims, Betsy –Par.Wm. Cave & Wm. Sims
Jan. 11	Porter, Benj	to	Newman, Patsy –Par., Wm. Newman, Sr.
Jan. 13	Boston (or Bolton)	to	Moseley, Sarah
Jan. 16	Atkins, Waller	to	Atkins, Sally
Jan. 19	Moore, James	to	James, Nannie –Bonds.,Richard Rhoades
Jan. 20	Morris, Thomas	to	Acree, Betsy –Bonds., Wm. Aery
Jan. 21	Tyler, Wm.	to	Homdon, Mary Ann
Jan. 24	Maury, Lenard H.	to	Campbell, Virginia M. –Bonds.,Robert Wilson
Jan. 24	Reynolds, Wm.	to	Quisenberry, Jane –Bonds.,George Quisenberry
Jan. 24	Wyne, John	to	Ahart(prob.E), Rachel, John Wyne, guardian
Feb. 1	Powell, John West	to	Bell, Eliza F. P., Par.,John Bell
Feb. 28	Duke, William	to	Gibbs, Line –Bonds., John H. Gibbs
Feb. 28	Rogers, John	to	Darnell, Lucy –Par., Mary Ann Darnell
Mar. 3	Terrill, Reubin	to	Gaines, Caty –Par., Robert Gaines
Mar. 14	Jonathan, John	to	Eluck, Polly –Bonds., George Smith
Mar. 14	Newman, Alexander	to	Sleet, Lucy –Par., James Sleet, Sr.
Mar. 17	Lane, Robert G.	to	Whitelaw, Polly –Par.,Thomas & Elizabeth Whitelaw
Mar. 31	Hawkins, Roddy	to	Chamberlane, Alice –Par.,Reubin Hawkins
Mar. 28	Gibson, Wm.	to	Cartey(?), Betsy –Bonds., Benjamin Holley
Apr. 5	Osborne, Fielding	to	Massey, Mary –Par.,Edmund Massey
May 18	Keith, Peyton	to	Petty, Sally –Par., George Petty
May 24	Wheeler, Jesse	to	Cash, Caty –Bonds., Joshua Tate
June 2	Moore, Wm.	to	Day, Susanna –Bonds., Pierce Sanford
June 9	Dodd, James	to	Cook, Nancy–Parson, Nathaniel Sanders
June 11	Elliot, Albin	to	Gaines, Urcilla –Bonds., Wm. Robinson
June 13	Nelson, Wm.	to	Smith, Sara –Par.,James Nelson,James Smith
June 30	Beazley, Valentine	to	Powell, Franky –Par.,Joice Powell
June 23	Hambleton, Thomas	to	Coleman, Margaret –Par., John Coleman
June 27	Overpack, George	to	Carns, Martha –George Walters,guardian
July 25	Holsapple, George	to	Hubbert, Pheobe –Par.,Peter Hubert
Aug. 3	Harrod, Richard	to	Arnold, Joanna –Bonds.,Willis Arnold

Date	Groom		Bride
Aug. 30	Johnson, Valentine, Capt.	to	Cave, Elizabeth -Parent, Belfield Cave
Sept. 14	Hawley, Benjamin	to	Edwards, Francis -Bonds., Joseph Edwards
Sept. 16	Camp, James	to	Wood, Mary
Oct. 20	Bradley, James	to	Wells, Elizabeth -George Wells signs permission
Oct. 24	Coppage, Charles	to	Wait, Lydia -Par., Wm. Wayt
Oct. 26	Blakey, Yelverton	to	Burton, Judith -Par., May Burton
Oct. 26	Morton, Robert	to	Curtis, Margaret -Bonds., James Morton
Oct. 27	Sanford, Stewart	to	Arnold, Anna -Par., Benjamin & Sally Arnold
Nov. 15	Ferguson, Vivbn	to	Mills, Mary A. -Par., Nathaniel Mills
Nov. 16	Bill, Wm.	to	Boston, Fanny -Par., Reubin Boston
Nov. 19	Pitcher, Wm.	to	Coleman, Fanny -Par., James Coleman
Nov. 2	Atkins, James	to	Atkins, Fanny -James Atkins signs permission
Nov. 29	Chapman, Thomas	to	Early, Elizabeth -Par., James Early
Nov. 28	Hite, Isaac	to	Maury, Ann Tunstall -Bonds., Leonard H. Maury
Nov. 2	Turner, James	to	Loyd, Sarah -Par., Wm. Loyd
Dec. 22	Hughes, Alexander	to	Mitchell, Elizabeth -Par., West Mitchell
Dec. 3	Dawson, James	to	Hughes, Nancy -Par., Francis Hughes
Dec. 8	Stone, John	to	Parrot, Judith -Par., Wm. Parrot
Dec. 8	Young, John	to	Reynolds, May -Par., Wm. Reynolds, Sr.
Dec. 27	Beach, Henry	to	Trus, Delila -Bonds., Joseph Beach
Dec. 26	Stephens, Wm.	to	Nelson, Elizabeth -Par., James Nelson
Dec. 27	Marshall, Thomas	to	Ancel, Nancy -Bonds., Wm. Ancell
Dec. 29	Piper, Wm.	to	White, Elizabeth -Bonds., Willis White
Dec. 28	Collins, John	to	Yager, Betty -Bonds., Ben Collins
Jan. 4	Sanford, Muse	to	Scott, Betty -Par., George Scott
Feb. 9	Graves, Wm.	to	White, Petty -Par., John White
Feb. 8	Clark, Nathaniel	to	Hall, Nancy
Feb. 12	Winslow, Valentine	to	Beadles, Ann -Par., John Beadles, Sr.
Feb. 13	Dodd, John	to	Johnson, Sally -Bonds., Wm. Dodd
Mar. 20	Clark, James	to	Payne, Sally -Bonds., Gabriel Payne
Mar. 5	Hamm, Joseph	to	Smoot, Nancy -Bonds., Cabel Smoot
Mar. 12	Fitz, Battaile	to	Taliaferro, Elizabeth -Bonds., Lewis Taliaferro

1804

Date	Groom		Bride
Mar. 26	Grasty, Goodrich	to	Morton, Elisabeth -Bonds., Thomas Coleman
Mar. 26	Petty, Zachary	to	Kendel, Polly -Par., John Kendel
Apr. 2	Moore, Wm.	to	Smith, Rebecca Hite -Par., John Smith
Apr. 4	Mallory, Elijah	to	Payne, Judith -Bonds., John Payne
Apr. 4	Todd, Wm.	to	Winslow, Catherine R. -Bonds., Joseph Chew
Apr. 23	Hawkins, Moses	to	Quisenberry, Joice -Bonds., Moses Quisenberry
May 3	Long, Wm.	to	Bickers, Elizabeth -Bonds., Joseph Bickers
June 6	Sampson, Elijah	to	Rogers, Amy -Par., John Rogers
July 3	Newman, John	to	Quisenberry, Sidnah(?) -Par., George Quisenberry, Sr.
July 3	King, John	to	Row, Cynthia -Par., Edmund Row
July 15	Medley, Jacob	to	Head, Fanny -Par., John Head

June 16	Smith, Absolem	to	McNiel, Martha -Bonds.,Wm.Terrill,Jr.
July 23	Arnold, Willis	to	Golden, Margaret -Bonds.,Julian King
July 23	Smith, Philip	to	Bickers, Matilda -Par.,Joseph Bickers, Mathias Smith
July 28	Golding, Reuben	to	Price, Polly -Par.,George Price
July 30	Martin, George	to	Sisson, Fanny -Par.,Sarah Sisson, Henry Martin
Aug. 16	Lamb, Wm.	to	Herring, Elizabeth
Aug. 17	Paggett, Wm.	to	Clark, Ann -Par.,Partick Clark, Ann Paggett
Aug. 16	Moore, Thomas R.	to	Crow, Elizabeth -Cladiah Overton,guardian
Aug. 27	Clark, John	to	Payne, Dillah -John Clark guardian
Aug. 27	Ancell, Robert	to	Pereson, Frances -Bonds.,Thomas Cox
Sept. 21	Grant, Jesse	to	Faulconer, Sally -Par.,John Faulconer
Sept. 24	Riddle, John	to	Seal, Elizabeth -Bonds.,John Ballard
Oct. 4	Barbour, Philip P.	to	Johnson, Frances T. -J. W. Barbour signs permission
Oct. 27	Sleet, James, Jr.	to	Petty, Rebecca -Par.,George Petty
Sept. 30	Gaines, Augustine	to	White, Polly -Bonds.,John White
Oct. 29	Mason, Samuel	to	Graves, Lydia -Bonds.,Thomas Graves
Oct. 10	Merryman, Wm.	to	Stevens, Elizabeth -Bonds.,Merryman Stevens
Oct. 23	Estes, William	to	Harvy, Polly -Bonds.,Anthony Harvey
Oct. 20	Stevens, Merryman	to	Grigry, Ann -Par.,John Grigry(?)
Nov. 8	Colyer, Preston	to	Hayna(?), Eliza
Nov. 12	Willis, John	to	Madison, Nelly C. -Bonds.,Paul Vidier
Nov. 19	Bell, Thomas	to	Milburn, Sarah -Bonds.,Robert F. Moore
Nov. 21	Abraham, Francis	to	Mallory, Jestin -Bonds.,Thomas Proctor
Nov. 25	Henley, Osborne	to	Winslow, Martha -Par.,Benjamin Winslow
Dec. 6	Taylor, Jonathan	to	McDaniel, Liza Ann -Bonds.,Alexander McDaniel
Dec. 4	Bell, John	to	Minton, Fanny -Par., John Minton
Dec. 18	Sanders, Benjamin	to	Jones, Nancy - Par.,Nathaniel Sanders & Francis Jones
Dec. 18	Lancaster, Edmund	to	Cooper, Dolly -Bonds.,Wm. Robertson
Dec. 18	Faulconer, Nicholas	to	Faulconer, Francis -Bonds., Reubin Faulconer
Dec. 18	Cooper, Benjamin	to	Lancaster, Susannah -Par.,John Lancaster
Dec. 20	Goodall, John	to	Davis, Sally
Dec. 20	Daniel, Reubin R.	to	Reynolds, Elizabeth -Bonds.,Thomas Daniel
Dec. 24	Acree, Wm.	to	Morris, Rebecca -Bonds., John Morris
Dec. 25	Austin, Richard	to	Snow, Mary
Dec. 25	Darnell, Rice	to	Ahart (?), Polly
Dec. 26	Hubbard, Joseph	to	Durrett, Deana -Par.,Joel Durrett
Dec. 27	Marshall, Henry	to	Wood, Ellen
Jan. 3	Spriggs, Ebenezer	to	Sanford, Mima -Bonds.,Stewart Sanford
Sept. 4 1805	Vernon, Isaac	to	Patterson, Nancy
Jan. 10	Payne, John	to	Mallory, Elizabeth -Bonds.,Elijah Mallory
Jan. 17	Banks, Gerard	to	Davis, Ann
Jan. 23	Bronsugh(?),Charley	to	Daniel, Mary -Bonds.,Cabel Lindsay
Jan. 28	Leavell, Lewis	to	Bell, Francis -Bonds.,John W. Powell

Date	Groom		Bride
Feb. 4	Mitchell, Thomas	to	Rumsey, Nancy -Par.,Thomas Rumsey
Feb. 14	Gibbs, Zacharias	to	Wayt, Lucy -Par., James Wayt
Feb. 19	Kelly, Spencer	to	Rumsey, Lianna -Bonds.,John Sleet
Mar. 1	Reynolds, Washington	to	Swan, Catherine -Bonds.,Wm. W. Reynolds
Mar. 18	Eves, Thomas	to	Jenkins, Fanny -Par.,Wm. Alkins
Mar. 20	Bickers, Joel	to	Atkins, Rosanna -Par.,John Atkins
Mar. 25	Clark, Henry	to	Johnson, Elizabeth -Bonds.Thomas Grasty
Apr. 2	Price, Thomas	to	Dohoney, Elizabeth -Par.,Hannah Dohoney
Apr. 19	Gosney, Reuben	to	McKenney, Elizabeth -Bonds., Wm. McKenney
May 30	Anderson, Joel	to	Reddish, Lucy
June 2	Baily, James	to	Mallory, Nancy
June 12	Graves, Walker	to	Rucker, Polly -Bonds., Wm. Rucker
July 30	Rumsey, Elijah	to	Hughs, Sally -Par.,Francis Hughs
July 30	Abell, John	to	King, Sally -Bonds., Cabel Abell
Aug. 10	Gatewood, Henry	to	Quisenberry, Amy -Par., Moses Quisenberry
Aug. 10	Quisenberry, Moses	to	Burnley, Sarah -Par.,Joel Durrett
Sept. 11	Hilman, Joseph	to	Abell, Susanna -Par.,Cabel Abell
Sept. 28	Taylor, William	to	Burnley, Sarah G. -Bonds.,John Taylor
1805			
Sept. 11	Terrell, Reubin	to	Morton, Susanna -Bonds.,William Morton
Sept. 23	Sherman, Jessie	to	Bruden, Sally -Bonds.,Berryman Bruding
Sept. 11	Trower, Solomon	to	Smith, Nancy -Bonds., John Smith
Sept. 25	Durrett, Achilles	to	Quisenberry, Lydia -Bonds., Moses Quisenberry
Oct. 5	Smoot, Jenifer	to	Malone, Rebecca -Par.,John Malone
Oct. 9	Herndon, Benjamin	to	Stevens, Mary -Par.,Benjamin Stevens, Sr.
Oct. 11	Hancock, James	to	Hancock, Elender -Par.,Wm. Hancock
Nov. 16	Ford, Wm.	to	Stubbling, Susanna -Bonds.,James Lanton
Nov. 17	Quisenberry, Aaron	to	Reynolds, Henrietta -Bonds., George Quisenberry
Nov. 18	Thompson, Wm. Jr.	to	Ellis, Rebecca N. -Par.,Wm.Thompson,Sr. & Thomas Ellis
Nov. 21	Lowry, Thomas	to	Dedman(R?), Nancy -Par. John Dedman
Nov. 20	Thompson, Wm.	to	Sinker, Catey -Bonds.,Brooks Sinker
Nov. 25	Cave, Richard	to	Poter, Maria -Bonds.,Abner Porter
Dec. 18	Loyd, George	to	Bell, Betsy -Bonds.,Wm. Pulliam
Dec. 19	Smith, William	to	Morris, Nancy -Parson,George Bingham
Dec. 25	Harris, James	to	Estes, Sally -Bonds., Wm. Estes
Dec. 24	Wells, Levi	to	Marshall, Charlotte -Parson, George Bingham
Dec. 26	Beckett, Richard	to	Thornhill, Nancy -Parson, George Bingham
1805			
Dec. 28	Fisher, James	to	Mason, Fanny -Bonds., Peter Mason,Jr.
Jan. 2	Lower, Peter	to	Ham, Judith -Parson, Nathaniel Sanders
Jan. 9	Snow, James	to	Harvy, Jenny -Parson, George Bingham
Jan. 25	Davis, Benjamin	to	Jones, Jane - Parson, George Bingham
Feb. 18	Fant, John T.	to	James, Fanny -Par.,Joseph & Lucy James

Feb. 4	Highlander, Jacob	to	Pittis, Fanny –Par., John Pittis
Feb. 18	Tulloch, Wm.	to	Whitelaw, Nancy –Par., Douglas Whitelaw
Dec. 27	Robinson, Moses	to	Jones, Fanny –Par., Richart Jones
Mar. 21	Marsh, Peter	to	Jollett, Lucy Walker – Par., James Jollett
Apr. 1	Herndon, George	to	Teale, Sarah – Par., Henry Teale
Mar. 22	Braden, Joseph	to	Neal, Polly –Par., Fielding Neal
May 3	Harrison, Lewis	to	Harrison, Nancy
May 19	Wood, Jesse	to	Page, Nancy
June 9	Smoot, John	to	Thornton, Lucy Buckner –Par., George Thornton
June 23	Mozings, James	to	Coleman, Mildred –Bonds., John Herndon
July 14	Philips, Conyers	to	Farneyhough, Elizabeth –Par., Thomas Fearney
July 18	Brockman, James	to	Turner, Milly
July 23	Waggoner, Wm. G.	to	Hansford, Lucinda –Bonds., James Garnett
1806			
July 31	Taylor, Robert	to	Taylor, Mary Conway –Par., Charles Taylor, Sr.
Aug. 19	Cave, Robert	to	Bradley, Lucy –Bonds., George Bradley, Jr.
Aug. 28	Wright, John J.	to	Wright, Nancy –Par., John Wright
Sept. 22	Oakes, Mainyard	to	Lancaster, Polly – Par., John & Susannah Lancaster
Sept. 22	Webb, Wm. Bennett	to	Lancaster, Martha –Par., John & Susannah Lancaster
Oct. 15	Anderson, Benjamin	to	Miller, Mary –Par., John Miller
Oct. 17	Woods, Richard	to	Cox, Tabitha –Par., Thomas Cox
Nov. 22	Stevens, John	to	Stephen, Ann S. Par., John Stephens, Jr.
Nov. 24	Snell, Joseph	to	Mansfield, Elizabeth C. –Par., Robert & Maurning Mansfield
Dec. 19	Jacobs, Nathan	to	Straghan, Nancy –Bonds., Albin Elliot
Dec. 12	Cave, Richard	to	Shelton, Lucy –Parson, Nathaniel Sanders
Dec. 20	Atkins, John	to	Campbell, Peggy –Guardian, Wm. Tatum
Dec. 20	Kenney, Wm.	to	Beale, Fanny –Bonds., Cornelius Devenney
Dec. 24	Morris, Reubin	to	Acre, Sally –Par., Wm. Acre
Dec. 24	Pendleton, John	to	Thompson, Fanny –Bonds., Jackson Tandy
Dec. 24	Davis, Elijah	to	Jones, Elizabeth –Parson, George Bingham
Dec. 25	Burton, Wm.	to	Goodridge, Ann –Bonds., Wm. Rucker
1807			
Jan. 4	Wood, James	to	White, Sarah –Par., Jeremiah White
Jan. 5	Fletcher, Washington	to	Payne, Elizabeth –Bonds., Willis Overton
Jan. 8	Hawkins, Elijah	to	Scott, Elizabeth –Bonds., George Scott
Jan. 12	Rogers, Keller	to	Ham, Mary –Par., Samuel Ham
Jan. 15	Wood, Nicholas L.	to	Key, Nancy –Parson, Wm. Douglass
Feb. 5	Clark, James	to	Graves, Elizabeth –Parson, Wm. Douglass
Feb. 5	Beadles, Robert M.	to	Winslow, Sarah –Bonds., Fertunatus Winslow
Feb. 11	Berry, Wm. S.	to	Row, Rachel –Par., Thomas Row
Feb. 12	Blakey, Reubin	to	Strother, Polly
Feb. 16	Twyman, Anthony	to	Davis, Sarah –Par., Isaac Davis

Mar. 17	Madison, Carlett	to	Routt, Winney –Bonds., Wm. Tinsley & Stewart Sanford
Apr. 14	Oaks, John	to	Graves, Joanna –Par., Thomas Graves
Apr. 29	Walters, Isaac	to	Pence, Elizabeth –Par., John Pence
Apr. 28	King, John	to	Yates, Francis –Par., Julien King
Apr. 26	Rollins, Richard	to	Herndon, Lucy –Guardian, John Herndon
May 8	Walters, John	to	Hambleton, Margaret –Bonds., John Coleman
May 21	Collins, Reubin	to	Riddle, Fanny –Par., James Riddle
May 15	Moore, Alexander	to	Ford, Lucy –Par., Wm. Ford
May 22	Johnson, James	to	Quisenberry, Nancy –Par., Mary Quisenberry
May 24	Daniel, Wm.	to	McCully, Jane –Bonds., Wm. Finnell
June 1	Webb, James	to	Clark, Nancy –Par., Joseph Clark
June 9	Frazier, Shadrack	to	Morris, Polly –Par., Wm. Morris
June 20	Adams, Thomas B.	to	Burnley, Judith –Par., Francis Burnley
July 1	Proctor, George, Jr.	to	Grady, Fanny –Par., Wm. Grady, Sr.
July 1	Strother, George F.	to	Williams, Sarah Green –Par., James Williams
July 27	Barton(Byrton?) John	to	May, Milly –Bonds., Joel May
July 28	Rumsey, Walker	to	Camike(?), Polly –Bonds., Spencer Kelly
Aug. 21	Wallis, John	to	Randel, Nancy –Par., Wm. Randel
Sept. 10	Bruce, Loudown B.	to	Estes, Milly –Bonds., Wm. Estes
Sept. 23	Leathers, Jonathan	to	Payne, Betsy –Par., Thomas Payne
Sept. 30	Lamb, Willis (Par.,Wm. Lamb, Sr.)	to	Slaughter, Rebecca –Bonds., Wm. B. Knight
Dec. 23	Garnett, James	to	Chiles, Frances –Par., James Chiles
Oct. 16	Bailes, Joseph	to	Olliver, Cency(?) –Par.,Frances Olliver
Oct. 17	Hawkins, Alexander	to	Scott, Anna –Bonds., George Scott
Oct. 15	Scott, George	to	Abell, Nancy –Bonds., George Smith
Nov. 11	Blakey, James	to	Branham, Nancy –Par.,Robert Branham
Dec. 4	Morris, Thomas	to	Wright, Sally –Bonds., Elisha Wright
Dec. 18	Grady, John	to	Proctor, Sarah –Par., John Proctor
Dec. 16	Smith, James	to	Smith, Caty –Bonds., Wm. Lindsay
Dec. 17	Fletcher, Wm.	to	Sullivan, Delila –Par., Wm. Sullivan
Dec. 30	Thornton, Charles	to	Ogg, Martha –Par., Alexander Ogg
Dec. 24	Austin, John	to	Burrus, Justina
Dec. 27	Hall, Ambrose	to	Marr, Elizabeth
1808			
Jan. 4	Bell, Jacob	to	Tatiaferro, Martha H., Par., Ann Taliaferro of Madison Co. Hay Taliaferro, guardian of Martha
Jan. 6	McFarlan, Wm.	to	Alsop, Fanny –Par., John McFarling?
Jan. 6	Lee, Abner	to	Lee, Sally –Bonds., Samuel Lee
Jan. 21	Hensley, Seder	to	Thompson, Winney –Bonds., George Thompson
Jan. 20	Goodall, Isaac	to	Huckstep, Milly –Bonds.,John Huckstep
Jan. 25	Cottom, Peter	to	Grymes, Judith R. –Bonds., James Pulliam
Jan. 28	Walton, Snow	to	Snow, Agnes –Parson, George Bingham
Feb. 2	Shelton, Thomas	to	Beadles, Clary –Bonds.,Robt. M. Beadles
Feb. 10	Wright, Alexander	to	Jones, Betsy –Bonds., Edward Holladay

Date	Groom		Bride
Feb. 11	Harvey, Anthony	to	Bingham —Bonds., Richard Golding
1807 May 21	Collins, Reubin	to	Riddle, Fanny —Par., James Riddle
1803 Dec. 28	Collins, John	to	Yager, Betty —Bonds., Ben Collins
1803 Jan. 4	Collins, John	to	Kirtley, Elizabeth
1799 Sept. 23	Robertson, Richard	to	Collins, Eliz. —Bonds., Edward Collins
1798 Dec. 26	Eddins, Thom	to	Collins, Frances —Par., Wm. Collins
1796	Graves, Benj.	to	Collins, Eliz. —Par., Wm. Collins
1803 Oct. 24	Coppage, Charles	to	Wayt, Lydia —Par., Wm. Wayt
1794 Apr. 24	Collins, Francis	to	Dahoney, Peggy —Par., Thom. Dahoney
1808			
Mar. 29	Terry, Overton	to	Garnett, Sarah —Bonds., James Morton
Mar. 31	Moody, John	to	Stowers, Betsy —Par., Mark Stowers
Apr. 10	Lamb, John	to	Watson, Polly
Apr. 12	Turner, Fleming	to	Clark, Jane —Par., John Clark
June 2	Taylor, Larkin	to	Hume, Elizabeth —Parson, George Bingham
June 2	Frye, John	to	Baugker, Catherine — " George Bingham
June 7	Miller, Christian	to	Beazley, Elizabeth — " George Bingham
June 9	Humble, Wm.	to	Overton, Mary —Par., Willis Overton
June 28	Gilmer, John	to	Minor, Sarah —Bonds., Dabney Minor
June 28	Rogers, Joseph	to	Newman, Malinda —Par., Wm. Newman, Sr.
Aug. 16	Gibbins, Thomas	to	Debord, Lucy —Parson, George Bingham
Sept. 13	Rogers, Benjamin	to	Lane, Mary —Parson, George Bingham
Oct. 30	Bruth, Kendal C.	to	Burton, Polly W. —Par., James Burton
Nov. 15	Lindsay, Reubin	to	Mills, Fanny —Bonds., Nathaniel Mills, Jr.
Nov. 19	Garnett, Andrew	to	Bell, Sally B. —Bonds., Wm. Bell
Nov. 17	Aery, George	to	Shiflet, Elizabeth
Nov. 24	Fredrick, Philip	to	Baughker, Betsy —Parson, George Bingham
Nov. 29	Barbour, Philip. C.S.	to	Pollock, Peggy —Bonds., John Moore Par., Wm. Pollock
Dec. 3	Martin, Wm.	to	Atkins, Patsy —Bonds., Lewis Harris
Dec. 9	Hunt, Robert	to	Darnell, Francis —Par., Mary Ann Darnell
Dec. 19	Jenkins, Wm.	to	Pettis, Sally —Par., John Pettis
Dec. 22	Thornton, Thomas	to	Wright, Elizabeth —Bonds., Wm. Wright
Dec. 30	Tucker, Thornton	to	Biggers, Betsy —Par., Mason Biggers
Dec. 30	Vealch(W?) John	to	Cooper, Nancy
Dec. 31	Eddins, Joseph, Jr.	to	Davis, Nancy —Par., Mary Davis
1809			
Jan. 13	Hicks, Charles	to	Watson, Judith —Parson, George Bingham
Jan. 12	Breedlove, Broaders	to	Powell, Nancy —Bonds., Martin Thomas
Jan. 5	Sems, Isaac	to	Catterton, Nancy —Parson, George Bingham
Jan. 8	Sampson, Wm.	to	Jollet, Sally —Parson, George Bingham
Jan. 11	Yager, Wm.	to	Chancellor, Jane —Par., Betsy & John Chancellor
Jan. 22	Melons, Wm.	to	Wayland, Mary —Par., Henry Wayland
Jan. 19	Rucker, Elzy	to	Turton, Mary —Par., Joseph Burton
Jan. 19	Whitelaw, Nicholas	to	Beasley, Elisabeth —Par., James Beasley
Jan. 19	Shifflet, Overton	to	Herring, Sally —Par., Wm. R. Herring
Jan. 19	Jackson, John	to	Herndon, Polly —Parson, George Bingham

Jan. 24	Darnell, Nelson	to	Mallory, Cynthia -Bonds. & Par., Henry Mallory
Feb. 1	Johnson, Richard	to	Alcocke, Lucy -Bonds., Joseph Alcocke
Feb. 4	Burke, Isaac	to	Miller, Jane -Bonds., Robert Miller
Feb. 9	Collins, Tandy	to	Beazley, Ann -Par., James Beazley, Sr.
Feb. 21	Goodall, David	to	Clark, Tibatha -Parson, George Bingham
Mar. 24	Evans, John	to	King, Nancy -Par., Julian King
Mar. 22	Quick, George	to	Raines, Mildred -Par., Reubin Rains?
Mar. 26	Goodridge, George C.	to	Burton, Fanny -Bonds., John Lucas
Mar. 27	Tandy, Jackson	to	Mills, Sara -Par., Nathaniel Mills, Sr.
Apr. 27	Shisler, Lewis	to	Clark, Saley -Par., Joseph Clark
May 14	Watts, Thomas	to	Head, Sarah -Parson, George Bingham
May 17	Gilbert, Aquila	to	Newman, Fanny -Par., Wm. Newman, Sr.
May 25	Anderson, Wm.	to	Hawkins, Lucy -Par., Reubin Hawkins
May 28	Rucker, Belfield	to	White, Nancy -Par., Richard & Nancy White & Joel Rucker
May 30	Stephenson, Charles	to	Hancock, Susan -Bonds., Willis Arnold & Francis Day
June 25	Beckham, John	to	Hancock, Rebecca -Par., Wm. Hancock
June 26	Mason, Joseph	to	Tandy, Anna -Par., Henry Tandy, Sr.
June 24	Payne, Robert	to	Collins, Ann -Bonds., Lewis D. Collins
July 29	Twyman, John	to	Wayt, Peggy - Par., Wm. Wayt
Aug. 4	Horsley, James	to	Chiles, Jane -Par., Robert Jones
Aug. 24	Newman, Wm., Jr.	to	Faulconer, Lucy -Bonds., Nicholas Faulconer
Sept. 10	Arnold, Wm. B.	to	Martin, Jane -Par., Wm. H. Martin
Sept. 15	Nalle, Martin	to	Nelly, Madison Barbour -Bonds., J. W. Barbour
Sept. 24	Thompson, John	to	Pierce, Julia -Bonds., Cypress Hensley
Oct. 15	Lloyd, Thompson	to	Moubray, Sarah -Parson, George Bingham
Oct. 27	Taylor, Robert	to	King, Fanny - Parson, Robt. Jones
Nov. 19	Terrell, Henry C.	to	Smith, Delpha -Bonds., Samuel Tell
Sept. 24	Hensley, Cypress	to	Thompson, Caty -Bonds., John Thompson
Oct. 14	Morris, John, Jr.	to	Dollins, Suky -Par., Wm. Dollins
Oct. 23	Longan, Edmund	to	Edwards, Sally -Bonds., Joseph L. Edwards
Nov. 9	Thompson, Thomas	to	Robinson, Frances -Par., Francis Robinson
Nov. 11	Riddle, Valentine	to	Goodall, Betsy -Par., James Goodall, Sr.
Nov. 27	Breedlove, Nathaniel	to	Mitchel, Eleanor -Bonds., Wm. Mitchell
Nov. 27	Davis, William	to	Boston, Sally -Bonds., Reubin Boston
Nov. 27	Reynolds, Wm.	to	Quisenberry, Joice -Par., Sally Quisenberry & Wm. Reynolds
Dec. 14	Bledsoe, John	to	Pitcher, Susanna -Par., Wm. Pitcher, Sr.
Dec. 15	Herndon, John	to	Adams, Nancy -Par., Wm. Adams
Dec. 18	McCoyle, Michall	to	McKinney, Nancy -Par., Wm. McKinney
Dec. 21	Boston, Reubin	to	Anderson, Mary -Par., Jacob Anderson
Dec. 24	Quinn, Garland	to	Smith, Dealem -Par., Hannah Hensley
Dec. 22	Grasty, George	to	Payne, Elizabeth -Par., John Payne
Dec. 23	Gibson, Peter	to	Estes, Fanny -Bonds., William Estes
Dec. 24	Rogers, Jermenius	to	Ferguson, Elizabeth -Parson, George Bingham
Dec. 25	Loyd, Willis	to	Ayheart, Felicia -Parson, George Bingham

1810

Date	Groom		Bride
Jan. 4	Herman, Fredrick	to	Jamerson, Mary (widow) -Bonds., Phellemon Davis
Jan. 15	Steward(?) John	to	Reynolds, Catherine -Par., Wm. Reynolds, Sr.
Jan. 15	Parrot, Wm.	to	Wayland, Judith -Par., Joshua Wayland
Jan. 17	Sanford, Hamlet	to	Biggers, Pheobe -Par., Mason Biggers
Jan. 25	Barker, Leonard	to	Robinson, Keturah -Par., Frances Robinson
Feb. 11	White, Richard	to	Wayt, Amey -Bonds., Wm. Wayt
Mar. 1	Stowers, Reubin	to	Jackson, Margaret -Par., Mark Stowers
Mar. 26	Batley, Alfred	to	Wright, Mishel -Bonds., Thomas A. Dempsey
Mar. 8	Schooler, Joseph H.	to	Quisenberry, Dolly -Bonds., Henry Quisenberry
Mar. 12	Yates(Yancy?) Charles	to	Loyd, Betsy -Par., Wm. Loyd
Mar. 14	Simpson, Aaron	to	Mullican, Mary -Bonds., John Richards
Apr. 3	Bronaugh, Charles B.	to	Brockman, Elizabeth -Par., Wm. Brockman
Apr. 6	Bell, Robert W.	to	Schenk, Anne T. -Parson, James Goss
Apr. 16	Henderson, Ambrose	to	Acre, Lucy -Par., William Acre
Apr. 24	Coleman, Ambrose	to	Hilman, Fanny -Par., Joseph Hilman
May 10	Marr, Joel	to	Miller, Betsy -Bonds., Robt. Mallory
May 17	Adams, James	to	Harper, Patsy -Bonds., Ellick Hawkins
July 16	Cave, Wm.	to	Snow, Sarah -Bonds., Bartlett Cave
Aug. 26	Estes, Abraham	to	Cox, Sally W. -Bonds., Wm. Cox
Aug. 27	Wright, Dabney	to	Bell, Sally - Brockman Bell, Guardian
Oct. 11	Blackwell, Leland	to	Burton, Nancy -Par., Wm. Burton
Sept. 13	Welsh, Oliver	to	Mallory, Betsy -Par., Nathaniel Welsh, Uriel Mallory, Sr.
Sept. 13	Terrell, Edmund	to	Smith, Susannah -Par., Oliver Terrill
Sept. 17	Bell, Brockman	to	Brockman, Rebecca -Par., John Brockman
Sept. 25	Sampson, Wm. Jr.	to	Sampson, Sally -Par., Wm. Sampson, Sr.
Sept. 26	Conway, Catlett, Jr.	to	Taliaferro, Virlinda -Bonds., George Conway
Sept. 22	Dickinson, Thomas	to	Wood, Nancy -Bonds., Reubin Twyman
Oct. 22	Rogers, Thomas	to	Chancellor, Penelope -Thomas Rogers, Guardian
Oct. 28	Hoard, Washington	to	Verdier, Susan -Wm. Shepherd, Guardian
Dec. 6	Kirtley, Joseph	to	Sims, Elizabeth -Par., Jeremiah Sims
Dec. 26	Jenkins, John	to	Terry, Sarah -Bonds., Reubin Oakes
Dec. 8	Hensley, John	to	Oliver, Elizabeth -Par., Francis Oliver
Dec. 14	McFarling, John	to	Dedman, Frances -Bonds., George Herndon
Dec. 17	Beadles, John, Jr.	to	Haymes, Jucinda -Bonds., Robt. M. Beadles
Dec. 27	Austin, David	to	Williams, Fanny -Par., Nancy Austin & John Williams
Dec. 28	Marr, Thomas	to	Harvy, Sally -Bonds., Thomas Harvey
Dec. 27	Martin, Wm.	to	Snell, Margaret -Bonds., John Snell

1811

Date	Groom		Bride
Jan. 2	Blakey, William	to	Branham, Polly -Par., Robert Branham
Jan. 3	Bowen, John	to	Seal, Sally -Par., Philip Seal
Jan. 17	Turner, Elisha	to	Seal, Mary -Bonds., Newman Faulconer
Jan. 21	Breedlove, Edward	to	Harvey, Haney -Bonds., Martin Thomas
Jan. 29	Collier, Hudson	to	Ham, Betsy -Bonds., Joseph Ham

Date	Groom		Bride
Feb. 11	Deane, George	to	Kindle, Mary -Par., Wm. Deane
Feb. 28	Shiflett, Edward	to	Herring, Joice -Par., Wm. Herring
Mar. 16	Vinniard, Alexander	to	Hensley, Polly -Bonds., John Hensley
Apr. 1	Wayland, Henry	to	Ara, Melone -Par., Henry Wayland, Sr.
Apr. 15	Rogers, James	to	Jackson, Elezabeth -Par., Drury Jackson
Apr. 16	Klu, John	to	Price, Catherine(widow) -Bonds., Thomas Sorrille
May 3	Beckham, Benjamin	to	Poter, Mary Ann -Par., John Porter
July 24	Conway, Reubin	to	Macon, Lucy H. -Par., Thom. Macon
Aug. 4	Reynolds, Wm.	to	Jones, Hannah -Bonds., Thom. Clark
Aug. 22	Black, Jacob	to	Cave, Nancy -Par., Jacob Black, Sr. & Wm. Cave, Jr.
Sept. 3	Ballard, David C.	to	Huckstep, Elizabeth -Par., John Huckstep
Sept. 26	Lindsay, Landon	to	Mills, Celey -Par., Nathaniel Mills
Sept. 12	Carter, Adcock	to	Daniel, Elizabeth -Bonds., John Corthone
Sept. 24	Palmer, Benjamin	to	Lefore, Judith -Bonds., Willis Overton
Nov. 11	Haney, May	to	Runkle, Mary Macklin -Par., Jacob Runkle
Nov. 7	Payne, Milton	to	Burton, Sarah -Par., May Burton
Nov. 20	Jones, Thomas	to	Overton, Peggy -Par., Willis Overton
Nov. 11	McGee, John S.	to	Harris, Lucy -Par., Francis Harris
Nov. 25	Beazley, Wm.	to	Graves, Susanna -Par., Charles Beazley & Thomas Graves
Nov. 26	Ralls, Robinson	to	Clark, Mary Ann -Par., Thomas Clark
Oct. 3	Abell, Alexander	to	Abell, Polly -Par., Cabel Abell
Oct. 16	Faulconer, Thomas	to	Jones, Elizabeth -Par., James Jones
Oct. 19	Wood, Levi	to	Estes, Susan -Par., Wm. Estes
Oct. 23	Raines, Wm.	to	Eddins, Frances -Par., Mildred Eddins
Oct. 28	Brockman, Curtis	to	Quisenberry, Nancy -Bonds., Wm. T. Burrus
Oct. 28	Quisenberry, Vivian	to	Wright, Sally -Bonds., Benjamin Wright, Geo. Quisenberry & Thomas Addams
Oct. 17	Smith, James, Jr.	to	Bell, May Hulda -Par., Henry Bell & James Smith, Sr.
Oct. 20	Cooper, Owen	to	Webb, Mary Mason -Par., Jesse B. Webb
Dec. 21	Chrenshaw, Thomas	to	Parrott, Nancy -Par., Wm. Parrott
Dec. 24	Morris, George	to	Simmons, Mary -Par., Bazzell Simmons
Dec. 23	Sisson, Abner	to	Chambers, Rachel -Par., Thomas Chambers
Dec. 25	Turnley, John	to	Pound, Patsy(widow) Parson, Robert Jones
Dec. 23	Gardner, Daniel	to	Harris, Malinda -Joseph Atkins, Guardian
Dec. 23	Bledsoe, George, Jr.	to	Pitcher, Joaner -Par., Wm. Pitcher
Dec. 23	Jones, John	to	Bickers, Susan -Par., Joseph Bickers
Dec. 23	Lansley, John	to	Pitcher, Catherine -Par., Wm. Pitcher
Dec. 25	Parrot, John	to	Simmons, Fanny -Par., John Simmons
Dec. 25	Smith, Tartan	to	Mallory, Luch -Par., Henry Mallory

1812

Date	Groom		Bride
Feb. 2	Keeton, John, Sr.	to	Chancellor, Elizabeth (widow) -Bonds., John Keelon, Jr.
Feb. 25	Nelson, Thomas	to	Quisenberry, Elizabeth -Bonds., James Nelson

Date	Groom		Bride
Jan. 26	Thacker, Henry	to	Terrill, Frances –Bonds., Reubin Terrill
Jan. 27	White, Willis	to	Wayt, Nancy –Par., Richard White & Wm. Wayt
Feb. 3	Whitelaw, Alexander	to	Chuvning, –Par., Robert Chuvning
Feb. 6	Breeding, Ezekiel	to	Haney, Betsy –Par., James & Nancy Haney
Feb. 5	Manpin, David	to	Davis, Jerusha
Mar. 3	Dewall, Claiborne	to	Faulconer, Polly –Par., David Faulconer
Feb. 26	Price, John	to	Sims, Elizabeth –Richard L. Sims Guardian
Mar. 24	Smith, Bradford	to	Jacobs, Nancy –Par., Robert Jacobs
Apr. 27	Tower, Mitchel	to	Gibbons, Ann –Par., Thomas Gibbons
May 12	Caza, Wm.	to	Slaughter, Mary –Bonds., Jeremiah Henry
May 19	Lee, Wm.	to	Terrill, Sally –Bonds., John Terrill
May 30	Woolfolk, Wm.	to	Woolfork, Susan –Par., Thomas Woolfolk
June 3	Long, Wm.	to	Farish, Mary Stevens –Par., Thomas Farish
June 18	Norris, Cabel	to	Harris, Olly –Parson, Geo. Bingham
June 18	Eaton, Wm.	to	Duniven, Elizabeth –Parson, George Bingham
June 25	Morton, Elijah	to	Webb, Mary G. –Bonds., Goodrich S. Grasty
Aug. 6	Baxter, James	to	Payne, Sally –Par., Reubin Payne
July 9	Early, James	to	Carr, Sarah
July 12	Bingham, Wyatt	to	Bingham, Rebecca –Par., Josiah & George Bingham
July 17	Young, Daniel	to	Rhoades, Elizabeth –Par., George Rhoades
Aug. 12	Jenkins, Quire(?)	to	Hawkins, Luch –Bonds., Alfred Battaile
Aug. 19	Mallory, Philip	to	Morton, Sally –Wm. Morton, Guardian
Sept. 2	Welsh, Nathaniel	to	Mallory, Mary –Bonds., Wm. Mallory
Sept. 3	Montague, Wm.	to	Perry, Sukey –Bonds., Wm. Dodd
Sept. 10	Shifflet, John	to	Raines, Polly
Oct. 4	Terrill, James	to	Middlebrook, Susan –Par., Nathaniel Middlebrook
Oct. 4	Hawkins, John B.	to	Ford, Ann –Bonds., Wm. Ford
Oct. 29	Bush, Cabel	to	Taylor, Lucinda –Bonds., St.Clair Taylor
Oct. 27	Walters, Mitchael	to	McFarland, Sally –Bonds., Robt. Mannan
Oct. 26	Yowell, Ephriam	to	Eddins, Polly –Bonds., Abraham Eddins
Oct. 29	Smith, Edward	to	Bess, Sally –Bonds., John Allbright
Nov. 8	Gregory, Obediah	to	Lancaster, Nancy –Par., Benjamin Lancaster
Nov. 10	Thomas, John	to	Ellis, Sally –Par., Thomas Ellis
Nov. 11	Sims, Reuben	to	Graves, Francis –Parson, Geo. Bingham
Nov. 12	Early, Wm.	to	Graves, Sarah – Parson, Geo. Bingham
Nov. 22	Osborne, Holland	to	Farneyhough, Sally –Par., Robt. Osborne
Nov. 26	Walton, John	to	Davis, Rhoda
Dec. 7	Hansford, John	to	King, Sarah –Bonds., John Evans
1813			
Jan. 1	Quisenberry, Daniel	to	Rhoades, Mary –Par., George Rhoades
Feb. 7	Atkins, Jonathan	to	Quisenberry, Milly –Par., George Quisenberry

Date	Groom		Bride
Feb. 14	Key, Walter	to	Daniel, Martha (widow) -Par., Martha Daniel
1812			
Dec. 20	Lay, John	to	Sebree, Elizabeth -Bonds., Wm. W. Johnson
Dec. 24	Morris, George	to	Simmons, Mary
Dec. 24	Lansley, John	to	Pitcher, Catherine
Dec. 27	Martin, Wm.	to	Fearneyhough, Nancy -Bonds., John Farneyhough
Dec. 31	Hume, James	to	Dodd, Margaret, -Par., James Dodd
1813			
Jan. 13	Osborne, Braxton	to	Taliaferro, Ann -Bonds., John Taliaferro
Jan. 27	Hughes, George W.	to	Harvy, Polly -Bonds., James Snow
Jan. 21	Terrill, Edmund	to	Morton, Ann T. -Bonds., Elijah Morton
Jan. 18	Jones, John	to	Faulconer, Milly -Par., Richard Faulconer & Thomas Jones
Feb. 12	Musgrove, Alexander	to	Morris, Polly -Par., George Morris
Feb. 4	Dunn, John	to	Maupin, Susanna
Feb. 7	Chapman, Richard M.	to	Verdier, Maria -Par., Paul Verdier
Feb. 14	Robinson, Thomas	to	Roach, Nancy -Par., James Roach
Feb. 16	Cox, Wm. D.	to	White, Fanny -Bonds., John White
Feb. 19	Morris, Wm.	to	Roach, Molly
Mar. 2	Sampson, John	to	Jollett, Clarisa -Bonds., Peter Marsh
Mar. 2	Williams, Wm.	to	Stubblefield, Mary Ann -Par., George Stubblefield
Mar. 15	Brock, Archibald	to	Moyers, Sarah -Par., Michael Moyers
May 5	Teel, Henry	to	Reed, Dicy (widow) -Bonds., George Herndon
Mar. 28	Bryan, Jeremiah	to	Long, Frankey -Bonds., Armistad Long
Apr. 26	Morris, David	to	Shifflett, Patsy -Par., Wm. Shifflett
May 10	Wood, Zachariah	to	Clark, Peggy -Bonds., Baylor Mason
May 10	Mason, Baylor	to	Clark, Caty -Bonds., Zachariah Wood
May 13	Shifflett, Merry	to	Snow, Lucy -Parson, Geo. Bingham
June 6	White, Benjamin	to	Twyman, Judith -Bonds., James White
June 18	Gray, Gabriel	to	Barbour, Sarah -Par., Thomas Barbour
July 14	Newman, Andrew	to	Wright, Eleanor -Bonds., Wm. Wright
Sept. 5	Clark, Thomas	to	Jamerson, Catherine R. -Bonds., John Clark & Philemon Samuel
Sept. 23	Waugh, Gores	to	Wright, Susan -Par., Wm. Wright
Sept. 23	Mitchell, John	to	Wood, Nelly -Par., Wm. Mitchell
Sept. 30	Yowell, John	to	Davis, Jane -Bonds., Cudden Davis
Sept. 30	Dixon, John	to	Rumsey, Lucy -Par., Wm. Rumsey
Oct. 13	Carter, Benjamin	to	Daniel, Polly -Bonds., Adcock Carter
Oct. 30	Holmes, Armistead, Capt.	to	Willis, Lucy M. -Par., Wm. C. Willis
Oct. 4	Wigglesworth, Wm., Jr.	to	Reynolds, Mary -Par., Joseph Wigglesworth & Joseph Reynolds
Oct. 18	Collins, Wm.	to	Quisenberry, Sally -Bonds., John Henderson
Nov. 1	Loring, Thomas	to	Vawter, Mary -Bonds., Benjamin Vawter
Nov. 18	Mansfield, James W.	to	Clark, Mildred -Par., Robert Mansfield & John Clark
Nov. 22	Trice, Jesse	to	Arnett, Liddia -Bonds., Wm. Arnett
Nov. 22	Sims, Brooks	to	Boswell, Polly -Par., Charles Boswell
Dec. 2	Shifflett, John	to	Martin, Francis -Parson, Geo. Bingham
Dec. 9	Early, Joab	to	Thompson, Elizabeth - " George Bingham

Date	Groom		Bride
Dec. 16	Parrott, George	to	Catterton, Elizabeth -Bonds., George Bingham
Dec. 28	Herndon, Benjamin	to	Lucas, Lucy -Bonds., George Bingham
Dec. 20	Berry, Anthony	to	Lee, Jane -Bonds., Nathaniel Lee
Dec. 27	Wright, Isaac	to	Smith, Agnes -Bonds., John Fisher
Dec. 27	Bowen, Ephriam	to	Leathers, Polly -Par., John Leathers
Dec. 30	Riddle, Tavernor	to	Goodall, Mary -Par., David Goodall
Dec. 29	Richards, Hezekiah	to	Lancaster, Elizabeth -Par., John Lanchaster
Dec. 29	Faulconer, Carter B.	to	Faulconer, Nancy -Bonds., John Tunley
Dec. 29	Ford, Benj.	to	Atkins, Rhody -Par., Annie Alkins
1814			
Jan. 4	Naylor, Thomas	to	Watton, Jane -Parson, George Bingham
Jan. 27	Walker, James	to	Powell, Joice -Par., Lewis G. Powell
Jan. 25	Oaks, Major	to	Oaks, Martha -Bonds., Reubin Oaks
Jan. 26	Ehart, Michael	to	Ehart, Sara -Bonds., Adam Ehart
Feb. 2	Walker, John	to	Porter, Frances (widow) -Bonds., Wm. Tinsley
Feb. 24	Harvey, Thomas	to	Goodall, Eleanor -Par., James Goodall
Mar. 13	Cave, Sinclair	to	Anderson, Sarah
Mar. 14	Roberts, Curtis	to	Chewning, Sally -Par., Robert Chewning
Mar. 17	Faulconer, Newman	to	Newman, Maria -Par., Wm. Newman, Sr.
Mar. 23	Herring, Jonathan	to	Hill, Polly -Bonds., Elijah Holbert
Mar. 26	Dickenson, Ralph	to	Quisenberry, Ann -Mary Quisenberry, Guardian
Mar. 28	Stringfellow, Robert	to	Plunkett, Mary -Bonds., Thomas Miller, Jr.
May 13	Davis, Lewis	to	Ham, Dashia -Bonds., Wm. B. Knight
May 23	Bremer, John F.	to	Demsey, Polly -Bonds., Allen Demsey
Aug. 11	Whitelaw, David	to	Davis, Mary -Par., Isaac Davis, Sr.
June 13	Sale, John W.	to	Coleman, Catherine -Bonds., Wilson Coleman
Oct. 6	Rhoades, Clifton	to	Ham, Milly -Par., Samuel Ham
June 27	Gregory, Isaac	to	Sampson, Lucy -Bonds. & Par., John Sampson
Aug. 10	Lee, Henry	to	Lamb, Fanny
Sept. 13	Perry, James Lewis	to	Perry, Jane -Par., Peter Perry
Sept. 22	Jamerson, Wm.	to	Maupin, Robecca
Oct. 6	Huckstep, Willis	to	Beazley, Mary -Par., Ann & James Beazley
Sept. 30	Black, Joshua	to	Raines, Alpha
Oct. 21	Mason, Thomas	to	Clark, Nancy -Par., Baily Mason
Oct. 27	Dunaway, George	to	Hainey, Peggy -Par., James Hainey
Nov. 13	Rogers, Jonathan	to	Twyman, Frances
Nov. 8	Payne, Charles	to	Jones, Lucy -Par., Francis Jones
Nov. 28	Peregoy, Moses	to	Newman, Sara -Bonds., Thomas Newman
Nov. 28	Parks, Richard H.	to	Burton, Clarissa -Richard H. Parks, Guardian
Dec. 25	Williams, John	to	Row, Hetty -Par., Thomas Row
1815			
Jan. 3	Becket, Richard	to	Kea, Jermima
Jan. 4	Crooks, Joseph B.	to	Hennesey, Kitty M. -Bonds., Wm. P. Routt
Jan. 6	Wharton, Joseph	to	George, Catherine -Bonds., Robert Moore
Jan. 12	Dunaway, John	to	Sutherland, Polly -Parson, Wm. Mason

Date	Groom		Bride
Jan. 14	Quisenberry, Benjamin	to	Groom, Sally —Parson, Jeremiah Chandler
Feb. 14	Mundy, Burrus	to	Crosthwaite, Elizabeth —Par., John Croswaith
Feb. 16	Hord, Killis	to	Perry, Elizabeth —Par., Nancy Perry & Daniel Hord(F?)
Mar. 23	Goodall, James	to	Riddell, Lucy —Bonds., Charles Goodall
Mar. 1	Thrift, Robert	to	Burton, Margaret —Bonds., Braxton Osborne
Mar. 1	Bledsoe, John	to	Perry, Margaret —Par., Peter Perry
Mar. 15	Edwards, John	to	Bickers, Selena Anna —Par., George Bickers
May 25	Brown, Bernis	to	Burton, Nancy —Par., James Burton
May 23	Head, Valentine	to	Huckstep, Eliza —Par., John Huckstep
Apr. 25	Jones, Benj. H.	to	Whitelaw, Elizabeth —Bonds., Alexander Whitelaw
Apr. 29	Williby, Tandy	to	Chiles, Polly —Par., James Chiles
June 1	Waller, James	to	Atkins, Elizabeth Y. —Par., Spencer I. Atkins
July 5	Shifflett, James	to	Herrin, Milly —Parson, Geo. Bingham
July 6	Roberson, Williams	to	Mallory, Elizabeth —Bonds., Robt. Payne
July 30	Herndon, James	to	Quisenberry, Elizabeth —Par., George Quisenberry
July 31	Smith, Owen	to	Jamerson, Dolly A. —Andrew Samuel, Guardian
Aug. 5	Estes, Elisha	to	Bingham, Maria —Par., George Bingham
Aug. 31	Snow, Holland	to	Mallory, Judith J. —Bonds., Thomas Mallory
Mar. 26	Dickinson, Ralph	to	Quisenberry, Ann —Par., Mary Quisenberry
Aug. 3	Marshall, Coleman	to	Bickers, Joanna —Par., Nicholas Bickers
Sept. 7	Landford, James	to	Martin, James
Sept. 7	Herndon, John	to	Pence, Mary —Par., John Pence
Oct. 5	Fisher, Wm.	to	Faulconer, Margaret —Bonds., Isaac Johnson
Sept. 17	Sanford, Hamlet	to	Clark, Nancy —Par., Wm. Clark
Sept. 25	Meriwether, Charles H.	to	Anderson, Ann Eliza —Par., Wm. Anderson
Sept. 16	Bickers, Benj.	to	Martin, Joanna —Bonds., Mallory Martin
Oct. 9	Macon, James M.	to	Newman, Lucetta T., Par., Wm. E. Newman
Oct. 12	Catterton, Francis	to	Clarkson, Nancy
Oct. 23	Cowherd, Francis K.	to	Henshaw, Sara A. —Par., John Henshaw
Nov. 8	Hilman, Joseph	to	Pitcher, Frances
Nov. 12	Vass, Walker	to	Lee, Francis —Par., William Lee
Nov. 28	Anderson, John	to	Lower, Nancy —Par., Jacob Anderson & Michael Lower
Nov. 28	Herring, George	to	Holbert, Sally —Par., Elijah Holbert
Dec. 4	Porter, Wm. (Capt.)	to	Henshaw, Mary Newman —Par., Edmund Henshaw
Jan. 2	Ancell, James	to	Estis, Francis —Bonds., Edmund Estis
Jan. 5	Wharton, Samuel	to	Waugh, Sara —Bonds., George Waugh
Jan. 19	Gibbs, Wm.	to	Wayt, Mary Ann —Par., William Wayt
Dec. 8	Meadow, Jacobs	to	Roach, Nancy —Parson, Geo. Bingham
Dec. 25	Clark, Henry James	to	Mansfield, Mary Lewis —Par., Robert Mansfield
Dec. 28	Wood, Zacharias	to	Estes, Nancy —Bonds., John Estes
Dec. 29	Page, Tandy	to	Smith, Judith —Par., Benj. Smith

1816

Date	Groom		Bride
Jan. 2	Shifflet, Bennett	to	Shifflett, Polly
Jan. 6	Miller, Robert	to	Jennings, Ann (widow) –Bonds., Geo. Witherall
Jan. 12	Dunaway, John	to	Sutherland, Polly –Bonds., Alex. Sutherland
Jan. 14	Quisenberry, Benj.	to	Groom, Sally B. –Par., Major Groom
Jan. 13	Yager, Thomas	to	Cauthorn, Fanny (widow) –Bonds., Noah Watts
Jan. 22	Mallory, Ichabod	to	Martin, Lucinda –Bonds., Mallory Martin
Jan. 11	Sandrige, Austin	to	Hall, Ann
Jan. 31	Elliot, George	to	Martin, Judith
Feb. 4	Chambart, Henry	to	Dawson, Fanny –Bonds., Baldwin Taliaferro
Feb. 6	Richardson, Josiah	to	Abell, Sarah –Par., Cabel Abell
Feb. 21	Peyton, James	to	Huffman, Anna –Par., Elijah Huffman
Feb. 13	Walton, Edmund P.	to	Watson, Letice
Feb. 27	Snow, Augustine	to	Mallory, Aggy Eggliston –Par., Henry Mallory
Feb. 28	Wallace, James	to	Oaks, Mourning –Par., Major Oaks
Feb. 26	Ship, Robert M.	to	Burton, Martha –Par., May Burton
Feb. 29	Bishop, Samuel	to	Via, Sarah
Feb. 29	Morris, Dabney	to	Petty, Morris –Bonds., Patrick Petty
Mar. 5	Hill, Henry (Capt.)	to	Payne, Matilda –Par., John Payne
Mar. 5	Lee, James	to	Sanford, Harriet –Wit., Pierce Sanford
Mar. 7	Wright, Alexander	to	Boston, Malinda –Bonds., Thomas Thornton
Mar. 22	Faulconer, Hugh	to	Faulconer, Elizabeth
Mar. 22	Boswell, Wm.	to	Sleet, Mary –Par., John Sleet & Charles Boswell
Mar. 25	Elles, James	to	Woolfolk, Mary C. –Par., Thomas Woolfolk
Apr. 1	Davis, Reubin	to	Grady, Luch –Far., Luch & Wm. Grady, Sr.
Apr. 4	Long, Armistad	to	Kendell, Betsy –James McCullan, Guardian
Apr. 8	Breeding, James	to	Gibbins, Rachael –Bonds., Lewis G. Powell
Apr. 4	Dowling, John	to	Lucas, Francis –Bonds., Benj. Herndon
Apr. 18	Davis, Mitchell	to	Harvey, Elizabeth –Bonds., Robt. A. Douglass
May 18	Davis, John	to	Dear, Sally –Bonds., David Goodall
May 4	Conway, Catlett	to	Taylor, Harriet –Par., Charles Taylor
May 15	Dean, Charles	to	Boston, Elizabeth –Par., John Boston
May 27	Rice, Henry	to	Bingham, Milly –Par., George Bingham
June 9	Deane, Wm., Jr.	to	Deane, Mary
June 5	Ball, Jessie	to	Payne, Frances E. –Bonds., Jessie Payne
June 12	Ball, Fayette	to	Williams, Francis –Par., James Williams
June 18	Crenshaw, Spotswood	to	Graves, Winifred –Par., Isaac Graves, Jr.
July 6	Lancaster, James	to	Lancaster, Nancy –Bonds., Richard Richards
Aug. 1	Ballard, Wilson	to	Goodall, Sarah –Bonds., Park Goodall
Aug. 6	Gentry, James	to	Gibson, Nelly
Aug. 26	Munday, Wilson	to	Oliver, Nancy –Par., Francis Oliver
Aug. 27	Swartswelder, Wm.	to	Sebree, Nancy – Bonds., Charles Goodall
Sept. 5	Black, Wm.	to	Sebree, Nancy
Sept. 5	Munday, Samuel	to	Crosswhite, Milly –Par., John Crosswhite

Date	Groom		Bride
Sept. 14	Hudson, Wm.	to	Childs, Nancy —James Childs signs permission
Sept. 5	Moore, Wm. A.	to	Wright, Mary —Par., Wm. Wright
Sept. 25	Powell, James	to	Shelar, Nancy —Bonds., John Shelar, Jr.
Sept. 22	Sleet, Philip	to	Petty, Ann —Wit., Weeden Sleet
Oct. 2	Jarrald, Jeremiah	to	Sims, Lucretia —Bonds., James Jarrald
Oct. 14	Harrison, Wm.	to	Sims, Polly —Bonds., Wm. Sims
Oct. 21	Lacy, Allen R.	to	Ancell, Elizabeth —Bonds., Robt. Ancell
Oct. 27	Thornton, Anthony	to	Twyman, Nancy —Bonds., Wm. Buckner
Oct. 3	Blackwell, James	to	Burton, Elizabeth
Nov. 12	Draper, Richard	to	Boston, Martha —Par., Beubin Boston
Nov. 17	Harris, Lewis	to	Smith, Martha —Bonds., Wm. Ellis
Nov. 25	Jones, Wm. L.	to	Arnett, Jane Ellen —Par., Wm. Arnett
Nov. 28	Moyer, Wm. H.	to	Beadles, Lurinna(?) Bonds., Thomas Miller, Jr.
Nov. 28	Woolfolk, Wm.	to	Ellis, Clarissa W. —James H. Ellis, Guardian
Nov. 26	Chapman, Joshua	to	Yancy, Catherine —Bonds., Stephen Yancy
Dec. 3	Walker, Thomas	to	Anderson, Frances —Par., Jacob Anderson
Dec. 12	Hutcherson, Washington	to	Lancaster, Elizabeth —Bonds., Thomas Lancaster
Dec. 12	Gardner, Zachariah	to	Martin, Lucinda
Dec. 12	White, James	to	Plunkett, Frances —Bonds., Willis White
Dec. 24	Wallis, George	to	Hilman, Susan —Par., Uriel Hilman
Dec. 24	Hawkins, Thomas	to	Perry, Mary —Par., Peter Perry
Dec. 23	Eddins, Wm.	to	Mansfield, Sarah H. —Bonds., Wm. Mansfield
Dec. 23	Ancell, Michael	to	Williams, Nancy —Par., Joseph Williams
Dec. 24	Shifflett, John	to	Shifflett, Vina
Dec. 26	Brown, Sanderson	to	Bickers, Nancy —Bonds., Abner Bickers
Dec. 30	Leathers, James	to	Mallory, Dolly —Bonds., Uriel Mallory
Dec. 22	Alexander, Samuel D.	to	Burrus, Anna
1817			
Jan. 13	Sullivan, Dawson	to	Payne, Lucy —Bonds., Berryman Cox
Jan. 14	Haney, Bazle	to	Dean, Elizabeth —Par., Wm. Deane
Jan. 19	Edwards, Wm.	to	Oliver, Olivia —Par., Francis Oliver
Jan. 30	Sanford, Lawrence	to	Ford, Catherine —Par., William Ford
Jan. 31	Davis, Evan	to	Hilman, Polly —Bonds., Joseph Hilman
Feb. 4	Grinnon, Wm. S.	to	Shepherd, Mary Miller —Par., George Shepherd
Feb. 11	Durritt, Davis	to	Davis, Elizabeth —Par., Isaac Davis, Sr.
Feb. 10	Jones, Fielding	to	Johnson, Mary —Par., Isaac Johnson
Feb. 22	Woirhaye, Francis	to	Hancock, Nancy —Par., Wm. Hancock
Feb. 26	Grigsby, Reuben	to	Porter, Berlinda A. —Bonds., Wm. Porter
Feb. 28	Hawkins, Roddy	to	Jones, Elizabeth —Par., Francis Jones
Apr. 12	Leckie, Wm. S.	to	Reddis, Ann V. —Bonds., John Miller
Apr. 14	Houck, Henry	to	Lucas, Mildred —John Lucas, Guardian
Apr. 30	Abell, Richard S.	to	Hilman, Sarah A. —Par., John S. Abell
June 14	Smith, Presley	to	Winslow, Frances —Par., Fortunatus Winslow
June 23	Stevens, Edward	to	Petty, Betsy —Par., John Petty

(42)

Date	Groom		Bride
Aug. 2	Scott, Larkin	to	Faulconer, Elizabeth -Bonds., Wm. Faulconer
Aug. 4	Wood, James	to	Mills, Ann -Bonds., Wm. S. Frazer
Aug. 22	White, John	to	Adams, Luch -Bonds., Wm. Clark
Aug. 22	Robinson, John	to	Melone, Susan -Par., John & Rebecca Melone
Sept. 4	Maden, Jacob	to	Davis, Julia -Par., John Davis
Sept. 5	Thomas, Henry	to	Wood, Henry -Bonds., Edward Thomas
Sept. 10	Brown, Bezabel	to	Price, Elizabeth -Par., George Price
Sept. 25	Williams, David	to	Row, Elizabeth -Par., Thomas Row
Oct. 29	Tyler, Richard	to	Scott, Jane T. -Bonds., John Scott
1818			
Nov. 14	Gibson, Wm.	to	Morris, Elizabeth -Par., Wm. Morris, Jr.
Nov. 6	Goodall, Fontaine	to	Teal, Peggy -Bonds., John Riddle
Nov. 10	Owen, Cheschester	to	Clark, Frances -Par., Philip Seal
Nov. 14	Shifflett, Richard	to	Morris, Nancy -Par., Wm. Morris, Jr.
Nov. 15	Beadles, James	to	Winslow, Elizabeth -Bonds., Edward Winslow
Nov. 26	Scott, Thomas	to	Henshaw, Virginia O -Par., Edmund Henshaw
Nov. 27	Jones, Mecajah	to	Wright, Susan -Bonds., Fielding Jones
Dec. 2	Walker, Benjamin	to	Henshaw, Elizabeth V. -Par., John Henshaw
Dec. 9	Jennings, John	to	Willis, Mary E. -Bonds., Augustine Jennings
Dec. 12	Riener, John	to	Overton, Fanny -Par., Obediah Overton
Dec. 26	Tell, John	to	Waugh, Nancy -Par., Elizabeth Waugh
? 1817			
Dec. 22	Simmons, George	to	Darnell, Mary -Bonds., Rice Darnell
Dec. 22	Collins, Francis T.	to	Williams, Margaret -Par., Jacob Williams
Dec. 28	Vaughn, Joseph	to	Dean, Eliza -Bonds., Archibald Barcus
Dec. 30	Gilbert, Joseph	to	Ferneyhough, Agnes -Bonds., John Ferneyhough
Dec. 31	Robinson, Thomas	to	Lancaster, Sarah -Bonds., Edmund Lancaster
Dec. 31	Mansfield, Wm. H.	to	Edins, Selina -Par., Thomas Eddins
1818			
Jan. 3	Riddle, Charles	to	Sims, Lucretia -Bonds., Jeremiah Jarrell
Jan. 9	Simpson, George	to	Goodridge, Mary -Bonds., Wm. Davis
Jan. 13	Jacobs, Benjamin	to	Faulconer, Ann -Par., John Faulconer
Jan. 11	Johnson, Peter R.	to	Alcock, Patsy -Bonds., Robert H. Rose
Jan. 15	Page, Sinclair	to	Long, Elizabeth -Par., William Long
Jan. 15	Clark, William	to	Terrill, Jane -Bonds., Eliphalet Johnson
Jan. 15	Brent, Daniel	to	Sampson, Elizabeth -Bonds., Daniel Norman
Feb. 11	Richards, Richard	to	Adams, Mary -Bonds., Ezekiah Richards
Feb. 26	McMullin, John	to	Walker, Peachy -Par., James McMullin & John Walker, Jr.
Feb. 12	Jacobs, Joel	to	Taylor, Mary -Par., Thomas Jacobs & James Taylor
Feb. 15	Emmerson, James	to	Tinder, Jemimah -Par., Ephriam & Jessie Tinder

Date	Groom		Bride
Feb. 23	Davis, William	to	Goodridge, Harriet –Wm. Davis, Guardian
Feb. 23	Estes, Littleton	to	Harvey, Frances –Sittleton, Estes, Sr., Guardian
Feb. 25	Shackleford, Uriel	to	Hilman, Deadema –Uriel Hilman, Guardian
Feb. 24	Davis, Wm.	to	Rogers, Auley –Par., John Rogers
Mar. 11	Wyatt, John	to	Baugker, Elizabeth
Mar. 12	Coons, John P.	to	Braidenheart, Susan –Bonds., James Virdier
Mar. 17	Jones, Burkett	to	Wright, Polly –Par., Nancy Wright
Mar. 25	Faulconer, Edward S.	to	Hord, Melinda –Par., Jesse Hord
Apr. 7	Collins, Wm. W.	to	Williams, Frances –Par., Jacob Williams
Apr. 8	Bryan, Daniel	to	Barbour, Mary T. –Par., Thomas Barbour
Apr. 21	Burn, James	to	Knight, Elizabeth –Wm. B. Knight signed permission
May 7	Campbell, Robert	to	Atkins, Ann Maria –Par., Spencer J. Atkins
May 5	Ballard, Garland	to	Burt, Eliza –Par., James Ballard
May 10	Crawford, Zachariah	to	Rains, Abbie
May 15	Sims, Wm.	to	Morgan, Eliza.
May 20	Smith, Daniel M.	to	Stubblefield, Frances –Par., George Stubblefield
May 25	Davis, Asa	to	Snow, Mary –Par., Byrd Snow
May 27	Williams, Sinclair	to	Colyer, Lucinda –Par., Martin Colyer, Sr.
June 2	Faulconer, Wm.	to	Jacob, Elizabeth –Par., Benj. Jacob
May 2	Newman, George, Jr.	to	Tutman, Elizabeth –John Tutman, Guard.
June 9	Welsh, Nathaniel, Jr.	to	Newman, Virandy –Par., Thomas Newman
June 24	Gaines, Richard	to	Sanders, Malinda –Bonds., John Sanders
Aug. 10	Seal, Thomas	to	Powell, Elizabeth –Par., Lewis G. Powell
Aug. 17	Estes, Samuel	to	Ogg, Jane –Bonds., James Ogg
Aug. 26	Baggott, James	to	Johnson, Justina –James Baggott, Guard.
Sept. 25	Jones, Mosias	to	Slaylor, Francis
Sept. 28	Cason, Benj.	to	Graves, Nancy –Bonds., Jonathan Graves
Oct. 2	Lamb, John	to	Knight, Lucy –Par., Wm. Knight
Oct. 14	Cross, Joshua	to	Daniel, Mary –Bonds., Jas. B. Daniel
Nov. 12	Row, Elhanan	to	Sanders, Mary D., –Par., John Sanders
Nov. 11	Hancock, Munroe B.	to	Overton, Sidney –Bonds., Wm. Mallory
Nov. 26	Norman, Daniel	to	Warkin, Betsy –Bonds., Peter Marsh
Nov. 15	White, Anderson	to	Huckstep, Lucinda –Par., Josiah Huckstep
Dec. 8	Henshaw, John	to	Cowherd, Sarah –Par., Francis Cowherd
Dec. 17	Sampson, George	to	Jollett, Drada –Bonds., Fielding Jollett
Dec. 26	Jones, John	to	Mason, Elizabeth –Par., George Mason
Dec. 31	Sims, James	to	Early, Lucy T. –Par., James Early, Sr.
Dec. 23	Gibbs, Wm. C.	to	Wayt, Kissy –Bonds., Christopher Cregler
Dec. 21	Shifflett, Slaten	to	Morris, Susanna
1819			
Jan.	Wren, John	to	Loyd, Esther –Par., Robert Loyd
Jan. 18	Brockman, Asa	to	Quisenberry, Lucy E. –Bonds., John Henderson
Jan. 25	Robinson, Achilles D.	to	Bell, Sally B. –Par., Roger Bell
Jan. 14	Dowell, John	to	Garitson, Elizabeth
Feb. 2	Sims, Richard	to	Wood, Mary –Bonds., Henry Herndon
Feb. 4	Norris, William	to	Watson, Margaret B.
Feb. 11	Shifflett, Archibald	to	Vaughn, Belinda –Par., Joseph Vaughn

(44)

Date	Groom		Bride
Feb. 18	Smith, Dudley	to	Lancaster, Susanna -Par., Benjamin Lancaster
Feb. 25	Hall, Thomas	to	Picket, Elizabeth
Feb. 18	Graves, Lewis	to	White, Fanny -Par., Richard White
Mar. 22	Dilly, Richard	to	Devenney, Mary M. -Par., C. Devenney
Apr. 1	Faulconer, Kemp	to	Perry, Elizabeth -Par., Peter Perry
Apr. 29	Dowell, Nathan	to	Vaughn, Lucy -Par., Richard Dowell of Albemarle County & Joseph Vaughn
Apr. 18	Newman, John	to	Alkins, Mildred -Bonds., Moses Peregory
Apr. 24	Taliaferro, Lawrence	to	Chewning, Eliza -Par., Robt. Chewning
Apr. 24	Rogers, James	to	Wood, Margaret
Apr. 28	Frazer, Wm. S.	to	Burrus, Ann -Par., William T. Burrus
June 3	Coly, William	to	McClary, Milly
June 30	Vaughn, Charles	to	Clayter, Elizabeth -Charles Vaughn, Guardian
July 14	Crigler, Peter	to	Pratt, Fanny -Par., Jonathan Pratt
Aug. 13	Blackwell, Wm.	to	Gordon, Ann S. -Par., Joseph Blackwell
Aug. 23	Wren, Edward	to	Lloyd, Lucy -Par., Robt. Lloyd
Aug. 26	Rhoades, John	to	Faulconer, Margaret -Bonds., Hugh M. Faulconer
Aug. 26	Rucker, Thornton	to	Snyder, Patsy -Henry Hill, Guardian
Sept. 11	Madison, Ambrose	to	Willis, Jane -Par., Wm. C. Willis
Sept. 15	Page, James	to	Long, Belinda -Par., Wm. Long
Sept. 22	Fearneyhough, John	to	Jones, Elizabeth -Bonds., Holland Osborne
Sept. 24	Merriweather, Garrett M.	to	Minor, Mary Ann -Par., Dabney Minor
Oct. 7	Sherick, Philip B.	to	Garton, Martha -Jacob Rumbough, Guard.
Oct. 4	Grymes, Peyton	to	Dade, Harriet (widow) Bonds., Blackwell Chilton
Oct. 6	Mayo, Robt. A.	to	Taliaferro, Sarah D. -Bonds., Lawrence T. Dade -Par., Wm. Mayo & Hay Taliaferro, Sr.
Nov. 10	Rains, Fielding	to	Williams, Elizabeth -Bonds., Mathew Lamb
Nov. 16	Parrott, Woodson	to	Williams, Elizabeth -Par., John Williams
Nov. 24	Luck, George A.	to	Kendall, Mary Louise -Bonds., Joshua Kendall
Nov. 22	Boswell, Garrett	to	Dolin, Patsy -Bonds., John Dolin
Nov. 23	Stowers, Winston	to	Lindsay, Rebecca -Par., Larkin Lindsay
Nov. 30	Williams, Joseph	to	Catterton, Mary
Nov. 23	Barrett, Patrick	to	Bridwell, Sally -Bonds., Edwin Holaday
Dec. 11	Hill, John	to	Lathan, Frances -Bonds., John Campbell
Dec. 23	Dunn, Fountain D.	to	Via, Nancy Craig
Dec. 20	Abraham, Booton	to	Clark, Babara -Bonds., Wm. Clark
Dec. 22	Hudson, Wm.	to	Vawter, Malinda -Bonds., Benj. Vawter
Dec. 24	Tyree, John	to	Lindsay, Nancy -Par., Larkin & Sarah Lindsay
Dec. 27	Montague, David	to	Herndon, Nancy -Bonds., Fielding Herndon
1820			
Jan. 9	Tinder, James	to	Shadrack, Elizabeth - Par., Sarah Shadrack & Anthony Tinder of Culpeper County
Jan. 8	Williams, Felix	to	Ham, Frankey H. -Franky Herring, Grandmother
Apr. 9	Wright, Alexander	to	Peacher, Luch -Bonds., Wm. Peacher
Apr. 24	Harris, Wm.	to	Gibson, Peggy -Bonds., Peter Gibson
Feb. 7	Moubray, Zachariah	to	Clatterbuck, Mary -Par., Wm. Clatterbuck
Feb. 8	Harrison, Jabez	to	Taylor, Elizabeth -Par., Wm. Taylor, Sr.

Date	Groom		Bride
Feb. 18	Beals, Charles	to	Gordon, Mary –Par., Nat Gordon
Feb. 22	Brown, John	to	Waller, Judith –Bonds., Spencer J. Atkins
Mar. 7	Melone, John	to	Golding, Nancy –Par., Richard Golding
Mar. 27	White, Wm.	to	Scrivner, Susan –Par., Samuel Scrivener
Apr. 11	Kennedy, Littleton	to	Hill, Martha –Par., Richard Hill & Reuben Kennedy
May 22	Thompson, David	to	Ellis, Maria –John Ellis, Guardian
May 29	Marshall, Willis	to	Whitelaw, Sarah –Bonds., Alex. Whitelaw
June 17	Lee, Moses	to	Terrill, Elizabeth –Bonds., Henry Clark
June 23	Hume, Francis	to	Jones, Lucy –Bonds., John Richards
July 24	Eddins, Smith	to	Burton, Maria –Par., May Burton
Sept. 4	Marr, Henry	to	Rucker, Francis –Par., Wm. Rucker
Sept. 20	Twyman, Thornel	to	Coleman, Sarah K. –Par., Thos. Coleman
Sept. 25	Lewis, Thomas M.	to	Twyman, Emaline –Walter Key, Guardian
Oct. 20	Woolfray, Richard	to	Battaile, Elizabeth –Par., Alfred Battaile
Oct. 21	Hardiman, James E.	to	Kinzer, Elizabeth –Bonds., K. Sturman Kinzor
Oct. 23	Watters, Jacob	to	Brooking, Belinda –Par., Robt. Brooking
Oct. 25	Conally, Patrick	to	Hill, Polly –Par., Richard Hill
Oct. 25	Lamb, John	to	Knight, Lucy –Par., Wm. Knight
Nov. 6	Blakey, James G.	to	Sorrill, Maria Ann –Par., Thomas Sorrille
Nov. 18	Terrill, John	to	Grasty, Susan A. –Par., G. S. Grasty
Nov. 27	Middlebrook, Archibald	to	Boswell, Lucy –Bonds., Chas. Boswell
Dec. 6	Snyder, Wm.	to	Jenkins, Sarah –Henry Hill, Guardian
Dec. 20	Newman, Charles	to	Chiles, Catherine –Par., James Child
Dec. 21	Yancy, Laton	to	Moyers, Lurina –Par., Michael Moyers
Dec. 22	Mason, Charles	to	Jones, Lucy –Bonds., George Mason
Dec. 22	Lancaster, Jonathan	to	Herndon, Sally –Bonds., Benj. Herndon
Dec. 25	Brown, Henry	to	Boston, Polly –Par., John Boston
1821			
Jan. 8	Clark, Wm.	to	Lee, Lucy –Bonds., Ambrose Lee
Jan. 13	Snell, Joseph	to	White, Annie –Bonds., John Campbell
Jan. 16	Long, Joshua	to	Dawson, Frances –Par., John Dawson
Jan. 25	Miller, James	to	Lloyd, Sarah –Par., Robt. Lloyd
Jan. 26	Ford, Harlin	to	Grady, Margaret –Par., Wm. & Margaret Grady
Jan. 29	Herndon, Ezekial	to	Jones, Sarah –Par., Elliot Jones
Feb. 5	Blakey, Geo. Smith	to	Davis, Susanna W. –Par., Isaac Davis
Feb. 6	Roach, Wm.	to	Row, Tincey –Par., Thomas Row
Feb. 10	Hord, Peter	to	Hord, Eliza –Par., Jesse Hord
Feb. 22	Brockman, Wm. Jr.	to	Graves, Elizabeth C. –Par., Claibourn Graves
Mar. 8	Pickett, Charles	to	Dowell, Jane
Mar. 15	Stephens, Newton	to	White, Susanna –Par., James White
Mar. 26	Hicks, John	to	Sleet, Lucinda –Par., John Sleet
Apr. 12	Ham, Bennett	to	Ham, Lurinna –Bonds., Samuel Ham
Apr. 6	Rogers, Wm.	to	Collier(or Colyer), Polly –Par., John Rogers & Martin Colier
Apr. 11	Craig, Sammuel	to	Thomas, Frances –Par., James Thomas
Apr. 16	Estes, John	to	Daniel, Maria –Par., Reubin Daniel
Apr. 19	Jenkins, David	to	Darnell, Elizabeth –Bonds., Rice Darnell

May 3	Webb, Lewis	to	Waller, Elizabeth -Bonds., James Waller
May 28	Graves, Isaac, Jr.	to	Plunkett, Elizabeth -Bonds., James White
June 11	Pratt, William	to	White, Nancy -Bonds, Wm. White
July 3	Baily, Samuel	to	Baily, Jane
July 24	Deane, John		
Aug. 18	Swindell, Joel S.	to	Anderson, Mary Jackson -Par., Joseph Swindell & Joel Anderson
Sept. 15	Graves, Charles Tandy	to	Webb, Ann Roger -Par., Augustine Webb
Oct. 6	Gambriel, Walter	to	Hutcherson, Martha -Bonds., Wash. Hutcherson
Oct. 5	Woodhead(?), Wm.	to	Mayo, Lettisa
Oct. 22	Wright, Benj.	to	Quisenberry, Eliza -Par., George Quisenberry
Oct. 23	Mallory, Nathan	to	Thompson, Elizabeth
Nov. 2	Porter, John A.	to	Crump, Mary -Par., John Crump
Nov. 22	Conner, John	to	Terrill, Sarah -Bonds., Robt. Terrill, Jr.
Nov. 26	Leathers, Alexander	to	Mitchell, Lucy -Par., Henry Mitchell
Dec. 18	Via, Jonathan	to	Via, Mary Elizabeth
Dec. 10	Mason, Sanders	to	Jones, Caty -Par., George Mason & James Jones
Dec. 14	Robertson, Willis	to	Dolin, Elizabeth -Bonds., John Dolin
Dec. 20	Elliot, Wm.	to	Hall, Mary Knight
Dec. 15	Herndon, John	to	Landram, Mahalo(?) -Par., Lewis Landram
Dec. 20	Gibson, Joshua	to	Stone, Elizabeth
Dec. 17	Bell, Wm. B. Jr.	to	Newman, Frances -Par., Andrew Newman
Dec. 19	Martin, Wm.	to	Faulconer, Melinda -Par., Elias Faulconer
Dec. 20	Via, Reubin	to	Garrison, Livinia -Par., John Garrison
Dec. 21	Wright, Robt.	to	Faulconer, Luch -Par., John Faulconer
Dec. 24	Roach, Wm.	to	Leathers, Sarah -Bonds., Alexander Leathers
Dec. 30	Davis, Mitchel	to	Mallory, Elizabeth -Bonds., John Mallory
1822			
Jan. 3	Catterton, Benj. W.	to	Price, Elizabeth Bonds., James Sims
Jan. 13	Stevens, George Jr.	to	Ball, Eliza Ann -Par., Jesse Ball
Jan. 14	Shepherd, Robert W.	to	Conway, Susan Fitzhugh -Par., Francis Conway
Jan. 24	Vawter, Benj.	to	Bell, Elizabeth -Bonds., Boswell Bell
Jan. 31	Gibson, John	to	Collins, Eliza
Mar. 7	Sherman, John H.	to	Rucker, Margaret S. -Par., Wm. Rucker
Mar. 8	Dennison, James	to	Lucas, Nancy(widow) Bonds., Jacob Rembough
Mar. 12	Webb, Wm.	to	Sampson, Mary -Bonds., Simeon Jollett
Mar. 12	Marsh, Thom	to	Jollett, -Par., James Jollett
Apr. 8	Brooking, Robt. U.	to	Wilhoit, Mildred -Par., Ezekiel Wilhoit
Apr. 10	Hales, John	to	Blackwell, Mary E -Bonds., John Hales
Apr. 10	Hughes, Wm. Jr.	to	Blackwell, Ann G. -Bonds., Wm. Hughes, Jr.
Apr. 10	Scott, John	to	Cowherd, Ann -Par., Colby Cowherd
Apr. 13	Shackleford, Zacharias	to	Cleave, Sarah -Philip C. Cave, Guard.
Apr. 25	Riddle, Tavney	to	Powell, Sally -Par., Lewis G. Powell
Apr. 22	Boswell, Samuel T.	to	Middlebrook, Martha -Par., Nathaniel Middlebrook
Apr. 30	Nichols, John	to	Pritchett, Sarah -Bonds., Robt. Pritchett

(47)

Date	Groom		Bride
June 15	Perry, Wm. W.	to	Rippeto, Ann G.
May 20	King, Reubin	to	Jollett, Elizabeth -Par., Jas. Jollett
May 27	Harris, Moses T.	to	Bowcock, Elvina M. -Bonds., A. M. Barksdale
May 7	Atkins, Davis	to	Mallory, Alice -Bonds., Joseph Edwards
May 14	Carter, James	to	Newcome, Jane
June 27	Taliaferro, John S.	to	Barbour, Maria -Bonds., Richard Taliaferro
June 27	Shifflet, Felix	to	Shifflet, Phoebe
June 19	Brown, Wm.	to	Hord, Ann -Par., Jesse Hord
July 8	Jollett, Simeon	to	Glass, Nancy -Par., James Jollett
Aug. 28	Webb, Ellis	to	Badger, Margaret -Bonds., Richard Richards, Wm. Wright
Aug. 6	Harvey, Layton	to	Dowell, Elizabeth -Bonds., Jeremiah Pierce
Aug. 15	Slater, Thom. M.	to	Lamb, Martha -Bonds., John Deane
Aug. 28	McClary, Wm. F.	to	Dempsey, Pheobe -Par., Daniel Dampsey
Sept. 11	Herndon, Fielding	to	Montague, Mildred
Sept. 21	Winslow, Moses	to	Long, Lucy A. -Par., Robert B. Long
Sept. 23	Sims, James P.	to	Beasley, Ann (widow) -Par., John Graves
Sept. 23	Leathers, James F.	to	Jenkins, Lucy -Bonds., Edmund D. Longar(?)
Oct. 19	Herndon, Edward	to	Bradley, Mary B. -Bonds., Pollard Bradley
Oct. 28	McClarney(?), Robt.	to	Long, Elizabeth -Bonds., Samuel Flinn
Oct. 29	Jones, Wm. W.	to	Farish, Elizabeth -Bonds., Thomas Gray
Nov. 7	Campbell, Alexander	to	Mallory, Ann -Bonds., Geo. Lawson
Nov. 5	Swiser, David	to	Banker, Christine W.
Nov. 12	Webb, John	to	Blakey, Judith -Bonds., John Collins
Nov. 14	Bibb, Wm.	to	Groom, Mourning(?) -Bonds., Solomon R. Groom
Nov. 25	Rucker, Minor	to	Head, Harriett -Par., John Head
Nov. 27	Sommerville, Harrison	to	Sleet, Nancy -Par., John Sleet
Dec. 7	Davis, Fredrick D.	to	Eddins, Mildred -Par., Theo. Eddins
Dec. 12	Wood, Wm.	to	Austin, Mildred
Dec. 9	Grymes, Thom. N.	to	Wormley, Rebecca Taylor -Bonds., Peyton Grymes
Dec. 3	Twyman, Pascal	to	Melone, Elizabeth -Bonds., Ely Melone
Dec. 17	Haney, John	to	Watson, Elizabeth
Dec. 17	Herndon, Benj.	to	Bledsoe, Hannah -Bonds., Moses Bledsoe
Dec. 23	Roberts, James	to	Whitehead, Catherine -Bonds., Thomas Sorrille
Dec. 23	Dickanson, Bennett	to	Carpenter, Mildred -Par., Plesant Carpenter
Dec. 26	Powell, Lewis G., Jr.	to	Smith, Jane -Lewis G. Powell, Guardian
Dec. 27	Robinson, Hugh	to	Johnson, Susan -Joseph Atkins, Guardian
1823			
Jan. 7	Conner, Wm.	to	Smith, Emily -Zeph Turner, Guardian
Jan. 3	Aery, Wm.	to	Dawson, Amanda -Par., Wm. H. Dawson
Jan. 6	Stone, Henry	to	Mitchell, Polly -Par., Wm. Mitchell
Jan. 7	Sorrille, John N	to	Stanard, Sarah Ann Ophelia -Par., Wm. H. Stanard
Jan. 18	Bickers, Proctor	to	Overton, Lucy -Bonds., Thomas Martin
Jan. 2	Shifflet, Edmund	to	Wlan(?), Milly
Jan. 21	Mitchell, Robt.	to	Parrott, Nancy Y., John Beasley signed permission

Jan. 23	Saunders, James W.	to	Blair, Barbara G. -Par., Helen Blair
Feb. 10	Hasey(?), Michael	to	Leathers, Elizabeth -Bonds., James T. Leathers
Feb. 18	Head, Wilton	to	Huckstep, Fanny -Par., Marshall Head & John Huckstep
Feb. 24	Kendal, Thom. G.	to	Merideth, Elizabeth -Bonds., Roger Slaughter
Mar. 5	Snow, Early	to	Mallory, Mary Payne -Bonds., John Mallory
Mar. 26	Shifflet, Trice	to	Snow, Raney -Par., John Snow
Mar. 4	Miller, Daniel	to	Sorrille, Elizabeth -Par., Thom. Sorrille
Jan. 2	Baukerand, Jacob	to	Davis, Polly
Mar. 8	Millir, John	to	Lloyd, Mary -Bonds., Henry Lloyd
Mar. 6	Early, John	to	Timberlake, Margaret
Mar. 17	Demsey, Lewis	to	McClarney, Polly -Bonds., Ike Richards
Mar. 24	Hume, John	to	Jones, Nancy -Bonds., Fielding Jones
Mar. 24	Eheart, Michael L.	to	Cave, Lavinia B. -Par., Robt. Cave
Mar. 27	Bryant, Charles	to	Snow, Polly
Mar. 25	Tinder, John	to	Shadrack, Frances M. -Bonds., Robt. Sanders
Apr. 10	Richards, Fountain	to	Mills, Sophia
Apr. 13	Geer, John	to	McDaniel, Betsy (widow of Simeon McDaniel)
May 24	Burrus, Joseph	to	Terrill, Nancy -Bonds., Wm. S. Fraser
June 2	Miller, John, Jr.	to	Miller, Ann -Par., John Miller
June 20	Morton, George	to	Williams, Elizabeth S. -George Pannill, Guardian
July 3	Jones, Edmund	to	Shecler or Shelar, Caty -Bonds., John Shelar, Jr.
July 11	Nelson, James	to	Adams, Ann (widow) Bonds., Richard Richards
July 12	Willis, Larkin	to	Gordon, Mary -Par., John C. Gordon
Aug. 18	Austin, Willis	to	Melone, Jane -Bonds., James Melone
Aug. 20	Carroll, Wm.	to	Clark, Elizabeth -Par., Wm. Clarke
Sept. 15	Groom, Soloman	to	Harris, Elizabeth -Bonds., Overton Harris
Sept. 29	Gordon, John H.	to	Grasty, Eliza -John Terrill, Guardian
Oct. 14	Sims, Wm., Jr.	to	Sorrille, Virginia -Par., Thom. Sorrille
Oct. 21	Scott, Charles	to	Cowherd, Harriet -Par., Francis Cowherd
Oct. 27	Battle, Alfred	to	Jones, Polly -Bonds., Fielding Jones
Oct. 3	Gentry, James	to	Langford, Peachy
Oct. 27	Atkins, John	to	Webb, Susan -Wm. T. Burrus, Guardian
Oct. 28	Atkins, Dickinson	to	Alkins, Margaret -Par., Gentry Atkins
Nov. 10	Eddins, Tandy	to	Sims, Amelia -Par., John & Elizabeth Sims
Nov. 25	Rumbough, Jacob	to	Southerland, Nancy -Bonds., Wm. Southerland
Nov. 27	Watts, Elijah D.	to	Sampson, Margaret -Bonds., Benson Henry
Dec. 5	Holbert, Richard	to	Kinzer, Catherine -Par., Lucy Kinzer
Dec. 15	Knight, Mathew	to	Haney, Nancy -Par., James Haney
Dec. 16	Wayland, Wm.	to	Miller, Frances -Par., Thom. Miller
Dec. 17	Southerland, John	to	Johnson, Mary -Bonds., John B. Johnson
Dec. 17	Jackson, John M.	to	Daniel, Nancy R. -Bonds., Landon Linds
Dec. 30	Sullivan, Everet	to	Dean, Nancy

Date	Groom		Bride
Dec. 17	Collins, John	to	Cave, Frances B. -Philip C. Cave, Guardian
Dec. 30	Herndon, James	to	Ferneyhough, Ester -Par., Thom. Ferneyhough
Dec. 22	Kennon, Philip	to	Hord, Sarah -Par., Jessie Hord
Dec. 22	King, Holcombe R.	to	Peacher, Mary Ann D. -Par., Wm. Peacher

1824

Date	Groom		Bride
Jan. 6	Weaver, Samuel L.	to	Lamb, Ann -Par., Richard Lamb
Jan. 15	Willoughby, Wm.	to	Stephens, Lucy -Bonds., Maurice Webb
Jan. 15	Nash, Thom. W.	to	Clark, Virginia -Par., Wm. Clark
Jan. 19	Twyman, Jonathan	to	Rucker, Lucy -Par., Wm. Rucker
Feb. 5	Rippito, Thom. P.	to	McAlister, Louisa -Henry Houk, Guard.
Feb. 3	Turner, Elisha	to	Goodall, Polly -Bonds., Park Goodall
Feb. 10	Jacobs, George	to	Smith, Catherine -Par., Benj. Jacobs & George Smith
Feb. 22	Houseworth, Valentine M.	to	Brooking, Martha A. -Bonds., James R. Brooking
Mar. 2	Breeding, Ephriam	to	Haney, Fanny -Bonds., Mathew Knight
Mar. 10	Beckham, Benj.	to	Porter, Nancy C. -Bonds., Benj. F. Porter
Mar. 12	Brock, Wingfield	to	Webb, Sarah Mason -Par., Jesse B. Webb
Apr. 13	Morris, Aden C.	to	Finnell, Nancy -Bonds., Wm. B. Webb
Apr. 13	Morris, John	to	Shifflett, Fanny -Par., Wm. Shifflett
May 3	Bourn, John	to	Newman, Jane -Par., Thom. Newman
May 23	Collins, James, Jr.	to	Johnson, Mildred C -Par., Valentine Johnson
May 28	Morton, George W.	to	Taylor, Evelina M -Robt. Taylor, Jr., Guardian
June 7	Scott, John	to	Hilman, Joannah -Par., Uriel Hilman
June 14	Maupin, Tyree	to	Beadles, Jane -Par., John Beadles
June 22	Pulliam, Absolem C.	to	King, Rhoda -Bonds., Thomas Row
June 29	Long, Spotswood	to	Harris, Sabina -Bonds., Thom. Harris
July 20	Henshaw, Philip T.	to	Scott, Sarah Ann -Par., Sarah Scott
Aug. 7	Shifflet, John	to	Shifflet, Polly -Bonds., Mordicai Shifflet
Aug. 18	Paul, John	to	Leathers, Eliza Ann -Par., Jonathan Leathers
Sept. 10	Watson, Benj.	to	Jacob, Frances -Bonds., George Smith
Sept. 15	Garth, D. C.	to	Head, Amanda -Par., John Head, Sr.
Sept. 25	Brown, Wm.	to	Hancock, Mary -Bonds., John P. Coons
Oct. 14	Shepherd, James	to	Taylor, Lucinda -Bonds., Philip Fry
Oct. 16	White, Winston	to	Harris, Elizabeth -Bonds., Wm. White
Oct. 16	Read, Carvel H.	to	Faulconer, Mildred -Par., Wm. Faulconer
Oct. 25	Cave, Wm. D.	to	Smith, Frances -Par., Abner Cave
Oct. 25	Smith, Thomas	to	Cave, Polly -Par., Abner Cave
Oct. 28	Lindsay, Robert	to	Daniel, Minerva -Wm. Reynolds, Guard.
Nov. 22	Goodwin, John M.	to	Stevens, Elisa T. -Par., Wm. Stevens
Nov. 22	Riddle, Thompson	to	Powell, Mary -Thomas Riddle, Guardian
Nov. 22	Oliver, James	to	Sims, Lucretia -Par., Margaret Sims
Nov. 24	Pendleton, John S.	to	Williams, Lucy Ann -Bonds., Philip Fry
Dec. 8	Brock, Absolom	to	Buckner, Elizabeth -Bonds., Horace Buckner
Dec. 10	Quisenberry, Hezekiah	to	Burrus, Emily Frances -Par., Wm. T. Burrus

Dec. 24	Perry, Wm.	to	Wood, Mary —Bonds., Lewis L. Poate(?)
Dec. 24	Jackson, Wm.	to	Miller, Ann —Bonds., Thom. Mitchell
Dec. 20	Johnson, Colin	to	Ellis, Mary Anne —Bonds., Thom. H. Ellis
Dec. 20	Sims, John	to	Walker, Nancy —Bonds., Wm. H. Sims
Dec. 24	Tinder, Thom.	to	Mason, Nancy —Bonds., Sanders Mason
Dec. 21	Parrott, George	to	Hartsook, Elizabeth —Bonds., Wm. Acre

List of Importations to Orange County, Virginia

Name	Date	Country Imported From
Anderson, Hannah	Feb. 1752	Ireland
Amberger, Conrade	May 1736	Great Britain
Abel, Joseph	Nov. 1736	Great Britain & Ireland
Anderson, John, and wife, Jane, and children, Esther, Mary, Margaret	May 1740	Ireland
Anderson, George, and wife Elizabeth, and children, Margaret, William, John, Francis	May 1740	Ireland
Appleby, Robert	May 1741	Great Britain & Ireland
Brown, John	Oct. 1751	Great Britain
Barley, Robert	Jan. 1754	Great Britain
Beasley, Bennet	July 1735	Great Britain
Branham, Francis	Mar. 1756	Ireland
Brown, Ann	May 1756	Great Britain
Burk, Thomas	1735	
Bryan, Dennis	1735	Great Britain & Ireland
Burke, John	1735	Great Britain & Ireland
Billingsby, Francis	1735	Great Britain & Ireland
Bickers, Robert	Mar. 1735	Great Britain & Ireland
Butler, John	Nov. 1736	Great Britain & Ireland
Bowrke, Martin	1735	Great Britain & Ireland
Byrd, George	Feb. 1737	Great Britain & Ireland
Blair, Alexander, Jane, James, Mary, John	Feb. 1739	Ireland
Breckenridge, Alexander, Jane, John, George, Robert	May 22 1740	Ireland
Byrne, Thomas		Great Britain & Ireland
Breckenridge, James, Smith, Jane, Letitia	May 1740	Ireland
Bell, James, John, Margaret, Elizabeth	May 1740	Ireland
Brown, William, Mary, Robert, Hugh, Margret	May 1740	Ireland
Black, Thomas and wife, Margaret	July 1740	Great Britain & Ireland
Brawford, Samuel	July 1740	Great Britain & Ireland
Baskins, William	July 1740	Ireland
Bambridge, Ann	Feb. 1740	England
Bayne, Henry	Mar. 1741	Great Britain & Ireland
Bradstreet, Francis	Mar. 1741	Great Britain & Ireland
Banks, William	Mar. 1741	Great Britain & Ireland
Brady, William, his mother, Judy, brother, Daniel	May 1741	Ireland
Brown, Thomas	July 1741	Great Britain
Buntine, William	May 1746	Great Britain
Bird, James	Mar. 1749	Great Britain

Name	Date	Country Imported From
Blankenbacker, Zachaim	1743	Great Britain
Cotton, Joseph	1735	
Cavanaugh, Philemon	Nov. 1736	Great Britain & Ireland
Cummins, Alex. (or Timmons)	Nov. 1738	Great Britain
Chambers, Thomas	Nov. 1738	Great Britain
Cathey, James, Ann, William, Elizabeth, Andrew, George, Margaret, Ann	Feb. 1739	Ireland
Camble, John, Elizabeth, Esther, Mary, Rachel, Jane	Feb. 1739	Ireland
Cross, Richard	Feb. 1739	Great Britain & Ireland
Carr, John, and wife, Lucy, and children, Jane, William, Barbara, Lucy, Martha	Feb. 1739	Ireland
Crocket, Robert, Margaret, John, Marshall, Jane, Samuel, Robert	May 1740	Ireland
Campbell, Patrick, Elizabeth, Charles, William, Patrick, Jr., John, Mary, Elizabeth, Gennet	May 1740	Ireland
Caldwell, James, Mary, Jean, Agnes, John, Mary, Sarah, Samuel	May 1740	Ireland
Carohant, John(German), Mary, Elizabeth, Daniel, Catherine	May 1740	Great Britain
Cole, William, and wife, Rachel	July 1740	Ireland
Caldwell, George, and wife, Mary, and children, William, Mary, John, Jane, David, Agnes	July 1740	Ireland
Crawford, Patrick, Ann, James, George, Margaret, Mary	July 1740	Ireland
Christopher, Nicholas	July 1740	Great Britain & Ireland
Crawford, John	July 1740	Great Britain
Cross, Elleaner	May 1743	Great Britain
Cooper, William	June 1743	England
Coleman, John, Margaret	Feb. 1744	Great Britain
Crawford, William	May 1744	England
Chambers, Elizabeth	May 1744	England
Cook, James	June 1746	Great Britain
Collins, James	Mar. 1749	Ireland
Cook, George	May 1750	Great Britain
Collins, Anne	Sept. 1750	Great Britain
Chancy, Joseph	Oct. 1751	Great Britain
Carney, Easter	Nov. 1752	Ireland
Cock, Charles George	June 1755	Great Britain
Cussine, Richard	Oct. 1756	Great Britain
Cole, Edward	Sept. 1751	Ireland
Carney, Timothy	May 1751	Ireland
Campbell, Dougall	Feb. 1746	Great Britain
Dyer, James	Feb. 1735	Great Britain & Ireland
Dunn, Authur	Feb. 1735	Great Britain & Ireland
Dealmore, John	Feb. 1735	Great Britain & Ireland
Drake, Samuel	Feb. 1735	Great Briatin & Ireland
Daniels, John	July 1736	
Dier, Jeremiah	Apr. 1738	Great Britain

Name	Date	Country Import'd From
Daley, James	July 1740	Ireland
Davidson, John, Jane, George, Thomas, William, Samuel	July 1740	Ireland
Davis, James, Mary, Henry, William, Samuel	July 1740	Ireland
Dunning, Elizabeth	July 1740	Ireland
Dungan, Margaret	July 1745	Scotland
Douglas, Elizabeth	Mar. 1749	Ireland
Durham, John	Mar. 1749	Great Britain
Drake, Hannah	Aug. 1751	Great Britain
Dooling, Thomas	May 1752	Ireland
Davis, John	July 1755	Great Britain
Duff, Arthur	Feb. 1746	Ireland
Dulling, John	Feb. 1746	Ireland
Duff, Mary	Feb. 1746	Ireland
Evans, John	Feb. 1737	Great Britain & Ireland
Edmiston, David, Isabella, Jesse, John, William, Rachell, David, Moses	July 1740	Ireland
Ewe, Joseph	May 1750	Great Britain
Finlason, John	May 1735	
Floyd, John	1735	
Floyd, Charles	Feb. 1735	Great Britain & Ireland
Frazer, Robert	May 1740	Ireland
Fox, James	July 1740	Ireland
Fink, Mark	May 1741	Great Britain & Ireland
Frazier, Alexander	July 1745	Scotland
Forester, John	May 1746	Great Britain
Fields, Mary	May 1750	Great Britain
Finley, Patrick	Feb. 1752	Ireland
Flanders, William	June 1755	Great Britain
Frazer, John	Feb. 1746	Great Britain
Green, Robert	1735	
Gray, William	Aug. 1736	
Grant, John	Nov. 1736	Great Britain & Ireland
Givins, Samuel, and wife, Sarah, and children, John, Samuel, James, Martha, Elizabeth, William, Margaret, Sarah, Jane	Feb. 1739	Ireland
Grady, Mary	Feb. 1739	Great Britain & Ireland
Glasby, Margaret, Matthew	Mar. 1740	Ireland
Gilasby, James, Jennet, Agnes, James, William, Jesse	July 1740	Ireland
Gay, Samuel, and wife, Margaret, and children, John, Thomas	July 1740	Ireland
Gibson, Margaret	May 1742	Great Britain & Ireland
Green, Edward	May 1743	Ireland
Gibson, Abel	May 1746	Great Britain
Gibbins, William	June 1746	Ireland
Galagan, Thomas	Mar. 1747	Ireland
Gulby, Thomas	May 1750	
Grant, Alexander	May 1752	Great Britain
Golder, John	Jan. 1755	Great Britain

Name	Date	Country Imported From
Goodin, Mary	July 1770	Great Britain
Grace, Ann	Feb. 1746	Great Britain
Hawkins, William	Feb. 1737	Great Britain & Ireland
Home, George	1735	
Humphries, George	Feb. 1735	Great Britain & Ireland
Hays, John, Rebecka, Charles, Andrew, Barbara, Joan, Robert, Patrick, Francis, Joan, William, Margaret, Catherine, Ruth	May 1740	Ireland
Hook, Robert and wife, Jane, and son, William	May 1740	Ireland
Harrell, John, Margaret, Mary, Edward	May 1740	Ireland
Hall, Edward	July 1740	Ireland
Hutchison, William, John, Sr., Margaret, John, Jr., Mary	July 1740	Ireland
Henderson, Thomas and wife, Dersas	July 1740	Ireland
Hawkins, Elizabeth	July 1740	Ireland
Honey, John	July 1740	Ireland
Hart, Henry Philip	May 1741	Great Britain & Ireland
Harris, Joseph	May 1741	Great Britain & Ireland
Hopkins, James	May 1743	Ireland
Honson, Thomas	June 1746	Great Britain
Hussee, Easter	Mar. 1749	Great Britain & Ireland
Herrenden, John	May 1750	Ireland
Henderson, Alexander	June 1755	Great Britain
Haney, Darby	Mar. 1756	Ireland
Johnson, William	Feb. 1735	Great Britain & Ireland
Jones, Thomas	Nov. 1736	Great Britain & Ireland
Johnston, William, Ann, Elizabeth, John	July 1740	Ireland
Johnson, Archibald	Mar. 1741	Great Britain & Ireland
Jennings, Edward	May 1746	Great Britain
Johnson, Peter	May 1750	Ireland
Jerman, Thomas	Nov. 1750	Great Britain & Ireland
Johnson, Peter	Oct. 1751	Great Britain
Johnson, William	July 1740	Ireland
Jones, Thomas	Feb. 1746	Great Britain
Irwin, Anthony	Nov. 1750	Ireland
Kerchler, Mathias	May 1736	England
Kemp, Richard	Feb. 1737	Great Britain & Ireland
Kendall, Henry	Mar. 1737	Great Britain
King, Robert, Catherine, John, Sarah, Elizabeth, William, Margaret, Jane, Elizabeth, Margaret	May 1740	Ireland
Kelly, Catherine	Mar. 1741	Great Britain & Ireland
Kines, John	May 1741	Great Britain & Ireland
Kelly, Michael	May 1752	Ireland
Kindal, Henry	June 1755	Great Britain
Kelly, William	Feb. 1735	Great Britain & Ireland
Kelly, William	June 1746	Ireland
Kindle, Thomas	July 1740	Ireland

Name	Date	Country Imported From
Latham, John	Feb. 1735	Great Britain & Ireland
Lamlotte, Edward	Aug. 1736	
Ledgerwood, William, Agnes, Martha, Jane, Eleanor, William, James	Feb. 1739	Ireland
Leppor, James, Margaret, Nicholas, Sarah, Jane, Andrew, James, Gerins, Isbell, Mary	Feb. 1739	Ireland
Lampart, Edward	Feb. 1739	Great Britain & Ireland
Logan, David, and wife, Jane, and children, Mary, William	May 1740	Ireland
Long, William, Elizabeth, Alexander, John, William, Jr.	July 1740	Ireland
Leonard, Patrick	July 1740	Ireland
Lynd, John	June 1746	Ireland
Lamb, Richard	Mar. 1749	Ireland
Lyon, Michael	May 1750	Ireland
Lerney, Thomas	Feb. 1745	Ireland
McCoy, John	1735	
McCulley, James	1735	
McKinney, John	Feb. 1735	Great Britain & Ireland
Mitchell, James	Feb. 1735	Great Britain & Ireland
McMurrin, David	Feb. 1735	Great Britain & Ireland
Man, John	Feb. 1735	Great Britain & Ireland
Moore, William	July 1735	
McCaddan, Patrick	Feb. 1739	Ireland
McKoy, James, Agnes, William	Feb. 1739	Ireland
Morphet, John, Mary, George, Mary, Catherine	Feb. 1739	Ireland
McDowell, Robt., Martha, Jane, Margaret, William	Feb. 1739	Ireland
Mitchel, David, Martha, Sarah, James, Eliza	Feb. 1739	Ireland
McDowell, John, and wife Magdalene, and son, Samuel	Feb. 1739	Great Britain
McMurrin, Margaret	Feb. 1739	Great Britain & Ireland
McDowell, Ephraim, John, James, Margaret	Feb. 1739	Ireland
Mullalan, John	May 1740	Ireland
McAlegant, James	May 1740	Ireland
McCanless, William, Elizabeth	May 1740	Ireland
McOnnal, Andrew, Jane, John, Agnes	May 1740	Ireland
McDowel, Robert	June 1740	Ireland
McGowin, Francis, and wife, Mary, and children, Markham, Elizabeth	June 1740	Ireland
McClure, James, Agnes, John, Andrew, Eleaner, Jean, James, Jr.	July 1740	Ireland
Maxwell, John, Margaret, John, Jr., Thomas, Mary, Alexander	July 1740	Ireland
McClean, William, Margaret	July 1740	Ireland
McDaniel, William	Mar. 1741	Great Britain & Ireland
McPherson, Robert, Margaret, Alexander, Susannah	May 1741	Great Britain & Ireland
Mills, James	July 1741	Great Britain

Name	Date	Country Imported From
Morgan, John, Mary	Feb. 1744	Great Britain
McNiel, Patrick	May 1745	England
McKensey, John	July 1745	Ireland
McCullock, Ann	June 1746	Ireland
Morris, William	Mar. 1747	Great Britain
Mason, Margaret	Feb. 1748	Ireland
Monroe, William	Mar. 1749	Ireland
Morris, Jane	Mar. 1749	Ireland
Mulholland, Owen	May 1750	Ireland
McGinnis, James	May 1750	Ireland
Mannen, Andrew	Sept. 1751	Ireland
McField, John	May 1752	Ireland
Morgan, Thomas	Feb. 1754	Great Britain
Mitchel, John	Feb. 1754	Great Britain
McDonald, John	May 1756	Great Britain
Nicholls, William	Feb. 1735	Great Britain & Ireland
Northan, James	Feb. 1735	Great Britain & Ireland
Neilson, David, and wife, Charity, and child, James	May 1740	Ireland
Newport, John	July 1741	Great Britain
Offrail, Morris, and wife Catherine	May 1740	Ireland
Overton, Mary	May 1750	Great Britain
Ogg, John, and wife, Mary	July 1752	Great Britain
Pitcher, Thomas	Feb. 1735	Great Britain & Ireland
Phillips, Joseph	Feb. 1735	Great Britain & Ireland
Parsons, Richard	Mar. 1735	Great Britain & Ireland
Patterson, Robert, and wife Frances, and children, Thomas, Mary, Elizabeth	May 1740	Ireland
Poage, Robt., and wife, Elizabeth, and children, Margaret, John, Martha, Sarah, George, Mary, Elizabeth, William, Robert	May 1740	Ireland
Pickins, John, Margaret, Gabriel	July 1740	Ireland
Parks, Thomas	Mar. 1741	Great Britain & Ireland
Phillips, Edmund	Mar. 1741	Great Britain & Ireland
Piner, Thomas	June 1746	Ireland
Price, Edward	June 1746	Great Britain
Parsons, George	June 1746	Great Britain
Phillips, Joseph	May 1750	Ireland
Parsons, Mary	May 1752	Great Britain
Poor, Michael	Nov. 1752	Ireland
Peacock, Thomas	June 1755	Great Britain
Parks, John	Nov. 1736	Great Britain & Ireland
Page, John	May 1746	Great Britain
Plunkett, Edward	Nov. 1746	Ireland
Rigby, John	May 1756	Great Britain
Ryan, John	Sept. 1756	Great Britain
Robinson, Charles	July 1735	
Rouse, Edward	Nov. 1735	Great Britain
Read, John	Feb. 1735	Great Britain & Ireland
Ray, Joseph	Feb. 1740	Great Britain & Ireland
Roach, David	Feb. 1735	Great Britain & Ireland

Name	Date	Country Imported From
Roberson, James	Aug. 1736	
Ryley, Mical	Nov. 1736	Great Britain & Ireland
Reed, James	Nov. 1736	Great Britain & Ireland
Ryan, Soleman	Mar. 1737	Great Britain
Ramsey, Robert	Feb. 1738	Great Britain
Rutter, John (servant)	Feb. 1739	Great Britain
Ralson, Robt., and wife, Martha	May 1740	Ireland
Read, Joseph, Elizabeth, Ann	July 1740	Ireland
Robinson, James, Jean, George	July 1740	Ireland
Raney, John	May 1746	Great Britain
Ross, David	Nov. 1747	Great Britain
Rosse, Alexander	Mar. 1747	Great Britain
Rowland, Edward	Mar. 1747	Great Britain
Rakestraw, John	June 1755	Great Britain
Rouse, Frances	June 1755	Ireland
Riche, Patrick	Oct. 1751	Great Britain
Stephenson, William	Nov. 1735	Great Britain
Small, Oliver	Feb. 1735	Great Britain & Ireland
Stockdell, John	Feb. 1735	Great Britain & Ireland
Stanton, Mathew	Feb. 1735	Great Britain & Ireland
Smith, John	July 1736	
Stewart, George	May 1738	Great Britain & Ireland
Stevenson, David, James, Jane, Thomas, William	Feb. 1738	Ireland
Smith, William, and wife Elizabeth	Feb. 1738	England
Stanton, Elizabeth	Feb. 1738	Great Britain & Ireland
Steavenson, Thomas, Rachel	May 1740	Ireland
Scott, Samuel, Ann, Jane, John, Robert, Ann (his wife), Mary, George, Esther	May 1740	Ireland
Steavenson, John, Sarah, Mary	May 1740	Ireland
Smith, John, and wife, Margaret, and children, Abraham, Henry, Daniel, John, Joseph	June 1740	Ireland
Skillirn, William, Elizabeth, George, William, Isabell, Sarah	July 1740	Ireland
Smith, William, and wife, Jean, and children, Mary, Margaret, John	July 1740	Ireland
Sevier, Valentine	May 1742	Great Britain & Ireland
Scott, James	Mar. 1749	Great Britain
Sims, Joanna	May 1750	Great Britain
Sheets, John	Feb. 1752	England
Sleet, James	June 1755	Great Britain
Smith, Thomas	June 1755	Great Britain
Stokes, Elizabeth	May 1756	Great Britain
Smith, Elizabeth	June 1755	Ireland
Sutherland, William	Mar. 1741	Great Britain & Ireland
Scales, Richard	Feb. 1744	Great Britain
Sims, William	Mar. 1749	Great Britain
Sleet, James	May 1750	Great Britain
Thomas, Joshua	Feb. 1735	Great Britain & Ireland
Thomson, John	Sept. 1738	Great Britain
Timmins (or Cummins), Alexander	Mar. 1738	Great Britain

Name	Date	Country Imported From
Turk, Robert, Margaret, Jane, John, Ann, Thomas, William	Feb. 1739	Ireland
Trimble, John, Ann, Margaret, Mary	May 1740	Ireland
Thomson, Wm., Isabelle, William	June 1740	Ireland
Thompson, Moses, Jane, William, Robert, John, Alexander, Mary, Thomas, Omy, Isaac, George	July 1740	Ireland
Thomson, Robert	May 1743	Great Britain
Thurston, Sarah	May 1743	Great Britain
Terrell, Hanner	Mar. 1749	Ireland
Tibbit, Matthew	Aug. 1751	Great Britain
Terret, Nathaniel	Nov. 1752	Ireland
Thompson, Alexander	Feb. 1754	Great Britain
Uxton, Henry, Mary	Feb. 1741	Great Britain
Vineyard, John	1735	
Vought, John Paul, and wife, Mary Catherine, and children, John Andrew, John Casper, Catherine Margaret, Mary Catherine	July 1735	
Wood, James	1735	
Warfin, Richard	Feb. 1735	Great Britain & Ireland
Welch, John	Feb. 1735	Great Britain
Walker, John	Mar. 1735	
Wilhite, Michael, John	May 1736	England
Wilhite, Tobias	1743	
Weaver, Peter	May 1736	England
White, John	Sept. 1738	Great Britain
Welch, Patrick	July 1740	Great Britain & Ireland
Williams, Thomas	July 1740	Great Britain
Wilson, John, Martha, Mathew, William, John, Sarah, Elizabeth	July 1740	Ireland
Walker, John	Feb. 1740	England
Wheeler, John	Feb. 1744	Great Britain
Walsh, Joseph	July 1745	Scotland
Wood, Thomas	May 1746	Great Britain
Wallace, Humphrey	June 1746	Great Britain
Wallis, Margaret	May 1750	Ireland
Willson, Mary	May 1750	Great Britain
Whitman, William	May 1751	Great Britain
Walker, Thomas	May 1756	Great Britain
Wilson, Richard	Feb. 1739	Great Britain & Ireland
Whiteman, William	Nov. 1746	Ireland
Warner, Daniel	Mar. 2, 1744	Great Britain
Young, Robert, Agnes, John, Samuel, James	June 1740	Ireland
Zinnerman, Jno. (alias Carpenter)	1743	

Military Commissions

Name	Date	Rank
Anderson, William	Aug. 1742	Ensign
Anderson, George	Feb. 1742	Captain
Ashby, Thomas	Mar. 1742	Captain of Foot.
Bryant, Morgan	June 1736	
Bell, William	Mar. 1741	Cornet
Beverley, William	Nov. 1741	Lieutenant of Orange and Agusta

Name	Date	Rank
Bush, Phillip	Feb. 1741	Ensign
Buchannon, John	June 1742	Captain
Breckenridge, Robert	Mar. 1742	Captain
Brown, John	June 1743	Lt. Col. of Foot.
Bell, Samuel	June 1743	Captain
Borden, Benj.	Aug. 1744	Captain of Foot.
Bird, Andrew	Feb. 1744	Lieutenant of Foot.
Bell, William	Mar. 1745	Lieutenant
Baylor, John (of Carolie County)	Apr. 1745	Major
Baylor, John	July 1749	Lieutenant
Baylor, John	May 1753	Lieutenant
Bell, William	July 1755	Captain
Barbour, Richard	Feb. 1758	Captain
Burnley, Zack	Oct. 1766	Major
Bell, John	May 1770	Captain
Bruce, Charles	June 1772	Captain
Brockman, John	Feb. 1777	Lieutenant
Burton, May. Jr.	Aug. 1777	Ensign
Burton, Ambrose	Sept. 1777	Ensign
Buckner, William	Sept. 1777	2nd Lieutenant
Burnley, Zack	May 1778	County Lieutenant
Barbour, Thomas	May 1778	Major
Burton, May, Jr.	May 1778	1st Lieutenant
Buckner, William	May 1778	Captain
Burton, May, Jr.	May 1779	1st Lieutenant
Burton, May, Jr.	May 1780	Captain
Burton, William	May 1780	2nd Lieutenant
Beadles, John	May 1780	2nd Lieutenant
Burton, James	July 1781	2nd Lieutenant
Burton, William	July 1781	Ensign
Barbour, Thomas	July 1781	Colonel
Bell, Mary	July 1781	Jailor of County
Burnley, Garland	Feb. 1783	Captain
Barbour, Thomas	Oct. 1784	County Lieutenant
Bell, Thomas	July 1786	Ensign
Burnley, Hardin	July 1787	Major
Burton, May	July 1787	Captain
Beadles, John	July 1787	Captain
Bell, Thomas	July 1787	Lieutenant
Bell, James	July 1787	Lieutenant
Beckham, James	July 1787	Ensign
Burnley, James	July 1787	Ensign
Burton, William	Sept. 1787	Lieutenant
Burnley, Hardin	Sept. 1790	Colonel
Bell, Thomas	Sept. 1790	Captain
Bledsoe, Miller	Sept. 1790	Ensign
Beadles, John	Apr. 1793	Captain
Bell, Thomas	Apr. 1793	Captain
Cave, Benj.	Nov. 1735	Capt. of troop of Hrs.
Chew, Thomas	Mar. 1735	Major
Chew, Thomas	July 1738	
Cave, Robert	July 1738	Capt. Troop of Horses

Name	Date	Rank
Chew, Thomas	Feb. 1741	Colonel of County
Curtis, Charles	Feb. 1741	Captain
Cathey, James	June 1742	Captain
Christian, John	June 1742	Captain
Clayton, Phillip	July 1742	Lieutenant
Campbell, Andrew	Feb. 1742	Captain
Carter, Joseph	Feb. 1742	Lieutenant
Coulton, Joseph	May 1743	Captain
Craven, Robert	July 1743	Captain of Horses
Carpenter, William	Aug. 1743	
Clayton, Phillip	May 1748	Captain
Covington, Thomas	Nov. 1748	Lieutenant of Foot.
Craig, Toliver	Feb. 1777	Captain
Conway, Catlett	July 1777	Captain
Chambers, Thomas	Oct. 1777	Ensign
Chambers, Thomas	Nov. 1778	2nd Lieutenant
Cave, Belfield	Apr. 1779	2nd Lieutenant
Cave, Belfield	May 1780	1st Lieutenant
Chambers, Thomas	May 1780	1st Lieutenant
Cave, Belfield	July 1781	Captain
Coleman, James	July 1786	Ensign
Cave, Belfield	July 1787	Captain
Coleman, James	July 1787	Lieutenant
Coleman, James, Jr.	July 1787	Ensign
Coleman, Thomas	July 1787	Ensign
Chapman, Joseph	Sept. 1787	Ensign
Campbell, William	Sept. 1790	Lt. Col. of County
Cave, Belfield	Sept. 1790	Major
Chapman, Joseph	Sept. 1790	Lieutenant
Coleman, James	Apr. 1793	Captain
Chapman, Joseph	Apr. 1793	Captain
Campbell, William	June 1793	Lieutenant Colonel
Conner, Timothy	May 1780	1st Lieutenant
Downs, Henry	Mar. 1741	Capt. Troop Horses
Doggett, George	Feb. 1741	Lieutenant
Dewitt, Charles	Aug. 1742	Lieutenant
Duncan, William	Aug. 1742	Ensign
Denton, John	Feb. 1742	Captain
Dunlap, Alexander	Aug. 1743	Captain of Horse
Dobbin, John	Feb. 1743	Lieutenant of Horse
Daniel, Reuben	Mar. 1755	Captain
Daniel, Reuben	May 1761	Captain
Daniel, Vivian	Sept. 1774	Captain
Daniel, Robert	Aug. 1777	2nd Lieutenant
Dawson, John	Sept. 1781	Ensign
Deering, James	Sept. 1781	Ensign
Davis, John	May 1784	Ensign
Daniel, John	May 1784	1st Lieutenant
Davis, Thomas	Sept. 1784	Ensign
Daniel, John	July 1787	Captain
Daniel, William	July 1787	Lieutenant
Davis, John	July 1787	Ensign

Name	Date	Rank
Dawson, John	Apr. 1793	Captain
Evans, William	June 1742	Lieutenant
Eastham, Robert	Aug. 1742	Captain
Early, James	Sept. 1781	Ensign
Early, Joseph	July 1787	Ensign
Emgram, William	May 1780	Ensign
Finlason, John	Mar. 1735	Captain
Finlason, John	Feb. 1741	Major
Field, Henry	June 1742	Captain
Ferguson, Samuel	Aug. 1742	Ensign
Funk, John	Mar. 1742	Lieutenant
Fortson, Thomas	May 1780	1st Lieutenant
Goodall, John	June 1757	Lieutenant
Green, Robert	July 1742	Captain
Gill, James	Aug. 1742	Captain
Guy, Henry	May 1742	Lieutenant of Foot.
Guy, Samuel	Aug. 1742	Captain
Garnett, Anthony	Feb. 1744	Captain of Foot.
Gibbs, Zackary	Aug. 1737	Lieutenant of Foot.
Graves, Richard	Oct. 1777	2nd Lieutenant
Graves, Richard	July 1778	Captain
Gaines, Richard	May 1784	2nd Lieutenant
Gibson, John	July 1786	Lieutenant
Gaines, Richard	July 1787	Lieutenant
Gaines, Richard	Sept. 1790	Captain
Gaines, Richard	Apr. 1793	Capt., 1st Regiment
Gaines, Reuben	Apr. 1793	Capt., 2nd Regiment
Grymes, Ludwell	May 1769	Captain
Howard, John	Feb. 1737	Captain Troop
Holt, Peter	Aug. 1742	Captain
Hite, John	Feb. 1742	
Hobson, George	Feb. 1742	Lieutenant
Hite, Jacob	Feb. 1742	Lieutenant
Harrison, John	Feb. 1742	Lieutenant
Harrison, Daniel	July 1743	Captain of Horse
Hays, Andrew	Aug.	Lieutenant of Foot.
Hudson, Rush	Nov. 1757	Lieutenant
Head, Benj.	1777	Captain
Head, James	Aug. 1777	Ensign
Hansford, Benoni	Aug. 1777	2nd Lieutenant
Hansford, Benoni	Aug. 1777	2nd Lieutenant
Hawkins, James	Aug. 1777	2nd Lieutenant
Hawkins, James	Oct. 1777	1st Lieutenant
Hawkins, James	Mar. 1777	Captain
Hansford, Ben	Sept. 1786	Lieutenant
Hawkins, James	July 1787	Captain
Hansford, Benj.	July 1787	Captain
Herndon, Zach	July 1778	Captain
Jones, Thomas	Sept. 1742	Lieutenant
Jones, Robt.	Feb. 1742	Ensign
Jameson, William	Apr. 1745	Captain
Jones, Thomas	June 1736	Captain
Jones, John	Mar. 1755	Captain
Jameson, Thomas	Jan. 1757	Captain
Jameson, Thomas	Feb. 1773	Ensign

Name	Date	Rank
Johnson, Robt.	Sept. 1777	2nd Lieutenant
Johnson, Robert	Apr. 1779	1st Lieutenant
Jameson, James	May 1780	Captain
Johnson, Martin	May 1780	Ensign
Johnson, Benjamin	July 1781	Lieutenant
Johnson, Benjamin	Apr. 1787	Lieutenant Colonel
Johnson, Benjamin	Sept. 1790	County Lieutenant
Jameson, Wm.	Mar. 1779	Ensign
Karr, John	May 1744	Capt., Troop of Horse
Lightfoot, Goodrich	Feb. 1735	Commission
Lewis, John	Feb. 1738	Commission
Lightfoot, Goodrich	Sept. 1740	Captain of Troop
Lightfoot, Goodrich	Feb. 1741	Captain
Lewis, John	Feb. 1742	Colonel
Low, Thomas	Feb. 1742	Captain
Lindsay, Caleb	Oct. 1777	1st Lieutenant
Lindsay, Caleb	Nov. 1780	Captain
Lindsay, Caleb	July 1787	Captain
Morgan, Morgan	Feb. 1735	Commission
Morton, George	May 1740	Commission
McCrackin, James	July 1740	Commission
Michael, Francis	Sept. 1740	Cornet
Michael, Francis	Feb. 1741	Ensign
Moffett, John	June 1742	Lieutenant
Morton, George	June 1742	Ensign
Moore, Frans	June 1742	Ensign
McDowell, John	Aug. 1742	Captain
Morgan, Morgan	Feb. 1742	Major
Morris, Samuel	Feb. 1742	Lieutenant
Morgan, Richard	Feb. 1742	Captain
McMure, Daniel	June 1743	Captain
Matthews, John	June 1743	Captain
Michael, Francis	Mar. 1745	Lieutenant of Foot
Moore, Francis	June 1745	Lieutenant of Foot
Mallory, John	June 1736	Ensign
Moore, Francis	June 1757	Major
Morton, Jeremiah	July 1755	Captain
Moore, Francis	Aug. 1749	Captain
Moore, Francis	Apr. 1761	Major
Madison, James	July 1767	County Lieutenant
Moore, Francis	July 1767	Lieutenant Colonel
Moore, William	Mar. 1768	Captain
Moore, William	July 1768	Captain
Merry, Thomas	July 1768	Lieutenant
McNeal, Patrick	May 1769	Ensign
Mills, Nath.	Feb. 1777	Captain
	(Rec. to Governor)	
Miller, Robt.	Aug. 1777	2nd Lieutenant
Martin, Robt. Jr.	May 1778	Ensign
Moore, Reuben	Mar. 1779	Lieutenant
Miller, Robert	May 1779	Captain

Name	Date	Rank
Morris, Reuben	May 1780	1st Lieutenant
Merry, Prettyman	Oct. 1780	2nd Lieutenant
Madison, James, Jr.	July 1781	County Lieutenant
Madison, Ambrose	July 1781	Major
Merry, Prettyman	May 1784	Captain
Miner, Jere	Sept. 1784	Captain
Miller, John	July 1787	Captain
Miller, John	Apr. 1793	Captain
Mallory, Uriel (resigned)	Feb. 1777	Captain
Neil, Lewis	Feb. 1742	Captain
Newman, Alex	May 1780	Ensign
Patton, James	Feb. 1742	Colonel Horse & Foot
Patton, James	May 1742	Colonel of Augusta
Pickins, John	Feb. 1742	Captain
Pennington, Isaac	Feb. 1742	Captain
Peyton, William	Nov. 24, 1743	Lieutenant of Foot
Pendleton, Jno.	Jan. 1757	Ensign
Pearce, Jeremiah	Aug. 1763	Lieutenant
Pearson, Henry	Aug. 1763	Ensign
Parish, Joseph	Feb. 1777	Ensign
Proctor, John	Sept. 1777	Ensign
Porter, John	July 1778	2nd Lieutenant
Porter, Abner, Jr.	Mar. 1779	Lieutenant
Price, Richard	Mar. 1779	Lieutenant
Porter, Charles	Mar. 1779	Lieutenant
Price, Rich. Moore	Mar. 1779	Ensign
Payne, Richard	May 1780	2nd Lieutenant
Pannill, John	May 1780	2nd Lieutenant
Quin, John	Jan. 1742	Lieutenant
Rucker, John	May 1740	Captain for County
Russell, Wm.	Feb. 1741	Captain
Roberts, John	July 1742	Ensign
Robinson, George	Aug. 1742	Captain
Roberts, Benj.	Aug. 1742	Lieutenant
Roberts, Benj.	Aug. 1746	Captain
Russell, Peter	Nov. 1743	Ensign
Roy, Mungo	May 1753	Colonel
Riddle, Lewis	May 1780	1st Lieutenant
Rucker, Jno.	May 1780	Ensign
Robinson, John	May 1780	Ensign
Row, Thomas	July 1786	Lieutenant
Row, Thomas	July 1787	Captain
Riddle, Lewis	July 1787	Ensign
Row, Thomas	Sept. 1790	Captain
Riddle, Lewis	Sept. 1790	Captain
Row, Thomas	Apr. 1793	Captain
Rutherford, Thos.	Feb. 1742	Captain
Smith, John	June 1739	Commission
Spencer, Edward	May 1740	Captain for Orange Co.
Sisson, Bryan	Sept. 1740	Lieutenant
Slaughter, Robert	Sept. 1740	Major
Slaughter, Robert	Feb. 1741	Lt. Colonel of County
Smith, John	June 1742	Captain
Spencer, Edward	June 1742	Captain

Name	Date	Rank
Smith, Justphonica	June 1742	Lieutenant
Scott, Robert	Aug. 1742	Lieutenant
Scott, George	Aug. 1742	Ensign
Swearinham, Thomas	Feb. 1742	1st Lieutenant
Smith, Jeremiah	Mar. 1742	Captain of Foot
Scott, Robt.	Nov. 1743	Captain of Foot
Smith, Wm.	Aug. 1744	Captain of Foot
Scott, Saml.	May 1744	Ensign
Slaughter, Thomas	May 1748	Lieutenant
Spencer, Edward	July 1749	Major
Scott, Johnny	Feb. 1758	Lieutenant
Suggett, James	Mar. 1762	Lieutenant
Scott, Johnny	Nov. 1767	Captain
Smith, Joseph	June 1768	Ensign
Smith, _____	May 1769	Lieutenant
Stevens, John	May 1769	Ensign
Singleton, Manoah	July 1777	2nd Lieutenant
Smith, Wm.	Aug. 1777	2nd Lieutenant
Stubblefield, Geo.	Oct. 1777	1st Lieutenant
Shackelford, Zachy.	Oct. 1777	2nd Lieutenant
Smith, Geo.	May 1778	(resigned as Captain)
Sisson, Caleb	Mar. 1779	Ensign
Scott, John	Apr. 1779	Ensign
Shackleford, Edmond	May 1780	Captain
Scott, John, Jr.	May 1780	1st Lieutenant
Sanders, James	May 1780	2nd Lieutenant
Shackleford, Zach	Nov. 1780	1st Lieutenant
Stevens, James	Nov. 1780	Ensign
Stubblefield, Robert	July 1780	Captain
Sleet, James	Sept. 1781	Ensign
Smith, Absalom	July 1786	Lieutenant
Shackleford, Edward	July 1787	Captain
Shepherd, Geo.	July 1787	Captain
Smith, Absalom	Sept. 1790	Lieutenant
Thomson, Hugh	Aug. 1742	Captain
Tayloe, George	Jan. 1742	Captain
Thompson, William	Feb. 1744	Company of Foot.
Taylor, George	Feb. 1748	Major
Taylor, George	June 1749	Lieutenant Colonel
Taylor, George	July 1755	Colonel
Thomas, Rowland	July 1755	Captain
Thomas, Richard	July 1755	Captain
Thomas, Robert	Jan. 1757	Lieutenant
Taylor, George	May 1757	County Lieutenant
Taliaferro, William	May 1757	Colonel
Taylor, George	Apr. 1761	Colonel
Thomas, Richard	Apr. 1761	Lieutenant
Thomas, Rowland	Apr. 1761	Lieutenant
Thomas, Robert	Apr. 1761	Lieutenant
Thomas, Robert	Apr. 1762	Captain
Taylor, James	Aug. 1763	Captain
Thomas, Robert	Nov. 1767	Captain
Taylor, James	Mar. 1768	Captain

Name	Date	Rank
Taylor, Zachary	Mar. 1768	Lieutenant
Taliaferro, Lawrence	July 1768	Captain
Taliaferro, Hay	July 1768	Lieutenant
Taylor, James, Jr.	May 1769	Captain
Taylor, Zachary	May 1769	Lieutenant
Taylor, Zacky	Sept. 1774	Captain
Taylor, Jonathon	Sept. 1774	Lieutenant
Thomas, Robert	Oct. 1777	Captain
Taliaferro, Lawrence	May 1778	Lieutenant Colonel
Thomas, Rowland, Jr.	May 1780	Lieutenant
Thomas, Robert (resigned)	Nov. 1780	Captain
Thomas, William	Nov. 1780	2nd Lieutenant
Thomas, Chs.	Sept. 1781	Ensign
Thomas, Jos. Jr.	Sept. 1784	Lieutenant
Taylor, Reuben	Sept. 1786	Captain
Thomas, Joseph	July 1787	Captain
Vance, David	May 1743	Lieutenant
Willis, Henry	Nov. 1735	Lieutenant for County
Wood, James	Feb. 1742	Colonel of Horse & Foot
Walter, Edward	Feb. 1742	Lieutenant
Watts, John	Feb. 1743	Ensign
Wilson, John	Aug. 1744	Captain
Walker, James	July 1755	Lieutenant
Walker, James	Apr. 1761	Lieutenant
Walker, James	Apr. 1762	Captain
Webb, Richard Crittenden	Feb. 1777	Lieutenant
Wright, Wm.	Aug. 1777	Ensign
Waugh, George	Oct. 1777	2nd Lieutenant
White, Benj.	May 1778	Captain
White, Richard	May 1778	Ensign
Waugh, Geo.	Mar. 1779	Lieutenant
White, Richard	May 1779	2nd Lieutenant
Waugh, Geo.	May 1780	Captain
Willis, Lewis	May 1780	2nd Lieutenant
Willis, Moses	May 1780	2nd Lieutenant
Webb, Richard Crittenden	May 1780	Captain
White, Thos.	May 1780	Ensign
Wright, John	July 1781	Ensign
Welsh, James	July 1782	Lieutenant
Wood, Joseph, Jr.	May 1784	Captain
Webb, Rich.	July 1787	Captain
White, Rich.	Sept. 1787	Captain
Wright, John	Apr. 1793	Captain
Winslow, Richard	Feb. 1741	Captain
Yarbrough, Richard	Sept. 1742	Ensign
Zimmeman, Christopher	Sept. 1740	Lieutenant
Zimmeman, Christopher	Aug. 1742	Lieutenant

Revolutionary Soldiers

Name	Date	Rank
Abell, John	Mar. 1785	
Atkins, John	Aug. 9, 1820	5th Va. Reg. & Order, Apr. 24, 1837

Adams, John	June 1785	
Almond, John	Sept. 27, 1847	
Brown, John	June 26, 1815	
Brown, John	Apr. 27, 1818	Capt. Francis Taylor Co., Monmouth & Siege of Charleston
Brown, James	1818	20th Va. Reg. Capt. Charles Gee
Bledsoe, John	Apr. 1783	
Bledsoe, Peachy		
Boye, William	Mar. 1785	
Barnett, John	Aug. 1785	
Burton, James (Capt.)	1811	
Bush, John	July 1786	
Bolling, John	Mar. 1792	
Clark, Robert	Feb. 28, 1848	
Cowherd, Francis	Oct. 25, 1779	
Chandler, Jere	Apr. 22, 1779	
Coleman, John	Sept. 1781	
Campbell, William, (Col.)	Sept. 26, 1852	
Cooke, Jos.	Oct. 1783	
Chiles, James	Aug. 27, 1832	(served over two years)
Chisham, William	Apr. 1785	
Clark, Robert	Feb. 28, 1848	
Douglas (son of Margaret)	Aug. 27, 1778	
Davis, John	Aug. 28, 1832	
Edmonson, Joseph	May 1788	
Finlasson, Sleet	1787	
Farguson, Joshua	June 1786	
FitzPatrick, John D.		(dead for bounty land)
Furnish, James	July 1786	
Gaines, James		
Goodall, Richard	Aug. 28, 1832	
Garrett, Soloman	Jan. 1779	
Groom, John	May 1783	
Head, Benj. (Capt.)	June 1778	
Hensley (son of Jane Hensley)	Apr. 22, 1779	
Hawkins, Moses (Capt.)	May 1784	
Haney, James	Aug. 28, 1832	
Jones, James	Aug. 29, 1832	
Jones, Joseph	Mar. 1784	
Janell, Wm.	1832	
Johnson, Martin		
James, Catlett	July 1786	
Johnson, John		
Knighton, Wm.	May 25, 1818	16th Va. Reg., Capt. Grant, Monmouth & Charleston
Kennedy, James	June 25, 1855	
King, Julius (prisoner)	Sept. 27, 1818	Order in Light Dragoons & Naval Service., Col. George Baylor, Battle of Germantown
Leech, Andrew	Aug. 1785	
Landrum, Josiah	Aug. 1785	
Linter, James	Oct. 1785	

Mansfield, Geo.	May 27, 1818	Light Dragoons, Capt. James Gunn - Guilford Court House
Marsh, Thomas	1785	
Miller, John	1789	
Montague, Peter	Jan. 22, 1818	2nd Va. Reg., Capt. Alexander Parker, Savannah
Murphy, Charles	May 25, 1818	10th Va. Reg., Capt. John Gillison -Brandywine, Germantown - Monmouth
McClarney, Frans	May 28, 1778	(wife, Usley McClarney)
Montague, Peter	1832	
Newman, George	1832	
Parrott, William	Nov. 28, 1836	
Palmer, William	July 1786	
Pierce, Zackariah	July 28, 1817	
Roach, Absolon	Aug. 28, 1732	
Rosencrants, Alex.	June 1779	
Richards, Philemon	Aug. 29, 1832	
Rosson, William	Apr. 1785	
Smith, John	1832	
Sheaman, Geo.	June 24, 1833	
Snow, John	May 25, 1818	2nd Va. Reg. -Brandywine & Germantown
Sutton, James	1784	
Sutton, John	1784	
Stanis	1778	(two sons of widow Stanis)
Sutherland, Kenneth	June 24, 1833	
Taylor, Zachariah	Aug. 27, 1832	
Trasey, John	July 1784	
Thomas, Joseph		2nd Va. Continental Reg., Capt. Francis Taylor, discharged at Valley Forge (July 28,1817 order)
Thornton, William	Aug. 1784	
Taylor, Dr. Charles	May 28, 1838	Surgeon Va. Continental Lines
Thornton, Jess.	Nov. 22, 1812	
Vawter, Herman	1817	
Watts, Robert	Jan. 1786	
White, Ambrose	Mar. 1786	
White, Jeremiah	Aug. 27, 1832	
Williams, John	Feb. 28, 1842	
White, Richard	1832	
Waugh, Geo., Ensign	May 24, 1852	
Miller, Robt., 1st Lieut.	June 1778	

Colonial Soldiers

Bullock, Richard	Oct. 1779	Soldier in 1758 in 1st Va. Reg., Colonel Washington's Regiment
Brook, William (Brockman)	Nov. 1779	Soldier in Colonel Steven's Regiment, 1782
Cowherd, James	Oct. 1779	Ensign in Colonel Boquitt's Reg.
Cave, William	Feb. 1789	Non-com in Colonel Byrd's Reg., 1759

Crosthwaite, Jacob	Aug. 1779	Soldier in Colonel Byrd's Regiment in 1758
Crosswaite, Isaac	Sept. 1779	Soldier in Colonel Byrd's Regiment in 1758
Fitzgarrett, Thos.	Sept. 1779	Soldier in Colonel Byrd's Regiment in 1758
Fisher, Patrick	Mar. 1780	Non-com officer —Colonel Byrd 1760
Gaines, James	Jan. 1780	Soldier in Colonel Byrd's Regiment, 1760
Gibbs, Francis	May 1780	Captain Hoggs' Rangers 1758
Hackley, Frans	Oct. 1779	Colonel Byrd's Regiment
Hervey, Henry	Oct. 1779	Captain Hoggs' Rangers 1758
Lucas, John	Nov. 1779	Colonel Byrd's Regiment
Lamb, John	Feb. 1780	Colonel Byrd's Regiment 1758
Lamb, Richard	Feb. 1780	Colonel Byrd's Regiment 1758
Lam, Littleberry	Mar. 1780	Colonel Byrd's Regiment 1760
Lamb, William	Mar. 1780	Colonel Byrd's Regiment 1760
Lamb, James	Mar. 1780	Colonel Byrd's Regiment 1760
Lamb, Jeremiah	Mar. 1780	
McClayland, Daniel	Oct. 1779	Colonel Byrd's Regiment 1759
Morris, Thos.	Feb. 1780	Colonel Byrd's Regiment 1759
Powell, Simon	Nov. 1779	Sargent in Capt. Hoggs' 1758
Powell, Thos.	Oct. 1779	Soldier in Colonel Byrd's Regiment 1758
Pearcey, Chs.	Feb. 1780	Colonel Byrd's Regiment 1759
Powell, Ambrose	Apr. 1780	Staff Officer in Virginia forces in 1755
Powell, Ben.	Sept. 1779	Sargent in Col. Byrd's Reg. 1758
Vawter, William	Oct. 1779	
Rice, Mich.	Oct. 1779	Non-com Officer in Colonel Byrd's Regiment 1758
Riddle, James	Feb. 1780	Non-com officer in Captain Hogg Regiment 1758
Roberts, James	Apr. 1780	Captain Wagoner's Company 1757
Rogers, Wm.	Oct. 1779	Soldier in 1758 in 1st Virginia Regiment, Colonel Washington's Regiment.
Shackleford, Henry	Oct. 1779	Soldier in Captain Hoggs' Reg.
Sims, William	Apr. 1780	Captain Hoggs' Rangers 1759
Smith, William	May 1780	Captain Hoggs' Rangers 1758
Thompson, David	Aug. 1779	Soldier in Captain Hoggs' Company of Rangers in 1758 & Sargent in Colonel Bouquett's Regiment in 1764
Turner, John	Oct. 1779	Soldier in Colonel Hogg's Company 1758
Vawter, William	Sept. 1779	Sargeant in Captain Hoggs' Company of Rangers 1758
Williams, Jacob	Aug. 1779	Soldier in Col. Byrd's Reg. 1758
Williams, John	Sept. 1779	Soldier in Col. Byrd's Reg. 1758
Walker, Thomas	Sept. 1779	Soldier in Captain Hoggs' Rangers 1758

Walker, Charles	Sept. 1779	Soldier in Captain Hoggs' Rangers 1758
Warren, John	Oct. 1779	Soldier in Colonel Byrd's Regiment 1758
Watson, William	Mar. 1780	Captain Overton's Company of Regulars 1755
Watts, David	Mar. 1780	Colonel Byrd's Regiment 1758
Watts, Chs.	Mar. 1780	Colonel Byrd's Regiment 1758

May, 1739, Nicholas Currer, prisoner of Chelsea College and formerly belonging to Lunsleys horse, served 18 years and wounded in right arm, 69 years old, home, Orange County, Virginia.

Bonds and Administrations

Garland Burnley, administrator of John Bell, July 26, 1790, Bondsman: Hardin Burnley

Nancy Brockman, administratrix of James Brockman, Feb. 23, 1795, Bondsman: Aaron Bledsoe

James Beazley, Jr., administrator of William Beazley, January 28, 1799, Bondsman: Robert Branham & John Melore

Samuel Brockman, Jr., guardian of Sarah Burruss and Mary Burruss, orphans of John Burruss, July 24, 1783, Bondsman: Geo. Morton

Oliver Banister, administrator of Arthur Banister, January 27, 1794, Bondsmen: James Coleman & Ludlow Branham

Samuel Brockman, Jr., administrator of John Burruss, July 27, 1780, Bondsman: John Oakes

Hardin Burnley, guardian of Mary Bell Burnley, orphan of Richard Burnley, Sept. 27, 1790, Bondsman: Zack Burnley

John Bledsoe, administrator of Howard Bledsoe, February 27, 1778, Bondsman: Richard C. Wells

Dec. 26, 1791 John Brockman, administrator of Samuel Brockman, Bondsmen: Thos. Bell, Thos. Barbour & John Alcock

Apr. 24, 1794 James Barbour, administrator of Philip Barbour, Bondsmen: Benjamin Johnson, Mordicar Barbour & Thomas Barbour, Jr.

July 28, 1794 James Barbour, guardian of Philip Barbour, orphan of Philip Barbour, Bondsman: Thos. Barbour, Jr.

Feb. 25, 1799 James Barbour, administrator of Philip Barbour, Bondsman: Wm. Moore

Mar. 29, 1796 Edward Cason, administrator of Delilah Beadles, Bondsman: Belfield Cave

Feb. 24, 1794 Alexander Dabney, guardian of James Bell, orphan of William Bell, Bondsman: Wm. Alcock

June 25, 1798 Alex. Dabney, administrator of Thomas Bell, Bondsmen: Henry Bell, Robert Alcock and Alex. Shepherd

Apr. 28, 1786 Alex Dobney, guardian of Miller Bell, orphan of William Bell, Bondsmen: Ben Winslow & Francis Madison

Oct. 22, 1792 Thos. Farish, guardian of Elizabeth Bruce, orphan of Charles Bruce, Bondsman: Chas. Bruce

Dec. 22, 1794 Thomas Farish, administrator of William Bruce, Bondsman: Camp Porter

Aug. 27, 1792 Charles Bruce, administrator of Charles Bruce, Bondsmen: Wm. Pannill and Thomas Farish

July 28, 1794 John Atkins, administrator of James Brockman, Bondsman: Caleb Lindsay

Apr. 28, 1786 Alex Dabney, guardian of William Bell, orphan of William Bell, Bondsmen: Ben. Winslow & Francis Madison

Sept. 27, 1752 Mary Haton, administratrix of Robert Blunder, Bondsman:
  Champ Terry
Sept. 23, 1799 Henry Hammer, guardian of Catherine Beasely, orphan of
  Wm. Beasely, Bondsman: George Price
May 26, 1778 Bartlett Bennett, guardian of William, Jno. and Sithe
  Cleveland, orphans of John Chaveland, Bondsmen: Bernard Franklin,
  David Gillasby and John White
Mar. 24, 1785 John Carroll, guardian of John, Edward, Molly and Wm.
  Cason, orphans of Edward Cason, Bondsmen: James Head & Anthony Foster
Apr. 28, 1786 Duncan Campbell, administrator of Archibald Campbell
  Campbell, Bondsman: John Willis
Oct. 24, 1796 Thomas Coleman, Jr., guardian of Wilson Coleman, orphan
  of James Coleman, Bondsmen: Thomas Coleman, Sr. & Spilby Coleman
  Betty Coleman, administrix of James Coleman, Bondsmen: Thomas Coleman, Jr.,
    Thomas Coleman, Sr., Spilby Coleman & William Moore
  Betty Coleman, guardian of Elizabeth, Sally, Nancy, Polly, Caty and
    Garner Coleman, orphans of James Coleman, Bondsmen: Thomas Coleman, Sr.,
    and Spilby Coleman
Sept. 26, 1796 Reuben Cowherd, guardian of John Cowherd, his child, a
  legatee of Nancy Woolfolk, deceased. Bondsman: Yelverton Cowherd
June 25, 1778 James Dawson, guardian of Milley Dawson, orphan of Robert
  Dawson, Bondsman: Robt. Dawson
May 28, 1778 John Dollens, administrator of Presley Dollens, Bondsmen:
  Josiah Bush and Thomas Jones
June 25, 1778 James Dawson, guardian of Benjamin Dawson, orphan of Robert
  Dawson, Bondsman: Robt. Dawson
Jan. 23, 1797 Ptolamy Powell, administrator of Robert Daniel, Bondsmen:
  Wm. Leavel and James Powell
Jan. 28, 1793 Lawrence Taliaferro, guardian of Lawrence, Francis and
  Mary J. Dade, orphans of Francis Dade, Bondsman: Ray Taliaferro
Feb. 27, 1783 Johnny Scott, guardian of John, Charles, Reuben, Nancy
  and Mary Eastin, orphans of Phillip Eastin, Bondsman: Thos. Barbour
Jan. 24, 1791 Jonathan Davis, guardian of Joseph George, orphan of
  Isaac George, Bondsman: Prettyman Merry
Feb. 22, 1796 Anthony Garton, administrator of Uriah Garton, Bondsmen:
  Lewis Brockman and Henry Chiles
Jan. 28, 1793 David Goodall, guardian of Isaac and Charles Goodall,
  orphans of John Goodall, Bondsmen: James Riddell, Garner Early &
  George Price
Feb. 23, 1795 John D. Grymes, administrator of Ludwell Grymes, Bondsmen:
  Wm. C. Webb and John Douglas
Apr. 23, 1792 Edm. Henshaw, guardian of Isaac & Joseph George, orphans.
  Bondsman: George Newman
Feb. 22, 1781 John Hawkins, guardian of Jane Gaines, orphan of William
  Gaines, Bondsmen: Law---Taliaferro
Feb. 28, 1791 Prettyman Merry, administrator of Catherine George,
  Bondsman: Wm. C. Well
Jan. 24, 1791 Prettyman George, guardian of Edward & Winnefred George,
  orphans of Isaac George, Bondsmen: Jonathan Davis & Geo. Newman
Jan. 24, 1791 William Pannill, guardian of William George, orphan of
  Isaac George, Bondsman: Wm. Morton
Mar. 28, 1782 Thomas Coleman, guardian of William Strother, Sarah Bagley,
  Lucy and Moses Hawkins, orphans of Moses Hawkins, Bondsman: Wm. Strother

Apr. 23, 1784 Edmond Dear & Robert Chandler, administrators of John Hiatt, Bondsman: George Morton

Dec. 23, 1793 Robert Daniel & Prettyman Merry, guardians of Sarah and Edward Hobdey, Bondsman: Wm. Moore

Nov. 23, 1769 George Eastham, guardian of Lewis Hipkins, orphan of And. Hipkins, Bondsmen: Johnny Scott & R. M. Martin

Nov. 23, 1781 Sarah Hiatt, administratrix of John Hiatt, Bondsmen: Robert Chandler and Edmond Dear

Sept. 27, 1790 Edward Hambleton, guardian of Ellis and Thomas Hamilton, orphans of Mathew Hambleton, Bondsmen: Chas. Douglas & Mathew Hambleton

Aug. 26, 1784 William Millikin, guardian of John, Thos., Ellis and Mary Hamilton, orphans of Mathew Hamilton, Bondsmen: Jas. Counelby & Mathew Hamilton

July 27, 1785 Robert Martin, administrator of Edward Hobdey, Bondsman: George Martin

1788 Ambrose Madison, guardian of John, Sarah, Martha, and Edward Hobdey, orphans of Edward Hobdey, Bondsman: James Taylor

June 25, 1792 Archibald Wilson, administrator of Alexander Henderson, Bondsman: Prettyman Merry

Sept. 26, 1796 Thomas White, administrator of James Head, Bondsman: Rich. White

Nov. 23, 1769 Matthew Davis, guardian of Frances and Mary Johnson, orphans of John Johnson, Bondsman: Wm. Bell

Mar. 23, 1769 Thomas Jameson, guardian of Wm. Jameson, orphan of Thos. Jameson, Bondsman: Taliferro Craig, Jr.

Oct. 28, 1779 Joseph Spencer, guardian of Philiman Kavanaugh, orphan of Philiman Kavanaugh, Bondsman: John Conner

Feb. 27, 1777 Reuben Lindsay, administrator of James Ker. Bondsman: John Walker

Sept. 27, 1775 William Lee, administrator of Charles Lee, Bondsmen: James Lee & John Dodd

Dec. 23, 1793 Nelly Lamb, administratrix of John Lamb, Jr., Bondsman: John Lamb & James Early

June 25, 1787 Hopkins Lewis, guardian of Edward and Charles Lewis, orphans of Edward Lewis, Bondsman: Francis Garner

Jan. 24, 1791 Henry Mallory, guardian of William and Elizabeth Long, orphans of Brown Long

May 23, 1769 Charles Neale, guardian of Phoebe Lenard, orphan of Walter Leonard, Bondsmen: Langhly Leonard & James Simpson

Jan. 26, 1795 Enoch Gully, administrator of Richard Land, Bondsman: Rich. Gulley

June 27, 1789 Reuben Moore, guardian of Alexander, Bernard and Francis Moore, orphans of Reuben Moore, Bondsman: Finlason Sleet

Aug. 26, 1762 Rich. Thomas, guardian of Thomas Merry, orphan of Thomas Merry, Bondsman: Elijah Morton

John Morrison, administrator of Thomas Morrison, Bondsman: Boswell Morrison

June 22, 1795 Mary Maury, administratrix of Walker Maury, Bondsman: Matthew Maury & Abraham Maury

Sept. 20, 1789 Elizabeth McAlester, administratrix of Alex McAlister, Bondsman: John Smith

Dec. 23, 1789 Hannah Morrison, administratrix of Thomas Morrison, Bondsmen: Adam Goodlet & James Colsman
July 27, 1786 Reuben Moore, guardian of Lucy Barbour Moore, orphan of Bernard Moore, Bondsmen: John Price & George Waugh
Oct. 24, 1796 Abraham Maury, guardian of Lenard Hill, Ann, William Grymes and Penelope(P?) Maury, orphans of Walker Maury, Bondsman: William Dade
Oct. 26, 1795 John Marr, administrator of Alexander Marr, Bondsmen: John Douglas & Augustine Webb
Sept. 24, 1794 James Madison, Jr., administrator of Nelly Willis Madison, Bondsmen: James Madison & Abner Porter
July 27, 1795 Mary Willis Madison, guardian of Nelly Conway Madison, orphan of Ambrose Madison, Bondsman: James Madison
Dec. 23, 1793 Mary W. Madison, administratrix of Ambrose Madison, Bondsmen: Francis Madison & Wm. Madison
Oct. 25, 1790 Charles Mason, guardian of James, George & Peter Mason, orphans of Charles Mason, Bondsmen: Rich. C. Webb & Thomas Row
Jan. 28, 1788 Micajah Mason, guardian of Samuel Mason, orphan of Charles Mason, Bondsmen: Charles Mason & Rich. C. Webb
Feb. 26, 1788 Rebecca Mason, guardian of Elizabeth Mason, James Mason, George Mason, Peter Mason, Joseph Mason & Nancy Mason, orphans of Charles Mason, Bondsmen: Thos. Row & Charles Mason
Oct. 28, 1779 Joseph Spencer, guardian of Lucy Barbour Moore, orphan of Bernard Moore, Bondsman: John Price
Nov. 25, 1762 Edward Thomas, administrator of William Mattox, Bondsman: Rich. Thomas
Oct. 25, 1790 Jesse B. Webb, guardian of Joseph Mason, orphan of Chs. Mason, Bondsman: Rich. C. Webb
Dec. 23, 1793 James Beazley, Jr., guardian of Polley Neale, orphan of Fielding Neale, Bondsman: James Early
Oct. 24, 1791 Mace Pickett, administrator of Fielding Neale, Bondsman: John Miller
Feb. 26, 1778 Alexander Ogg, administrator of John Ogg, Bondsman: James Early
Aug. 24, 1790 John Miller, guardian of Lewis Gordon Powell, orphan of James Powell, Bondsman: Churchill Gibbs
Oct. 22, 1792 Charles Pearcey, guardian of Elizabeth & Frankey Pearcey, orphans of Charles Pearcey
Sept. 28, 1795 Camp Porter, guardian of Mary Porter, orphan of Charles Porter, Bondsman: Thomas Wood
Dec. 28, 1795 Camp Porter, guardian of Benj. Porter, Jr., orphan of Charles Porter, Bondsman: John Porter
Jan. 23, 1797 Ann Perry, administratrix of John Perry, Bondsmen: Charles Massey & Allan Massey
Feb. 28, 1781 Henry Perry, administrator of Benjamin Perry, Bondsmen: Rich. C. Webb & Thos. Lantor
Jan. 27, 1774 James Walker, guardian of Richard Price, orphan of Ajalon Price, Bondsman: Bernard Moore
May 23, 1765 John Boston, Jr., guardian of Catherine Petty, orphan of George Petty, Bondsman: Alex Waugh
Feb. 23, 1795 John Chiles, guardian of Nancy Page, orphan of John Page, Bondsman: Elijah Page

Feb. 23, 1795 Aaron Quisenberry & Moses Quisenberry, administrators of Aaron Quisenberry, Bondsman: Wm. & George Quisenberry
Jan. 28, 1788 Reuben Zimmiman, guardian of James Roach, orphan of John Roach, Bondsman: James Gordon
July 28, 1794 Wm. Riddell, administrator of Lewis Riddell, Bondsman: Uriah Anderson
Sept. 24, 1794 Salley Riddell, administratrix of Lewis Riddell, Bondsman: Benj. Head
Dec. 23, 1783 May Burton, Jr., administrator of Mary Scott, Bondsman: William Clark
Mar. 27, 1793 Thomas Coleman, administrator of William Dabney Strother, Bondsman: James Coleman
Nov.   1775 Benj. Finnell, guardian of Patey & _____ Sleet, orphans of Weeden McCawley Sleet, Bondsman: Hadley Head
Sept. 27, 1790 James Gordon, administrator of William Sisson, Bondsman: Francis Dade
Jan. 23, 1797 Valentine Johnson, guardian of Elizabeth Sebree, orphan of John Sebree, Bondsman: Benj. Johnson
Mar. 25, 1784 William Sutton, administrator of Samuel Sutton, Bondsman: Thomas Stevenson
Nov. 23, 1775 John Sleet, guardian of James & Weden Sleet, orphans of Weden McCauley Sleet, Bondsman: James Newman
May 23, 1776 Ignatius Trueman, administrator of
Bondsman: James Madison
July 22, 1793 Samuel Thompson, administrator of Samuel Thompson, Bondsman: Benj. Hyde
Apr. 25, 1791 Edmund Terrill, guardian of Robert, James, Nancy, Fanny & Lucy Terrill, orphans of Edwd. Terrill, Bondsmen: Joseph Clark & Reuben Picher
Feb. 22, 1790 John Netherland, administrator of Ann Thurston, Bondsmen: Benj. Porter & Jos. Smith
Sept. 26, 1794 Thomas Bryant, guardian of Janey Thornton, orphan of James Thornton, Bondsman: James Sleet & George Petty
July 28, 1788 Joseph Clark, guardian of Robert, James, Nancy, Fanny & Lucy Terrill, orphans of Edmund Terrill, Bondsman: James Coleman
Dec. 23, 1779 Jonathan Cowherd, guardian of Chapman, Richard & Mary Taylor, orphans of Richard Taylor, Bondsman: Jonny Scott
Apr. 24, 1792 Thos. Bryant, guardian of Sarah & Rosa Thornton, orphans of James Thornton, Bondsman: Sanford Ransdell
Nov. 24, 1785 Hugh Jones, administrator of William Thornton, Bondsman: Henry Brown
Oct. 24, 1796 William White, guardian of Elizabeth White, orphan of Jeremiah White, Bondsman: White
          1788 Francis Moore, Jr., guardian of Lucy Ward, orphan of Peggy Ward, Bondsman: John Brown
Jane Wharton, administratrix of Thomas Wharton, Bondsmen: Tully Choice & John Finney
July 25, 1791 Margaret Wood, administratrix of Joseph Wood, Jr., Bondsman: Francis Madison
July 25, 1791 Margaret Wood, Alexander Downey & Francis Madison, guardians of William Bell Wood, John Scott Wood & Mary Miller Wood, orphans of Joseph Wood, Jr.
Apr. 22, 1799 Wm. C. Webb, guardian of Benjamin Webb, orphan of John C. Webb, Bondsman: Prettyman Merry
Feb. 22, 1796 William White, administrator of Jeremiah White, Bondsmen: John White, Richard White and Belfield Cave

Mar. 24, 1774 Thos. White, administrator of Joseph White, Bondsman: Conyers White
Jan. 27, 1794 Elizabeth Walker, administratrix of Thomas Walker, Bondsmen: Thomas Walker & Sanders Walker
Oct. 24, 1796 Sarah Wright, administratrix of James Wright, Bondsman: Archibald Rawson, John Robison, Reuben Hawkins
June 27, 1796 Catherine Woodford & Daniel Woodford, administrators of Frederick Woodford, Bondsmen: Philip Seal & Jacob Kiblinger
Oct. 24, 1796 Jno. White, guardian of Jeremiah White, orphan of Jeremiah White, Bondsman: Wm. White
Jan. 1742 Naturalization of Foreign Protestants
Andrew Garr, John Adam Garr, Lawrence Garr, Lawrence Frays, Eewald Christle, Martin Vallick, John Zimerman, Peter Fleshman, Zachaniah Blankenbaker, John Zimmerman, alias Carpenter, John Thomas, Christopher Whle & Frederick Bambgardener, under the hand of George Samuel Klug minister of the German Congregation in Orange County
Feb. 1742 Christopher Broyle, Tobias Wilthite, Jacob Manspite, John Wilhite, Jacob Miller, German Protestants under hand of Rev. John Thomson of St. Marks & George Samuel Klug of Minister of the German Congretation

Chancery Suits

June Worthington, Mary Worthington vs Robert Ex. (Youan). Mary, wife of Robert Worthington, married July 31, 1729 (nee Mary Burtis of Burlington, N. J. Richard Burtis, brother of Mary (a Quaker of Middlesex N. J.
Sarah Connelly, wife of Silvester Connelly & mother of Mary Worthington (nee Burtis) (Sarah Connelly being a Quaker)
July 1739 Nicholas Christopher vs Lawrence Taliferro (heirs dead at this time). Suit about land taken at the southwest mountains by Lawrence Taliferro and his brother.
July 1739 Lawrence Taliaferro, a son named John & Frances Taliferro (deposition of Colonel John Taliaferro in papers, his nephews John & Francis having come of age). Doc. James Currie, M.D. 1737 (Doctor)
Mar. 1742 John Thornton & Jemima his wife, Luke Thornton & Milicent his wife (administrator of Wm. Sargents) daughter & only surviving child of William Longworth, late of Westmoreland County (who died in 1724).
Sept. 1742 Richard Thomas & Benj. Cave (Church wardens St. Thomas)
Wm. Triplet & Wm. Payton (Church wardens St. Marks)
Sept. 1743 Robert Worthington vs Jacob Worthington, Robert Worthington, Jr., Martha Worthington, Samuel Britain & Mary his wife, Robert Worthington, son & heir of Samuel Worthington who was son & heir Robert Worthington the Elder Robert's grandfather.
Robert Worthington the older was seized of 3000 acres called "Quarry Bank" formerly called "Every's Marsh". Division of land in Nov. papers 1746
June 1746 Jemimah Botts vs John Botts -Suit of divorce, abates by defts. death
June 1746 Mary Lightfoot, widow & relict of Goodrich Lightfoot, who died in the year 1739, leaving Goodrich Lightfoot as eldest son & heir.
Mar. 1, 1747 Hannah Drake vs Samuel Drake (divorce granted)
Mar. 1749 Randall Fugate vs Edm. Rowland, etc.
Randall Fugate, who intermarried with_____the daughter of Mary Deelwood, and sues for marriage portion.
May 1750 Mary Taliaferro, widow of John Taliaferro, vs Willaim Taliaferro, herson suit for dower, which is assigned her.

Oct. & Nov. 1758
Francis Boswell vs Gatewood, Boswell & Foster Frances Boswell youngest daughter of John Boswell, late of Spotsylvania County & Anne his wife (John Boswell died May 5, 1741, & Anne his widow intermarried with William Gatewood.
Children of John & Anne Boswell viz Ransom, John, George, James, Dorothy & Francis

Morton vs Morton, Jr. Est.
Aug. 1760 Jeremiah Morton children, Ann, Jane & William.
July 1759 Abraham Crothwaite vs William Crothwaite in re Timothy Crothwaite, his brother will. (all three brothers)
Apr. 1760 Samuel Rice, Thomas Shackelford & Margaret Shackelford his wife, Henry Rice, Joseph Smith & Mary Smith, his wife, Anne Rice, William Rice, Michael Rice, Fisher Rice, Sarah Rice, Milly Rice & Armon Bohanan Rice infants, by Samuel Rice their Guardian, children of Henry Rice, deceased, vs John Gollosthen & Margaret his wife (widow of Henry Rice).

Bonds

May 1735 Robert Green, administrator of Joseph Step
June 1735 Jacob Prosie, administrator of Barbara Cooper
July 1735 Robt. Cave, administrator of Elizabeth Cave
 Benj. Cave & Wm. Phillips, Surety.
Feb. 1735 Mary Rush wife of Wm. Rush, administratrix
Feb. 1735 Thomas Lewis, administrator of James McCullough
July 1735 Robert Slaughter, administrator of Augustine Smith
Aug. 1736 Mercio Vickory, Relict of Hezekiah Vickoy, administratrix
Sept. 1736 Sarah Jones, wife of Josiah Jones, not being found, Sheriff admr. on Estate of Josiah Jones
Feb. 1736 Betty Kirk, relict of James Kirk, adminstratrix
May 1737 Margaret Gay, administratrix of Wm. Gay, her husband
May 1737 Elizabeth Taylor relict of Wm. Taylor, administratrix
Apr. 1738 Isaac Perkins, administrator of Joseph Hollingsworth
May 1738 Wm. Jackson, administrator of John Biswell in right of Wm. Jackson, wife daughter of the Sd. Biswell
July 1738 John Carpenter, administrator of Andrew Kercher
July 1738 Henry Thornton, administrator of Richard Parsons
Aug. 1738 Patrock Boggini, administrator of Niel McSwain
Sept. 1738 Mary Lightfoot, relict of Goodrich Lightfoot, guardian to Wm. Lightfoot
Sept. 1738 Elizabeth, the relict of John Pitts, administratrix
Sept. 1738 Jane Smith, relict of John Smith, administratrix
Nov. 1738 Wm. Russell, administrator of Wm. Hoskins. Anne the widow surrendered right.
Feb. 1738 Camelus Cornegis, administrator of John Sargeant
Mar. 1738 Goodrich Lightfoot, administrator Goodrich Lightfoot
Mar. 1738 Nathaniel Chapman, administrator of Peter Faulconer
Mar. 1738 Ress Smith, administrator of John Smith (his father)
June 1739 Sarah Worthington, widow of Samuel Worthington, administratrix of Samuel
May 1740 Thos. Grayson, administrator of Robert Grayson
May 1740 Robert Poage, administrator of Seth Poage
May 1740 Samuel Brittan, guardian of Martha & Robert Worthington, orphans of Robt. Worthington
July 1740 John Shost, administrator of Micha Sheppard
Sept. 1740 Edward Spencer, administrator Simon Raine

Feb. 1740 Jacob Stover, administrator of Jacob Stover, dec'd Margaret Widow
Mar. 1741 Ann Lilborne, relict & Jost Hite, administrator of John Lilbourne
May 1741 Wm. McDonough, administrator of Jeremiah Bryant
May 1741 Martin DeWit, administrator of Charles DeWit, his father. Mercy DeWit, widow & relict relinquishes right
June 1741 Henry Huffman, administrator of John Huffman
July 1741 Wm. Glover, administrator of Edward Glover
July 1741 Mary Curtis widow of Thomas Curtis administratrix
July 1741 Wm. Crawford, administrator of James Wright
Sept.1741 Wm. Thomson, administrator of John Campbell
Oct. 1741 Thomas Stanton, guardian of Mary & Sarah Staunton
Oct. 1741 Thomas Stanton appraisers appointed
Nov. 1741 Reuben Allen (eldest son) administrator of Reuben Allen Benj. Allen, Surety.
Nov. 1741 Geo. Wheatley, guardian of Elizabeth Stanton
Nov. 1741 Henry Field, guardian of Sarah, William & Jane Stanton
Jan. 1741 Elizabeth, widow of Miles Murphy, administratrix
Feb. 1741 Michael Holt, administrator estate of his father Michael Holt
Feb. 1741 Henry Field, guardian of Sarah, Wm. & Jane Stanton
Feb. 1742 Thomas Stanton, guardian of Mary Stanton
Feb. 1742 Thomas Ewall, guardian of Thomas, John & Agatha Ewall vs Sam Ferguson
June 1742 Zackary Taylor, guardian of John Jones
July 1742 On motion of Mary Holladay, relict Samuel Holladay, administrator of Wm. Holladay
July 1742 Barbara Ambuger relict, admininstratrix of Cornade Ambuger
July 1742 David Kirkhead, administrator of John Hobson
Sept.1742 Culvert Anderson, guardian of Wm. Holliday's children
Nov. 1742 Esther Blackbourn, relict of Arthur Blackbourn, Admx. Wm. Blackbourn, surety.
Feb. 1742 Isaac Smith, administrator of James Thurston
Mar. 1742 Magdale McDowell, relict administratrix John McDowell, Jas. McDowell, surety.
Mar. 1742 Barnet McHenry, guardian of Samuel Baker
Mar. 1743 Anthony Strother, administrator of John Corley
           Robert Turner, administrator of Thomas Durham
July 1743 James Allan, administrator of his brother Wm. Allan
July 1743 Reuben Rutherford & Anne his wife, administrators of Harry Hunt (Anne his late widow)
Aug. 1743 Eliza Coger, relict of Michl. Coger, relinquish right to adm. to his brother Jacob Coger
Aug. 1743 Silas Hart, administrator of his brother John Hart
Mar. 1743 Mary Teater, relict of George Teater, administratrix
Mar. 1743 Wm. Hobbs, administrator of Higgin Axford
Apr. 1744 Susannah Axford, relict of John Axford, relinquish her right of adm. Wm. Keley, Adm.
May 1744 Jane McDaniel, relict of Randolph McDaniel, administratrix
May 1744 Jane Brackenridge, relict of Alex Brackenridge, relinquish right to her son George Breckenridge
June 1744 Margaret Tilly, administratrix of Lazarus Tilly
Oct. 1744 Jeremiah Morton, administrator of George Morton
Oct. 1744 Miss Francis Madison, Jr. chose Erasmer Tayler, Jr.
Oct. 1744 Miss Mary Layton chose Gabriel Jones, guardian
Nov. 1744 Hannah Sculthrop, relict of Anthony Sculthrop

(76)

Nov. 1744 Susannah Anderson, administratrix of Geo. Anderson (relict)
Nov. 1744 Margaret Evert, administratrix of Geo. Evert (relict)
Nov. 1744 Edward Spencer, guardian of Wm. Lightfoot, minor son of Goodrich Lightfoot.
Jan. 1744 Martin DeWit, guardian for Charles Neale, minor son of Wm. Neale
Jan. 1744 Thomas Jackson, administrator of James Halloway
Feb. 1744 Ann Dunlap, relict of Alex Dunlap, administratrix
Feb. 1744 Sarah Thomas, relict of John Thomas, administratrix
Feb. 1744 Timothy Crothwaite, administrator of Wm. Crothwaite (Suit-Crothwait vs Russell)
Mar. 1744 Margaret Gibson, administratrix of Jonathan Gibson (her husband)
May 1745 Elizabeth Strother, administratrix of Wm. Taylor (order inre)
July 1745 Philip Glayton, administrator of John Bonner
Aug. 1745 Henry Field, guardian of William Stanton, Acct.
Sept. 1745 Thomas Story, brother & heir of John Story, administrator
Sept. 1745 Robert Pemick, adm. William Pidgeon, adm.
Jan. 1745 Jeremiah Morton, appointed guardian of Berryman Davis, infant orphan of John Davis
Jan. 1745 On motion of Jeremiah Newton, guardian of Berryman Davis, with assent Wm. Minor who has intermarried with Mary the widow, John Davis, commissioner, appointed to divide estate.
Mar. 1746 Sarah Russell, widow administratrix of Peter Russell
Mar. 1746 Jane Wiley, widow, administratrix of David Wiley
May 2 1746 Antoinet Montague, widow, administratrix of Peter Montague
May 2 1746 Robert Eastham, Gent., administrator of John Fulcher
May 1746 Sarah Chapman, administratrix of Isaac Chapman
July 1747 Henry Downs, Jr. Petition to be relieved of surety of Joana Sims, administratrix of Richard Sims.
July 1747 Christopher Zimmerman, administrator of John Newport
May 1748 Anne Goerge, widow, administratrix of John George
Nov. 1748 Sheriff, administrator of Jane Wiley
Feb. 1748 Jane Wharton, administrator of Thomas Wharton, her husband
June 1749 Stokesley Towles who has intermarried with the administratrix of Thomas Wharton, settlement.
Mar. 1749 Elizabeth Willis, widow, administratrix John Willis
Mar. 1749 Mary Rowland, widow of Edward, removed will
Mar. 1749 Jeremiah Morton, administrator of James Thornton
Nov. 1750 Sarah Tubufield, widow, administratrix Edward Tubufield
Sept. 1751 Samuel Rice, guardian of Michael Rice & Fisher Rice, Sarah Rice & Milley Rice, his brothers and sisters, orphans of Henry Rice
Sept. 1751 Walter Shropshire, guardian of John & Anne, his brother & sister, orphans of John Shropshire.
Feb. 1752 Mary Hayton, administratrix of Robert Blunder
May 1752 Timothhy Crothwait, surety for Hannah McClayland, late Hannah Rhodes.
May 1752 Richard Sebree, administrator of Richard Jeoffrys
Nov. 1752 James Madison, guardian of Mary Willis, orphan of John Willis
May 1753 Edward Spencer, widow, adm. Edward Spencer died her husband
May 1753 Martin & Sarah Benion, orphans of William Benion, chose John Murrell guardian
Aug. 1753 Ann Stodghil, widow, administratrix of James Stodghill, her husband
Nov. 1753 William Johnson, administrator of Andrew Harrison
Nov. 1753 Samuel Rice, brother & heir of Henry Rice, administrator of Harry Rice.

Feb. 1755 Betty Mallory, wife & administratrix of Henry Hick Mallory
Feb. 1755 Jeremiah Morton, guardian of Urial, Mary & Roger Mallory, orphans of Roger Mallory
June 1755 Martha Grayson, relict of John Grayson, administratrix
Sept. 1756 Reuben Daniel, guardian of Elizabeth Montague, orphan of Peter Montague, Owen Thomas
Oct. 1756 Elizabeth Cowerd, relict of James Cowerd, administratrix
Feb. 1757 Elijah Morton & Andrew Bourn, administrators of Jeremiah Morton
Feb. 1757 Robert William, administrator of Cornelius Reynolds
Feb. 1757 John Stewart, administrator of Francis Henley
June 1757 Andrew Bourn, administrator of Robert Bourn
Sept. 1757 Martha Gillum, relict of Richard Gillum, administratrix
Sept. 1757 Andrew Manner, administrator of Patrick Leonard
Nov. 1757 Rush Hudson, administrator of Isaac Miller
Feb. 1758 Joshua Step, guardian of Elizabeth Lucas, orphan of William Lucas
Feb. 1758 Francis Moore, guardian of Edward Spencer, orphan of Edward Spencer
Feb. 1758 William Lucas, guardian of Thomas & Elizabeth Lucas, orphans of John Lucas
Apr. 1758 Lucy Mary Marshall, relict of Mingo Marshall, clerk, administratrix of Minigo Marshall
May 1758 Wm. Lucas, guardian of John Lucas, orphan of John Lucas
May 1758 Urial Mallory, guardian of Mary & Roger Mallory, orphans of Roger Mallory
Nov. 1758 Kelly Jennings, guardian of William & Sarah Brockman, orphans of John Brockman
May. 1759 William & Sarah Brockman, orphans of John Brockman, chose Samuel Brockman, their brother, guardian, and court appointed him guardian to Elizabeth, Hannah, Mary, Joseph, Rachel & Major Brockman.
Sept. 1759 Thomas Montague, guardian of Elizabeth, the orphan of Peter Montage
Nov. 1759 Zackary Burnley, guardian to Elizabeth Trawin Jones & Susan Jones, orphans of John Jones
Feb. 1759 Thomas Rucker, administrator of William Pearce
Feb. 1759 Richard Thomas, administrator of John Lyrial
Aug. 1761 Thomas Douglas, guardian of Elizabeth & Ann Embrey, orphans of Wm. Embry
Aug. 1761 Thomas & Betty Lucas, orphans of John Lucas, chose Ambrose Coleman, guardian
Mar. 1762 William Bickers, administrator of Robert Bickers, Jr.
Mar. 1762 Rowland Thomas, guardian of Catherine Thomas, orphans of Richard Thomas, Bondsman: Richard Thomas
Mar. 1762 Edward Thomas, administrator of William Mattox
Mar. 1762 Isaac Rucker, guardian of Benjamin & Sarah Plunkett, orphans of John Plunkett
Mar. 1762 Sam. Rice, guardian of Milley Rice, orphan of Henry Rice
Aug. 1762 Richard Thomas, guardian of Thomas Merry, orphan of Thomas Merry
Aug. 1762 Prettyman Merry, orphan of Thomas Merry, chose William Walter, guardian
Feb. 1763 Martin Hacket, administrator of Chesley Hacket
Feb. 1763 Zach Burnley & Andrew Shepherd, administrators of James Taylor
Mar. 1763 Mary Taylor & Andrew Shepherd, administrators of John Taylor

Mar. 1763 Roger Bell, guardian of Lucy & Francis Wisdom, orphans of Francis Wisdom
June 1764 Lucy Mary Marshall, guardian to James, William, Lucy and Susannah Marshall, orphans of Mingo Marshall
Aug. 1764 Jonathan Gibson, administrator of Jonathan Gibson, administered by Margaret Gibson
June 1765 James Coleman, guardian of James Coleman, son of Ambrose Coleman
June 1766 William Mallory, orphan of Henry Mallory, chose Rowland Thomas, guardian
June 1766 William Scott, administrator of Benj. Martin
July 1766 Catherine, failing to qualify as administratrix of Walter Lenard, her late husband, Rowland Thomas, sheriff, guardian.
Sept. 1766 Andrew Shepherd, administrator of William Whitman
Aug. 1767 Edward Franklin, administrator of Edward Frankley father
Oct. 1767 Robert Baker, administrator of James Ellen
Nov. 1767 Charles Beale, orphan of Tavernor Beale, chose Tavenor Beale his guardian and court assigned him guardian of Francis, Elizabeth & Ann Beale
Feb. 1768 Simon Powell & Francis Kirtley, administrators of Honorias Powell
Mar. 1768 John Griffin, guardian of Thomas Harper, orphan of Samuel Harper
Mar. 1768 Zackary Taylor & Thomas Bell, administrators of Zackary Taylor
June 1768 Robert Boston, guardian of Catherine Pitty
June 1768 Charles Yates, administrator of Genard Banks
July 1768 Thomas Jameson, administrator of Thomas Jameson
Sept. 1768 John Griffin, administrator of Samuel Harper
Mar. 1769 Wm. Jameson, orphan of Thomas Jameson, chose his brother Thomas guardian
Mar. 1764 Benj. Cave, administrator of David Cave
Mar. 1765 Moses Lucas, guardian of Ann Farguson, daughter of Joshua Farguson
May 1765 Catherine Pettey, orphan of Geo. Petty, chose John Boston, Jr. guardian
June 1767 John Bousey chose John Stockdell guardian
Sept. 1769 John Neale chose his father Ch. Neale guardian
Sept. 1769 James Marshall, orphan of Roy Mungo Marshall, chose Peter Marqi (Marye?) guardian
Oct. 1769 Hugh Morrison, orphan of Fenlason Morrison, chose Taliaferro Craig guardian
Oct. 1769 Margret Morrison chose orphan of Fenley Morrison
Oct. 1769 Catherine Reynolds, mother, relinquishes right as guardian, of Taliaferro Craig & Charles Bruce appointed guardians of Wm., John, Sarah, and Lucy Morrison, orphans of Fenley Morrison
Nov. 1769 Francis & Mary Johnson, orphans of John Johnson chose Mathew Davis guardian
Nov. 1769 Lewis Hipkins, orphan of Andw. Hipkins, chose Geo. Eastham guardian
Oct. 1770 Grace Johnson & Andw. Shepherd, administrators of Robt. Johnson
Feb. 1771 Joseph Martin, administrator of Joseph Holladay
Mar. 1771 Edward Dearing, administrator of Fran Sykes
Apr. 1771 Benj. Spicer, guardian of Sarah & Joseph Spicer, orphans of Rawsen Spicer
Apr. 1771 Philmon Snell, guardian of Rawsen Spicer & Lucy Ellen Spicer, orphans of Rawson Spicer

(79)

Aug. 1771 James Gibbs, administrator of Wm. Johnson
Sept. 1771 Tabetha Oliver, administratrix of Durrett Oliver
Jan. 1772 Beverly Winslow, administratrix of Rich. Winslow
Feb. 1772 Sheriff administrator of Charles Smith
Apr. 1772 John Bowling, administrator of Wm. Bowling
Feb. 1773 Eliz. Jennett Powell, orphan of Simon Powell, chose Wm. Riddle her guardian
Apr. 1773 Francis Kirtley, guardian of Eliz, Jannet Powell & Salley Powell, orphans of Simon Powell
May 1773 Lucy & Susannah Marshall, orphans of Mungo Marshall, chose Thos. Bell guardian
May 1773 Cath. Smith, orphan of Chas. Smith, chose Jas. Smith, guardian
July 1773 John Marshall Johnson, orphan of Robt. Johnson, chose Martin Johnson, guardian
July 1773 Sarah Lanter, administratrix of Peter Lanter
Sept. 1773 Mary & Susa Davis, orphans of Bereman Davis, chose Lewis Conner guardian
Sept. 1773 George Mitchell, administrator of Wm. Cruther
Jan. 1774 Richard Price, orphan of Sylvia Price, chose James Walker, guardian
Feb. 1774 Thos. Robbins, administrator of Wm. Robbin
Feb. 1774 Thos. White, administrator of Jos. White
Feb. 1773 William Dangerfield, guardian of Molly & Anne Beale, orphans of Richard Beale
Sept. 1774 Francis Kentley, administratrix of John Kentley
Jan. 1775 George Proctor, administrator of Geo. Proctor, Jr.
Jan. 1775 Benj. Johnson, guardian of William Robert Johnson, orphan of Wm. Johnson
Feb. 1775 James Walker, administrator of Ambrose Gusham
Feb. 1775 John Johnson, orphan of Robert Johnson, chose Grace Johnson, guardian
Nov. 1775 Benj. Furrill, guardian of Lucy, Patsy & Susie Sleet, orphans of Weeden Sleet
Apr. 1776 Wm. Wright, administrator of John Weatherspoon, Jr.
May 1771 Ignatius Trueman, administrator of George Trueman
Sept. 1776 Elizabeth Reynolds, administratrix of Benj. Reynolds
Feb. 1777 May Burton, Jr., administratrix of Stephen Shiflett
Feb. 1777 Reuben Lindsay, administrator of James Kerr
Feb. 1777 John Bledsoe, administrator of Howard Bledsoe
Nov. 1774 Thos. Bell, orphan of Roger Bell, chose Thos. Bell, guardian
Jan. 26, 1775 James Gibbs, guardian of Wm. Robert Johnson, lives out of this government, Benj. Johnson appointed guardian
Apr. 25, 1777 Jack Burnley, administrator of James Powell
June 26, 1777 Lucy Mary Manden, administratrix of James Manden
July 24, 1777 Thos. Gardner, administrator of John Road
May 28, 1778 James Dawson, guardian of Milly Dawson, his sister & James Dawson
Mar. 28, 1778 John Dollings, administrator of Presley Dollings
—Sept. 24, 1778 Joseph Smith, administrator of Geo. Smith, his son
—Sept. 24, 1778 Joseph Smith, guardian of Rueben Smith, orphan of Joseph Smith
Nov. 26, 1778 Bartlett Bennett & Bernard Franklyn, guardians of Wm. & Jno. Cleaveland & Sithe Cleveland, orphans of Jno. Cleaveland, dead.

Aug. 26, 1779 John Conner, appointed guardian of Mary, John, Eliza, Philimon & Ch. Conner, orphans of Philimon Conner
Oct. 28, 1779 Joseph Spencer, guardian of Lucy Barbour Moore, orphan of Bernard Moore
Oct. 28, 1779 Joseph Spencer, guardian of Philomon Cavanagh, orphan of Philinus Cavanaugh
Dec. 23, 1779 Jonathon Cowherd, guardian of Richard, Chapman & Mary Taylor, orphans of Richard Taylor
May 25, 1780 Francis Moore, Jr., administrator of Wm. Gaines
May 25, 1780 John Shiflett, guardian of Lewis Powell, orphan of James Powell
July 27, 1780 Sam. Brockman, Jr., administrator of John Burrus
Feb. 22, 1781 John Hawkins, guardian of Jane Gaines, orphan of Wm. Gaines
Oct. 25, 1781 Caty & Archibald Oliver, orphans of Durrett Oliver, chose Tabitha Oliver, guardian, also guardian of Caleb & Nancy Oliver, orphans of Duret Oliver
Nov. 22, 1781 Sarah Hiatt, administrator of John Hiatt
Feb. 28, 1782 Henry Perry, administrator of Benj. Perry
Mar. 28, 1782 Thomas Coleman, guardian of Wm. Strother Hawkins, Sarah Boyle Hawkins, Lucy Hawkins & Moses Hawkins, orphans of Moses Hawkins
Jan. 25, 1782 Mildred Beasley granted adm. of John Beesley
Feb. 27, 1783 Johnny Scott, guardian of John ch. Reuben, Nancy & Mary Eastin, orphans of Philip Eastin
Sept.25, 1783 Abbe Jones, administrator of Nich Jones
Mar. 25, 1784 William Sutton, administrator of Saml. Sutton
Alice & Mary Hamilton, orphans of Martha Hamilton
Apr. 22, 1784 Francis Earley, orphan of John Earley, dec'd, chose Theodore Early her guardian
Apr. 23, 1784 James Robb, administrator of Fran. Moore, Jr.
Aug. 26, 1784 Thos. Cook, administrator of Fielding Cook
John Thomas, Ellis & Mary Hamilton, orphans of Matha Hamilton, chose Wm. Milikin guardian
Sept.23, 1784 Ambrose Madison, guardian of Philip & Alice Taylor
Jan. 27, 1785 Robt. Martin, administrator of Edward Hobday
Mar. 24, 1785 Massa Gresham, administratrix of John Gresham
Mar. 24, 1785 John Carroll, guardian of John, Edwd, Molley & Wm. Cason, orphans of Edwd. Cason
Mar. 24, 1785 Wm. Vauter, administrator of David Vauter
May 26, 1785 Lawrence Taliaferro, administrator of Wm. Hunter
July 28, 1785 George Payne, guardian of Joseph Arnold
July 28, 1785 Nathl. McAlister, administrator of Wm. Bickers
Oct. 28, 1785 John Croxton, administrator of Rich Croxton
Nov. 24, 1785 Hugh Jones, administrator of Wm. Thornton
Mar. 24, 1786 Mary Alcock, late wife of William Bell, guardian to Thomas & James Bell, orphans of Wm. Bell
Apr. 28, 1796 Duncan Campbell, administrator of Archibald Campbell
Apr. 28, 1796 Alexander Downey, guardian to Thos. & James M. Bell, orphans of Wm. Bell (Mary Alcock declines to act)
July 27, 1786 Lucy Barbour Moore, orphan of Bernard Moore, chose Reuban Moore, her guardian
Sept.28, 1786 Mary Branham, administratrix of John Branham
Oct. 26, 1786 Joseph Smith, guardian of John Sebree for the purpose of dividing Wm. Johnson estate

(81)

Nov. 25, 1786 Robert Sanford, guardian of Reuben Sanford
Nov. 25, 1786 Wm. C. Webb, guardian of Vivian Webb
Feb. 22, 1787 Coleby Rucker, administrator of Peter Rucker
Apr. 23, 1787 Joel Stodgill, administrator of Martha Pearcey
June 25, 1787 Hopkins Lewis, guardian of Edward & Charles Lewis, orphans of Edwd. Lewis
Jan. 28, 1788 Micajah Mason, guardian of Samuel Mason, orphan of Charles Mason
Jan. 28, 1788 Reuben Zimmerman, guardian of James Roach, orphan of John Roach
Feb. 26, 1788 Rebecca Mason, guardian of Eliz, James, George, Peter, Joseph & Nancy Mason, orphans of Charles Mason
Apr. 28, 1788 Francis Moore, Jr., guardian of Lucy Ward, orphan of Peggy Ward
July 28, 1788 Ambrose Madison, guardian of John, Sarah, Martha & Edward Hobday, orphans of Edward Hobdey
July 28, 1788 Reubon Rucker, guardian of Sarah & Jane Terrill, orphans of Edm. Terrill
July 28, 1788 Joseph Clark, guardian of Robert, James, Nancy, Fanny & Lucy Terril, orphans of E. Terrill
Sept.23, 1788 Reuben Moore, guardian of his sons, Robert & Francis Moore, Legatees of Robert Terrill
Dec. 22, 1788 Alex Downey, guardian of Thos. Bell, orphan of Wm. Bell, William Webb, Garland, Webb, Chs. Webb & Wiatt Webb his children, for the purpose of renewing their proposition of John Vivian, dec'd.
June 22, 1789 Reuben Moore, guardian of Alexander & Bernard Moore, children of Reuben Moore for the purpose of renewing legally under the will of Robert Terrill.
Dec. 28, 1789 James Coleman, guardian to his son, Tho. Coleman, for purpose of receiving legacy left by And. Manning.
Dec. 28, 1789 Hannah Morrison, administratrix of Thos. Morrison
Feb. 22, 1790 John Nethertan, administrator of Ann Thursteirn
July 26, 1790 Garland Burnly, administrator of John Bell
Aug. 24, 1790 Mary Maury, guardian to Mary Maury, Jno., Mathew Ludwell Maury, Leonard Hill Maury, Wm. Grymes Maury, Penelope Maury & Ann Maury, infants of Walker Maury, to defend them at the suit of John Glassell in chg.
Aug. 24, 1790 John Miller, guardian of Lewis Gordon Powell
Sept.27, 1790 Hardin Burnley, guardian of Mary Bell Burnley
Sept.27, 1790 John Snell, guardian to Durrett Sanford for purpose of acting for said Durrett Sanford in division of lands of Robt. Sanford
Sept.27, 1790 James Gordon, administrator of Wm. Sisson
Sept.27, 1790 Edward Campbell, guardian of Ellis & Thomas Hamilton
Oct. 25, 1790 Charles Mason, guardian of James, George & Peter Mason
Oct. 25, 1790 Jesse B. Webb, guardian to Joseph Mason, orphan of Charles Mason
Oct. 25, 1790 Ch. Mason administrator of Rebecca Mason
Jan. 24, 1791 Alex Downey, administrator of Jas. Wood
Jan. 24, 1791 Henry Mallory, guardian of William & Elizabeth Long
Jan. 24, 1791 Wm. Pannill, guardian of Wm. George, orphan of Isaac George
Jan. 24, 1791 Prettyman Merry, guardian of Edwd. & Winifred George
Jan. 24, 1791 Jonathan Davis, guardian of Joseph George, orphan of Isaac George
Feb. 28, 1791 Prettyman Merry, administrator of Catherine George

Feb. 28, 1791 Mary Clark & Joseph Clark, administrators of James Clark
Apr. 24, 1791 Edm. Terrell, guardian to Robt. James, Nancy, Fanny & Lucy Terrill, orphans of Edm. Terrill
July 25, 1791 Margaret Wood, administratrix of Joseph Wood
July 25, 1791 Margaret Wood vs guardian to Wm. Bell Wood, John Scott Wood and Mary Miller Wood, orphans of Jos. Wood
Oct. 24, 1791 Townshand Dade, guardian to Reuben Berryman
Oct. 24, 1791 Thomas Bryant, guardian of Jeremiah & Jenny Thornton
Oct. 24, 1791 Mace Pichett, administrator of Fielding Neale
Dec. 26, 1791 John Brockman & Thos. Bell, administrators of Sam Brockman
Apr. 23, 1792 Caty Neale, administratrix of Fielding Neale (his widow) Mace Pickett adm. annulled
June 25, 1792 Sanford Ransdell, administrator of Jessee Ramsdell
Aug. 27, 1792 Charles Bruce, administrator of Ch. Bruce
Sept. 24, 1792 Sarah & Rosa Thornton chose Thomas Bryant guardian
Oct. 22, 1792 Tho. Farish, guardian of Elizabeth Bruce, orphan of Ch. Bruce
Oct. 22, 1792 Ch. Pearcey, guardian of Eliz. & Frankey Pearcey, orphans of Ch. Pearcey
Jan. 28, 1793 Lawrence Taliaferro, guardian to Lawrence, Francis & Mary I. Dade, orphans of Francis Dade
Jan. 28, 1793 David Goodall, guardian to Charles & Isaac Goodall, orphans of Jno. Goodall
Mar. 27, 1793 Thomas Coleman, administrator of Wm. Dabney Strother

July 22, 1793 Samuel Thompson, administrator of Samuel Thompson
Dec. 23, 1793 Mary Madison, administratrix of Ambrose Madison
Dec. 23, 1793 Nelly Lamb, administratrix to John Lamb, Jr.
Dec. 23, 1793 May Burton, Sr., administrator of Mary Scott
Dec. 23, 1793 James Beasley, guardian of Polly Neale, orphan of Fielding Neale
Dec. 23, 1793 Robt. Daniel & Prettyman Merry guardians of Sarah & Edwd Hobdey
Jan. 27, 1794 Oliver Barnster, administrator of Arthur Banister
Jan. 27, 1794 Prettyman Merry & Robert Daniel, guardians of Martha Hobdey
Jan. 27, 1794 Elizabeth Walher, administratrix of Thomas Walker
Jan. 23, 1794 Ptolemy Powell, administrator of Robert Daniel
Jan. 23, 1794 Ann Perry, administratrix of John Perry
Jan. 23, 1794 Eliz Sebree, orphan of John Sebree, chose Benj. Johnson, guardian
Jan. 23, 1794 Alex Downey, guardian of Alex Downey
Apr. 28, 1794 James Barbour, administrator of Philip Barbour
Jan. 23, 1794 Sheriff administrator of Benone Twentyman
July 28, 1794 John Atkins, administrator of James Brockman
July 28, 1794 William Riddell, administrator of Lewis Riddell
July 28, 1794 James Barbour, guardian of Philip Barbour, orphan of Philip Barbour
Sept. 22, 1794 Thos. Bryant, guardian of Nancy Thornton, daughter of James Thornton
Dec. 22, 1794 Thomas Farrish, administrator of Wm. Brice
Dec. 22, 1794 Sarah Day, administratrix of Henry Day
Dec. 22, 1794 Enoch Gulley, administrator of Richard Land
Feb. 23, 1795 Nancy Brockman, administratrix of James Brockman

Feb. 23, 1795   Sheriff, administrator of Walker Maury
Feb. 23, 1795   Aaron & Moses Quisenberry, administrators of Moses Quisenberry
Feb. 23, 1795   John Shelton, guardian of Nancy Page
Feb. 23, 1795   John D. Grymes, administrator of Ludwell Grymes
June 22, 1795   Mary Maury, administratrix of Walker Maury
July 27, 1795   Nelly Conway Madison chose Mary Willis Madison, her mother, her guardian
Sept. 28, 1795 Champ Porter, guardian of Mary Porter
Oct. 26, 1795   John Marr, administrator of Alex Marr
Dec. 28, 1795   Champ Porter, guardian of Benjamin Porter
Feb. 22, 1796   William White, administrator, Jeremiah White, Richard & John White & Belfield Cave, sister, & Mary Barbour, Jr., Benj. Head Geo. Thornton app.
Feb. 22, 1796   Anthony Garton, administrator of Uriah Garton
Mar. 27, 1796   Edward Cason, administrator of Delilah Beadles
June 27, 1796   Daniel & Frederich Woodford, administrators of Frederick Woolford
Sept.26, 1796   Thomas White, administrator of James Head
Sept.26, 1796   Reuben Cowherd, guardian to John Cowherd, his child, and legatee of Nancy Woolfolk
Oct. 24, 1796   Sarah Wright, administratrix of James Wright
Oct. 24, 1796   Betty Coleman & Thomas Coleman, Jr., administrators of James Coleman.
Oct. 24, 1796   Thomas Coleman, guardian of Wilson Coleman
Oct. 24, 1796   Betty Coleman, guardian to her children Elizabeth, Sally, Nancy, Polly, Caty & James Coleman
Oct. 24, 1796   Abraham Maury, guardian of Leonard Hill Maury, Ann Maury, Wm. Grymes Maury & Penelope Maury, orphans of Walker Maury
Oct. 24, 1796   John White, guardian of Jeremiah White
Oct. 24, 1796   Wm. White, guardian of Elizabeth White, orphan of Jeremiah White
Sept.25, 1797   Sheriff, administrator of Beryman Twentyman
Dec. 25, 1797   John Wright, administrator of John Sebree, dec'd.
Feb. 26, 1798   Alexander Ogg, administrator of John Ogg
June 25, 1798   Administration granted Henry Bell of Thomas Bell, dec'd.
Dec. 24, 1798   Johnny Herndon, orphan of L. Herndon, chose Johnny Scott guardian
Dec. 24, 1798   Joseph Herndon, orphan of L. Herndon, chose John Scott, guardian
                Polly Dade, orphan of Fras. Dade, dec'd.
Jan. 28, 1799   Jas. Beazley, administrator of Wm. Beazley
Apr. 22, 1799   Benj. Webb, orphan of Jno. C. Webb, chose Wm. C. Webb, Guard.
Nov. 25, 1799   Lucy James, orphan of Dav. James chose George James, Guard.

Miscellaneous

Aug. 1738   On application of Anthony Strother for a view of improvements on a tract of 600 acres of land granted to him by patent dealer the 23rd day of Jan. MDCCXXIV etc.
Aug. 1738   On motion of Anthony Strother to have names of his tithables viz Anthony Strother, Charles Kitchen, Sam Frank & Sarah inserted into the list of tithables vs granted & they were inserted accordingly.

May 22, 1742 Jeremiah Strother appointed overseer of the C. H. road
Feb.   1740 Joseph Thomas Gent. app. to value improvements on his land in the Goard Vinia Fork
May 28, 1747 Marriage contract between Thomas Wiatt & Sukey Edmonson. Gabriel Jones & Mary his wife, mother of the said Sukey Philip Edmonson
Jan. 26, 1748 Hanah Rhodes, widow of William Rhoades, named Daniel McClealand, petition of Timothy Crothwait & Wm. McDraugh. Relief from bond.
Nov.   1752 Perry vs Robert Thomas dismissed
Apr.   1753 Thomas Browning vs Mitchell
June 28, 1753 John Medley one gun
July   1755 Geo. Taylor (Col.) Rowland Thomas & Richard Thomas Captains.
Silthant of Peter Montague estate shows that John Stevens intermarried with Sarah, daughter of Peter Montague.
Feb.   1757 Geo. Taylor Co. Lieutenant, Wm. Taliaferro, Colonel.
Aug. 28, 1759 On motion of John Stevens who has intermarried with Sarah, one of the daughters of Peter Montague, by the assent of Reuben Daniel, guardian to Elizabeth Montague, the other daughter of the said Peter Montague, partitioneers appointed.
June 25, 1761 May Burton allowed to
Oct. 23, 1762 Partitioners appointed to divide land Thomas Merry between Thomas Merry, orphan of Thomas Merry & Elizabeth Daniel, late Elizabeth Merry, mother of said orphan.
Apr.   1763 On motion of William Pannill who intermarried with Ann Morton, daughter of Jeremiah Morton, Appointed to set aside said Pannill's share.
Jan. 2, 1763 William Terrill presented into court a receipt for provisions which he supplied the Orange Militia with on their march into Augusta which he made oath to as the law requires and ordered to by recorded.
Jan. 2, 1763 Wm. Johnson same claim on return from Augusta
June   1764 Jane Buckner, relict of Philip Buckner, Dower assigned
Oct. 1764 Edward Thomas, brother of Capt. Thomas
May 22, 1786 John Groom lost a leg at the Siege of Yorktown in Oct. 1781
Oct. 23, 1783 Jos. Cooke soldier in continued service (brother & heir Thos. Cook)
Feb. 26, 1784 Benj. Alexander died a soldier in Continental Army (Brother & heir James Alexander)
Feb. 26, 1784 Jos. Jones died a soldier in Continental Army (Hugh Jones next of kin)
Mar. 25, 1784 Lucy Moore, widow of Francis Moore, Jr., ordered to produce will (if any).
June 24, 1784 Moses Hawkins Captain in Continental (Wm. Strother Hawkins heir).
June 24, 1784 John Sutton & James Sutton who were soldiers in the Georgia Battallion & died in the service (Wm. Sutton heir at law)
July 22, 1784 John Tracey, who died a soldier in the Continental Service, leaving no issue, widow is Mary Tracey.
Aug. 26, 1784 Wm. Thornton died in Continental Service, his heir at law is Daniel Thornton
Aug. 26, 1794 Dower of Mary Milikin, late widow of Doctor Mathew Hamilton) laid off
Sept. 24, 1784 Jere Minor appointed captain in room of Geo. Waugh. Joseph Thomas, Jr., Lieutenant, & Thomas Davis, Ensign.

Mar. 24, 1785. John Boze proved he is heir at law of Wm. Boze who died a soldier in the Continental service in July 1780

March 24, 1785 John Gresham died soldier in Continental service in February, 1778.

Margaret Abell, widow of Jno. Abell died a soldier in Continental service

Wm. Chisham proved he is heir at law of James Chisham who died a soldier in Continental service in March 1778

Apr. 28, 1785 Thomas Rosson proved that he is heir at law to Wm. Rosson died a soldier in Continental service

May 26, 1785 John Spotswood, County Lieutenant, Francis Cowherd, Major, and Wm. White, Major

June 23, 1785 James Adams proved heir at law of John Adams who died a soldier in Continental Army in August 1783

Aug. 28, 1785 Nathaniel Sanders, Baptist, right to celebrate marriage

Aug. 28, 1785 John Barnett, soldier in Regiment of Guards at Albermarle Barracks

Aug. 28, 1785 Thomas Landum proved he is heir at law to Josiah Landum who died a soldier in 2nd Battle of Continental Troops for the State of Georgia

Oct. 27, 1785 Hardin Burnly, sworn Major for County

Soldiers War of 1812

George Burus
Joseph Stephens
Reuben Newman
Abram Eddins in Calvary
John Terrill, 1st Sargant
Gorie Waugh
Thomas Davis
Edward Collins
Peter Grymes, paymaster

Soldiers in Mexican War

John Edwards (of New Hope)
Andrew B. Grymes
John Henderson
Harry Richerson
Frank Carroll
Joshua Long
Robert Stogdall

Miscellaneous

Oct. 29, 1785 James Linton proved he is heir at law to James Linton who died a soldier in the 2nd Regiment of the Continental troops for the State of Georgia.

Number of taxable property & tithables for the year 1785

Free Males	Slaves	Horses	Cattle	Tithable
703	3371	2517	5882	2450

Number of white people & buildings in 1785

Number people	Dwelling houses	Out houses
3985	605	1792

Nov. 24, 1785 Aaron Bledsoe, Baptist (celebrate marriage)

Jan. 26, 1785 Johnson Watts, heir at law to Robt. Watts & Benj. Watts, soldiers who died in service in Continental Army; Benj. in Militia

Mar. 23, 1786 Henry White, heir at law to Ambrose White, who died a soldier in the Regiment of Guards

June 22, 1786 John Farguson, heir at law to Joshua Farguson

July 27, 1786 Dower assigned to Margaret Landrum, wife of Thos. Landrum, late Margaret Miller, relicit of Benj. Miller

July 27, 1786 John Wright, Captain in the room of Robt. Stubblefield Wm. Daniel, lieutenant, & John Chandler, ensign, John Gibson, Lieutenant, in Capt. Graves company; Thos. Row appointed lieutenant & James Coleman ensign in Capt. Wilber company.

July 27, 1786 Absalom Smith, Lieutenant, & Thos. Bell, ensign in Capt. Lindsay's company

July 27, 1786 James Furnish, orphan of John Furnish, proved that he is heir at law to his uncle William Furnish, dec'd., who died a soldier in the Continental service in the South Virginia Regiment, etc., the time of the death of the said William, his mother Jane, & Samuel, Jacob Thos. & James his brothers & Mary and Elizabeth his sisters were still living.

July 27, 1786 Ann Powell proved that she is heir & mother to John Bush who died a soldier in the Continental Service in the 7th Virginia Regiment.

July 27, 1786 Catlett James mentioned in the pension list, not continued on pension list.

July 27, 1786 John Groom lost a leg & entitled to pension.

July 27, 1786 And. Leach, dead

July 27, 1786 Wm. Palmer lost a leg - entitled to pension

Sept. 28, 1786 Reuben Taylor, Captain in room of Jos. Wood, Bon. Hansford, Lieutenant

Dec. 28, 1786 Assignment of dower of Mary Adams widow of Benj. Adams, dec'd.

Dec. 28, 1786 Archibald Wilson, naturalized

Feb. 23, 1787 John Bell, attorney

Mar. 26, 1787 James Howarth & Robert Wilson, naturalized

June 25, 1787 Wm. Palmer, made oath that has obtained a pension warrant.

Apr. 28, 1788 Catlett James a pensioner

Aug. 25, 1788 Thos. Walker proved he was wounded in the arm in Gates defeat, he being in the militia in Capt. Daniels company from Orange, Gen. Stevens Brigade in the year 1780

Dec. 22, 1788 Johnny Scott & Catlett Conway, coroner for County

Apr. 28, 1789 John Spotswood, a pensioner

June 22, 1789 John Groom, a pensioner

Oct. 26, 1798 Judith Miller, widow of John Miller who died of wounds in service of U.S.

Sept. 27, 1790 Wm. Campbell Lieutenant Colonel for County

Oct. 25, 1790 Proved in court that Eliz. McDaniel, wife of Alex. McDaniel, was the natural daughter of James Taylor and also, Dorothea Taylor widow of Wm. Taylor

Oct. 26, 1790 John Groom in militia from Orange at seige of York - lost a leg

Mar. 28, 1791 Judith Miller widow of John Miller, a pensioner still living

Mar. 27, 1792 John Bolling, heir at law & brother to Wm. Bowling who enlisted a soldier in the 20th S. Regiment in February 1777 in the company commanded by Capt. Dudley, said Wm. died in July 11

Aug. 1778 While in the service which was proved by Peachy Bledsoe who was a sargeant in So. Regiment

Feb. 24, 1795 Thomas Ellis, coroner in room of Catlett Conway, resigned

Aug. 24, 1795 James Blackerly, legal inspector of Thomas Blackerly, a soldier in the late Continental Army and who died in same.

Robert Thomas, signature, in Wm. Sawyer petition for mill, March Court 1754

1755 Nov. Court Benj. Cave expenses to Williamsburg as Burgess

1755 Nov. Court Geo. Taylor expenses to Williamsburg as Burgess
Nov. 1760   Benj. Cave expenses to the Assembly May & October
Oct. 1764   James Taylor, Burgess January 1764
June 1746   Joanah Sims, administratrix of Richard Sims
July 1746   Christopher Zimminan, administrator of John Newport
May & June 1757 Margaret Douglass petition for adm. of her father, Geo. Douglas
Sept. 1759   Zack Burnley, guardian bond of Eliz. Swan Jones & Sivan Jones, orphans of John Jones
Nov. 1762   Wm. Walker & Richard Thomas, guardian bond Prettyman Merry, orphan of Thos. Merry
Mar. 1764   Benj. Cave, bond as administrator of David Cave

Supplements to Previously Published Genealogies
by W. E. Brockman

The earliest Brockman record that I have found is that of John Brokeman, Chaplain of the Free Chapel of Brokenfold, 1379. That there were earlier Brockmans, there can be no doubt. The satisfying feature is that in all that period few, if any of the name, has come into prominence because of dishonest or criminal acts. The record is one of good citizenship and why should one look further? The Brokman or Brockman family gained its historical importance through participation in the Crusades, and activity in the last Crusade led by Richard the 1st was recognized by a grant of certain estates in Essex to John Brokeman by the College of Heralds, and this emblem can be found only in the arms of those who participated in the Crusades.

In the 13th year of the reign of Richard II, 1390, John Brokeman was granted lands in Essex including the Manor of Pirre extending into Romney and old Medley with other lands in Stowting and Crundale. The other name of the Manor was Wymondesse, mentioned in the Valor Ecclesiastics and held a one-eighth fee from the Archbishop in 1347. From here the family spread into what in recent years was Brockmanland County, near Bremen, Germany, and in later years into Holland, following the beginning of the reign of Oliver Cromwell, to escape his wrath. As a matter of fact the Brokman property in England extended to the sea, and there was a cavern that led down to the ocean, and was used in the escape to Europe and was likewise used by Charles II and his supporters in an effort to overthrow Cromwell.

William Brockman, son of John, appears to have lived at Powers Hall, which he may have come into possession of through his wife, Elizabeth, whose mother was the wife of Robert Power, Esq. through her second marriage of John Fryar, her first husband having been John Rikedom. The Manor of Powers Hall is still standing (1955) and the picture of it may be found in the "Brockman Scrapbook", by the compiler of this.

John Brockman, Brokeman, died August 22, 1500, at Witham, Essex. His wife was Florence St. Leger, daughter of John and widow of John Clifford. She also died 1500. The tombs of husband and wife are in St. Nicholas Church, Essex.

Thomas, son of John Brockman, married a Miss Rochester and had two children whose descendants cannot now be traced, and it could well be that this family located in North Germany, where the Brockmans have always lived and borne the names of John, Henry, William.

William, second son of John Brokeman, succeeded to his father's estate, which in itself is proof that the elder son had left the country, since he lived long enough to have children and grandchildren, prior to the succession of the estates of his father by brother William. William died in 1525 and his Will has heretofore been published. His wife was Margaret Chapman, a widow. This is proven by his will, in which he mentions a child of his wife. He is buried in the Chancel of Newington Church, as the family had moved to Kent and his son Henry had acquired Beachborough.

Henry, son of William purchased Newington and Cheriton Manors, as well as Beachborough. He died 1573 and is buried in the church at Newington. His wife was the daughter and heiress of Thomas Chilton (Sheltons of Virginia).

William, son of Henry, married Margaret, eldest daughter of Humphrey Clark, and he died April 16, 1605 at age 74, and his wife died February 5, 1610, age 73, and both are buried at Newington.

The first wife of Henry, son of William Brockman, was Helen Sawking, daughter of Nicolas. He died March 27, 1630 and she in 1642. Henry's tablet is at Newington church.

William, the first of the family to known as Sir, was knighted by Charles I in 1632. He was born 1595, educated with a degree at Oxford, was sheriff of Kent 1643, and died December 6, 1654. He was not deported or punished by Cromwell, but was heavily fined for his defense of Maidstone and Leeds against Cromwell forces. Henry, eldest son of Sir William, died in 1622 at the age of 4. James, the second son, was born in 1621, and it was his grandson James, son of William who died without issue leaving the Brockman estates to Rev. Ralph Drake who had married Caroline, a daughter of Henry Brockman of Cheriton and wife Elizabeth Randolph, son of William and wife Mary, son of Zouch and wife Jane Evering. Zouch was a brother of Sir William of Beachborough. The condition of the bequest was that the family take the name of Brockman, and this was approved by the Crown. The court procedures undoubtedly show that, Henry, the second son, of Sir William born 1623 who was given the name of his deceased brother, was no longer a British resident having left for Holland and therefore being a refugee was no longer entitled to consideration. James, died in 1767, and I still hope to uncover this court procedure in the British Museum.

Henry, the refugee, who settled in Maryland, apparently had a ventursome life for it is not believed that he married until after he landed in Maryland. Our first record of him was in 1674 when he sold land to Thos. Salmon. When Fletcher Simms Brockman visited England in 1905, he called on Mr. Alfred Brockman of Folkstone, and was told that the records at Beachborough showed the birth of Henry Brockman November 8, 1623.

The children of Sir William Brockman, of Beachborough, then, were:
1. Henry, born 1618, died 1622
2. Martha, died April 3, 1646, single
3. Helen, died 1633, single
4. Anne, married Sir John Boys, December 12, 1650, died 1656
5. James, born about 1622, married Lucy Young, died without issue February 22, 1683
6. Henry, born 1623, and apparently went to Holland to escape Cromwell. (It was the practice of the Brockmans to name children after a deceased child
7. Helen, married Roger Gipps.
8. Margery, married Sir William Hugeson, August 27, 1644

The pattern of immigration, while disorganized by political pressures is definite. The St. Leger's settled in King and Queen County, Virginia. Florence St. Leger, who married John Brockman, had a brother Thomas who married Anne Plantagnet, sister of King Edward IV. Henry, grandson of John Brockman, married a Chilton, and the Sheltons became one of the early wealthy Virginia families, and had the first brewery in Albermarle County, Virginia. Elizabeth, sister of Sir William, married Robert Curteis, and the Curtis family came in droves to Virginia. John Curtis led immigrants from the Barbados and on one trip about 1670 he was shipwrecked and returned on a passing ship to Barbados, finally landing in Maryland and went over to the adjoining counties of Northumberland and Middlesex in Virginia and right up to Orange County with the Brockmans. The Robertson, Robinson and Potter families had their own sloop running from Barbados to Virginia and they became one of the prominent families of the state, and of course the Randolphs need no comment. Anne, daughter of James Brockman, baptized January 25, 1652, married Sir Miles Cooke, and the Brockmans of Virginia had land transactions with the Cooks in Louisa and Orange. They intermarried with the Henderson (Joseph Miles Henderson) and a daughter of Joseph Collins married John Cook. Julian, daughter of Henry Brockman (d1573) married Thomas Broadnax, and this family settled in Virginia. Thomas changed his name to May and later to Knight in 1738. Henry Brockman registered into Maryland and with his adventurous career, it is not curious that he did not marry till late in life and that there was one child only, Samuel. (I discount the report that Henry was son of Thomas). The family after his purported marriage to Rebecca Salmon lived in Maryland for awhile, where the son was born, and I think it most likely that Henry died there, and that Samuel came on over to Virginia with his mother who remarried, probably a Pettie, and he Samuel married Mary, daughter
of John, who was grandfather to President Madison. The close tie of the Madisons, Sims, Petties and Brockmans is indisputable. The elder Thomas Madison, left a will November 4, 1674, recorded in Rappahannock where he leaves property to his godchild Rebecca Pettie, daughter of Robert Pettie. He left to his wife his real estate except the 300 acres he wold to Richard White, and a parcel sold to Richard Sims. The Sims and Petties intermarried in Orange as well as in Richmond county. The second Thomas Madison father of Mary, we believe patented his land in King William, later King and Queen in 1719 and Thomas Salmon in King and Queen 1727. Here we find Richard and Joseph Woolfolk, John Madison, William Mays, the Craddock family, all in King William and later cut off into King and Queen. The Madisons, Hendersons, Woolfolks, Sims, Petties or Petty's all came on to Orange and had land adjoining, and the first mill of John Brockman was adjoining Petty's mill stream and I have fished and bathed in this old Mill race many times. When Richard Woolfolk, in anticipation of death in 1770, transferred land to John Burrus, John Henderson and Samuel Brockman, it is obvious that these three were getting their share of the estates to which they were entitled after the death of Joseph Woolfolk, father of Joseph of Orange who married Christian Bibb.

It is apparent that William, son of Samuel I, married Elizabeth Mason and this evidence has piled up, finally culminating into a decision when in Albermarle this year I discovered that William Mason Brockman, son of old William had witnessed a will, prior to the birth of the children of

Ambrose Brockman, all of the sons of which carried Mason as their middle name. This leaves me to conclude, that Agatha, second wife of William Sims of Albermarle, was Agatha Robinson, born 1737, daughter of William Robinson and wife Agatha Beverley, who were married February 17, 1737. The first of the Robinson family was John, of Cleasly, Yorkshire, who married Elizabeth, daughter of Christopher Potter. Christopher was in Middlesex and his wife was Agatha, daughter of Bertram Obert. Colonel Christopher Robinson was a son of John and wife Elizabeth. Again we have the Robinson and Curtis families uniting when Anno, widow of John Curtis, married Richard Robinson and in 1684 a deed from Richard and wife Anne to John Curtis, son by her marriage to John Curtis, Sr. Will of John Vaus September 8, 1691, names daughters Agatha and others and James, Averilla and Chichley Curtis children of "my loving sister Elizabeth Curtis by James Curtis." Also mentions nephew Christopher Robinson. Colonel Christopher Robinson was Secretary of State for the Colony of Virginia. He was brother to John Robinson, Bishop of London and they were sons of John Robinson of Cleasby. All of these lines down to John Roberson of Albermarle, who will was witnessed by Samuel and Caty Brockman, are proven. John Robinson of St. Mary's Parish, Spottsylvania, for nominal amounts transferred in 1744 and 1745, 400 acres to Joseph Collins, 300 to Thomas and 200 to William Collins, and then to Joseph Collins again 254 acres. William Collins and wife Elizabeth then transferred to James Haley of Orange his 200 acres, and the deed it witnessed by several of the Collins brothers. It is fair to assume that the mother of Joseph Collins, (will 1757) was a Robinson, and this was a division of the estate. Benjamin and John Robinson settled in Albermarle and Benjamin was always on hand to give a bond when one of the Brockmans married.

To summarize the Robinson connection, I quote from authoritative sourced: John Robinson, of Sleasby, England, in Yorkshire married Elizabeth Potter. It will be remembered that it was Mrs. Harriet Potter's slave Letty that poisoned Richard Sims. Elizabeth was the daughter of Christopher Potter. The fourth son of John Robinson, was John of Bristol, Bishop of London and envoy to Sweden. He died 1723, leaving no children, but he devised his real estate to his brother Christopher who emigrated to Virginia. Christopher was in the first vestry book of Middlesex county in 1664. His wife was Agatha, daughter of Bertram Obert; his second wife was Catherine, widow of Robert Beverley, who was daughter of Theo Home. The children of Christopher were:

 John Robinson, born, 1683, became President of the Council of Virginia. Married Catherine Beverley, daughter or Robert, who was author of the History of Virginia.

The other children including, Henry, Christopher and Benjamin. Benjamin, son of Christopher was Clerk of Caroline County. He married a Miss King and had a son William, minister of Stratton Major Parish, King and Queen County, who married Agatha Beverley, February 17, 1737, daughter of Robert, and had Clara, who married James Walker; Ann, who married Dr. John Hay and Agatha, who must have married William Sims, as his second wife, and she was born before the end of the first year of her father's marriage. To the wedding of Benjamin Robinson and Miss King, there was born a son Joseph, and Joseph had a son Benjamin who married Susannah Brock, and this Benjamin was executor to the will of his brother John and Samuel and sister Caty Brockman, were witnesses.

It all looks quite plain when it is down on paper and I am indebted to Mrs. Pauline Brandt of Norfolk, and Mrs. Crystal Willard of Baxter Springs, Kansas for working this out, although neither know the extent of my conclusions.

I finally obtained the complete deed from John Henderson of King and Queen to Samuel Brockman, for 300 acres of land, and this deed was prefaced by a lease for the land, and the consideration was "one ear of Indian corn yearly" and from other sources Samuoll Brockman gave the 300 acres of Land he had in King and Queen in exchange and instead of the usual "one dollar" consideration, and ear of corn sufficed. The very next day a complete deed was given to "Samuoll" Brockman by John Henderson, but the deed in King and Queen County executed by Samuoll Brockman went with the burning of the other records.

From Mrs. Major Morecock, Jr., Richmond, we find that the land of Samuel Brockman in King and Queen was on "Port Tobago Road which ran from the bay of Port Tobago on the Rappahannock River in upper Essex passing through Elevon, Beasley, and King and Queen Line and continuing south through the latter county.

Mary M. Singleton, daughter of Samuel Brockman I

Mary, daughter of Samuel I must have married Richard Hunt Singleton, instead of John as previously reported. Henry Singleton came to York in 1650 and it suggests that he may have lived in York before coming to that part of King and Queen which was cut off from Kent, from York.

"Virginia Gazette, Williamsburg, March 24, 1774"
'All persons indebted to the estate of Mr. Richard Hunt Singleton, deceased, are desired to make immediate payments; or, farthest (??) by ensuing general court, as his affairs will not admit of any longer indulgence. Those who fail paying by that time may depend on having their accounts put into a lawyer's hands.
                                            Mary Singleton' "

Charles Parish —York County, Va.
History and Register 1648-1789

Singleton, Anne, daughter of Richard Hunt, by Mary, b. Nov. 29, bap. January 11, 1746.
Singleton, Frances, daughter of Ambrose by Frances, b. Jan. 13, bap. March 17, 1716.
Singleton, Mary, daughter of Ambrose by Frances, b. May 31, bap. July 2, 1732.
Singleton, Rachel, daughter of Richard Hunt and Mary, b. Dec. 23, bap. Jan. 5, 1747.
Singleton, Samuel, son of Ambrose by Frances, b. Jan. 5, bap. Feb. 13, 1724.

Virginia Historical Magazine
Notes from Records of Richmond Co.

Will of Cuthbert Webb, dated January 25, 1781, proved August 2, 1782. Legatees: Mother Frances, sister-in-law Winny Webb, brother Charles, brother Isaac, to Godson James Cuthbert Williamson, two negroes at the death of "my sister Singleton", nephew George Harrison, niece Frances Harrison, Goddaughter Priscilla Webb, Godson John Hill and John Edmundson, brother and friend, Robert Singleton, executors.

Will of Robert Singleton, dated September 2, 1781, proved August 5, 1782 —Legatees: Wife Priscilla, son James Cuthbert Singleton, brothers James, Joshua and Samuel Singleton.

Henry Singleton and brother John came to York County in 1637. Robert, son of Henry, made his will April 15, 1724, probated 1725. Names wife Elizabeth, children Robert, Joshua, Mary, wife of George Foster, Susannah wife of Thos. Smithers, Isaac, Averilla, last two minors. Henry Singleton had also sons Henry, (sold land Oct. 21, 1687, next to brother Samuel. Also had a son Joshua. Richard Hunt Singleton was also in York, which suggests that Samuel Brockman I also lived there before coming to King and Queen.

"Virginia Gazette Index"

"To be sold at the plantation where Mrs. Mary Brockman, dec'd., lately lived, in the County of Orange, on the 15th of Nov. next (1776) for ready money, all personal estate of Mr. Samuel Brockman, dec'd., consisting of horses, hogs, cattle, sheep, crops, household furniture by the executors.

Samuel & William Brockman"

"Brockman, Samuel, 8th Nov. 1776 -Taken up in Orange, a red cow with a middle size bell on, and marked in each ear with a crop & slit posted and appraised to 55°.

Samuel Brockman"

The Estate of Samuel Brockman II

It is now quite apparent that Samuel II left a Will as a close study of the court records indicate this, plus the power of attorney executed by his daughter Mary Crossthwaite in 1815. For some reason the Will was not admitted to Probate, and John Brockman, son, and Thos. Bell, son-in-law, were appointed administrators. The Will probably showed preference to William, and was finally settled by all of the land being transferred to son William but with a payment to each of the children. Mary, Sally and John were probably the dissenting heirs, although John as administrator was later pressured by court to complete the division of the estate. William did not get along with John as indicated by the affidavit filed by Rebecca* his mother, and it is most likely that William was the first son of Rebecca and John was a child by his father's first marriage, probably to Mary Woolfolk. There was a deep seated enmity between John and William which carried down to my generation.

The records for this area are scarce and incomplete, but it is obvious that Richard Sims married a Potter, and was staying with Mrs. Harriet Potter when Letty, the Potter slave, got tired of him and fed him some poison. There were Tandy and Brockman, and Burris and Brockman, marriages, and Dolly Payne Madison was related to the ALBERMARLE Brockmans and the Dickinsons, and one of the Paynes who married Mary Major, built a new house in Culpeper in 1798, and named it Bleake Hill, the same name William Brockman gave to his Albermarle home at Burnleys.

DB 28, P.36 Orange County

I, Mary Crossthwait of the County of Clark and State of Kentucky, have made constituted and appointed my beloved son Elijah Crossthwait of the county and state aforesaid my agent and attorney for me and in my name to transfer a certain piece of business in Orange Co., State of Virginia, to wit. Whereas my father Samuel Brockman, decd., later of the aforesaid County of Orange, Virginia, bequeathed to me a certain legacy by his last will and test, a part whereof remains unpaid and in

---

*most likely Rebecca Salmon and not Rebecca Graves as previously reported.

the hands of John Brockman executor of the last will and testament of my said father Samuel Brockman.

Now this is therefore to authorise and empower my said attorney for me and my name to receive, transact any such other business, sign acquittals, releases or commense such for the recovery of the said legacy which remains unpaid or either any other lawful step which would be necessary for me to take where I present, hereby ratifying and confirming whatsoever my said attorney shall lawfully do for me in as complete and perfect a manner as if done by myself.

In testimony whereof I have hereto set my hand and seal this 7th of June 1815.

State of Kentucky -Clarke Co.   Mary Crossthwait

Following is one relatives idea about the Salmon connection. One Thos. Salmon left a will at St. Mary's County, Maryland, and another one in Cecil County. Another was County Clerk of Baltimore County. It is assumed the one that purchased the land of Henry Brockman took up a papent in Spottsylvania in 1727.

While in Washington in 1953 I rented a car and drove over to Annapolis and in the Hall of Records, I found the Will of Thos. Salmon dated Nov. 24, 1695, in which he mentioned no children. In his estate settlement he was referred to as a Cooper. Samuel Brockman II was a Cooper.

Greenway of the Brockmans

We have wondered the source of the name Greenway, the home of the Brockmans in Orange County, and we know that Sarah Greenway who married G. T. Grasty lived there, and that the old home was moved from the Linsay property to its present site.

"Legends of the Skyline Drive & Great Valley of Virginia by Carrie Hunter Willis and Etta Belle Walker. 'The proprietor of the Northern Neck, Lord Fairfax, lived at Greenway Court after first having a country seat at Belvoir near the Potomac River in what is now Fairfax County.... It may be of passing interest to learn that Lord Fairfax, although proprietor of thousands of acres, lived in a comparatively simple way. His home was an unpretentious story and a half frame building, situated in a large grove of trees, and surrounded by smaller homes for servants and tenants. Greenway Court the name given the home, very probably lacked more indications of elegance and grace because of Fairfax's bachelor state.......His domain called the Northern Neck of Virginia comprised the present counties of Lancaster, Northumberland, Richmond, Westmoreland, Stafford, King George, Prince William, Fairfax, London, Fauquier, Culpeper (part of Culpeper was cut off into Orange) Clarks, Madison and Page in Virginia and numerous counties in what is now West Virginia."

Miss Annie Laurie Hill
937 Juniper Street, N.E.
Atlanta 5, Ga.

My dear Mr. Brockman: December 8, 1954

At last I am sending you a certified copy of the Grant proving that Lewis Brockman was a Revolutionary Soldier. (R.Sol.).

Please note the erasures on lines near the bottom of the Grant. This is not an error of the typist, but just as in the original Grant. Every Grant in this particular Book of Grants has the same erasures.

I regret that so much delay has occurred in connection with sending you this copy of the Brockman Grant but it is the definite proof that Lewis Brockman was a Revolutionary Soldier.

Sincerely

Annie Laurie Hill

STATE OF GEORGIA.
    By his Excellency Wilson Lumpkin Governor and Commander in Chief of the Army and Navy of this State, and of the Militia thereof.
TO ALL TO WHOM THESE PRESENTS SHALL COME GREETING.
    KNOW YE, That in pursuance of the several acts of the General Assembly of this State, passed the 9th of June, and 24th December, 1825, and the 14th and 27th of December, 1826, to make distribution of the land acquired to the Creek Nation of Indians, by a Treaty concluded at the Indian Springs, on the 12th day of February, 1825, and forming the Counties of Lee, Muscogee, Troup, Coweta and Carroll, in this state, I HAVE GIVEN AND GRANTED, and by these presents, DO GIVE AND GRANT unto LEWIS BROCKMAN, R Sol, of Dix's District Oglethorpe County his heirs and assigns forever, all that tract or lot of land, containing two hundred two and a half acres, situate, lying and being the the ELEVENTH District, of the Third Section, in the County of TROUP in said State, which said tract or lot of land is known and distinguished in the plan of said District by the number One hundred and fifteen - - having such shape, form and marks as appear by a plat of the same hereunto annexed: To have and to hold the said tract or lot of land, together with all and singular the rights, members and appurtenances thereof whatsoever, ~~except all valuable ores, mines and minerals, which have been reserved to the State by an act, passed the 24th of December, 1825,~~ unto the said LEWIS BROCKMAN his heirs and assigns, to - - - - and their proper use, benefit and behoof forever in fee simple.
    GIVEN under my hand and the Great Seal of the said State this fifteenth day of June in the year one thousand eight hundred & thirty-five and of the Independence of the United States of America 39th

Signed by his Excellency the Governor,)   Wilson Lumpkin
  15th day of June 1835   )   R. A. Greene   S.E.D.
Registered the 15th   day of   July   1835

STATE OF GEORGIA
OFFICE OF SECRETARY OF STATE
DEPARTMENT OF ARCHIVES AND HISTORY

    I hereby certify that I am State Historian and Director of The Department of Archives and History of the State of Georgia, duly and regularly appointed by the Secretary of State of Georgia, in accordance with the provisions of Chapter 40-8 of the Code of Georgia, and that, as such, I am authorized and empowered to make and sign this certificate and to attach the official seal of The Department of Archives and History of the State of Georgia;
    I further certify that The Department of Archives and History is the official depository of all of the original books and records containing the grants of land, with the plats of surveys thereof, heretofore made by the State of Georgia;

(95)

I further certify that the typewritten copy attaced is a true and correct copy of the record of the grant of a 202½ acre tract of land in Dix's District Oglethorpe County, made by the State of Georgia, as the same appears in the official records in this office, known as Page. No. 317 of the Secretary of State's book of Grants entitled "TROUP", DISTRICT 11-12;

In witness whereof, I have hereunto set my hand and affixed the sale of The Department of Archives and History of the State of Georgia, this 14th day of July 1954.

                     Mrs. Mary Givens Gryan
                     Director of Department of Archives
SEAL   and History

* * *

                                               1101 West Second St.
                                               Arlington, Texas
Dear Mr. Brockman: May 7, 1955

I sent in my application for membership in the D.A.R. and I need additional information to complete it. I think they are mixed up about Major Brockman -I will quote exactly from the letter they sent. Quote:

"There are two Major Brockmans who were living during the Revolutionary period -one the uncle of this Major Brockman, who married Jessie Jones and moved to Guilford Co. N.C. Various records state that he was the man who rendered the Revolutionary service. The Major Brockman who married Mary Patterson, his nephew, is the Revolutionary ancestor on whom Mrs. Lebo has filed her papers and she is claiming for him the service that has been thought to be that of his uncle.

Since there is so much confusion as to the identity of the Major Brockman who rendered the service claimed, it is our suggestion that you file a new set of papers on the record of John Brockman, father of Major Brockman, for Mrs. Lebo to which her dues and fees can be transferred. Mrs. Lebo's line, of course, would come through Major, born Dec. 18, 1760. John Brockman served as a soldier, North Carolina". Unquote.

Your book, Virginia Wills and Abstracts, has Major Brockman, born in 1755, as the son of John Brockman and Mary Collins. The John Brockman who married Amelia Martin was Major Brockman's brother. There's no record in the book that John and Amelia Brockman had a son, Major.

I thought maybe you could help me straighten this out. If I should file a new set of papers, claiming that Major was John and Amelia Brockman's son I have no claim whatsoever to prove it.

I hope this won't be too much trouble for you but I just don't understand their statement.

Thanking you very much, I am

                                     Sincerely yours,
                                     Gussie Brockman Lebo
                                     (Mrs. M. B. Lebo)

Secretary
Daughters of American Revolution   May 12, 1955
D.A.R. Memorial Hall
Washington, D.C.

Dear Madam Secretary:

I have had access to your correspondence on the subject of the application of Mrs. M. B. Lebo of Arlington, Texas. You state there were two Major Brockmans, one the son of John and Mary Collins Brockman (born about 1756) and the other a son of John and Amelia Martin Brockman (born December 18, 1760. The existence of the two Major Brockmans is recorded in my book "Hume, Kennedy, Brockman Families" 1916.

The existence of Major born 1755 is proved by the Will of his father John, dated August 8, 1755, and the Executor's Bond 1756. The existence of the second Major is not documented but came from the family of Col. Thos. Patterson Brockman of Spartanberg, S.C., a grandson of John & Amelia Brockman.

Major the son of John and Mary Collins Brockman inherited land in Louisa County; sold his land in 1776 at which time he was living in Guilford, N. C. and had just reached the age of 21. One Major Brockman married Mary Patterson at Goochland, Nov. 11, 1779. Major Brockman and Major B. Brockman are recorded as being Revolutionary Soldiers from Louisa County.

Were there two Major Brockmans and did the second one marry Jessie Jones? This second marriage is hearsay, no proof has been found although records at Louisa, Virginia, suggested this marriage.

When I published the "Brockman Scrapbook" I had located the Will of John Brockman, wife Amelia Martin, probated in Laurens County, S. C., and this will made no mention of a son Major, dead or alive, and the conclusion reached was there was just one Major Brockman, perhaps, who may have married Jessie Jones as his second wife.

Mrs. Lebo's records show that Barney Brockman, supposed son of one Major was born _____ 1819, and this of course would be possible as child of the second wife.

Your record that one Major was born December 18, 1760, if correct, proves that there were two Major Brockmans, but not father and son as Major of Orange was not born until 1755. The second Major could have been, statistically, a son of John and Amelia Brockman or a son of Samuel and Mary Bell Brockman who had land in Louisa, Virginia, and had a son, Lewis, Revolutionary Soldier who died in Georgia.

You refer to the death of John Brockman taken from the Bible of Col. Thos. Patterson Brockman as having taken place August 13, 1825. I believe this John was the son of Henry and grandson mentioned in Will of John Brockman 1801 but not mentioned in the will of Henry Brockman dated July 19, 1834 and probated at Spartanberg, S. C. June 11, 1842. More information is needed to verify this line.

              Sincerely yours,

              W. E. Brockman

* * *

Stephen Brockman and Elizabeth Embre

         C. A. Brockman
         Iago, Texas   Aug. 26, 1952

Mr. W. E. Brockman
Minneapolis 1, Minn.

Dear Sir:

We sure have enjoyed reading the book we have about the Brockmaans. We would not have known much if did not have this book and am sure will learn more when the new book comes off the press and we are sure hou have worked to get this together. We trust what we have sent you will give more information. I was married in Camden Ray Co., Mo. Dec. 20, 1905 came to Texas Jan. 1907. Texas has been good to us. All the generation of Father and Mother have died except my Mother and her half sister now lives in Richmond, Mo. My Mother will be 91 yrs. old Dec. 24, 1952. Mother lives in Sweeny, Texas, about 30 miles from me. I try to see her each week.

My wife does not have very good health -high blood pressure. She is a member of D.A.R., The Colonial Dames of America, Daughters of American Colonists, eligible to others.

My wife was born in Brown Co., Ohio, April 14, 1881

Please find enclosed my check for $11 as follows; $10 The Brockman Scrapbook; $1 supplement you sent sometime ago.

                         As ever,

                         C. A. Brockman,
                         P. O. Box 53, Iago, Tex., Wharton Co.

Asa Brockman, possessing a farm in township 51, Range 28, Ray County adapted to the growing of grain and the raising of stock. Our subject pursues both departments of agriculture with assediuty and success. His position in the community is one of prominence and he is held in esteem by all who know him.

He was born in Clark County, Kentucky, April 19, 1826 and is the son of Joseph E and Mary J (Culbertson) Brockman. His parents were natives of Kentucky. The father born June 1, 1805 and the mother March 20, 1801. The father of our subject was educated in the district common school and remained with his parents until his marriage, which occured when he was but eighteen years of age. Afterward he rented land for one year and then removed to Howard County, Mo. where he raised one crop.

In the year 1828 he came to Ray Co., Mo. and bought the farm now occupied by our subject consisting of one hundred and sixty five acres. The country was new, he being one of the first settlers, and his farm was heavily timbered with white oak and walnut, in which deer, turkey and bears were plentiful. He drove hither across the county with horse teams. His first house was built of logs and was roofed with boards weighted with poles which the floor was of puncheon. The children of his marriage were Asa our subject; Milton, Clifton, Harmon F Israel who died in early manhood and three who died young. He and his wife were devoted members of the Christian Church. The principles of the Whig party were very dear to him and he was an enthusiastic follower of Henry Clay.

His parents were Stephen and Elizabeth (Embree) Brockman, natives of Virginia who settled in Ky. at an early day. Being but a child when he came to the wilderness the educational advantages of our subject were very limited.

The primitive schoolhouse in which he gained a rudimentary education was constructed of logs, with a log cut out of the whole length of the side for a window. A log split in two with sticks for uprights answered for seats and desks. The teachers of those early days were not as thoroughly trained for their work as those of the present time, and "lickin" went along with "larnin". Our subject left his parents for the first time in 1849 when he went to California making the journey with an ox team in company with seven others. The party was on the road from April 10 to August 20 when they arrived at Sacramento. The hardships endured in the journey were many but bravely borne. Our subject began work in the Golden State by chopping wood at $8.00 per cord and soon thereafter went into the mines where he remained a few months. Later he proceded to the Sonoma Valley where he worked at fencing for a large land company. In the spring of 1850 Mr. Brockman returned to the mines and there made sometimes as much as $100 a day with the pan. In a few months he went back to the valley and worked for $100 a month after which to took to the mountains as a hunter of deer and elk.

In 1851 he returned home by the way of the ocean and upon resuming his former occupation purchased his father's farm. Previous to this, in 1850, his parents went with him to California where they resided until their death, the mother passing away in 1888 and the father in 1890. Our subject remained in the East after his return in 1851. In 1852 he married Sarah F. daughter of Ballard and Nancy (Jackson) Hudgins a native of Ray Co., Mo., her parents being natives of Kentucky. The children of this marriage were ten, two of whom died when young.

Joseph E. Brockman	married	Victoria Ballew
John C. Brockman	married	Mary. A. Rush
Harvey M. Brockman	married	Hattie Keller
James A. Brockman	married	Maud Jones
Asa B. Brockman	married	Ida Smithey
Nancy J. Brockman	wife of	James W. Rosell
Lou Isabell	wife of	Joseph A. Brown
Sarah A. Brockman	wife of	Luther Phillips

Mr. Brockman and his wife are earnest and active members of the Christian Church. In politics he is a Democrat, voting and working with the party. In 1861 he entered the Union Mo. Militia under Col. Barr and was in the Battle of Glasgow where he was captured but fortunately remained a prisoner only a short time. Soon afterward he was paroled and discharged.

Returning home he resumed the duties connected with the management of his well appointed farm of two hundred and eighty seven acres upon which he carries on general farming and stock raising.

This history from Portrait & Biographical Record of Clay-Ray-Carroll-Chariton and Co. of Missouri. Printed in Chicago, Ill., by Chapman Bros., 1893.

(Clarence A. Brockman)

Asa Brockman

Born April 19, 1826, died October 19, 1905. His wife Sarah F. (Hudgins) Brockman; born October 9, 1829, died Nov. 27, 1910. Children and their families of Asa & Sarah Brockman:

Derwood Brockman, decd.
Gertrude Brockman
Robert Brockman
John C. & Mary (Rush) Brockman (my parents). their children:

Clarence A. Brockman, born Oct. 30, 1880, married Dec. 20, 1905 to Etta Ann Mick. We have one son, Dr. Asa Mick Brockman, born April, 1st, 1907. He married Mary Belle Dockrell Jan. 1, 1948. They have one son born July 15, 1952 (adopted)

Virgil, born June 16, 1886; died Oct. 12, 1891
Blanche, born Dec. 12, 1892; died Aug. 8, 1893
John Creel Brockman, born April 4, 1896, married Willie Grey
   Arrington August 18, 1916; their children:
      Mary Louise Brockman   married Archie Haggard
      Eleanor Creel Brockman   married Fred Barton
      their children -boy named Brockman & girl named Gay
      John C. Brockman III married Roberta Niblik
         their children:
            John N. Brockman
            Mollie Ann Brockman
      Billy Francis Brockman married Eugene Arnold, their children
         Jane Arnold
      Harvey M. Brockman married Hattie Keller Brockman; children
         Sallie, Mattie, Zenobia, Mildred, Tommy (died)
      Nancy J. Brockman married James W. Roselle; children
         Harvey (decd), Vesta, Francis, Louella, Mina, May,
         Arthur (died)
      James Arthur Brockman married Maud Jones; children
         Rosia (died)
         Carral
      Lou Isabell Brockman married Joseph A. Brown; children
         Jesse
         Smith) twins
         Tabiatha)
         William -died about two yrs. ago
         Joda
         Jennie
         Charles
            and they have eight children deceased in infancy
      Sarah A. Brockman married Luther Phillips; no children
      Asa B. Brockman married Ida Smithey; their children
         Guthrie
         Susie
         Grandville
         Harmon

Clifton Brockman of Camden, Mo., born in 1831 was 86 years old when he
died. Clifton was a brother of my grandfather Asa Brockman. They
married sisters. Clifton's wife's name Mary Ann Hudgins.
Asa Brockman (my grandfather) omitted one thing in his record in regard
to his sister - have forgotten her name since he told me.
   She married a man by the name of Hendley. She and her husband were
in the party that went to California in 1849 and she died enroute and
was buried in middle of road on account of wild animals destroying the
body.

                                                    C.A.B.

                          * * *

                   ASA T. BROCKMAN FAMILY

                                             July 30, 1952
Mrs. G. V. Proctor
R. R. 6
Columbia, Missouri

My dear Cousin:

The Brockman Scrapbook is just going to press, and I am, therefore delighted that your letter came in time so that I can include the data which it contained. You will find the ancestry of your father, James Wesley Brockman, on page 96 of my book entitled, ORANGE COUNTY FAMILIES, and on page 242 of the Brockman Scrapbook.

This record shows the marriage of Asa T. Brockman and Lucy Quisenberry and I note that your Bible records show that his wife was Mary J. Quisenberry. I am glad to have this information as I never believed that his wife was Lucy as suggested in previous books.

W. E. Brockman

* * *

Columbia, Missouri
August 25, 1952

Mr. W. E. Brockman

Dear Mr. Brockman:

I am sorry I have been so long writing to you, but we have had company. My cousin, Mrs. A. L. Samuels, from Princeton, N. J., spent last week with me. She was telling me she had met you and I believe has given you the information about our great-grandfather. My father was James Wesley Brockman, born Feb. 14, 1858, in Clark Co., Ky., near Winchester. Came to Missouri in 1877. Married Mary Catherine Spence, Oct. 12, 1886. They lived on a farm northeast of Centralia, Mo. for 46 years. I was born Oct. 4, 1887. Married Graham W. Proctor May 4, 1907.

OUR CHILDREN

James Emmett Proctor, born Sept. 19, 1910. Died Jan 20, 1911.
Roger Lee Proctor born May 31, 1912
Madge Proctor Kennedy, born Oct. 28, 1914
Marion Glenn Proctor, born Jan. 17, 1919. Died Mar. 26, 1919
Roger Lee Proctor, married Mary C. Smith of St. Louis, Sept. 9, 1939. They have the following children:
    Roger Lee Proctor, Jr., born June 28, 1942
    Michael Spence Proctor, born July 19, 1943
    Mary Ellen Proctor, born Nov. 29, 1944
    Karen Elizabeth Proctor, born Aug. 20, 1947

Our daughter Madge married Mell D. Kennedy in Kansas City, Mo., Sept. 6, 1942. They have no children. Madge is supervisor in the Welfare office of Jasper Co., in Joplin. They live in Webb City. She was Vital Statistician in the State Health Dept. of Mo. when she was married.

Our son lives near us, and is in the Broiler business with his father.

I have made a copy of the births, marriages and deaths of my grandfather's family from the family Bible.

Margaret L. Proctor
(Mrs. Graham V. Proctor)

BIRTHS

Asa T. Brockman, Jr., was born Mar. 18, 1823.
Mary J., wife of Asa T. Brockman, was born Jan 22, 1826

Susan Ann Huguely Brockman, wife of Asa T. Brockman, was born June 16, 1834
Roger Jacob Brockman, son of Mary J. and Asa T. Brockman, born Oct. 5, 1843
James Francis Brockman, son of Mary J. and Asa T. Brockman, was born Sept. 3, 1846.

CHILDREN OF ASA T. and SUSAN

Flora Anna (called Mickie) Brockman, born March 1, 1856
Mary E. Brockman, born April 24, 1852
John H. Brockman, born May 27, 1854
James Wesley Brockman, born Feb. 14, 1858
Alice Brockman, born March 18, 1860
Roger Lee Brockman, born Jan. 9, 1864
Rachel H. Brockman, born Jan. 19, 1868
Asa T. Brockman, Jr., born Jan. 31, 1870
Infant son born Aug. 25, 1874
Maggie D. Brockman, born Oct. 31, 1877.

GRANDCHILDREN OF ASA T. and SUSAN

Ann Brockman
Ora Myrtle Brockman, dau. of John H.
Florine Brockman, born March 24, 1884
Asa Dawson Brockman, son of John H.
Florine Brockman, born June 12, 1887
Margaret Lee Brockman, daughter of James W. and Mary C. Brockman, born Oct. 4, 1887
Lynwood Hodgkin Dawson, son of Rachel and Nathaniel Dawson, born Oct. 26, 1897

MARRIAGES - MY GRANDFATHER

Asa T. Brockman and Mary J. Quisenberry, married Nov. 24, 1841
Asa T. Brockman and Susan Ann Huguely, married June 3, 1851
Willis Green and Mary E. Brockman, married June 22, 1871
John H. Brockman and F. Florine Dawson, married Oct. 3, 1882
James W. Brockman and Mary C. Spence, married Oct. 13, 1886
Nathaniel L. Dawson and Rachel H. Brockman, married Dec. 12, 1893

GRANDCHILDREN - MARRIAGES

John L. Lowery and Myrtle O. Brockman, married Jan. 1, 1901
Graham V. Proctor and Margaret Lee Brockman, married May 4, 1907
Asa D. Brockman and Mary Frances Proctor were married in Aug., 1911

DEATHS

Mary Jane Brockman -April 12, 1847
James Francis Brockman -May __, 1848
Roger Jacob Brockman -Aug. __, 1862 (He was killed in the Civil War)
Rachel Alice Brockman - Aug. 17, 1868
Mary E. Brockman Green -Dec. 25, 1874
Infant son -Feb. 11, 1875
Flora Ann Brockman -March 27, 1880
Asa T. Brockman, Sr. -Sept. 11, 1880
Roger Lee Brockman -Mar. 8, 1887
Maggie D. Brockman -Jan. 28, 1888
Asa Thomas Brockman, Jr. - May 22, 1890
Rachel H. Brockman Dawson -Nov. 7, 1897
John H. Brockman -Oct. 8, 1899
Susan Ann Brockman -Feb. 23, 1907

(102)

James Wesley Brockman -April 22, 1929
Mary C. Brockman -wife of James W. Brockman -May 2, 1935
Linwood H. Dawson, son of Rachel H. Brockman Dawson and Nathaniel
Dawson -July 25, 1898

* * *

WILLIAM BROCKMAN, JR. and WIFE LUCY SIMMS BROCKMAN

William Brockman, Jr. was son of William Brockman of Orange and wife Elizabeth Brockman, daughter of William Brockman, Sr. of Albermarle, and wife Elizabeth (probably Masons). Lucy Simms Brockman was, I believe, daughter of Ambrose Brockman and wife Nancy Simms Brockman.

William Brockman, Jr. b. 1/18/1777 -married to Lucy Simms, b.1/18/1787
      d. 6/5/1844 (2/17/1806)   d.1/24/1852
          Albermarle Co. (All buried at Mt.Vernon
          Va. by Jacob cemetery, 1 mi. E of
          Watts   Eldon, Mo. on N. J.
                Shepherd farm.)

" children:
Berlinda, b. 10/22/1807, married to Geo. Moore on May 31, 1825 by Rev.
Willis, b. 8/13/1809   Ebenezer Rogers
Nancy, b. 9/4/1811, d. 11/8/1896
Simms, b. 5/22/1813 -married (on 2/26/1837) Rachel Gartin, b. 5/18/1818
                   d. 11/27/1869
  d. 9/21/1856 (in Cole Co.,Mo.)Buried 1 mi. E Eldon,Mo.
              N. J. Shepherd farm
Dr. John, b. 1/11/1816
Elizabeth E. b. 3/25/1818 married to Uriah Dooley. Buried at Dooley
              Cemetery, Eldon, Mo.
Ellen, b. 8/28/1822
William, b. 1/25/1820

 Children of Sims and Rachel Gartin Brockman:
  Nancy Elizabeth, b. married to John M. T. Miller on 1/9/1859
  Martha A. b. 4/24/1844. d.5/24/1876 (married Samuel Dresser, buried
                   Eldon, Mo.
  James Mason, b. 1 -- 1841 d. 8/22/1908, buried in Ellensburg,Wash.
       (Ellen Adcock)
  Lucy Jane, b. 2/20/1838. d. 7/14/1902 (buried Mt.Pleasant,Eldon)
  William Simms, b. 8/11/1853 d. 8/19/1911. Buried at Mt.Pleasant,
                  Eldon, Mo.
  John Willis, b. 1/28/1848 d. 11/ /1926 Buried in Pasadena, Cal.
             m. Mrs. Abigail Padgett
  Dr. Henry Hugh, b. 2/7/1850 d. 8/25/1925 Buried in Eldon, Mo., m.
              Mahala A. Walker
           later to Mrs. Alice Harbison Brockman

Lucy Jane, 2/20/1838 married to William T. Franklin -Eldon, Miller Co., Mo.
  d. 6/14/1902   Merchant and banker
" " and Wm. T. Franklin's children:
James Simms Franklin, b. 10/2/1858 married to Elizabeth Cross b. 8/8/1850
          d.1/29/1921 (10/27/1881) Mt.Pleasant,Mo.(Eldon)
         buried at Eldon, Mo.
 Maude, b.1/30/1886 married Dr.Warren Logan Allee, son of Sen. Alee,
              Olean, Mo. (Eldon,Mo.) homeplace
 Jesse b. /13/1888 " Harry Kraus,widowed, m. Lynn Gearhardt.
 Ellen b. 9/12/1890 " Thomas Cuthbertson(NY), 1 dghtr Jeanne
              b. 3/9/1918
 Cirrelda, b.11/11/1894 married Dr. Otis E. Burris, 3 children(Okla.)
                in recent yrs.

Children -
                                    Martha Elizabeth b. 11/11/1922
                                    Cirrelda Franklin b. 9/14/1922
                                    Otis E. Jr., b. 1/18/1928
    William Thomas, b.6/ /1897,
              d. in service, Camp Pike, Ark. World War I, buried Eldon

      Dr. W. L. Allee and Maude Allee's children-
         Dr. James William Alee, b. 10/31/1907, m. to Elizabeth Galt
               James Galt, b. 4/8/1941; Sidney, b. 10/4/1942
         Laura Elizabeth Allee, b. 8/16/1912, married Robert Hinz
               Nell Franklin, b. 12/23/1945
Mary Cirrelda Franklin, b. 12/15/1860 (married Robt. S. Harvey-Eldon, Mo.
    b. 12/15/1860   (1/15/1880)   Merchant & banker now
                                              retired and living in
                                              Pomona, Calif.
    Children: (Mary Cirrelda Franklin and Robt. S. Harvey)
       Ralph S. Harvey, b. 1/15/1883, married Norah M. Penn of KC. (in recent
                                                   yrs. -Pomona, Calif.)
            1 son Robt. S. Harvey, b. 3/27/1914, m. Marie Persons 9/14/37
                 1 son, Robt. S. Harvey, Jr., b. 5/15/1943
       Bertram T. Harvey, b. 10/26/1885, married Antoinette Webber, 6/5/1907
                 Mary Elizabeth, b. 2/27/1911, m. Henry Persons, 9/8/32
                          Antoinette, Ellen, & Henry Harvey
                                                          Persons
                 Bertram T. Harvey, Jr., m. Marjory Hayden
                          Bertram T. Harvey, III, b.
                                                         12/31/41
                          Susan   b. 9/6/1943
       Opal Harvey, b. 12/10/1889, married Elmer Hale, 6/5/1913 (McAlester, Okla)
            Cirrelda Hale, b. 2/19/1916, m. Thomas Barnard
                          Cirreldia Barnard
                          Francis Ann "
                          Mary
            Elmer Hale, Jr., b. 2/7/1919
Mary Ellen Franklin, b. 12/21/1862 married Richard G. Spalding, b. 1/17/1864
                                                                    (Okla)
    Roscoe H. Spalding, b. 2/22/1887, married Loraine McCoughey
    Bessie, died in childhood
    Charles Spalding, b. 8/22/1891, married Leona Peck
Nancy Melcena Franklin, b. 12/20/1865, married Edward Nathaniel Harvey, Eldon
                    d. 2/ 5/1934   and Aurora Spgs., Miller Co., Mo.
    Bernice Lucille Harvey, b. 2/9/1889, married Ray McMeans 6/7/1910.
                                                                 He d. 11/1919
         (born in Aurora Spgs., Mo.)   " Vernon Young in 1929
    Harry Franklin Harvey, b. 8/29/1897 married Marion Correll
              Herbert Edward, b. 2/15/1926 -served in World War II. Eldon,
                                                                       Mo.
              Jeanette, died in infancy, 2/ /1931
              William Franklin, b. 10/20/1932
              Walter Logan, b. 5/16/1936

John Byron Franklin, b. 7/10/1870, d. 2/15/1930 (Eldon & Olean, Miller Co., Mo.)
    Eulah B. Franklin, b. 3/9/1895, married Charles Hardy of Vandalia, Mo.
         Mary Hardy.

Charles Perry Franklin, b. 8/25/1873, d. 8/5/1929, married Katherine Lesher,
                    buried Eldon Cemetery.   b. 1/10/1875
                                                          d. 12/25/1945
  Harry John Franklin, b. 1898, d. 11/17/1946, married Mary Leslie,
    Jeannine Leslie Franklin, b.6/6/1938   Russelvelle, Mo.
  Lucy Waldon Franklin, b.7/14/1906, married Howard Bridges 2/4/1933-
    Jane Franklin, b. 11/24/1933   St.Louis, Mo.
    William Edward, b. 1/30/1936
    Howard Kisner, b. 8/3/1943

William Simms Brockman (son of Simms & Rachel Gartin Brockman)
  b. 8/11/1853, d. 8/19/1911   married to   Lou Anne Reed -
  (Their children)
  James Arthur Brockman, b. 12/3/1870 married to   Dora Hendricks
                      d. 6/8/1947 in Ft. Scott, Kans., buried at Ulman,
                                                          Miller Co., Mo.
        Basil, died in service, World War I, 1918
        Alfred
        Mrs. W. T. Mead
  Clinton Oliver Brockman, b. 9/16/1872 married   Martha McGorder
    (Physician)   d. August, 1929   (Miller Co. Mo.)
    Bernice Brockman, b. 3/30/1903 married Maurice Boguard,
                                    later Richard Wallace (Ill.)
    Mildred Brockman, b. 6/29/1907 married Walter Nelson (Conn.)
        Barbara Nelson, b. 12/20/1931
        Ann Nelson   b. 5/17/1937
(William Sims Brockman, later married Mrs. Alice Harbison. They had two
        children: (Later, widowed, she married Dr. Henry
                                                Hugh Brockman)
    Helen Brockman -b. 1889, married McClanahan, had one daughter,
    Dr. William Henry Brockman, b. 1892, single,   Billy
        served World War I. (Eldon, Miller Co., Mo.)

- - - - - - -

Mary C. Brockman, b. 12/12/1874, married Dr. W. Spalding, 2/24/1897,
  Elmo Spalding, b. 1/1/1900   Jefferson City, Mo.
Walter Brockman, b. / 1876 married Daisy Slifer -Bagnell Miller,Co.,Mo.
- - - - - - -
Dr. Henry Hugh Brockman (son of Simms & Rachel Brockman)
  b. 2/7/1850, d. 8/25/1925   married   Mahala A. Walker, b.7/3/1851
                          (4/3/1872)   d. 5/11/1912
                  Both buried at Eldon Cemetery, Eldon, Mo.
  Lucy Leona Brockman, b. 1/24/1873 -died as a child.
  Eliza Ellen "   b. 8/2/1875 -married Frank Haynes(he died 4/7/
                                      no children   1935
  Laura Brockman, b. 5/10/1878, d.1937 -married Robt.E.Thornsberry
                          (8/8/1896)   b. 4/15/1878
                                                               d. 12/31/1915
                                                Ulman, Miller Co., Mo.
    Harry Elmo Thornsberr, b. 8/29/1897 -married Opal Clark
    Mabel Ethel Thornsberry,b.8/29/1898 " Stanley Keyes 5/12/1918
    Henry Ray Thornsberry   b.9/29/1901 " Blanch Reed
    Lulu Ann Thornsberry   b.8/24/1903 " Donald McClaskey
    Ralph Franklin Thornsberry, b. 3/24/1905 married Pauline Steeley

James Clinton Thornsberry, b. 1907 married Ruth Campbell
Susan Marie Thornsberry, b. 4/24/1910 " Donald Meeks
Perry Thornsberry   b. 1913

Dr. John Alonzo Brockman, b. 5/17/1882, married Bertie Cooper 5/17/1905
   Cedric Alonzo Brockman, b. 4/21/1906, married Jeannetta Marshal(Cal.)
      Susie Brockman, b. 8/1943 (Lonnie married Mrs. Daisy Choppell,
      Sally Brockman, b. 3/9/45   1940)
   Henry Franklin, b. 1/25/1913 -single, served World War II overseas
   Mary Genevieve, b. 9/12/1918 -married James Curnett, later Thos.
                                   Digman, no children
                                   Loretta Curnett, b. 2/12/1937
Dr. Wm. Henry Brockman, b. 5/30/1885 -married Flora Randalf (b. 7/26/1887)
                           m. 9/12/1906
   No children, but raised Flora's sister's daughter Dorothy Snayman,
                           b. 12/2/1907
                           " married J. P.
                           Banks, 11/12/1940
Mahala Ethel Brockman, b. 5/12/1887 -married John Perry Self, b. 10/28/1883
   Kenneth Brockman Self, b. 10-8-1910, married Marjorie Ewer in Oct.
                           26, 1940
                         " born in Hamadan, Persia,
                         11/4/1906
                         while her father was teach-
                         in boys' school there.
                         The Sharene (wife of
                         ruler) sent for Marjorie's
                         mother to bring the babe
                         to her so she could see
                         the first white child
                         (American) born there.
     Brockman Campbell Self, b. 1/11/1942
     Helen Ewer Self, b. 3/9/1945
   Virginia Lorraine Self, b. 1/9/1913 -single-at home-Kansas City
   James Howard Self, b. 8/5/1915 -married Helen Craig.
                         James Howard Self, b. 10/24/1939
                         Pamelai Jeanne Self, b. 3/9/1944

* * *

COLLINS OF KING and QUEEN

Prior to her death, Mrs. Virginia Baker Mitchell wrote a book on the Gholson Family which was published by Mrs. Margaret Scruggs Carruth, 3715 Turtle Creek Boulevard, Dallas 4, Texas, in 1950. This book dealt with the Gholson family and stated that the wife of Joseph Collins, who died in 1757, was Sussannah Lewis. She states that Sussannah was a close relative of the Zachary Lewis family and cites certain deeds witnessed by Zachary Lewis I and Zachary Lewis II and Waller Lewis who was a son of Zachary Lewis II, born on January 1, 1702, and who married Mary Waller in 1725.

Zachary Lewis I came to Virginia in 1692; had two sons, John and Zachary. He also had daughters but all trace of them has been lost. Sussannah Lewis Collins would have been about the right age to be the daughter of Zachary Lewis I. It is interesting to note that on January 6, 1768, Sussannah Collins was still alive and signed over her interest in her personal estate to her children. She had already signed over her real estate to her children prior to November 13, 1760, at which time William, Thomas and Lewis sold to their brother John all the interest which they expected to have in the real estate of their father, Joseph, at the death of their mother, Sussannah. This deed was witnessed by Lewis, Sr. and Jr., and Waller Lewis and several others.

WILL OF ELIZABETH COLLINS

In the name of God Amen

I Elisabeth Collins of the County of Kershaw and State of South Carolina very weak and in a low condition but of sound mind and memmory cauling to mind the mortallity of my body and knowing it is appointed for all persons once to die. I do make ordain this my last will and testament in the manner and form as followeth....

Imprimis...First I give and bequeath to my eldest son Edward Collins one shilling sterling...

Secondly I give & bequeath to my son Lewis Collins one shilling sterling.

Thirdly I give & bequeath to my daughter Lowis Gayden one shilling sterling and no more...

Fourthly I give and bequeath to my Gran Son Jackey Pery Son of Lamud Pery deceased..one negro woman by the name of Nancy..and her child by the name of Milley..My own lodging feather bed and furnature..one Flimnap Fhilley with a blase face..two cows and calves four head of ...

Fifthly I give and bequeath to the gran daughter Betsy Gayden daughter of George Gaydens..one negro girl by the name of Claricy..

Sixthly I give and bequeath to my youngest son Willie Collins my plantation and tract of two hundred acres of land whereon I now live to him and to his heirs and assigns for ever..also my living stock of every kind exclusive of my husbands will..

Seventhly I constitute and appoint my youngest son Willie Collins and Thomas Gardner Executors to this my last will and testament disannuling and revoking all other testaments wills codecils of wills by me made ratifying this my last will and testament...

Witness my hand and Seal this....day of....1796...and in the Twenty first year of the independence of the United States.

Signed sealed and acknowledged in presence of us/...

	her
C. Gayden	Elizabeth E Collins
Mary Platt	mark
Peggy Johnson	

A TRUE COPY
ATTEST: William R. Gettys
Probate Judge for Kershaw
County, South Carolina

* * *

LEWIS COLLINS WILL

In the name of God Amen, I Lewis Collins of the State of North Carolina in the County of Granville being in sound health and memory but calling to mind the uncertainty of this life do make and ordain this my last will

& testament in manner & form following:
First & principaly I give my soul to God who gave it trusting in the merits of Saviour Jesus Christ for perfect remission of my sins and my body to the ground to be disposed of at the discression of the exr. hereafter named.
Item. I lend to my dearly beloved wife Elizabeth the tract of land and plantation whereon I now live during her natural life and six negroes viz, Cupid, Plimoth, Peg, Amey, Peter & Plimeth with the whole of my stock, household furniture and she my said wife complying with my following bequests. viz -
Item. I give and bequeath to my daughter Louis Gaton a negro wench named Violet, a feather bed and furniture, one horse and saddle, two cows & calves, the same being already delivered but if it should please God that my said daughter die without lawful issue then the estate given her to return & be divided among my other children.
Item. I give and bequeath to my daughter Betsey Robinson in Virginia two negroes Feedy & her youngest child which child I don't know the name of as it's born since I delivered the wench with their future increase. Also cattle, bed & furniture which things are already delivered to her heirs and assigns forever.
Item. I give and bequeath to my son Edward Collins a negro girl named Choice, one mare and saddle already delivered, one bed and furniture, two cows & calves to him his heirs and assigns forever.
Item. I give and bequeath to my son Lewis Collins, a negro boy named Jack with one horse and saddle, one bed and furniture, two cows & calves to him his heirs and assigns forever.
Item. I give and bequeath to my son Wiley Collins a negro girl named Phillis, one horse and saddle, one bed & furniture, dollars at six shillings, to him his heirs and assigns forever.
Item.. I give and bequeath to my daughter Diannah Carter Collins One negro boy named Isom, with one horse & saddle, one bed & furniture, two cows & calves, also a seal'd skin trunk to her, her heirs and assigns forever.
Item. After the death of my said wife the estate left or lent her I give to be divided amont my five children Louis, Fdward, Lewis, Wiley & Diannah Carter or their representatives, but if any of them die with out lawful issue, then to those living or leaving issue except my land which I leave to my oldest son or his heirs and assigns forever.
Item. & lastly I constitute and appoint my loving wife Elizabeth & my sons Edward & Lewis Collins executrix & Executors of this my last will & testament, given under my hand & seal this 16th day of September in the year of our Lord 1783.

                              Lewis Collins (Seal)

Sealed signed & published by the said Lewis Collins to be his last will & testament before us. John Taylor Mourning x Matlock
                              her mark
This will was duly proved by the oath of John Taylor esq. and ordered to be recorded then Flizabeth Collins qualified as Executria & Fdward Collins & Lewis Collins qualified as executors to the said will.
                              Reuben Searcey, C.C.

THE GAYDEN -COLLINS FAMALIES
by Mrs. Benjamin Robertson
5855 North Four Mile Run Drive
Arlington, Virginia

The first Geo. Gayden's estate was probated Richmond, Co., July 2, 1718. George Gayden, II, will proved the 5th of September, 1764 of the County and Farnham Parish, Virginia. Married first Elizabeth _____? and had: George, born 4 Jan. 1739; Elizabeth, born 19 June, 1742. After Elizabeth died George Gayden remarried Hannah _____? and had: Winny, born Mar. 1750; John Gayden, born 19 Apr. 1753. In George Gayden's will the following children are listed: George Gayden; Elizabeth Nixson; John Gayden. Winny probably died young. (The name is also spelled Gaton, Graydon, Gayton, Gaiden, Gaydon). John Nixson presented the will into court and it is likely he is the husband of Elizabeth (Gayden) Nixson.

George Gayden, born 4 Jan. 1739 is next found in Orange County, Virginia, in which he purchases 100 acres of land on the West side of Mine Run from Nicholas Porter and wife Sarah in Oct. 1772. No wife is mentioned. In Sept. 1775 George Gayden and his wife Nanny sell this 100 acres in Orange County, Virginia, to William Cave.

John Gayden son of George Gayden, born 19 April 1753 North Farnham Parish, Richmond County, Virginia, son of George Gayden (died 1764) and Hannah _____? He is a half brother to my 4th great grandfather, George Gayden who went to Amite County, Mississippi.

He married 9 March 1773 Catey Collins, daughter of William and Elizabeth (Bashaw) Collins, in Orange County, Virginia. He gave his place of residence as St. Thomas Parish. John and Catey evidently moved to S. C. to be near the parents of Catey. Their records have been pieced in various ways. Their children:

1. George Gayden born S. C.
2. Sarah Gayden born 14 Feb. 1775 Kershaw County, S.C. died 20 June 1849 in Carroll County, Miss. Married Jesse Duren
3. Abner Gayden born in S. C. died in 1803
4. Charles Gayden born in S.C. (I havenot been able to find him but he is listed in a "Gayden History" compiled by Robert A. Love)
5. William Gayden born 16 April 1784 Lancaster Co., S.C. died 5 July 1815 Married Tempey Titus Pipkin. (Mr. Robert A. Love's ancestors)
6. George Gayden, Jr., born in S.C. died in 1818. Married Frances Rutledge. The 1810 census of Lancaster Co., S.C. shows 2 George Gaydens and 2 John Gaydens as heads of families. (None of these are children of my George Gayden of Amite Co., Miss.)
7. Uriah C. Gayden age 62 in 1850 (1788) born in S.C. Married first Miss McWaters; 2nd Malinda____? Went to Lumpkin County, Georgia.
8. Elijah Gayden age 60 in 1850 born in S.C. died 8 Jan. 1863. Married Sarah Gladden. Resided in Fairfield County, S.C.
9. Susanna Gayden age 60 in 1850 born in S.C. died in Yazoo Co., Miss. Married James D. Russell
10. John Gayden age 59 in 1850 (Coosa Co., Ala.) (1791) born in S.C. Married (a sister of Miss McWaters') Margaret McWaters. Was in Carroll Co., Ga., in Heard Co., Ga., 1850 in Coosa Co., Ala., 1860 in Coosa Co. and died in Sunflower Co., Miss.
11. Spencer Gayden age 55 in 1850 (1795) born in Lancaster Co., S.C. Married first Mary ____? 2nd the widow of his brother, George Gayden, who died in 1818, Frances (Rutledge) Gayden.
12. Reuben Gayden born in S.C. 1798 died in Carroll Co., Miss. Married first Susannah Boyd, 2nd a widow, Jane Hearn, (nee?) Note: that Sarah (Gayden) Duren went to Carroll Co., Miss., also.

The 1790 census shows that John Gayden had 7 males and 3 females in the household. The tradition is that Catherine (Collins) Gayden outlived her husband and remarried again.

The next we find George Gayden is where he signs the Oath of Allegiance 22 May 1778 in Nutbush District, Granville County, North Carolina. It is evident that Nanny Gayden went with her husband George Gayden as we know that their third child, Agrippa Gayden was born in South Carolina. So, we know she must have been with him when he took the Oath of Allegiance.

The next we find that Nanny must have died and George Gayden married Lois Collins, daughter of Lewis and Elizabeth Collins 4 Dec. 1782, in Granville County, North Carolina.

We find that George Gayden is a signer of an Indenture in which John and Catherine (Collins) Gayden are selling land to Elizabeth Collins, the widow of Lewis Collins. A short history of what we know of Lewis Collins is in order:

Lewis Collins signed a petition 17 Jan. 1770 in which the Inhabitants of Island Creek, are praying for a road, etc. It was in this same District in which he signs the Oath of Allegiance 22 May 1778, in Granville County, North Carolina. Both of these can be found in N.C. State Records. Lewis Collins made his will 16th Sept. 1783 and it was proved May court 1785 in Granville County, North Carolina. He left his wife who appears to have been a second wife, Elizabeth. The following children are listed: Louis(Lois) Gaton; Betsey Robinson of Virginia; Edward Collins; Wiley Collins; Lewis Collins; Diannah Carter Collins.

Now, to pick up where we find that Elizabeth Collins, widow of Lewis Collins, of Granville Co., N. C. has purchased land from John Gayden and his wife Catherine. This is an abstract of this record:

(Office of the Clerk of Court, Lancaster County, S.C.)
OLD DEED BOOKS   LANCASTER DISTRICT
A-192 Recorded July 16, 1788
    This indenture made March 24, 1787, between JOHN GAYDEN & CATHERINE, his wife, and ELIZABETH COLLINS. - - -200 acres on both sides of White Oak Creek ---to James McCullough's line---being part of a tract to Reason Nelson.

Wit. Fd Collins   John Gayden
    Willia Collins   Her
    George Gayden   Catherine o Gayden
                                        Mark
                         John Lowery, J.P.   July 12, 1788

Of course this John and Catherine Gayden are half-brother and sister in law of George Gayden. The Elizabeth Collins is George Gayden's mother in law and the two Collins boys are the brother in laws of George Gayden. I feel that there is a kinship between Lois Collins' father and the father of Catherine Gayden. That remains to be proven.

Betsy Gayden was willed the slave girl Claricy, the final link proving that she was the daughter of the George Gaydens who came to Amite County, Mississippi in 1801. So, Lewis Collins who died in Granville County, N.C. and his wife, Elizabeth are also my ancestors. In fact, 5th great grandparents on my maternal line. George Gayden who died in 1764 in Faranham Parish, Richmond County, Va. and his first wife, Elizabeth are my 5th great grandparents on my maternal line. The Betsy Gayden married William Morgan and they are my 3rd great grandparents on maternal lines. I carry the Morgan, Gayden and Collins name twice.

In the inventory of Lewis Collins there is this mentioned:
"6 negroes to wit Plimoth Cupid Pegg Peter & Plimoth & Amey the last mentioned one now in possession of William Robinson of Culpepor County, Virginia. I wonder if this isn't the husband of "Betsey Robinson of Virginia", daughter of Lewis Collins?

George Gayden was not in the 1790 census. I have not been able to find where he and his family were. But he is listed in the 1800 U. S. census of Kershaw County, S.C. But before a year was up he and his daughter Rebeccah (who already had two marriages) Wrenn left and were supposed to have been a year in Tenn. In the Memoirs of Louisana, however, a grandson Iveson Greene Gayden states that they came to Amite County, Mississippi in 1801. They were listed in the 1805 U. S. Census which was taken prior to the forming of the county of Amite from Wilkinson County.

"I. G. Gayden, Esq., is a prominent planter of East Feliciana Parish, La., but is a native of Amite Co., Miss. where he was born in Jan. 1825, a son of Agrippa and Margaret (Lea) Gayden, the former born in South Carolina and the latter in Tennessee. Agrippa Gayden came west with his parents in 1801 and settled in Amite County, Miss. ten miles south of Liberty several other families coming thither at the same time. They went overland to the muscle shoals of the Tennessee River, there built a flatboat and floated down the river to Natchez, when they came across country to Amite County, Miss. Agrippa was born in 1779, a son of George Gayden, a native of South Carolina and a soldier of the Revolution War." etc. (Taken from Memoirs of La.)

We have not been able to prove that George Gayden had a service in Revolutionary War. We have already shown that he was born in Virginia and not as stated in S. C. Many in East Feliciana Parish Louisiana tells the same story. A book by Henry Skipworth on "East Feliciana Parish, Louisiana" tells of the early pioneers of this area. In one part of the book it tells of a son of Edward Collins (brother of Lois Collins) "who was killed by a drunken Indian". This was a son of Edward and Elizabeth (Lee) Collins, named Wilie. His widow, Elizabeth (Perry)Collins married Agrippa Gayden before she reached Mississippi. Wilie Collins was killed "enroute". He left 4 Collins children.

George Gayden and Nanny had:
1. Rebeccah Gayden, b. 27 Feb. 1774 probably born in Orange County, Va. Married first Mr. Leith and had: Parthenia. Mr. Leith was from Va. Married 2nd Francis Wren and had John Wren; Elizabeth Wren; Francis Wren; George Gayden Wren. All these children born in S.C. Married 3rd Thomas Batchelor 26 Dec. 1805 in Amite County, Miss. They had: Victoria Caroline Batchelor; Mary Ann Harriet Batchelor; James Madison Batchelor; Thomas Agrippa Gayden Batchelor; Napoleon Bonaparte Batchelor; Rebecca Batchelor died 14 Jan. 1836 Amite Co.
2. Gadesbey Gayden. He was a Justice of Peace in Amite County, Miss. I believe his wife was Polly, judging from a land record. He is listed as having children but I have not been able to learn their names. He died in 1841 in Amite Co.
3. Agrippa Gayden was born 21 July 1779 in South Carolina. He married first the widow of Wilie Collins, Elizabeth (Perry) Collins and had one child. I have not learned the name or sex of this child. He married second Margaret Muse Lea, daughter of David & Nancy (Clay)

Lea. Nancy Clay is a relative of Henry Clay. (see Memoirs of La.)
Agrippa Gayden died 7 Jan. 1845 in Amite County, Miss.
4. Martha Gayden (Patsey) married Lewis Perkins 12 May 1808. The marriage bond will be found at Woodville, Miss.

George Gayden and Lois Collins had:
  a. George L. Gayden. He married Sally Evans, daughter of Archibald and Charlotte Evans, of Claiborne County, Miss. Their marriage bond is in Natchez, Miss.
  b. Elizabeth Gayden age 65 in 1850 census of Amite County, Miss. was born in S. C. married William Morgan. She is the "Betsy" of Elizabeth Collins will which was proven 10 April 1804 in Kershaw County, S. C. Elizabeth Morgan's will was proved in 13 Feb. 1854. The will was made 1 April 1852 in Amite County, Miss.
  c. Diana Gayden married Charles Davis. I believe this is a record of their marriage: "At the River Amite, on the 23rd Mr. George Davis m Diana Gaydon 1808(?). (See "Wills and Other Records" Magnolia State Chapter DAR Miss. Vol. 2 1947 issue)
  d. Griffen Gayden married first Dorcas Wade at Natchez. He married second Mary Ann (McClendhan) Cooper, the widow of Hugh W. Cooper.
  e. Nash Gayden married Hannah Howard 6 June 1811 in Amite Co., Miss. He died in 1812 leaving one child, Serefina(or Seresina) Gayden.

This is the way I think the children are in order. I could be in error as to just whom some of these children belong. I mean to the wives. They are all George Gayden's children.

GEORGE GAYDEN'S WILL

In the Name of God, Amen. I, George Gayden, of the State of Mississippi and the County of Amite, Being of perfect mind and memory (blessed be God) do this 29th day of May in the year of our Lord 1819, make and publish this my last will and testament in manner following; that is to say:
First, I give and bequeath unto my beloved daughter, Rebeccah Batchelor, a negro girl named Violet.
Secondly, I give and bequeath unto my dutiful son, Cadesbey Gayden, two negroes, towit: Lyphex, a negro man, and Mariah a negro girl; and one small desk.
Thirdly, I give and bequeath unto my dutiful son, Agrippa Gayden, two negroes, towit: a negro man named Meriday and a boy named Simon.
Fourthly, I give and bequeath unto my beloved daughter, Patsey Perkins, a negro woman named Ferriby and her increase.
Fifthly, I give and bequeath unto my dutiful son, George L. Gayden, two negro men, towit: Frederick and Peter, and one half of the cows, horses and hogs.
Sixthly, I give and bequeath unto my beloved daughter, Elizabeth Morgan, one negro by the name, Isaac, two cows and calves and one hundred dollars, the money to be paid to her at the expiration of five years.
Seventhly, I give and bequeath unto my beloved daughter, Diana Davis, two negroes, towit: Isum, a negro man and Owen, a negro boy.
Eightly, I give and bequeath unto my dutiful son Griffen Gayden a negro man named Tom, and one half of the stock of cattle, hogs and horses; also one waggon and gears; also a negro man named Solomon and two beds and steds.
Ninthly, I give and bequeath unto my daughter in law Hannah Gayden $20.00 to be paid to her at the expiration of five years.

Tenthly, I give and bequeath unto my loving granddaughter Seresina Gayden $360.00 to be paid to her at the expiration of five years.
Eleventhly, I give and bequeath unto my grandson, George Gayden Wren $360.00 to be paid at the expiration of five years.
Twelfthly, I give and bequeath unto my grandson, Francis Wren $360.00 to be paid to him at the expiration of five years.
I hereby make and ordain my beloved sons, Gadesbey Gayden, Agrippa Gayden and George L. Gayden executors of this my last will and testament, hereby revoking and disannulling all and every other will and testament, legacies, bequests and executors by me in anywise before named, willed or bequeathed, ratifying and confirming this and no other to be my last will and testament.
IN WITNESS WHEREOF. I have hereunto set my hand and seal the day and year above written.

George Gayden

Signed, sealed, published and declared
by the said George Gayden, testator, in the
presence of us who was present at the time of
signing and sealing hereof, and testified by us in the
presence of the divisor.
Daniel Wilkinson
William Morgan

State of Mississippi
Amite County
Personally appeared in open court Daniel Wilkinson and William Morgan, who being duly sworn, saith that they saw George Gayden, Dec'd sign, seal and acknowledge the within will and testament and that they signed the same in the presence of the testator and in the presence of each other.

Daniel Wilkinson
William Morgan

Sworn to and subscribed in open court June 8, 1819

Thos. Batchelor, Clerk

* * *

Elizabeth Gayden married William Morgan. Their children were:
1. Phoebe Morgan m Daniel Myres
2. William Morgan. He evidently died young. When his father died in 1830 he was mentioned in the will but in the settlement he was not.
3. Hiram Morgan age 25 in 1850 census. He married Augusta E. Hamilton.
4. Fielding Bradford Morgan was age 38 in 1850 census. He married first _____? and had three children; 2nd Amanda Elvina Duck, dau. of James and Mary (Peoples) Duck 4 Jan. 1844 Amite Co., Miss. Fielding Bradford Morgan and Amanda Elvina Duck are my 2nd great grandparents, on the maternal side.
5. James Morgan, I know nothing of him.
6. Benjamin Morgan, I know nothing of him.
7. John G. Morgan age 32 in 1850. He was born in Amite County, as all of William and Elizabeth (Gayden) Morgan's children were. John G. Morgan married first Sarah A. E. Sites, dau. of Leonard and Cynthia (?) Sites. They had one child, Cynthia Elizabeth Morgan. John G. Morgan and Sarah A. E. Sites are also my 2 great grandparents. John G. Morgan married 2nd Clorinda (Sleaper) Torrance, the widow of Robert L. Torrance. I have always wondered if John G. Morgan's full name wasn't John Gayden Morgan.

8. Wiley Morgan was age 43 in 1850 census of United States. He married Margaret M. Wilson, dau. of Daniel & Mary (?) Wilson, 15 July 1831 in Amite County, Miss.

Fielding Bradford Morgan and his second wife, Amanda Elvina Duck had the following children:
1. Fielding Brandford Morgan b. 31 July 1846 Amite County, Miss. He married his first cousin, Cynthia Elizabeth Morgan, dau. of John G. Morgan, 13 Dec. 1866
2. Gayden Wrenn Morgan Morgan age 2 in 1850 census (1848) born in Amite County, Miss. married 4 Jan. 1872 Mary A. Brabham
3. William Hamilton Morgan age 1 in U. S. census (1849) born in Amite County, Miss.
4. Hiram Morgan, age 7 in 1860 U. S. census (1853) Amite Co., Miss.
5. Robert H. Morgan age 5 in 1860 U. S. census (1855) Amite Co., Miss. Married Alice A. Neyland.
6. Priscella Morgan age 3 in 1860 U. S. census (1857) Amite Co., Miss. Married Ray Callender.
7. May Morgan age 22 in 1880 U. S. census (1858) Amite Co., Miss.
8. Marshall Morgan age 15 in 1880 U. S. census (1865) Amite Co., Miss. Married 2 June 1891 Ella McKey.
9. Amanda Morgan age 13 in 1880 U. S. census (1867) Amite Co., Miss.

Fielding Bradford Morgan by his first wife, name unknown, were:
1. Victoria C. Morgan age 13 in 1850 (1837) Amite Co., Miss. She married Jefferson D. Anderson 20 July 1859
2. Benjamin F. Morgan age 10 in 1850 (1840) Amite Co., Miss.
3. John Morgan age 6 in 1850 (1844) Amite Co., Miss.

Fielding Bradford Morgan, Jr. b. 31 July 1846 Amite County, Miss. married his first cousin Cynthia Elizabeth Morgan, dau. of John G. and Sarah A. E. (Sites) Morgan, 13 Dec. 1866. They had the following children:
1. Beatrice Morgan, b. 13 Sept. 1867 Amite Co., Miss. married Jimmy Duck
2. Claude Udeave Morgan b. 14 Dec. 1869 Amite Co., Miss. married Alice Ophelia Beasley 19 April 1889 (My grandparents on maternal line.
3. Loyola Morgan age 5 in 1880 U. S. census (1875) Amite Co., Miss. Married Seamore Lilly 25 June 1889. She died 23 June 1890.
4. Mittie Morgan born abt. 1877 Amite Co., Miss.
5. Eulalia Morgan age 2 in U. S. census 1880 (1878) Amite Co., Miss.
6. Leonard Fielding Morgan b. 18 June 1860 Amite County, Miss. Married 1st Della Hogans 21 Aug. 1902
(Note: Benjamin F. Morgan, brother of Fielding Bradford Morgan is shown as a single man in the 1880 census, age 41.)

The wife of Fielding Bradford Morgan, Cynthia Elizabeth (Morgan) Morgan was born 16 July 1843 Amite Co., Miss. She died 10 May 1905. She was the only child of her parents, John G., and Sarah A. E. (Sites) Morgan.

Fielding Bradford Morgan, Jr. married a second time to Sarah Elizabeth Goodman, dau. of George and Rhoda (Glasscock) Goodman 8 June 1905. They had:
1. Hinds Hartstein Morgan b. 7 Apr. 1906; d. 28 July 1924. Married Rhoda Freeman 4 July 1923 Amite Co., Miss.

2. Fielding Bradford Morgan b. 24 Feb. 1908; d. 19 Feb. 1914 Amite Co., Miss.
3. Clarence Morgan b. 23 June 1910 married Maggie May Blalock 16 April 1930 Amite Co, Miss.
4. Rufus Morgan b. 23 July 1913 Amite Co., Miss. married 23 June 1936 Eva Edna Tarver.
5. Sarah Madeline Morgan 24 June 1917 Amite Co., Miss. married 16 April 1932 Edgar Lilly
6. Drew Morgan b. 13 June 1920 Amite Co., Miss. married 22 Nov. 1939 Julia Mae Brabham

Claude Udeave Morgan was born 14 Dec. 1869 Amite Co., Miss. He died Sunday 7 May 1950. He married Alice Ophelia Beasley, dau. of Cornelius A. and Delila Jane (Woodall) Gammons. They had the following children:
1. Donnie Morgan b. 19 Jan. 1890 died 1897 Born Amite Co., Miss.
2. Pearla Ann Morgan b. 20 Jan. 1892 Amite Co., Miss. Married 25 Dec. 1909 Van Cavin
3. Mattie Delila Morgan b. 9 April 1893 Amite Co., Miss. married Moses Marlven Blalock 6 Oct. 1909 (My parents)
4. Elois Middle Lean Morgan b. 13 Jan. 1895 Amite Co., Miss. Married 22 Dec. 1915 Smyley Callender.
5. Willie Morgan 4 Jan. 1897 Amite Co., Miss. died July 1898
6. Frank Eugene Morgan b. 21 Jan. 1898 Amite Co., Miss. Married Thelma Jeraldine Welch 20 Dec. 1917
7. Hattie Rosebell Morgan b. 28 Nov. 1900 Amite Co., Miss. Married 18 Jan. 1915 G. B. Blalock
8. Howard Thomas Morgan 27 Mar. 1902 Amite Co., Miss. Married 18 July 1926 Velma A. Lilly
9. Gladys Alice Morgan b. 28 Mar. 1904 Amite Co., Miss. Married 10 Dec. 1919 Lloyd Callender
10. Myrtice Morgan b. 28 Dec. 1905 Amite Co., Miss. died 17 Mar. 1909
11. Claude (CE) Morgan b. 24 May 1907 Amite Co., Miss. Married 30 April 1930 Loraine Bass
12. Fannie Lee Ola Morgan b. 18 Feb. 1909 Amite Co., Miss. Married 24 Dec. 1925 Frank Lilly
13. Jannie Morgan b. 31 Jan. 1911 Amite Co., Miss. Married 27 April 1929 Monroe Johnson
14. Alma Hazel Morgan b. 31 Jan. 1912 Amite Co., Miss. Married 25 July 1928 Cornelius Hatch.
15. William Aughty Morgan 12 Jan. 1916 Amite Co., Miss. Married Reba Jewell Blalock 8 Jan. 1937

Mattie Delila Morgan born 9 April 1893 Amite Co., Miss. Married Moses Marlven Blalock (really is Blaluck) b. 6 June 1890, Centreville, Wilkinson County, Mississippi, the son of John Milton and Amanda Jane (Hastings) Blaluck. The following children were born of this union:
1. Amanda Ophelia Blaluck b. 14 July 1910 Amite Co., Mississippi. Married Benjamin Otis Robertson 1 Jan. 1927 in Dayton, Ohio
2. Lola Lydia Blaluck, b. 15 Sept. 1911 Amite Co., Miss. married William Joseph Martin 15 Aug. 1932 in Buffalo, N. Y.
3. Daisy B. Blaluck b. 12 Feb. 1913 Amite Co., Miss. Married 1st Earl Shandrew 19 Sept. 1930 in Xenia, Ohio. Resided in Kenmore, N.Y.
4. Moses Blaluck, Jr. b. 11 April 1920 Dayton, Montgomery County, Ohio; died 11 April 1920. He lived one half hour. Mother had the measles and when he came into the world, he too, had the measles.
5. Morris LaSalle Blaluck b. 12 Dec. 1921 Dayton, Ohio, married Zula Belle Hayes 9 Dec. 1943. Reside in Washington, D. C.

6. Al Charles Blaluck, b. 27 Aug. 1924, Dayton, Ohio, married Mary Louise Green 24 Oct. 1946 in Arlington, Virginia. Reside in Springfield, Va.
7. John William Blaluck b. 2 Sept. 1926 Dayton, Ohio married 24 Dec. 1947 Lula D. _____?, a widow. They are now divorced.
8. A. B. Blaluck (That is his full name) b. 20 Dec. 1914 Amite Co., Miss. married 1st _____? and divorced, married 2nd Elizabeth Jane Proff 8 Jan. 1942. Reside in Duluth, Minnesota

Note: Most of the ones listed as living in Amite County, Miss. lived near Liberty.

Amanda Blaluck. b. 14 July 1910; Liberty, Amite County, Miss. married Benjamin Otis Robertson b. 2 Feb. 1902, Peru, Indiana, son of Booker Jefferson and (his first wife) Laura Luella(Gable) Robertson, Jan. 1, 1927 in Dayton, Ohio. Their children are:
1. Arthur Paul Robertson b. 11 Oct. 1928 Buffalo, N. Y. He married Helen Louise Batchelor 3 May 1947. Reside in College Park, Md.
2. Joyce Muriel Robertson b. 9 July 1931 Buffalo, N. Y. Married James Clifford Tiedt 9 June 1950. Reside in Fullerton, Calif.
3. Inex Helen Robertson b. 26 Sept. 1934 Buffalo, N. Y. Married 30 Nov. 1954 Edward Rose. Reside in Los Angeles, Calif.
4. Carol Jean Robertson b. 6 Sept. 1938 Washington, D. C.
5. Frances Camille Robertson b. 23 Feb. 1940 Washington, D. C.
6. Benjamin Otis Robertson b. 9 Dec. 1950 Arlington, Va.

Arthur Paul Robertson, son of Benjamin Otis and Amanda (Blaluck) Robertson was born 11 Oct. 1928 Buffalo, N. Y. He married Helen Louise Batchelor b. 29 April 1927 Rocky Mt. N. C., dau. of Carl Lot and Mallie David(Carey) Batchelor, 3 May 1927 in Folkston, Ga. Their children:
1. Susan Valli Robertson 12 Oct. 1951 Washington, D. C.
2. Ginger Ileen Robertson b. 30 Sept. 1954 Washington, D. C.

Joyce Muriel Robertson born 9 July 1931 Buffalo, N. Y. and married James Clifford Tiedt, son of John Edward and Reba May (Gotellus) Tiedt, born 5 Oct. 1919 El Reno, Okla. Married 9 June 1950, Santa Ana, Orange County, Calif. Their child:
1. James Clifford Tiedt b. 8 Oct. 1954 Santa Ana, Orange County, Calif.

* * *

WILLIAM MORGAN'S WILL

In the name of God, Amen-
    I, William Morgan of the County of Amite in the State of Mississippi being weak of body but of perfect mind and memory calling to mind the mortality of the body, that it is appointed for all once to die, do make, ordain and constitute this and no other my last will and testament in manner and form following, that is to say-
    First of all it is my will and desire that all my just debts be paid out of my estate after which the following disposition be made of the same, to wit: Second
    It is my will and desire that all my estate shall remain and be kept together on my plantation for the maintenance and education of my

children, until my youngest sons William and Hiram Morgan arrives at the age of fourteen years, at which time I wish all my estate both real and personal to be equally divided among my dearly beloved wife Elizabeth Morgan and all my children, towit, Phoebe Morgan, Willie Morgan, James Morgan, Fielden Morgan, Benjamin Morgan, John Morgan, Diana Morgan, William Morgan and Hiram Morgan, each one to share and share alike in equal degrees and should my dearly beloved wife marry before the aforesaid William and Hiram Morgan arrives at the age of fourteen years, then and at that time, or as soon thereafter as may be convenient I wish the aforesaid division to take place, each one sharing alike, in manner aforesaid, in all my estate both real and personal-

It is my further will and desire that my son Fielden Morgan shall have the care and management of my plantation and hands, until a division shall take place, the proceeds of which to go to the maintenance of my family. Lastly

I do hereby nominate, constitute and appoint My dearly beloved wife Elizabeth Morgan my Executrix, until a division shall take place, and my son Willie Morgan my Executor to carry into effect this my last will and testament.

Signed, Sealed, pronounced and declared by the aforesaid William Morgan as his last will and testament the Twenty eighth day of May, in the year of our Lord one thousand eight hundred and thirty-
in presence of
Tho. Batchelor
Griffen Gayden   WILLIAM MORGAN   (SEAL)
William Spinks

* * *

Agreeable to an order from the Hon. the Probate Court in and for the County of Amite, in the State of Mississippi, directed to the undersigned, we have this 14th day of Apr. 1839, proceeded to value and appraise the following property belonging to the estate of William Morgan, deceased and allotted to his last will and testament in the manner following, viz,

To Mrs. Elizabeth Morgan
Clarisa, a negro woman	$400.00	
Betty and her child Elmira	$800.00	
One feather bed and furniture	$ 30.00	total $1230.00

To Mrs. Phoebe Myers, formerly Phoebe Morgan
Pender, a girl	$800.00	
Horace, a boy	$450.00	
One feather bed and furniture	$ 30.00	total $1280.00

To Willie Morgan
Bob, a boy	$850.00	
Mereday, a boy	$375.00	
One feather bed and furniture	$ 30.00	total $1255.00

To Fielding Morgan
Sarah, a girl	$750.00	
Aron, a boy	$175.00	
One feather bed and furniture	$ 30.00	total

To John Morgan
Solomon, a negro man	$850.00	
Alford, a boy	$250.00	
One feather bed and furniture	$30.00	Total $1130.00

To Diana Corcoran, formerly Diana Morgan
Mary, a girl	$475.00	
Joe, a boy	$750.00	
one feather bed and furniture	$30.00	Total $1255.00

To Hiram Morgan
Asker, a negro boy	$750.00	
Amelia, a girl	$475.00	
One feather bed and furniture	$30.00	Total $1255.00

The whole amount of appraisement and estate of $8360.00
Seven Legatees, each one's share is $1194.24 and ½

Mrs. Elizabeth Morgan, will pay to Fielding Morgan $34.10
Mrs. Phoebe Myers, formerly Phoebe Morgan to pay to Fielding Morgan $85.71
Wilie Morgan will pay to Fielding Morgan $60.71½
Mrs. Diana Corcoran, formerly Diana Morgan to pay to Fielding Morgan $60.71
Total $230.28 and ½
The above sums is over their respective shares.

* * *

MORE ABOUT SIMS

While indications are that Agatha, second wife of William Sims of Albermarle was a Robinson, the name of her first child Anester suggests that Agatha was sister of the first wife of William Sims. Other evidence suggests that Agatha was daughter of Thos. Hill and wife Elizabeth Gray. In January 18, 1723 William Beverly bought from William Cleveland 118 acres near Tandie's Mill, formerly Rouse's, now Brooks Mill, also 210 acres nearby. Agatha Beverly married William Robinson. Just how this land got into the possession of Francis Gray is not known, but on the death of William Sims, 1799, 104 acres of the 118 were transferred to Samuel Brockman of Albermarle and 14-3/4 acres to brother Ambrose Brockman. These brothers married sisters daughters of William Sims and wife Agatha. The first wife of William Sims was Anester Stap or Step, daughter of Joshua who was son of Abraham of Essex, will Oct. 20, 1710, wife Dorothy.

VIRGINIA HISTORICAL MAGAZINE

"On May 26th, 1748, Letty, a negro slave belonging to Mrs. Harriet Potter, of Middlesex County, Virginia, for some unknown reason, probably for change of venue, was tried by an Orange Court of Oyer and Terminer for mingling poison, water, bread and meat, and giving it to one Richard Sims, who ate and drank thereof, and did languish from the first of August, 1746, until the fourth day of January 1747, then he died in Middlesex County; and did also give poison to a negro man, Simon, a negro slave of John Grymes of said County, who languished from September 30, 1746, to May 1747, when he died. The court decided that Letty was not guilty and ordered her release; probably leading to her acquittal was the feeling that the horrible scene so recently enacted at the burning of Eve should not be repeated in Orange County.

Dr. A. G. Grinnan"

* * *

FROM MOTHER'S RECORDS
by Pauline Brandt
Norfolk, Virginia

George Weston Mitchell, Sr. is a graduate and post graduate of the Miller Manual Labor School, Albemarle County, Va., awarded the Miller Scholarship at the University of Virginia (mathematics, physics and applied mathematics). Afterwards took the senior year in the Mass. Institute of Technology in mechanical engineering, 1911-1912. Summer semester at the University of Michigan and also at Columbia University, New York City.

Served as instructor in mathematics at Miller School and taught drawing, Virginia Mechanics Institute, Richmond, Va., Head of Drawing Dept. at the Rose Polytechnic Institute, Ind., Head of Drawing Dept., Springfield Technical School, Mass., Associate Professor of Descriptive Geometry and Drawing at the University of North Carolina (4) years. In charge of Math. Dept., the Baron de Hirsch Trade School, and head instructor of the West Side Y.M.C.A. in Engineering Drawing, Machine Design and applied Mathematics, 1921-32.

George W. Mitchell, Sr. married Mrs. Lucy McAllister Brown, a widow, one son., George W. Mitchell, Jr., born Aug. 2, 1913. He graduated from Plant High School of Tampa, Florida, graduated from the State University of Florida, Gainsville, Fla.

* * *

For your records -
My nephew - Howard Carlyle Mayo and Norma Motley Ramsey were married January 16, 1954. -Mrs. Pauline Brandt.

* * *

1441 Oxford Rd.
Charlottesville, Va.
Jan. 20, 1956

Dear Mr. Brockman,

Mrs. Pauline Brandt, Norfolk, Va., asked me to send you my family data. I obtained her name from your "Brockman Scrapbook" in my research of the Rhodes family. I am the great, great granddaughter of Thomas Rhodes who married Mary Brockman April 5, 1813.

I hope you will be able to understand my notes as I am very new at this hobby. With the help of my mother's (Meta Rhodes Miller, age 75) knowledge of the family I started my research of the family one year ago. Prior to that time I knew very little of my ancestors. I am a housewife and mother and my spare time is limited. As you can see my family data is far from being complete. I hope to be able to add missing names and dates in the future.

I haven't found any relationship of my family of Rhodes to the Rodes who settled in the western part of Albermarle County and Rockfish Valley (now Nelson Co.) or the Rhodes (sometime spelled Roth) who settled in the upper Shenandoah Valley of Virginia.

I have read part of both of your books and enjoyed them very much. Prior to "finding" your "Brockman Scrapbook" I did not know anything about my gr. gr. grandmother, Mary Brockman, except the date she married my gr. gr. grandfather Thomas Rhodes.

Sincerely,
Mildred Marshall (Mrs. W. G.)

THE RHODES FAMILY
"The Old Middlesex Parish Register" (Va.)

Ezehias Rhodes m. Elizabeth Nicholls Oct. 22, 1684. Children:
1. Mary Rhodes b. Jan. 5, 1685
2. Alice Rhodes b. July 18, 1687
3. John Rhodes b. Feb. 12, 1689
4. Elizabeth Rhodes b. July 1693 d. July 22, 1706
5. Ezeckias Rhodes b. April 6, 1696
6. William Rhodes b. April 23, 1698
7. James Rhodes baptised Dec. 9, 1702
8. Seth Rhodes b. Jan. 2, 1705

Ezekias Rhodes died April 14, 1720
Elizabeth Rhodes died July 18, 1727

William Rhodes m. Hanner Miller Sept. 13, 1722, children:
1. Hezekiah b. Oct. 8, 1723
2. William b. Dec. 3, 1724
3. John Rhodes b. Nov. 4, 1727
4. Christopher Rhodes b. Nov. 25, 1730
5. James Rhodes b. Feb. 1, 1734, d. April 11, 1738

Orange County Clerk's Office - April 2, 1744 Will Book No. 1 P. 313
William Rhodes names wife Hannah - children:
1. William Rhodes
2. John Rhodes
3. Christopher Rhodes
4. Hezekiah Rhodes
5. Benjamin Rhodes

March 8, 1762 Will Book No. 2 P. 333
Hezekiah Rhodes names wife Ann - children:
1. Epophrodites Rhodes
2. Hannah Daughaumey
3. Mary Rhodes
4. Jane Dickinson
5. Grandson John Dickenson

Epophrodites Rhodes m. Ann White (See "Early Settlers of Alabama" by Sanders & Stubbs)

"Early Settlers of Alabama" by Sanders & Stubbs" - (White Family) p.458
Conyears and Mary White of Legistershire, England, had a son John
White, who came to Virginia and married Ann Widsom of King and Queen
County, Va.

Orange County Records - Orange Courthouse, Va.
Will of John White, date Aug. 8, 1787, names wife Ann White, children:
1. Thomas White
2. John White
3. Conyear White
4. Heirs of daughter Mary Shacklford, deceased
5. Theodosia Early
6. Francis Phillips
7. Ann Rhodes
8. Sarah Leathers

Albermarle County Records, Charlottesville, Va. Nov. 17, 1772 Deed Book 6
Epphrodites Rhodes and wife Ann bought 300 acres from George Waller
on Jacobs Run. (near the present Advance Mills, Va.)
Aug. 21, 1780 - Epphrodites Rhodes bought 200 acres (Glebe land) from
Thos. Johnson & Wm. Sims, church wardens of Fredericksville Parish of
Albermarle County. (this land bordered his other property.) DB 12, p.225

Epphrodites & Ann Rhodes children:
1. Nancy Rhodes (unmarried at time of her father's death)
2. *Theodosia Rhodes m. James Riddle March 27, 1788
3. Susan Rhodes m. Thomas Marshall Dec. 13, 1792
4. Sally Rhodes m. Richard Marshall 1809 (moved to Missouri)
5. Mary Rhodes m. Benjamin Nailor Nov. 1804
6. Franky Rhodes m. Andrew Fleak Oct. 22, 1795
7. Milly Rhodes m. James B. Watson 1810
8. Hezekiah Rhodes m. Mary Watts (daughter of Rev. Jacob Watts)
9. John Rhodes m. Mary Martin Nov. 2, 1815
10. Reuben Rhodes m. Tabitha ____ (?) (dec'd)
11. Thomas Rhodes m. Mary Brockman April 5, 1813

* Most of the above information came from a booklet "Some Descendants of
Thomas Marshall & Susannah Rhodes" by Mrs. Obadiah Boss, Lexington, Ky.,
Dec. 31, 1939, now owned by Dr. J. W. R. Smith, Charlottesville, Va.
(This is not a published book).

Albermarle County Records Will Book 6 -
April 5, 1816 - Epphrodities Rhodes names wife and the above children.

Epophrodities Rhodes divided his land among his four sons.
Jan. 19, 1797 Epphrodities Rhodes & wife Ann to Reuben Rhodes (son) DB12, p.23
  95 acres - 20 pounds
Jan. 13, 1797 -Epphrodities Rhodes & wife Ann to John Rhodes (son) DB12, p.236
  101-3/4 acres   20 pounds and gift.
Jan. 19, 1797 -Epphrodities Rhodes & wife Ann to Hezekiah Rhodes (son), p.240
  114 acres   20 pounds and gift
Aug. 17, 1810 -Epprodities Rhodes & wife Ann to Thomas Rhodes (son) DB17, p.163
  198 acres   gift

In 1820 Reuben, Hezekiah and Thomas Rhodes sold their land and seemed
to have left the country. However in 1834 Thomas Rhodes and wife Mary

Brockman signed deeds for property left by her father William Brockman, Jr. If Thomas Rhodes did leave the country they came back and lived (or it would seem) at Burnleys, Va.

Thomas Rhodes m. Mary Brockman April 5, 1813, children:
- Horace Rhodes m. Sarah Jane Spicer Dec. 20, 1838; children:
  - Daniel Rhodes m. Mildred Catherine Poindexter Dec. 23, 1868 children:
    - William Rhodes m. Kate Pyler (Pence Springs, W. Va.)
      - William Rhodes m (?)
      - Virginia Rhodes m. Theodore Ripberger, Kenbridge, Va.
      - Ashly Rhodes
    - Florence Rhodes m. David Jacobs 1916 (both dead, no heirs)
    - Charlie Rhodes m. Annie Noeland in W. Va.
      - Lawrence Rhodes -single (Hamlet, N. C.)
      - Elaine Rhodes - single (Hamlet, N. C.)
      - Regionald Rhodes m. Amy __(?) (Charlotte, N. C.)
    - Lossie Rhodes m. Fannie Noeland (W. Va.)
      - Mary Rhodes - single
    - Meta Rhodes m. David Miller Jan. 17, 1917
      - Mildred Catherine Miller b. Apr. 17, 1918, married Woodie Gordon Marshall Nov.28,1935
        - David Marshall b. Jan. 7, 1937
        - Adele Marshall b. Sept. 21, 1950
  - James Rhodes - (died in Civil War - unmarried)
  - Catherine Rhodes (died unmarried - lived Burnlys, Va.)
  - Martha Jane Rhodes (died unmarried -lived Burnlys, Va.)
  - Boy (?) -died unmarried
  - Samuel Epophrodities Rhodes m. Gilly Clark (Somerset, Va.)
    - Clyde Rhodes m. Robert Roberts
    - Maggie Rhodes m. ____(?) Watson
    - Virgie Rhodes m. ___(?) May
  - Nannie Rhodes m. Austin Domron
    - Leslie Domron (They lived at Burnley, Va. All are dead now. No heirs)

Daniel Rhodes died 1906 (my grandfather)
Mildred Catherine Poindexter Rhodes died 1921 (my grandmother)

My mother Meta Rhodes Miller lives at Barboursville, Va. She and my uncle Lossie Rhodes, Talcott, W. Va., are the only living children of my grandfather, Daniel Rhodes.

My grandfather Daniel Rhodes married my grandmother Mildred Catherine Poindexter at Burnley, Va. My grandmother was reared by her aunt and uncle Mary Mitchell who married Samuel Edward, Vurnleys Va. after the death of her parents Classisa and Joseph Poindexter. A few years after my grandparents marriage they moved to Illinois and lived two years (my grandmother had uncles in Illinois) They they moved to Missouri (my grandfather had uncles in Missouri). My grandfather's health became poor and the doctor advised him to return to Virginia. They came back to Virginia and later bought property in Albermarle County near Barboursville Va. There they spent their remaining years.

Thomas Rhodes and Mary Brockman Rhodes children cont'd:
  William Rhodes (he married twice, no heir, moved to Missouri. My mother thinks it was near Marshall Missouri.
  Sally Rhodes m. William Wood Aug 1, 1843.(lived at Barboursville,Va).
    1. John Wesly (died age 2 yrs)
    2. Jim Wood m. Jenny Mahoney
    3. Thomas Wood m. Marion May
    4. Jane Wood m. Jim Brown

              Orange County Records
  Mary Ann Rhodes m. Brice Edwards Dec. 23, 1848, lived Stony Point,Va.
    1. Brice Edward, Jr. (they had other children but I do not know their names. Brice Edwards was the son of Thomas Edwards who married Agatha Brockman. Brice, Mary Ann, Brice, Jr. Edwards are buried at the old Mitchell Brockman cemetery Burnleys Va. Some of Brice Jr. descendants live in Baltimore, Mr.

              Albermarle County Records
Epophrodities Rhodes m. Julia Edwards Aug. 30, 1855. She was the daughter of Thomas Edwards who married Agatha Brockman. They moved to Missouri (near Marshall, Mo.) I do not know any of their descendants).

I do not know the year my gr. gr. grandmother Mary Brockman Rhodes died but in 1843 Thomas Rhodes and wife Christian signed a deed for the same of property belonging to quote: "Mary Brockman, first wife of Thomas Rhodes, and daughter of William Brockman, Jr."
              Albermarle County Records

Thomas Rhodes m Christiane ____(?) (have been told she was a Drumright but I haven't found their marriage license). Children:
  Thomas Rhodes m. Sarah Beck June 30, 1868
    1. William Rhodes b. Nov 30, 1868
    2. Olivia Rhodes b June 26, 1871
    3. James Rhodes b Jan. 11, 1873
    4. Julia Rhodes b. Nov. 26, 1874
    5. Herbert Rhodes b. Dec. 1876
    6. Osar Lee Rhodes b. Jan. 1, 1879
    7. Eugene Rhodes b. March 15, 1881
    8. Peyton Rhodes b. 1883
    9. Hugh Rhodes b. Jan. 1885
  George Rhodes m. Emma Hicks Feb. 7, 1868
    1. Ervin Rhodes m. Molly Perry
      children:
      Raymond, Robert and Julia (they live in Hamlet, N.C.)
    2. Alex Rhodes
    3. Charlie Rhodes
    4. Julia Rhodes m ____(?) Head
  John Rhodes m. Alice Harris
    (9 daughters -moved to Richmond, Va)

I do not know when my gr. gr. grandfather Thomas Rhodes died but I think that he, his first wife Mary B. Rhodes and son Horace Rhodes (my gr. grandfather) were buried at Burnley, Va. in the old Mitchell-Brockman Cemetery. Of this I have no actual proof.

Records from Priddy's Creek Baptist Church, Albermarle
by Mrs. Mildred Marshall of Charlottesville, Va.

"Priddy's Creek Church Organized in 1781 -
Thomas Smith bapt. Aug. 11, 1876
Mary F. Brockman Sept. 10, 1866
Mary A. Rhodes now Edwards 1871 (I think she was the daughter of
   Mary Brockman Rhodes)
James W. Brockman received by letter Aug. 1891, dismissed by letter
   March 17, 1895 (probably son of Walter D. Brockman and wife Ann
   Fergerson Brockman)
William S. Brockman
Brice W. Edwards Sept. 12, 1890, dismissed by letter March 1898 (either
   son or grandson of Agatha Brockman Edwards)
Leonard Edwards bapt. Aug. 20, 1893
Robert A. Edwards Aug. 15, 1902
Ann E. Brockman (perhaps the wife of gr. uncle Walter D. Brockman)
Mrs. Elizabeth Brockman (I imagine this was great grandmother)
Mrs. Sarah Rhodes
Miss Martha Jane Rhodes Oct. 1876
Mrs. Ann E Brockman died Dec. 1895 (wife of Walter D. Brockman??)
Mrs. Mary F. Brockman died April 26, 1906
Mary A. Edwards died 1903

   Elizabeth Brockman died April 3, 1888 (I am sure this was great
grandmother, Elizabeth Catterton Brockman as she died shortly after
my mother's marriage March, 1888. The Mrs. Elizabeth Brockman listed
above may have been a record of her membership in the church)
Mrs. Mary F. Edwards dismissed by letter March 19, 1898
Fannie Brockman 1893

Mrs. Marshall copied the following from Edwards tombstones in our
cemetery at Burnleys. -
Mary A. Edwards born Dec. 22, 1827 - died 1903 (she was Mary Ann
Rhodes daughter of Mary Brockman who married Thomas Rhodes. Mary
Brockman Rhodes was daughter of William Brockman Jr.)
Brice Edwards born 1823 died 1899 (Brice Edwards was the son of
Agatha Brockman & Thomas Edwards)
Brice Edwards, Jr. born 1854 died 1909 (son of Mary Ann Rhodes and
Brice Edwards, Sr.

Poindexter Family
   Joseph D. Poindexter married Clarissa Jane Mitchell June 15, 1833
(Clarissa Jane Mitchell was a sister of my grandfather Andrew Jackson
Mitchell. Their parents were Nelly Wood and John Mitchell, who were
married in 1813 Orange Co., Va.)
Children of Clarissa Jane Mitchell and Joseph D. Poindexter:
   1. Mary Margaret Poindexter b. Dec. 25, 1834
   2. William S. Poindexter b. Jan 12, 1837 -moved to Ill.
   3. Jane P. Poindexter b. Aug 15, 1839 died 1840
   4. Martha Alice Poindexter b. Nov. 6, 1844 m. Robert Rohr and had
      two children, Alice and Joe (both dead)
   5. Mildred Catherine Poindexter b. 1844 m. Daniel Rhodes (I gave
      you their descendants in the Rhodes data & was named for her)
   6. Isaac Newton Poindexter b. Aug. 1847
   7. John Andrew Poindexter b. March 6, 1850 -moved to Ill.
   8. Sarah Ann Poindexter b. April 8, 1855 - m. John Thompson

and had eight children all dead now but some descendants in Orange Va. After Sarah Ann died John Thompson married a cousin of hers and my grandmother, Susan Poindexter)
9. Joseph D. Poindexter b. May 1, 1809 d. Nov. 3, 1854
10. Clarissa Jane Mitchell b. 1819 died 1856

The above information came from an "Age Book" but my mother doesn't know what became of it. Our Poindexters were from Louisa County but so far I have not been able to connect them with "The Poindexter Family" in the History of Louisa County by Harris.

* * *

WOOLFOLKS OF VIRGINIA

Richard Woolfolk lived in Abingdon Parish, Gloucester 1678-1761. He was on the Quit Rent Rolls in 1704, with 125 acres. He moved to Holly Hill, Caroline and his brother Robert moved to Shepherd Hill, Caroline. His oldest child Richard II born 1684 lived in Spottsylvania, Orange and Albermarle, and is thought to have died in Albermarle between 1770 and 1775. He is believed to have married Catherine Benson daughter of Chas. and Eleanor Benson. His children are believed to have included Richard III, who married Mary Coleman, according to one source, but he may have married a daughter of Thomas Sowell, of Albermarle as his first wife and had Sowell or Soyell, Joseph, Richard, and Sukey. All apparently went to Woodford County, Ky. The other children of Richard II are believed to have included, a daughter, who was first wife of Edmund Burrus, brother of Thomas Burrus, who married Frances Tandy; Mary, the first wife of Samuel Brockman II. Proof is not available, but certain events suggest this conclusion. Richard II was the approximate age of Samuel Brockman I. He owned 920 acres in Orange County which was patented either by himself or his father Richard. Richard II of Albermarle disposed of his Orange County land, apparently in anticipation of death, since he left no will and no estate was entered for probate. He was 86 in 1770. The land transfers were June 28 of that year: 400 acres to Samuel Brockman II; 300 acres to John Henderson; 200 acres to John Burrus, son of Edmund and the wife of John Burrus was Ann Henderson, daughter of John, who then deeded 100 of his 200 acres to Samuel Brockman II. These deeds coincide with the death of Joseph son of Richard I therefore it would appear that the land patent of 1726 in Orange County was by Richard I, and then passed on to the sons and granddaughters. These transfers are significant including the transfer of 161 or 165 acres to Samuel and William Brockman and Rebecca, wife of Samuel, for their lives, in 1785 which coincides with the death of Elizabeth the mother of Joseph who made the transfer. This transfer did not increase the taxable land of Samuel of 800 acres, therefore it was clearly a deed by Joseph to give up any claim his mother Christian had in this land as widow of Joseph father of Joseph. In 1772, when Richard II was then deceased, Richard III came into 300 acres in Albermarle from Robert Hardwick, and in 1784 he sold it to Ephiram Boeing, leaving then for Kentucky.

Other children of Richard I of Gloucester include Robert, born 1688, died 1744, wife Frances, children Robert married Ann George, Richard and John, who died 1766; Betty, born 1690, married Ambrose Bullard; Joseph, born 1696, and had children John, who married Elizabeth Wigglesworth, and 2nd Mrs. Sarah Tartlow; Elizabeth, who married Henry Chiles and second Chas. Dibb, whose son Thomas married Sarah Brockman; Augustine, who married Ann Harris 1st and 2nd Mrs. Broun; Joseph, who married Christian Bibb, and died by 1771, when his widow Christian married Samuel Brockman, whose first wife was Mary Bell; Captain Thomas W. (Waller) who married Miss Southerland and lived in Orange County, and finally Robert of Caroline, who married Mary Hackett, dau. of Garrett.

The other children of Richard I were Mary, baptized 1696, Martha baptized 1703 and Justine, baptized 1706 and had daughter Justin who married Timothy Chandler. Mary may have been the mother of John Henderson, since there is a Henderson-Woolfolk connection and John Henderson brought his mother, a widow, to Orange when he came, having patented land there in 1728, and he named one son Richard I Henderson and this Richard married Peggy Brockman of Albermarle. Richard Woolfolk showed tithes in Orange County as follows, 1737...6; 1753...6; 1754...9 and 8 in 1758, so that the supposition that he had daughters who married Samuel Brockman II and Edmund Burrus has foundation. I have accounted for only two of the daughters of Richard II and others I believe may have been the wife of John Oakes, Sr., executor to Joseph Woolfolk and legatee of Edmund Burrus; the wife of John Fmlrey, Sr. whose will 1786 named Samuel Brockman, Thomas Woolfolk and son Richard Embree, executors, along with Richard Woolfolk the latter having been guardian of the children of John Burrus. Another daughter may have married Lawrence Young, who was witness to the will of Joseph Woolfolk whose wife was Christian Bibb.

* * *

Comments on Woolfolk Chart owned by Mrs. Ann Waller Reddy, Richmond, Va.

Richard Woolfolk of Albermarle, son of Richard (2) sold 400 acres of land in Orange County to Samuel Brockman, June 28, 1770. This land had been mortgaged to Mitchell and Associates in 1764. The deed recites that it is part of a 1728 patent of 920 acres.

Robert Woolfolk of Orange married Ann George. His son Richard went to Jefferson County, Ky., before 1800. Married in Virginia probably 1st a daughter of Thomas Sowell and 2nd Sarah, daughter of Capt. Zachary Taylor and wife Alice Chew. John H. Woolfolk, Will Woodford September 12, 1813 (son of Sowel) named as legatees, Samuel Cox (wife, Mary), brother Thomas, brother Sowell, Jr., brother Joseph and sister America Baker. Sowell Woolfolk, Sr. went to Woodford after the Revolutionary War. Married Mary Harris, in Virginia. Their children: Joseph Harris, m. Mariah Mitchum; John, in War of 1812, illed in action; Sowell, Jr. married Sallie Barnum, was in War of 1812; William; a daughter m. Givens.

Joseph (2) may have died 1770 instead of 1771, for in 1770, Richard transferred land to Samuel Brockman. Elizabeth, widow of Joseph, died 1785, and that year Joseph Woolfolk, son of Joseph and Christian confirmed the transfer of 161 acres to Samuel Brockman and wife Rebecker for life then to William Brockman. This was a part of the 400 acres that Samuel bought from Richard Woolfolk in 1770 and was probably the dower interest of Elizabeth, mother of Joseph.

Joseph Woolfolk, wife Christian Bibb, Will at Orange 1778. Named his wife, John Oakes and brother John as executors, and brother Thomas W. (Waller?) as alternate executor. John Woolfolk died 1778, administration at Halifax, wife Lucy, daughter Anne, also administration at Orange, November 27, 1778. Thomas Woolfolk, Sr. in 1795 DB 20, P.503 (could not have died 1794) gave 500 acres in Orange to son Thomas "land given me by my father Joseph". Thomas Woolfolk's children included William, m. Ellis; Col. John, m. Mary Champe Stannard; Thos. m. Frances Thompson.

DB19 p.133 1787 Thomas Woolfolk of Orange to Thomas Jr., and Patsy, John, Nancy, Fanny and Fendall, sons and daughter of the said Thomas Woolfolk, Jr. Nancy died single; left property to nephew John Cowherd (see order book Orange); Patsy m. James Alan, Fanny, m. Reuben Cowherd. Woolfolk legatees meet to make division of slaves among heirs of Thomas Woolfolk; Thos. Jr., Nancy, James Alan, Reuben Cowherd. DB 20, p.503

* * *

THE MERRY FAMILY

Interest in this family has been stimulated by the frequent appearance of the association of Brockman, Collins, Merry and Daniel. Just what the connection between these names is not known. One Thomas Merry, born in England, married Ann APPIHIRA Prettyman, according to Mrs. C. M. Crafton, one of the descendants. They settled in Norfolk County, near Merry's Point out of Newport News, and their coming to Spottsylvania and Orange is evidenced by Merry's mountain near Gordonsville. Relatives say that he had only one son Thomas, but the will of Prettyman Merry of Norfolk County, mentions one son John, under 21, sister Elizabeth, sister Mary, brother Thomas, Mary Tucker, daughter of William, (probated March 16, 1744). It seems apparent that this Thomas Merry and wife Ann Prettyman had at least four children.

It seems apparent that this Thomas Merry, son of Thomas and Ann Prettyman, married Elizabeth Stephens. Order Book of Oct. 23, 1762 calls for the division of property of "Thomas Merry, orphan of Thomas Merry and wife Elizabeth Daniel, late Elizabeth Merry". A son of Thomas Merry, Thomas married Agnes (Agatha) Thomas, since Owen Thomas left a will at Spottsylvania Nov. 8, 1759, and named wife Mildred and children Owen, Jr., whose wife was Elizabeth, and his will 1772 mentioned daughter Sarah Kenner Thomas, so we assume his wife was Elizabeth Kenner. Other children of Owen Thomas were James, Robert and Agatha. Dec. 14, 1768, Mildred, widow of Owen Thomas gave property to son James, and daughter Agnes, "wife of Thos. Merry". In 1769, Thos. Merry and wife Agnes of Orange sold 300 acres to Samuel Brockman, Jr., part of the estate of Thomas Merry, deceased. Also in 1769 Thos. Merry and wife Agnes and Reuben Daniel and wife Elizabeth (Elizabeth Merry) sold land in Spottsylvania to John Holliday. James Jones, in his will 1776 left a legacy to granddaughter Elizabeth Merry, but he does not indicate the name of Elizabeth's mother or father. Now Thos. Merry whose wife was Elizabeth left a will at Orange June 21, 1754, naming wife Elizabeth, children Elizabeth, Ann and Mary, all minors and sons Thomas, Prettyman and John, Owen Thomas and William Smith and wife Elizabeth were executors. When the will was probated Oct. 23, 1756, widow Elizabeth came into court and disclaimed any interest in the estate, October 23, 1760, Elizabeth Merry stated that she would marry Reuben Daniel, and that she gives to her youngest son James, one negro girl. The agreement was signed by Elizabeth Merry and Reuben Daniel. In 1771 Reuben Daniel, Thomas Merry and Prettyman Merry, for "love and affection", gave a negro boy to James, son of Thomas Merry, deceased. It is apparent that Elizabeth Merry, widow of Thomas had a child James born after the death of her spouse Thos., and with the consent of her new husband, Reuben Daniel, she gave the slave to her youngest son James. I am not sure of the various Merry connections, and am not a Merry student, but I will submit authoritative data that others interested may study and arrange.

Will of Prettyman Merry, county of Norfolk, Dec. 23, 1743: "To son John land when he arrives at age 21, and if he should die, the same to go to the eldest child of sister Elizabeth; 25 pounds, also 25 pounds to the eldest child of sister Mary and residue to brother Thos. Merry and to their heirs; a negro girl to Mary Tucker, daughter of William if son John dies."

Will of Thomas Merry, Spottsylvania (Orange) county, June 21, 1754, sons Thomas and Prettyman, land in Orange county, "and when my son Prettyman comes of age, he is to lay it off in two parts and give my son Thomas his choice. My three daughters Ann, Elizabeth and Mary, certain property when they come of age or marry". The rest of my property to my "three sons, Thomas, Prettyman and John". Executors, wife Elizabeth, Owen Thomas and William Smith. The will of Thomas Merry was presented into court Sept. 23, 1756, and Elizabeth Merry appeared in court and declared she would not join in the probate and that she would not accept any legacy given to her and did renounce all advantages she might claim by the said will. One Elizabeth Merry was licensed to marry Reuben Daniel November 7, 1756. Elizabeth Merry, widow, on Oct. 23, 1760 came into court and stated that she was going to marry Reuben Daniel and that she gave to her youngest son James a negro girl and the contract was signed by Reuben Daniel and Elizabeth Merry, proving that she was a widow, and likely, Elizabeth, widow of Thomas Merry. Jan. 19, 1763 a court order was issued dated Nov. 23, 1762 assigning to Elizabeth Daniel, supposed widow of Thomas Merry and the wife of Reuben Daniel, her dower rights. Elizabeth must have been deceased by 1771, as Reuben Daniel, Thomas Merry, Dec. 31, 1771, for love and affection gave a negro boy to James Merry, son of Thomas Merry, deceased.

The children of Thos. Merry and Elisabeth Merry were Thomas, who married Agnes Thomas, Ann who married William Walker, 1758, Mary who became of age 1762, and married John Walker, Elizabeth, Prettyman, who married Katherine Suggett in 1769, and had ten children including John, James and Samuel and went to Ky. In 1769, Thomas Merry and wife Agnes, transferred 300 acres to Samuel Brockman, and a few years later Samuel Brockman, Jr. and wife Mary sold this land to Robert Daniel, June 1771, as part of the estate of Thomas Merry, deceased. Owen Thomas made his will Nov. 8, 1759, and mentioned wife Mildred and children, Owen, and his wife Elizabeth and daughter Sarah Kenner Thomas, James, Robert and Agatha. Nov. 11, 1768, Mildred Thomas of Spottsylvania, transferred to son James and daughter Agnes, wife of Thomas Merry, certain property. In 1769 Thomas Merry and wife Agnes and Reuben Daniel and wife Elizabeth sold land to John Holliday. Incidentally, Thomas Merry and wife had a daughter Frankky, who married John Henderson.

Oct. 13, 1787, Harry Bartlett sold to Prityman Merry of Orange 500 acres in Fayette County, Ky., and this Prettyman who married Nath Suggett.

The confusion that exists is apparent, indicated further by this from Mrs. C. M. Crafton, Orange, Virginia. "I know something about the Merry family since my maternal great grandmother was Mary Merry daughter of Thomas and Elizabeth Merry. She married Thomas Walker of Culpeper. I have a copy of his will of 1824 and his wife Mary was still alive. John Walker's brother, William Walker, married Ann Merry (born 1740) sister of Mary Merry, in 1758. William died in 1807 and wife Ann in 1818. He served in the Revolutionary War. One Mary Merry married William Russell Mar. 12, 1789. There is much confusion of the marriages of the two Mary Merrys and the two Elizabeths. Thomas and Ann Prettyman Merry had children Prettyman, Elizabeth and Mary, also Thomas". There were two Mary Merrys who married John Walker and William Russell. This solution I leave to descendants as I have enough to work on in the Brockman line and my exploration has been due to the land transfers from Thomas and Agnes Merry to Samuel Brockman, suggesting that Mary first wife of Samuel might have been a Merry, which apparently is not the case, and then the three Daniels, Reuben, Vivian and one other that witnessed so many documents that involved the family of Joseph Collins, and this Collins connection with the Merrys and the Daniels I have not yet accounted for. Since Susannah Collins was a daughter of Zachary Lewis, and there was a Lewis Daniel, and the Daniels and Merrys intermarried, it might appear that this is the connection, and that one Lewis married a Daniel. Mrs. C. M. Crafton has worked out a chart which shows that Thomas Merry II, son of Thomas and Ann Prettyman married first Elizabeth Stephens, and on his death Elizabeth married Reuben Daniel. There is the marriage bond of Elizabeth Merry and Reuben Daniel in November 1756, which was only two months after the probate of the will of Thomas Merry, deceased husband of Elizabeth. The fact that she declined to participate in the estate of her husband Thomas in September 1756, might indicate that she had planned her marriage to Reuben Daniel shortly after the death of her husband Thos. Merry. In her statement Oct. 23, 1760 Elizabeth Merry said she was about to marry Reuben Daniel, but then says that Reuben consented to the gift to James, her youngest son, "before" the marriage was solemized", in effect saying that the marriage had already taken place (1756 ?)

* * *

CORRECTIONS TO ORANGE COUNTY FAMILIES VOLUME I

Page 64 Andrew Brockman married Milly (Amelia) or Milla Brockman, daughter of William Brockman of Orange and not Milla Leek.

Barney Brockman, born 1819 married Telitha Landrum.

Page 99. Oswald Brockman went to Christian County, Ky. Children were: Martha, John L., Sarah, Joseph, Virginia and Samuel. Wife, Frances (Shishler) Brockman.

Page 41. Brockman Scrapbook. Richard Simms married Mary Towles.

The land consisting of 350 acres in Albermarle County, left to sons Samuel and William by father Samuel, which was sold to John White, was sold by the executors of John White in 1806 to Jason Bobock, and was along his line, which establishes the location, as having been near the line between the present boundary of Orange and Albermarle, formerly in Fredericksville Parish, Louisa and possibly extending over into what was then Spottsylvania, hence the land must have been acquired by Samuel Brockman by inheritance, when that area was Hanover.

The will of John Hill, at Albermarle June 1793, mentions wife Jane and Ambrose Brockman as executors. Witnesses were Ambrose and William Mason Brockman, his brother, which supports the conclusion that their mother was Elizabeth Mason, before her marriage to the father of William and Ambrose.

James Brockman of Albermarle, died at Goochland Nov. 12, 1823.

Page 24 O.C.F. Margaret (Peggy) Brockman, daughter of old William, married Richard I. Henderson, son of John and wife Sarah Brockman Henderson. Frances, her sister, perhaps married James instead of John Taylor.

Page. 125 O.C.F. Mrs. Ellis R. Hall, (Mary Ethel Brockman) died in June of Leukeuma in Iowa, and Clarence Aubrey Brockman died of cancer in Parke Ridge, Illinois in the Fall of 1955.

BROCKMAN REVOLUTIONARY SOLDIERS

Ambrose, Charles, and Joseph of Albermarle; James, John, Lewis, Samuel and William of Orange; Major of Louisa; Joseph of Amherst; Jessie and Thomas, probably of Orange and Albermarle.

(130)

THE CAVES OF VIRGINIA

Mrs. Dale M. Thompson
6435 Pennsylvania Avenue
Kansas City, Missouri

February 7, 1956

Mr. W. E. Brookman
Minneapolis, Minnesota

Dear Mr. Brookman:

    I am descended from Benjamin Cave (d. 1762) Burgess from Orange County who married Hannah Bledsoe, dau of William Bledsoe by his first wife Anne. What I am especially trying to find is the proof of Benjamin Cave's parentage, and some information about his brothers and sisters, and his possible relationship to other Virginia families named Cave. Such Orange and Culpeper records as I have are tantalizing in the extreme--telling just enough to keep me looking always for more.

    My descent from Benjamin Cave is through his daughter Anne, who is often given, erroneously, as having moved to North Carolina. Anne married (1) Philemon Cavanaugh (Kavanaugh, Cananah, in her father's will Cavender) by whom she had Benjamin, Philemon and Elizabeth. The sons died unmarried. Elizabeth married the Rev. John Taylor and went to Kentucky. Their youngest daughter Sally, who married Joseph Smith (son of Temple Smith and wife Lydia Lane) was my great-grandmother. Anne(Cave) Cavanaugh married (2) William Strother of Orange and went to Woodford County Kentucky where he died in 1808; no children of second marriage. I know she survived him, but can find no record of her death.

    I have done several articles for the KENTUCKY REGISTER on the Rev. John Taylor who married Elizabeth Kavanaugh (Cavanaugh), and have become very much interested in her grandfather Benjamin Cave. A chart made by the English genealogist Tyrrell is preserved in some branches of the family, which gives Benjamin Cave's parents as the Rev. William Cave and his wife Anna Stonehouse (dau the Rev. Walter Stonehouse). The Rev. William and his father the Rev. John Cave (ejected clergyman in Cromwell's time) are both written up in Dictionary of National Biography, but I can find no evidence that Benjamin was the Rev. William's son; an abstract of the Rev. Wm's will does not mention him. It could be that he had received his portion and was already in America, but what I am inclined to believe is that the descent is from that family perhaps a generation earlier, and that still eludes me--which is why I want to check the possible brothers and sisters of Benjamin in Virginia. Green's CULPEPER COUNTY mentions a sister of Benjamin Cave who had written a devotional book called SPIRITUAL SONGS. It has also been suggested that the first wife of William Bledsoe may have been a Cave; her given name was Anne. William Bledsoe's second wife was Elizabeth, widow of Charles Stevens; her maiden name is also unknown. And his father George Bledsoe (Blettsoe, Pletso) also married an Ann and an Elizabeth (neither maiden name known). (one record says erroneously that one of William's wives was Mary).

    I am also interested in the Mallory family because one of Benjamin's daughters married Uriel Mallory, and the co. Leicester Caves in England also married Mallorys in several instances, so it might serve as a link to bridge the ocean.

If your book can help me in solving these several problems, I shall be most happy to know about it. Or, failing that, if you happen to know of any line of research which might lead to the material I am looking for, I shall appreciate any suggestion. A self-addressed envelope is enclosed. And thank you very much.

                Hopefully,

                Dorothy Brown Thompson
                (Mrs. Dane M. Thompson)

As far as the Mallory family is concerned, the woods around Orange are full of them in the early ages and I lived about two miles from the famous Mallory's Hill which led almost straight down over a rocky ridge to the North Anna River which separates Louisa and Orange. This subject is a large one and would require special study and that I am not prepared to do at this time.

                                          February 10, 1956

Mrs. Dale M. Thompson
6435 Pennsylvania Avenue
Kansas City 13, Missouri

Dear Mrs. Thompson:

    I have never worked on the Cave family, but have been interested because Benjamin Cave was witness to the Will of Samuel Brockman 1762, and there was a William Cave in the lower Counties the same period as Benjamin, Sr. Mention of the Cave family brings back to me the family that lived in Orange just across the North Anna River from my father's house. There was a Reverend Cave about the age of my grandfather who had a reputation for good spirits and being able to "curse like a sailor" during my time. But my thoughts go back to "cousin" Irene Cave and a dance given at the home of "Cousin" Charlie Mills, when as a teen ager I squired to this dance Rosa Lee Graves, daughter of Lewis, who is now married to a Kite and lives at Orange. Just why we called the Caves and Mills "cousin" I don't know. Charlie Mills was well-to-do and democratic but the Caves were haughty, and I recall staring at Irene who was a stunning brunette with off-the-shoulders evening black gown, who looked at me contemptuously in my farmer Sunday-go-to-meeting clothes. In those days only the sophisticated girls did "round" dances with men, but that night Charlie Mills, escort of Irene Cave, broke through the tradition and waltzed with my sister Josie.

    All the people down there married each other so we were all Cousins and it is fair to assume that one of the women who married a Cave was a Brockman, or else a Brockman married a Bledsoe, whose child married a Cave.

    In the chart prepared by D. N. Davidson and a Rawlins, 1734, Benjamin Cave is shown as having been born in 1680 and died 1790, which must be incorrect, as the Will of Benjamin Cave was dated 1762 (date of probate not available) and it is not likely he lived to 1790, so that it was Benjamin II who died 1790. David Cave, son of Benjamin I, left a Will at Orange July 7, 1752.

Legatees of Benjamin Cave, spouse of Hannah Bledsoe, were: wife Hannah, sons John, who had a son William who married Frances Christy June 10, 1783; William Cave who had a daughter Frances who married William Knight August 23, 1791; Benjamin II who had a daughter Elizabeth who married Nehemiah Hundly July 31, 1790; and Richard Cave. Daughters were Elizabeth who married William Johnson, and in 1786 married second William Brockman Bell; Sarah, Ann Cavender and Hannah.

Benjamin Cave II married Elizabeth Bellfield, born 1735 at Montebello, Orange, but must have died 1790. And it must have been Benjamin III who died 1832. Elizabeth Bellfield was daughter of Thomas Wright Bellfield and wife Mary Meriwether. The Benjamin who died 1832 had son Richard, born 1780 and died 1863, married Maria Porter; son Captain Bellfield, married Mildred Christy; and Benjamin Cave IV, married Elizabeth White January 21, 1794. Bellfield Cave was a Major in 1790. One Benjamin was a Colonial soldier in 1742. Robert Cave was administrator to Elizabeth Cave, 1735; and Benjamin Cave administrator of David Cave, 1764.

Frances Cave married William Knight August 23, 1791, bonds by William Cave. Bartlett Cave married Jenny Snow, December 22, 1796. Reuben Cave married Mary Ramsey January 1781, a daughter born May 13, 1781. Hannah Cave married Richard Parker June 2, 1781, daughter Mary born June 2, 1781. A Reuben Cave married Lucy McGee October 21, 1790. William Cave married Judy Jollet November 22, 1791.

Orange Deed September 22, 1768, Benjamin Cave to Samuel Brockman, 13 pounds for part of tract Brockman bought of Abraham Mayfield which said Cave recovered, gave him good title to 176 acres.

William Brockman Bell, Will Orange 1780, "to children of sister Milly Cave".

Sarah Bledsoe, daughter of William and wife Elizabeth Stevens, must have been deceased by 1769, since she was not mentioned in her father's Will, but her husband Benjamin, Ambrose and Robert Powell were witnesses to Bledsoe's Will. This from a Bible record.

Orange County Order Book October 28, 1779. Joseph Spencer, guardian of Philemon Kavanaugh, orphan of Philemon, bond by John Conner, 2000 pounds.

I have spent sometime on this Cave data but instead of charging you for it, perhaps you would like to buy one of my books described on the enclosed sheets. BROCKMAN SCRAPBOOK $10.00 ORANGE COUNTY FAMILIES $8.00. Messrs. Bryce O. Templeton, 11 Howell Road, Mountain Lakes, New Jersey and Robert Coleman Siegfried, 2202 Steples Mill Road, Richmond 23, Virginia have typed M.S.'s on the Bledsoe family.

               Cordially yours,

               W. E. Brockman
               c/o Midland National Bank
               Minneapolis 1, Minnesota

GAYDEN - MISCELLANEOUS

The first record of the surname Gaton-Gayton-Gayden-Gaiden-Graydon is that of Georg Gaton 1638, by Richard Maion, Charles River County, Virginia. "Early Virginia Immigrants" by Greer F225. G81

Ann Gedon, 1636, by Wm. Bibby, Accomack County, Virginia. "Early Virginia Immigrants" by Greer F225. G81

In "Hottens Emigrants to the American Plantations" appears this: Richard G. Gayton (Barbadoes) 26 acres of land 1 hired servant 1 bought servant 26 negroes. A list of owners and possessors of land Hired Servants and Apprentices, Bought Servants in ye Parish of St. Michael's.
<u>Wills of Rappahannock County, Virginia by Sweeney</u>:
Page 21 Ralph Greaydon wit. will of William Hodgkin 22 Mar. 1671/2
                                                 7 May 1673

Page 129 Joanna Graydon wit. will of William Travers Gent. 14 Feb. 1686/7
2 Mar. 1686/7

Page 124 Ralph Graydon wit. will of John Palmer 16 Sept. 1686
                                                 8 bris 1686

Taken from North Farnham Parish Register at Warsaw, Richmond, County, Va.:
   Born Ralph the son of Ralph Gayton and Joanna Gayton Oct. 2, 1680 Gayton
   Born George the son of Ralph and Joanna Gayton 22 Dec. 1682 Gayton
   Born John the son of Ralph and Joanna Gayton 14 Sept. 1684.

Susanna Gaden died 4 Feb. 1730/1
   Born George son of George and Elizabeth Gayton 4 Jan. 1739
   Born Elizabeth daughter of George and Elizabeth Gayden 19 June 1742 Gayden
Died George Gayden son of George Gayden 8 July 1744 Gayden
   Born Winney daughter of George and Hannah Gayton 7 Mar. 1750
   Born John son of George and Hannah Gayden 19 April 1753

Northern Neck Grants No. 5 1713-1719 George Gayden purchased 92 acres from Catherine Lady Fairfax 13th day of February.

Old Rappahannock County, Virginia Deeds No. 7 1682-1688
   Charity Webster by and with consent of Henry Webster her husband gives unto George Gayden the son of Ralph Gayden and Johanna his wife one young heifer and increase; if sd George Gayden die then to fall to Ralph Gayden, Jr. Signed 2 day of Sept. 1685.
Signed in presence of   sign
Francis Settle   Henry H Webster
James Taylor   sign
                                               Charity M Webster
Charity and Henry Webster are presumed to be the parents of Johanna, the wife of Ralph Gayden and the grandparents of Ralph, Jr., John and George.

28V 279 (23) Deed Sept. 3, 1756, from Ann Barber and Thomas Barber, Executors of Thomas Barber, gent., dec'd in Pursance of his will, make Conveyance to George Grayden, Richmond County, Va.

THE BLALOCKS

The preceding data on Gaydens and the following data on Blalocks was

(134)

supplied by Mrs. Amanda Blaluck Robertson:

John Milton Blaluck, born Feb. 30 about 1830, at Manchester, England, married Amanda Jane Hastings, May 14, 1864 at Woodville, Mississippi. He died Dec. 1905 at Centerville. His wife was born May 16, 1852 at Centerville, was daughter of Andrew Hastings and wife Mary Jane McGraw. She died near Liberty, Amite County, Mississippi, Jan. 20, 1929. Children:

1. William D. Blaluck, b. May 16, 1868, married Mar. 13, 1892, Irie Arnold, and died Aug. 4, 1895
2. Elonza Blaluck, b. May, 1870, married Mar. 24, 1892, Ella Elizabeth Welch, and died Dec. 27, 1934
3. Mary Jane Blaluck, b. Aug. 16, 1872, married Dec. 6, 1887 Sylanus McGraw (2) William Brown (3) Mr. Booth, died June 16, 1947
4. Emma Blaluck, b. Sept. 1873 died an infant
5. Jim Blaluck, b. Sept. 1873, died an infant
6. John James Blaluck, b. Feb. 8, 1875, married (1) Marie Welch (or Clara) (2) Katherine Delle McGraw, and died June 13, 1944
7. Ann Bell Blaluck, b. 1877, married May 11, 1894 Napoleon Brown, and died May 6, 1928
8. Corine Blaluck, b. Feb. 11, 1879, married June 11, 1896 John Melton Brown
9. Carrie Elizabeth Blaluck, b. Jan. 11, 1881 married Dec. 20, 1896 Archie Welch, (2) Mr. Lilly (3) Mr. Sherald, and died Jan. 15, 1937
10. Amanda Drusilla Blaluck, b. Mar. 6, 1883, married Sept. 30, 1900 Van Cavin and died Dec. 8, 1908 or Dec. 21, 1907
11. Reuben Blaluck, b. June 16, 1885, married Feb. 21, 1911 Cola Mae Wilson
12. Maggie Blaluck, b. May 10, 1887, married Feb. 25, 1906 Willie McGraw (2) John Willard Messer and died Nov. 27, 1928
13. Moses Marlven Blaluck (my father) b. June 6, 1890, married Oct. 6, 1909 Mattie Delila Morgan and died June 18, 1953. Buried in Baton Rouge La. Died at Veterans Hospital in New Orleans.

In 1870 Wilkinson County, Mississippi P. O. Woodville
J. M. Blaluck 34 born in England, father and mother of foreign birth.
Amanda Jane 18 born in Mississippi
William D. 2 Mississippi
Alonzo 1/12 Mississippi

In 1880 U. S. Census Wilkinson County, Mississippi
John Blaluck 44 husband born in England. Father and Mother born in Turkey
Amanda J. Blaluck 26 wife born in Mississippi. Father in Mississippi Mother in Mississippi
William D. Blaluck 13 son born in Mississippi. Father born in Turkey Mother born in Mississippi
Alonzo Blaluck 10 son born in Mississippi. Father born in Turkey, Mother born in Mississippi
Mary J. Blaluck 8 daughter born in Mississippi. Father born in Turkey, Mother born in Mississippi
John M. Blaluck 6 son born in Mississippi. Father born in Turkey, Mother born in Mississippi
Annie L. Blaluck born (4) in Mississippi. Father born in Turkey, Mother born in Mississippi
Corine 15 months born in Mississippi. Father born in Turkey, Mother born in Mississippi

(135)

Tithables in the precincts of James Pickett, Constable, 1738

Name	#	Name	#	Name	#
Thomas Rucker	3	John McDaniel	2	Mathias Castler	1
John Howard	1	David Phillips	2	Michael Cook	1
Wm. Crawford	2	John Zackary	2	Henry Snider	1
Benj. Coward	3	Wm. Phillips	5	Robt. Tenner	2
Rich. Mouldin	3	Thos. Zachary	1	Geo. Tenner	1
Thos. Morgan	2	David Zackary	2	Ludwich Fisher	1
Benj. Thomson	1	Ann Stogdill, Jr.	2	Geo. Teter	1
Major Levaune	3	Wm. Offill	1	Phillip Roots	15
Thos. Jackson	6	Jonas Archer	2	Henry Mccoy	1
Thos. Coleman	1	Jas. Stevens	1	Anthony Strother, Jr.	5
Fra. Pickett	1	Walter Vaughn	1	John Kelly	2
Michael Gary	2	David Ford	1	Wm. Stone	0
Isaac Tinsley	1	Anthony Head	3	Geo. Simmons	2
Henry Ware	3	John Haresripe	1	John Simpson	3
Wm. Rucker	1	Geo. Bruce	2	Thos. Jones	3
Wm. Pirce	1	Abraham Bledsoe	3	Joshua Yarbrough	2
Peter Rucker	6	Abraham Bledsoe, Jr.	1	Mark Wonnell	1
John Garth	3	Thos. Downer	1	Rich. Yarbrough	2
Thos. Stanton	1	Isaac Smith	1	Henry Sparks	1
Walter Vaughan	1	Wm. Terrill	2	Rich. Holcomb	3
John Rogers	1	Mark Stowers	1	Sam Creel	2
Walter Lenard	3	Sam Taliaferro	1	Cortney Browel	1
Thos. Brown	2	Guy Meek	1	Adam Carr	3
John Shelton	1	Henry Downs	2	Wm. Carpenter	4
Wm. Loggins	1	Michael Pearson	1	Rich Yager	5
Jonathon Gibson, Jr.	4	Robert Morgan	1	Thos. Watts	4
Martin Trapp	1	Benj. Cave	5	Edw. Watts	2
John Bush	2	Blair Ballard, Jr.	2	Thos. Edmondson	1
John Forrester	3	John Grymes Esq. Jr.	15	Geo. Thompson	1
Wm. Williamson	1	John Stone	1	John Phillips	3
John Farrow	1	Michael Holt	3	Wm. Henderson	3
Moses Battley, Jr.	5	George Long	1	Thos. Coker	1
Leonard Phillips	2	John Hoffman	1	John Edins	1
Patrick Walsh	3	John Carpenter	2		

Tithables in precinct of James Pickett, Constable, 1739

Name	#	Name	#	Name	#
Dogwall Crister	1	Adam Yager	1	Mathew Smith	2
Henry Crowder	1	Christley Browel	1	Wm. Rice	1
Chas. Blunt	1	John Hansborgow	1	Michael Smith	3
Daywat Crisher (Cristley)	1	Michael Kieffer	1	Geo. Moyers	2
		Thos. Wayaldn	1	Mark Finks	2
Joyn Rowsee	2	John Blueford	2	John Wisdom	3
Henry Haws	5	Wm. Eddins	4	John Scotts	3
Wm. Jackson	2	James Barbour	8	David Bruce	1
Elias Smith	1	Thos. Bledsoe	1	Robt. Cave	2
Wm. White	1				

Tithables in precinct of Henry Rice, 1739

Name	#	Name	#	Name	#
Henry Isbell	2	Wm. Griddin	2	James Haley	1
Edward Haley	3	Wm. Cox, Jr.	1	George Cox	2
Obediah Aererbon	1	Wm. Cox	5	Daniel Singleton	1
Col. Willis	4	Capt. Wm. Bledsoe	2	Isaac Bledsoe	2
Wm. Thompson	1	George Brasbone	6	Capt. George Hardin	5

Name	#	Name	#	Name	#
Maj. Aylett	7	Rich. Bradley	2	John Evens	1
John Cook	3	Moses Harris	1	Jos. Woolfolk	6
John Henderson	1	Wm. Matthews	1	John Brock(man)	1
Thos. Dewson	2	Col. Aug. Moore	4	Sag. Tilley	1
Thos. Burgess	1	Saml. Smith	6	Backnel Alverson	1
Geo. Steward	1	Jeremiah Dear	1	John Collins	1
Nathaniel Clayborn	4	Wm. Wood	2	Daniel Cook	1
Malachi Chiles	3	Abraham Mayfield	2	James Stephens	4
Rich. Lamb	1	John Stephens	1	Larkin Chew	5
John Thomas	2	Daniel White	3	Wm. Pratt	1
Wm. Taylor	1	George Smith	3	Charles Stephens	4
Jos. Shears	1	Sam Brock(man)	2	Roger Bell	1
Thos. Cook	2	John Bixing	4	John Goldson	3
David Cave	3	Jostophonica Smith	1	James Elliot	3
David Griffin	1	Wm. Jones	1	John Griffin	1
John Clayborn	7	Wm. Stephens	1	John Hiatt	5
Henry Rice	3	Capt. Wm. Beale		Joseph Thornell	
Stephen Cubbon		James Coleman		Thomas Jones	
Thos. Hill		Charles Curtis		Rich. Bridge	

Tithables in precinct _____ for the year 1739

Name	#	Name	#	Name	#
John Christopher	9	Wm. Davis	3	John Hawkins	13
Alex Waugh	6	Rannill George	6	Vallentine Morgin	6
Willm. Clark	3	Benj. Horn	1	Capt. Spenser	13
Willm. Chroncker	4	James Thornton	1	John Wells	1
John Dizen	5	Thos. Night	1	Att. Coll Willis	4
Will. Davis	2	Jonathon Yowell(Orrell)	5	Wm. Hakins	1
John Smith	3	Nathan Turner	3	James Whitun	2
William Minor	2	John Branham	9	William Morton	14
William Smith	1	John Yowell	2	John Walton	1
Soloman Ryan	1	William Christopher	2	George McHolt	2
? Christopher	2	? Adam		Thos. Wharton	3
Sharly Water	3	Edward Price	7	Thos. Fox	12
Alex Newman	4	Brient Sisson	3	Robt. Terrell	11
Thos. Sims	42	John Ingram	4	John Mark	4
Saml. Graves	4	John Pettey	3	Thos. Pettey	1
Wm. Hawkins	1	John Morin	1	John Edwards	
George Whorton	3	Benjamin Porter	3	James Stanard	
Simon Bourne	1	George Anderson, Sr.	4	John Underwood	
George Anderson, Jr.	1	Sam Pound	2	John Manowell	
Rich. Sims	7	John Dolwood		Eddins Thefolus	
Thos. Russell	1	John Curtis	1	Peter Russell	
Luke Thornton	2	John Ramdal(Ranfield)	2	Thos. Micharl	
George Wills	1	Matthias Plunkabeamer	2	Nicholas Plunkabeamer	
George Shirley	1	Conrad Kather(Hater?)	1	Jacob Beorill(Beorid?)	
Zackaniah Fleshman	2				

Tithables in John Michell Precinct Year 1739

Name	#	Name	#	Name	#
Mr. Frys, Jr.	10	John Smith	1	Alexander Mcphearson	
Joshua Yarborough	2	Zackarias Sparks	1	John Layton	
John Toles	2	Thomas Waker	3	Tyentoe Bobon	
Henry Fields	3	Francis Michell	1	Mathew Stanton	

(137)

Wm. Durrett............ 2	John White............ 1	John Durett............ 1
James Morgan........... 1	Tobias Wilhite........ 1	John Holt............. 1
Frederick Bungarnes.... 1	Christopher Moyers.... 1	Peter Weaver..........
Michaell Wilhite....... 2	George Wood...........	Peter Fleshman........ 2
Richard Birdini........ 2	John Wilhite.......... 1	Michaell Cloare....... 2
Martin Dalluck......... 1	Michael O'Neall....... 1	George Taylor......... 1
Wm. Martin............. 2	Zachary Martin........ 4	Tenby Solester........ 1
Nicholas Coplin........ 3	David Quell........... 1	John Kyner............ 3
Christopher Y. Owell... 2	Thomas Fargison....... 1	John Thomas........... 1
Henry Shiter........... 1	John Zimmerman........ 1	

Tithables in John Mitkett Precinct, 1739

John Dotson............ 1	John Sutton........... 1	Robert Hutchison...... 1
Joseph Bloodworth...... 3	Thomas Cavely......... 1	John Friett........... 2
Christian Slemon....... 1	Jacob Neappoille...... 1	

Tithables in Precinct of Thos. Callaway, 1739

Geo. Braxton........... 8	Robt. Brook........... 6	Sarah Brook........... 5
Madam Stannard......... 6	James Lindsay......... 3	M. Lawson............. 5
Mrs. Rippon............ 2	Wm. Callaway.......... 1	Jeffry Crowley........ 2
Joseph Keatton......... 1	James Keatton......... 1	James Meredith........ 1
John May............... 1	Geo. Douglass......... 1	John Goodall.......... 2
Fran. Williams......... 2	John Ennis............ 1	Wm. Smith............. 1
James McKinney......... 1	James Stogdhill....... 1	Thos. Buttery......... 1
Honoros Powell......... 2	John Hunt............. 1	Thos. Wood............ 1
Trueman Fry............ 1	William Bunch......... 1	David Rock............ 1
Wm. Herren............. 1	Joseph Phillips....... 1	James Ireland......... 1
Henry Findell.......... 1	James Dier(?)......... 1	James Liley........... 1

Tithables in Elijah Daniels Precinct, 1739

Richard Thomas.........16	John Botts............ 9	Richard Durrett.......
Cap. Rucher............ 4	John McCoy............ 5	John Lucas at Madam
Thomas Red............. 6	Robert Desrm.......... 2	Told's Qr............
Mark Thornton.......... 7	Ambrose Powell........ 7	Mrs. Battaile........ 7
Samuel Drake........... 3	James Colady at Col.	William Clark........ 7
Zackary Gibbs.......... 3	Willis................	George Byrd.......... 1
Joseph Mollen(Morton).. 6	James Coleman......... 6	William Bell......... 3
William Rhodes......... 1	Edward Walker......... 2	Hezekiah Rhodes...... 2
George Anderson........	Wm. Crodewait......... 3	John Barnett......... 4
John Goss.............. 3	Earcey Taylor......... 3	Robert Bohanaugh.....17
Zachary Taylor.........10	Richard Kemp.......... 5	Thomas Jones......... 7
Mrs. Madisons.......... 6	Capt. John Scott...... 9	James Coward......... 6
Kenwood Winslow........ 3	George Ephriam(Eastham)6	Thomas Gresham....... 7
Wm. Clark.............. 7	Robt. Dear............ 2	Mark Thornton........ 7
Col. Chew.............. 8	Samuel Canady......... 8	

Tithables in the Precinct of Geo. Smith, 1736 or 1737

Chas. Stevens.......... 4	Daniel Cave........... 3	Thos. Cook............ 1
Roger Bell............. 1	Lazarus Tilley........ 2	Dame Cook............. 1
Coine Moore............ 4	Tho. Dudson........... 3	Mr. Brockman.......... 2

(138)

Jno. Brockman... 1	Jno. Henderson... 1	no. Shiflett... 1
Rich. Phillips... 2	Wm. Matthews... 1	no. Vivion... 4
Wm. Stevins... 1	Rich. Bradley... 1	nd. Hanson... 5
Mad. Fleet... 5	Jno. Hiatt... 1	ames Cox... 3
Edward Haley... 2	Charles Oakes... 2	ol. Braxton... 5
Corn. Willis... 10	Capt. Bledsoe... 2	saac Bledsoe... 1
James Haley... 1	Jno. Cook... 2	Chas. Curtis... 3
M. Hill... 5	Robt. Biggers... 1	Jno. Collins... 2
Geo. Stewart... 1	M. Taylor... 6	M. Larkin Chew... 5
M. Sletts... 4	John Griffin... 2	Wm. Jones... 1
Wm. Bohannan... 5	Henry Rice... 2	Wm. Codden... 2
Saml. Smith... 8	Geo. Smith... 1	

Tithables in the Precinct of Samuel Pound, Constable, 1736-37

Col. Willis... 15	Mrs. Conway... 14	George Whorton... 2
(Macerley Overseer)	John Branham... 8	John Curtis... 1
Alex Waugh (Overseer for	Stovin Bacon... 1	William Morton... 7
John Taliaferro)... 8	Luke Thornton... 3	James Thornton... 1
Will. Williams... 1	John Randall... 2	Will. Pattey... 1
Thomas Pattey... 1	Will. Wood... 2	John Kindell... 3
Wm. Hawkins... 3	Will. Hawkins... 3	John Walker... 1
John Walker... 1	Nicholas Christopher... 1	Wm. Davis... 2
M. Taliver, Jr... 4	Thos. K. Night... 1	John Christopher... 6
Thos. Wharton... 4	Will. Pannell... 3	John Eddins... 1
John Smith... 2	Ambrose Jones... 1	Thos. Russell... 1
Daniel Underwood... 2	John Marks... 4	George Wols... 1
Thos. Pattey Son... 3	John Pattey... 2	Thomas Sorrel... 2
Wm. Rose... 12	James Thornton... 1	John Porter... 1
John Floyd... 1	Joseph Morton... 5	Will. Edings... 5
George Anderson... 3	Mary Dolwood... 1	Thos. Nichol... 1
Chas. Davis... 1		

Tithables, 1736-37 _____ Constable

John Davison... 1	George Taylor... 3	Samuel Drake... 3
Capt. Daniel Mecarties... 5	James Taylor... 7	Samuel Baker... 5
James Thursion... 1	Capt. John Tallifearves 8	Zac. Gibbs... 2
Nicklas Baittails... 7	Elijah Daniel... 2	Edward Walker...
M. Richard Thomas... 7	Richard Thomas... 8	Edward Tinsley... 4
John Barnet... 5	Ezekiah Roades... 2	Wm. Crossthwait... 5
M. Bailors... 5	John Goss... 4	George Anderson... 5
Capt. Hill... 9	Capt. Rucker... 3	M. Thos. Jones... 7
Ed. Walts... 5	M. Beales... 5	Doct. Gordon... 3
Mrs. Mattisons... 6	Coe. Ginnes... 18	M. Jru. Minor... 5
James Coleman... 5	Capt. Todd... 9	Mad. Todds... 10
Col. Willis... 6	M. Thos. Edmonson... 5	M. James Barbour... 6
Thos. Scott... 9	Col. Chew... 10	Joseph Eve...
Robert Martain... 1	Mrs. Mattison... 8	Rich. Winslow...
Robert Adams... 2	John Moran... 1	Zach. Taylor...
Bryan...	John Branham... 10	Thomas Fox... 1
William Minor... 12	Ed. Price... 7	Nathan Turner...
John Smith... 3	Stoven Wolls... 2	William Connico...
William Cronchon... 3	James Thaston... 1	Shirley Watley... 3

(139)

Briant Sison............ 4	John Wols.............. 1	John Dolwood........... 1
Theofolus Edings....... 2	William Morton......... 8	James Wilson........... 2
William Tomson......... 1	Thomas Wharton......... 4	John Fenell............ 6
Sam. George............ 6	Will. Clark............ 3	John Davis............. 2
John Christopher....... 7	John Hockins........... 4	Simon Biccome.......... 2
Thos. Russell.......... 1	Robert Deering......... 1	Capt. Benj. Winslow.... 6
Thos. Knight........... 2	Alex Waugh............. 5	John Dozen............. 5
Will. Smith............ 6	Jonathan Tirrill or	B. Porter.............. 3
Thomas Simes........... 3	Pannell............. 5	Thomas Pattus, Jr...... 4
John Imgram............ 5	Will. Stevens.......... 1	M. Strother............ 1
P. Nichol.............. 1	John Marks............. 5	John Poth.............. 2
Sam. Green............. 3	Tho. Shambols.......... 1	Robert Terrell........12
Rich. Powell........... 4	Thos. Petty, Jr........ 3	Will Petty............. 1
Luke Thornton.......... 2	George Wols............ 1	Will. Christopher...... 2
John Curtus............ 1	Stoven Beecone......... 1	Nicholas Christopher... 1
Soloman Rion........... 1	-----Anderson.......... 2	John Underwood......... 2
Will. Biccon........... 3	George Whotun.......... 3	John Edwards........... 1
Will. Hopkins.......... 2	Will. Davis............ 2	Samuel Pound........... 2

Tithables in the Precinct of Isaac Haddock, 1736-37

Edward Spencer......... 7	Eliz. Kirk............. 2	Geo. Whitney........... 4
Sam. Wright............ 2	Zachariah Putnam....... 2	Jno. Pondgrass......... 2
Frederick Cobbler...... 1	Margret Grey........... 1	Christopher Zimmerman. 1
Eliz Taylor............ 1	Lenard Woofnol......... 1	Wm. Rumsey............. 1
Jno. Newport........... 1	Wm. Wats............... 3	Thos. Wright........... 2
Thos. Wats............. 2	Thos. Parks............ 3	Jno. Bond.............. 3
Sim Miller............. 7	Sam. Ball.............. 9	Thos. Stanton.......... 6
Jas. Pollard........... 9	Rodger Abbot........... 8	Capt. Jno. Finlason....11
Wm. Clift.............. 5	Timothy Fink........... 2	Henry Field............ 8
Thos. Byrn............. 2	Wm. Rosson............. 4	Richard Wright......... 2

Tithables in Isaac Haddoch Precinct Entered

Thos. Yeats............ 1	Jno. Campbel........... 1	Jno. Asher............. 1
Edward Teal............ 1	Wm. Russell............ 3	Wm. Lacey.............. 1
Peter Russel........... 1	Jno. Lillard........... 1	Jno. Morphus........... 1
Geo. Thomas............ 4	Col. Charles Carter.... 7	Wm. Moore.............. 2
Jno. Donely............ 1	Col. Goodrich	Edward Ablet........... 1
Col. Wright Belfield... 4	Lightfoot..........10	Wm. Burton............. 1
Geo. Underwood......... 3	Jno. Hadon............. 1	Col. Alex. Spotswood..14
Francis Thornton....... 5	Wm. Kelly.............. 1	Robert Slaughter......10
Jno. Carder............ 1	Wm. Ray................ 1	Wm. Johnson............ 1
Rev. Jno. Bicket....... 5	Chas. Morgin........... 1	Bryan Thorne........... 1
Christopher Walters.... 2	Jas. Conner............ 3	Wm. Wood............... 1
Minor Win.............. 1	Jno. Anford............ 1	Jacob Miller........... 1

Tithables in the Precinct of David Phillips, Constable, 1737

James Barbour.......... 7	James Dyer............. 1	Benj. Cave.............
Charles Blunt.......... 1	Col. John Grymes......17	Benj. Coward........... 3
Thomas Watts........... 5	William Crawford....... 1	John Wisdom............ 2
Benj. Thompson......... 1	Zackary Gibbs.......... 3	Anthony Head........... 1

(140)

Anthony Strother	6	Thomas Wood	1	Phillip Roots	
William Stone	2	Peter Rucker	5	William Piam	
William Offill	2	Henry Haws	2	William Pirce	
Richard Halsonn	3	John Garth	9	Thos. Binns	
Thomas Stanton	1	John Scott	3	Edward Ferrell	
John Wise	1	John Skilton	6	John Rogers	
Samuel Bird	5	Thomas Colman	1	Walter Lenard	
John Harsnap	2	Thos. Zackry	2	Cornelius Blake	
John Zackry	1	Larance Crise	2	Thos. Jackson	
John Hufmon	1	William Jackson	1	Courthney Broyle	
William Phillips	4	Andrew Careker	2	John Maccall	
Andrew Cair	3	Robert Cave	3	William Carpinter	
Thomas Downer	1	Michale Cook	2	George Myers	
Thomas Bledsoe	1	Michael Capher	2	George Myers	
Abraham Bledsoe	1	Michale Capher	2	Michale Smith	
Nicholas Yeager	5	Adam Yeager	1	John Bradford	
Mathias Caselear	1	George Long	1	Mark Fink	
Mathues Smith	1	Christopher Taner	1	Michale Holt	
William Rice	1	David Bruce	1	Frye Meeks	
David Phillips	1				

A list of Tithablers that Phillip Bush,
Constable, have viewed in his Precinct Nov. 1749

John Askew	5	Ed. Franklin	1	Thos. Ballard	
Lou Franklin	2	Will. Bryant	2	Reuben Franklin	
Will. Ballard	1	Will Gusum	5	Rich. Barbour	
John Gutridge	1	Phillip Bush	2	Thos. Garman	
Robt. Blunder	5	George Head	2	Sam Head	
James Coffee	2	John Hardwick	2	John Coffee	
Ed. Cleveland, Jr	1	Thos. Harral	1	John Cleveland	
George Murral	3	Brad Crimbs		Ransom Offield	
Ed. Coffee	1	John Page	5	Elx. Cleveland	
Joseph Phillips	2	Ed. Dearing	1	John Randall	
Robt. Dearing	2	Will. Richards	5	Capt. Downs	
John Snell	5	Rich. Durrett	20	James Towsend	
John Douglas	4	Henry Turner	8	Thos. Bohunne	
Fran. Wisdom	2	John Eubank	1	Phill Eastin	1
James Isbell	15	George Eastham	13		

Tithables in James Mitchell's Precinct, 1749

John Allens, Jr	2	Larkin Chew, Jr	7	James Adkins	
John Collins	2	George Bledsoe	3	George Cook	
Margarett Belk	3	Joseph Chamber	3	George Braxton	
Malliki Chiles	6	Robert Bagen	2	William Cook	
Thomas Burbridge	3	John Chinton(Clayton)	10	Rich. Bradley	
David Cave	3	Lawrence Battett	8	John Cave	
John Boutwell, Jr	2	Daniel Cook	2	John Beaveen	10
Edward Carter	1	Lawrence Battitt, Jr	3	Turley Choice	
Roger Bell	2	James Coleman	10	John Brockman	
Reuben Daniel	1	Samuel Brockman	1	John Evins	
Samuel Brockman, Sr	3	James Elett, Jr	3	Isaac Bradburn	
John Embrey	3	Capt. Beale	12	Mary Fleet	

(141)

James Cox............ 1	John Golson........... 3	William Cox........... 1
Capt. Garnet, Jr...... 6	William Cox........... 1	Thomas Gahagon........ 2
William Cox, Sr....... 3	John Graves........... 1	George Cox............ 1
Stephen Gupton........ 1	William Codden........ 2	Thomas Graves......... 2
Charles Curtis........ 3	James Siner........... 1	Edward Healy.......... 3
Stephen Smith......... 3	John Heighat.......... 1	Anthony Harrison...... 4
William Smith.........75	Joseph Holden......... 2	John Stevens, Jr...... 4
Reuben Harris......... 3	Elizabeth Thomas...... 4	James Healy........... 2
Widow Thomas, Jr...... 3	John Hinderson........ 3	Margret Tilly......... 1
Moses Harris.......... 1	John Wormley, Jr....... 8	Thomas Kenberry....... 2
John Willis, Jr....... 5	William Long.......... 2	John Wisdom........... 2
Raeff Morris.......... 1	William Moran......... 1	John Mallory.......... 4
Robert Woolfolk, Jr... 7	William Millers, Jr... 3	Jeremiah Whatson...... 1
William Millers, Jr... 3	Thomas Meacry, Jr..... 4	John Willis...........16
Thomas Moore, Jr...... 7	James Madison, Jr..... 6	James Mitchell........ 3
John Neall, Jr........ 5	William Pratt......... 2	Thomas Philpot........ 1
Joseth Reynolds....... 2	John Shackelford...... 3	Phillip Singleton..... 1
Daniel Singleton...... 2	Stephen Smith......... 2	George Smith.......... 7

A List of Tithables for the Year 1752

Isaac Arnold.......... 3	John Dodd............. 2	George Anerson........ 4
John Daniel........... 1	John Dolewood......... 1	Wm. Anderson.......... 3
Thomas Eavens......... 1	Robert Boston......... 2	Thomas Eavens......... 1
Henry Bowen........... 4	Boreman Davis......... 3	James Slate........... 5
Mrs. Fitstugh......... 8	Robert Beggs.......... 7	Charles Foushee....... 4
Mrs. Battley.......... 6	Charles Foushee....... 4	Stephen Beckham....... 1
Wm. Gaines............ 1	James Brazer.......... 1	M. Gibson............. 4
John Branham.......... 9	Benj. Hawkins......... 8	John Rakesbraw........ 1
Wm. Hawkins........... 3	Robert Brown.......... 3	Thos. Hughes.......... 6
Thomas Beckum......... 1	Bott Baker............ 1	Ben. Baugham.......... 1
Abraham Chambers...... 4	Valentine Crawley..... 1	Archibald Campbell.... 2
Wm. Choncher.......... 3	John Christopher...... 6	Charles Lee........... 1
John Morgan........... 3	Andrew Manner......... 2	Jeremiah Morton.......10
John Morton........... 6	Elijah Morton......... 6	Wm. Minor............. 2
Fran Moore............ 4	David Moore........... 1	George Morton, Jr..... 7
Thos. Moore........... 1	Henry Nixon........... 2	Alexander Newman...... 3
John Pound............ 1	George Nix............ 1	John Pattey...........
Archibald Price....... 7	Thos. Hughes, Jr...... 3	John Hammock.......... 1
John Harvey........... 2	John Jennings......... 1	Thomas Jameson........ 3
James Kelly........... 1	Hugh Jones............ 1	James Slate........... 1
Thomas Sharp.......... 8	Thomas Sharp.......... 8	Thomas Sharp, Jr...... 3
Owen Smith............ 1	Bryan Sisson.......... 4	Isaac Sartan.......... 1
Edward Spencer........13	Wm. Scott............. 5	John Taliaferro....... 9
Mrs. Taliaferro.......13	T. Phillips.......... 1	Wm. Taliaferro........ 7
Ann Thornton.......... 2	Luke Thornton......... 2	Thomas Turner......... 3
John Underwood........ 3	Wm. Withis............ 1	Jennine Patty......... 2
Mrs. Rose.............14	John Ramdel........... 2	Mrs. Robinson......... 4
Doctor Roy............11	Ned White............. 1	John White............ 1
Thos. Wills...........	John Williams, Jr..... 1	Robt. Williams, Jr.... 1
Wm. Whitman........... 1	John Wood............. 1	Alexander Waugh.......
John Willis........... 9	Robert Williams....... 6	To. Williamson........ 1
Herr. Wood............13		

(142)

A List of Tithables in the Folk of Pamankey, 1753

Jas. Atkins............ 1	John Goldson........... 3	Rich Bradley........... 2
James Garnet.......... 9	John Brockman......... 3	John Graves........... 3
Wm. Bradburn.......... 2	Thomas Graves......... 3	Sam. Brockman......... 3
John Groom............ 1	Richard Beal.......... 5	Stephen Gupton........ 2
Tavenor Beal..........14	Reuben Harris......... 3	Charles Beal.......... 6
John Henderson........ 3	John Bell............. 1	John Jones............11
Isaac Bradburn........ 2	Wm. Lea............... 1	Roger Bell............ 2
Thos. Merry........... 5	David Cave............ 4	Thos. Montagne........ 4
Jonathon Coward....... 1	Thomas Moore..........13	Maliki Chiles......... 8
James Madison, Jr..... 7	Dan. Cook............. 2	John Noel............. 3
Thomas Cimbro......... 2	Lewis Pine............ 1	James Coleman......... 9
Edw. Smith............ 2	Ambrose Coleman....... 4	John Stephens......... 6
John Dealwood......... 1	Robert Slayter........ 6	Thomas Dansley........ 3
Reuben Daniel......... 2	Sam. Daniel........... 1	Vivion Daniel......... 2
Jas. Daniel........... 2	John Embre............ 2	Capt. Frogmorth....... 4
Isaac Arnold.......... 2	George Anderson....... 3	Wm. Anderson.......... 1
Robert Boston......... 2	Robert Beggs..........10	Thomas Beacham........ 1
John Branham, Sr...... 7	Henry Bourn........... 1	Spencer Branham....... 1
Benj. Buchan.......... 1	Mrs. Battles, Jr...... 6	John Christopher...... 5
Arch. Campbell........ 2	Isaac Certain, Sr..... 3	Isaac Certain, Jr..... 1
Arch Chambers.........14	Valentine Crosby...... 1	Widow Chizin.......... 1
William Crowder....... 1	John Bodo............. 1	Berryman Davis........ 3
Robert Edwards........ 1	Thomas Evans.......... 1	Robert Slayter........ 6
Wm. Spear............. 1	Margaret Tilley....... 2	Richard Woolfolk...... 2
Joseph Woolfolk....... 6	Wm. Warin............. 1	Mr. Glass, Jr......... 5
Benjamin Hawkins...... 6	Thomas Hopkins........ 1	Rich. Hill............ 2
Thomas Hughes......... 4	Thomas Hughs, Sr...... 5	John Harvey........... 2
William Hawkins....... 1	William Hawkins,Jr.... 3	John Hammock.......... 1
Thomas Jameson........ 4	William Jones......... 1	Charles Lee........... 2
Patrick Leonard....... 1	Patrick Lanthon....... 1	David Moore........... 1
Elijah Morton......... 5	Capt. Francis Moore... 6	John Morgan........... 4
John Morton........... 5	William Minor......... 2	Geo. Mortons, Jr...... 5
Jeremiah Morton.......12	Charles Foushee....... 5	John Foushee.......... 6
Col. Henry Fitzhigh,Jn.8	Thomas Morgan......... 1	Andrew Mauner......... 1
Alexander Newman...... 3		

A List of Tithables for Year 1753

Henry Nixon........... 2	Jermnia Pettri........ 1	John Pettri........... 2
John Pound............ 2	Edward Price,Jr....... 6	Madam Rose............14
John Ransdale......... 2	Doc Rogs, Jr..........11	John Rakestraw........ 2
Mr. Robinsons,Jr...... 5	John Reynolds......... 1	Widow Russell......... 1
Madam Spencer.........10	Bryan Sisson.......... 5	Owen Smith............ 1
James Sleet........... 1	Wm. Taliaferro........ 9	Mr. Taliaferro........ 7
Luke Thornton......... 3	Ann Thornton.......... 2	Thomas Tharp,Sr....... 6
Thomas Tharp,Jr....... 3	Mr.John Taliaferro.... 9	Charles Tinsley....... 1
Thomas Turner......... 3	John Underwood........ 4	Alex Waugh............ 5
Henry Wood............ 1	William Willis........ 1	John Willis...........12
John Wood............. 1	Robert Williams....... 5	William Williams...... 1
Robert Williams,Jr.... 1	John Williams......... 2	Joseph Williams....... 2
John Williams......... 1		

(143)

Robert Deering List of Tithables, 1754

Richard Barbour....... 4	Robt. Blunder......... 5	Will. Ballard......... 1
Thos. Ballard......... 1	Will. Bryon........... 1	John Bryon............ 1
Phillip Bush.......... 3	John Cleveland........ 4	Alex Cleveland,Jr..... 1
John Coffee........... 4	Edwd. Coffee.......... 4	Alex Cleveland........ 1
Henry Downs........... 6	Mr. Dyllen............11	John Douglas.......... 1
Presley Dollens....... 1	Robt. Deering......... 1	Edwd. Deering......... 1
Rich. Durrett......... 4	Jos. Eve.............. 5	John Eubanks.......... 1
Reuben Flannagen......11	John Foster........... 4	Lawrence Franklyn..... 1
Jas. Fitzgerrell...... 1	Edwd. Franklyn........ 4	Wm. Gresham........... 1
Thos. German.......... 3	David Griffith........ 2	John Haskew........... 7
George Head........... 5	Will Johnston......... 5	Bradley Kembrow....... 1
John Layn.............10	Will Lucas, Jr........ 4	Robt. Martin.......... 5
John Page............. 3	George Roebuck........ 5	Jos. Phillips......... 4
Wm. Richards.......... 6	John Randolph......... 1	John Scott............ 7
Edwd. Spencer......... 5	John Snell............ 5	Rich. Sebree.......... 2
Henry Turner..........10	Jas. Townsen.......... 6	Len. Williams......... 8
Frances Wisdom........ 1	Mrs. Willis...........18	Richard Wilson........ 9
David Watts........... 1	Thos. Warren.......... 1	Rich. Winslow......... 1

Thomas Graves Tithables, 1754

Jas. Adkins........... 1	John Bell............. 2	Richard Bradley....... 2
Battle Harrison....... 6	Wm. Brockman.......... 6	Tavener Beal..........12
Wm. Bradburn.......... 4	Richard Brock......... 1	Robert Biggins........ 3
Saml. Brockman,Sr..... 2	John Brockman,Jr...... 1	Roger Bell............ 2
Malack Chiles......... 8	James Coward.......... 5	Ambrose Coleman....... 4
John Conner...........11	James Coleman.........10	Benj. Cave............ 1
David Cave............ 3	Reuben Davis.......... 5	Jack Davis............ 1
Jas. Daniel........... 3	Vivian Daniel......... 2	Jos. Davis............ 9
John Embre............ 2	John Alderson......... 1	Robt. Thomas.......... 5
Beckrol Alderson...... 1	John Vivian...........10	Stephen Gupton........ 2
Jos. Graves........... 6	David Griffin......... 4	John Graves........... 2
John Gholston......... 4	John Groom............ 1	Thos. Graves.......... 1
John Henderson........ 3	Reuben Harris......... 3	Thomas Kimbro......... 2
Richard Lewis......... 8	Wm. McDono............ 1	Thos. Montague........ 5
John Noch(Gouch?)..... 4	Abraham Mayfield...... 4	Wm. Richards.......... 3
John Stevens.......... 5	Robt. Slayter......... 4	Wm. Sims.............. 2
Saml. Sutton.......... 1	Edwd. Smith........... 2	John Thomas........... 5
John Tilley........... 3	Marg. Tilly........... 2	John Wright........... 1
Jos. Woolfolk......... 9	Jos. Haly............. 2	Thos. Healy........... 3
Battailes,Jr..........16	Robert Begore......... 1	Boutwills, Jr.........
Jos. Billinps(?)...... 1	George Bledsoe........ 2	Breckson.............. 4
Thomas Brown.......... 1	Joseph Chandler....... 4	Charles Curtis........ 5
John Crandam.......... 1	Thomas Curgio......... 3	Chews,Jr.............. 8
Richard Cousins....... 1	Benj. Cave............ 5	Marthy Cox............ 1
William Cox........... 1	Elliotts, Jr.......... 4	Joe. Evans............ 2
Fleet................. 8	Thomas Gohagon........ 1	John Hiaett........... 2
Wm. Hudson............ 1	Law. Harrison......... 3	Francis Lamb.......... 1
Merry................. 8	Elijah Morton......... 3	John Mallory.......... 3
Miller................ 5	John Wisdom........... 3	Harry Wood............ 1
Wormley...............12	Willis, Jr............ 5	Marshall.............. 5
James Mitchel........ 3	And. Manner........... 2	Zackary Price......... 1
Benj. Poe............. 1	John Rakstraw......... 2	Larne Ray............. 1

Stephen Smith......... 4	James Sidnor.......... 1	Wm. Sawyer............ 2
George Smith.......... 5	Charles Smith......... 7	William Stephens...... 1
Jos. Stephens......... 1	Daniel Singleton...... 1	Phillip Singleton..... 3
Stephen I.K.Smith..... 3	Richard Thomas........ 7	Robt. Thomas.......... 5
John Vivion...........10		

Tithables in Thos. White's Precinct, 1755

Col. John Baylor......32	Richard Beal..........11	---Braxton............ 5
Nicholas Battaile..... 8	Bohannon.............. 6	Widow James........... 2
Robert Martain........ 4	James Madison.........13	Mrs. Frances Madison.. 5
Murgo Marshall........ 7	Benj. Porter.......... 7	Richard Barbour....... 5
Mrs. Barnet........... 7	David Bruce........... 1	Wm. Christifor........ 1
John Christifer....... 4	Col. Thos. Chew....... 4	Timothy Crostwait..... 5
Bradley Cunbrow....... 2	Robert Dearing,Sr..... 2	Edward Dearing........ 2
Robert Dearing,Jr..... 1	Thos. Edmonson........ 8	Jos. Eave............. 3
John Finney........... 3	Benj. Grymes..........53	Zach Gibbs............ 2
Thos. Gully........... 2	Wm. Golden............ 6	Benj. Hubbard......... 4
Jos. Molton...........14	Peter Rucker.......... 4	Rucher................ 5
Wm. Spear............. 2	Johnny Scott.......... 5	Andrew Shepherd....... 6
Richard Todd.......... 8	Edmond Taylor......... 7	Capt. Thomas Row...... 7
Wm. Taliaferro........18	Joseph Thomas......... 7	Joseph Towles......... 3
Wm. Taliaferro........ 5	Col. George Taylor....16	Erasmus Taylor........ 6
Madam Taylor..........16	James Taylor.......... 9	Zackary Taylor........11
Col.Francis Taliaferro.27	Beverly Winslow....... 5	Edward Tinsley........ 7
Richard Vernon........ 5	Richard Winslow....... 3	Lt. James Walker...... 9
Edward Walker......... 4	Thomas White.......... 5	

Tithables, Thomas Graves Precinct, 1755

Thomas Atkins......... 1	Tavenner Beal......... 7	Wm. Bradburn.......... 4
John Brockman......... 2	Sam. Brockman,Sr...... 2	Sem Brockman,Jr....... 2
Richard Bradley....... 2	Robert Biggers........ 3	Roger Bell............ 3
Richard Brock......... 2	Capt. Frogmorton...... 5	Wm. Flanagin.......... 1
John Graves........... 2	Jos. Graves........... 6	Stephen Gupton........ 1
John Groom............ 1	John Gholson.......... 4	John Gibbins.......... 1
Thomas Graves......... 2	Wm. Howard............12	James Coward..........
William Cleveland..... 1	John Conyers..........10	Ambrose Coleman....... 4
James Coleman.........10	Malaki Chiles......... 3	David Cave............ 4
Abraham Cook.......... 1	Wm. Coaling........... 2	Zacharia Davis........ 1
James Daniel.......... 2	Vivian Daniel......... 2	Reuben Daniel......... 6
Philomon Easten....... 3	Joseph Eve............ 2	Samuel Sutton......... 1
Margaret-Tilley....... 2	Rich Woolfolk......... 3	James Wagoner......... 6
Wm. Warrin............ 1	Joseph Woolfolk....... 3	John Wright........... 1
Wm. Watson............ 3	Lawrence Young........ 4	John Henderson........ 3
Joseph Henderson...... 2	Reuben Haris.......... 3	Wm. Long.............. 1
Richard Lewis......... 2	Wm. McDonold.......... 1	Thomas Merry.......... 4
Abraham Mayfield...... 2	Thomas Montague....... 5	John Novel............ 2
Thomas Purim.......... 7	William Sims.......... 2	John Stevens.......... 5
Charles Smith......... 9	Edward Smith.......... 2	

John Williams Tithables, 1755

George Anderson...... 4	Benj. Davis........... 1	Isaac Arnold.......... 3
John Daniel........... 1	William Anderson...... 2	Mr. Fitzhughs,Jr...... 6
James Arnold.......... 2	John Foushee.......... 4	Isaac Anderson........ 1
Charles Foushee....... 4	John Branham,Sr....... 8	Joseph Foushee........ 1
Robert Boston......... 3	Jehew Glass........... 8	Henry Bowen........... 3
Benj. Hawkins......... 6	Sarah Bowen........... 2	Thomas Hughes,Sr...... 6
Benj. Bohon........... 2	Thomas Hughes,Jr...... 2	Stephen Beckham....... 2
John Harvey........... 3	Mrs. Battailes,Jr..... 7	Richard Hill.......... 2
John Branham,Jr....... 1	Francis Hensley....... 2	Thomas Brown.......... 1
William Hawkins....... 2	Henry Beckham......... 1	William Hawkins....... 4
Robert Boston,Jr...... 1	John Hammack.......... 1	Thomas Balkon......... 1
Thomas Hopkins........ 1	James Frazer(?)....... 1	Thomas Jameson........ 7
John Christopher...... 6	Wm. Johnson........... 4	Benj. Cave............ 5
Hugh Jones............ 1	Archibald Campbell.... 3	Wm. Jones............. 1
Wm. Croucher.......... 3	Mr. Jones,Jr..........11	Abraham Chambers...... 3
James Kelley.......... 1	Mary Chisson.......... 1	Patrick Leonard....... 2
Robert Dorson......... 3	Charles Lee........... 2	Moses Lindsay......... 2
James Roach........... 2	Thomas Larney......... 1	John Rains............ 1
Peter Lanthorn........ 1	Joshaway Stepp........ 9	Jeremiah Morton,Jr....19
Mr. Spottswood........ 9	Francis Moore......... 8	Mr. Spotswood
Mr. Morton............ 6	Windfield Shopshire... 1	(River Jr.)...........11
John Morton........... 8	Bryan Sisson.......... 6	Peter Montague........ 3
James Sleet........... 2	John Morgan........... 3	Lin Smith............. 2
Wm. Minor............. 3	Mrs. Spencer.......... 6	Alexander Moore Daniel 1
John Martain.......... 3	Danl. Megrigri........ 1	Wm. Taliaferro........20
Thomas Martin......... 1	Mrs. Taliaferro,Jr....10	John Martin........... 1
Francis Taliaferro,Jr. 9	Henry Nixon........... 2	Joseph Thomas,Jr...... 5
Thomas Newman,Jr...... 4	Luke Thornton......... 4	Alexander Newman...... 1
Thomas Sharp.......... 2	Joseph Phillips....... 1	Charles Tamkersley.... 1
John Pound............ 1	James Thornton........ 1	Archibald Price,Jr....10
Daniel Thornton....... 1	M. Roy................10	William Thornton...... 1
M. Robinson........... 5	Alexander Waugh,Jr....15	Richard Reynolds...... 2
John Willis...........13	Cornelius Reynolds.... 1	Robert Williams....... 6
Tho. Walsh............ 2	John Rensdal.......... 2	Robert Williams,Jr.... 1
John Wood............. 1	John Whitman.......... 1	Joseph Williams....... 1
Thos. Wells........... 1	Edward White.......... 1	William Whitman....... 1
John Williams......... 2		

John Williams Tithables, 1758

Andw. Manner.......... 8	John Deer............. 8	William Brock......... 8
Geo. Bledsoe.......... 2	John Vivian........... 9	John Kerchnall........ 8
Wm. Cymon............. 3	John Bledsoe..........	Francis Wisdom........ 6
George Smith.......... 4	Lawrence Young........ 5	Danl. Singleton....... 3
Roger Bell............ 4	John Cooper........... 8	John Cason............ 8
Peter Montague........ 4	Ambrose Smith......... 1	William Walker........ 3
John Smith............ 6	Zack. Allen........... 2	Edmond Burruss........ 1
William Sawyer........ 3	Vivian Daniel......... 1	John Alcock........... 5
Thos. Graves.......... 5	Henry Wood............ 1	John Talbird.......... 6
Charles Harrison...... 1	John Wisdom........... 2	Jos. Pratt............ 1
Joe Talbird........... 1	Wm. Cooke............. 1	John Anderson......... 9
John Mallory.......... 4	John Embrey........... 2	John Grove............ 1
John Branbane......... 1	Rich. Martin.......... 1	John Wright........... 1

(146)

Name	#	Name	#	Name	#
Thos. Walker	8	Robt. Martin	1	Lazarris Tilly	1
Robt. Bickers	2	James Coleman	9	Maliki Chiles	6
Wm. Bicker	1	Ambrose Coleman	4	John Martin	1
John Collins	4	John Conner	17	John Atkins	3
James Alverson	1	Jos. Busher	5	Samuel Brockman	7
Jos. Chanlor	3	Jos. Eve	8	James Atkins	1
Stephen Smith	5	James Griffin	7	David Cave	1
Samuel Kuchnall	11	Robt. Richards	7	Benj. Cave	2
Elijah Morton	3	John Hiatt	1	Reuben Daniel	2
John Henderson	5	Wm. Hiatt	1	Richard Bradley	4
Jos. Woolfolk	8	Robt. Smithe	1	Jos. Edmonson	4
Mrs. Bradburd	1	James Cozer	6	John Makes	5
John Gibbins	1	Jos. Reynolds	3	William Look	5
John Noel	2	James Davis	10	Rich. Broaduss	5
Thomas Kimbrough	4	John Wright	1	John Bell	1
William Brown	2	William Haley	1	Will. Bolling	5
Mrs. Cowherd	1	Robt. Lancaster	1	John Stevens	6
John Brockman		Phil Singleton	1	Richard Woolfolk	5
Samuel Sutton	2	Peter Montague	2	Robt. Thomas	4
Wm. Webb	7	Thos. Haley	3	Charles I. K. Smith	8
Wm. Howard	13	Charles Campbell	3	Col. Taylor	16
Lawrence Taliaferro	21	Rowland Thomas	10	Wm. Finnel	5
Eras. Taylor	6	Wm. Christopher	1	Martha Taylor	16
Charles Smith	6	Joseph Thomas	9	James Taylor	12
Benj. Winslow	11	Andrew Shepherd	9	Jos. Walker	10
Thos. Edmonson	7	Edward Walker	3	Richard Barbour	
Robert Terrill	6	Jno. Norton	11	Battell Harrison	
Jno. Beckston	5	Joseph Towles	4	Richard Todd	
Thos. Wright	1	James & Frances		Abraham Croswhite	1
M. Rucker	5	Madison	17	James Thomson	
Peter Rucker	3	James Megines	1	Bradley Kimbrom	
Edward Tinsley	8	David Bruce	1	Marion Barnett	6
Robert Dearing	1	Jack Gibbs	3	Edward Deering	
Grigsby	3	Wm. Crothwait	2	Jonathan Finnell	
Philip Easten	2	Joshua Step	1	Thos. Burgiss	
George Smith	17	Mildred James	2	William Whitman	
Wm. Morris	3	Mrs. Marshall	7	Benj. Porter, Sr.	
Alexander Waugh	3	Charles Lee	2	John Boston	
William Price	2	Elijah Morton	7	Wm. Jones	
Joseph Hopkins	1	John Wood	2	James Thornton	
Daniel Thornton	1	William Thornton	1	Joseph Williams	
William Croucher	3	Madam Taliaferro	6	Peter Lantor	
Hugh Jones	1	Benj. Cave	7	Henry Beckham	
John Williams	1	Robt. Dawson	3	Edward Watts	
Lawrence Taliaferro	7	Edward Spicer	5	Robisons, Sr.	
Francis Moore	6	George Morton	5	Spotswood	
Benj. Hawkins	8	Thos. Foster	3	Thos. Thorp	
John Willis	12	John Weatherspoon	1	Spotswood Ger	
Arch Campbell	2	Wm. Strother	4	James Roach	
James Arnold	2	Lewis Toone		Mungo Price	
Thos. Jones	1	John Dealwood	1	Wm. Pound	
Joshua Hudson	4	Thos. Hughs	6	Thos. Jameson	
John Pettey, Jr.	1	Solman Ryan	1	John Bramham	
John Finnel	1	James Stepp	3	John Bramham, Jr.	
David Moore	1	Abraham Chambers	3	Thos. Newman	
Lewis Willis	13	Rachel Reynolds	2	Henry Bourn	

Rose Quar............ 6	Thos. Larney.......... 1	Owen Thomas........... 3
Benj. Bohaon.......... 2	Widow Taliaferro, Jr.. 5	Henry Fitzhugh........ 5
James Sleet........... 3	Fenly Morris, Jr...... 3	Sarah Battle.......... 8
John Simson........... 2	Wm. Ball, Sr.......... 5	Angelon Price......... 7
William Simson........ 1	Joseph Sertain........ 1	John Foushee.......... 5
Alexander McDonald.... 1	John Sertani.......... 1	Richard Hill.......... 2
John Ransdel.......... 2	Joel Sertani.......... 1	Thos. Hughes, Jr...... 2
Luke Thornton......... 2	Thos. Welch........... 1	Bryan Sisson.......... 8
Presley Thornton...... 1	Isaac Sertani......... 1	John Morton........... 6
Col. Wm. Taliaferro...12	William Hawkins....... 2	Richard Morton........ 2
Samuel Thompson....... 2	Thos. Brown........... 1	Sarah Morton..........12
Arthur Hopes.......... 1	Bereman Davis......... 5	John Jones............ 9
Frances Conaway.......12	Joel Harvey........... 3	Wm. Minor............. 3
Alexander Waugh....... 7	James Kelly........... 1	Joseph Thomas, Jr..... 5
Col. Mongo Roys, Jr...11	Owen Smith............ 1	John Morgan........... 3
John Petley........... 3	Matthew Garrett....... 1	Rush Hudson........... 4
Robt. Boston.......... 2	William Hawkins....... 1	Richard Coal.......... 1
Robt. Boston, Jr...... 1		

(148)

9201 Imperial Avenue
Garden Grove, Calif.

Sunday, 20 January 1957

THE CROSTHWAITES

Dear Mr. Brockman:

Enclosed are copies of information that should have interest for you. The old Bible record herein copied and extracted was mailed to me by Dr. Crosthwait of Waco, Texas. All he informed me concerning the record was that he came across it among some of his wife's papers, that it was sent to them about 1900 from Tennessee, and that it came from one of the old family Bibles.

Here are recorded the births and deaths of some more of Jacob and Mary (Brockman) Crosthwait's descendants. The information in the record proves that Dr. Crosthwait of Waco is definitely a descendant of Jacob.

Items of interest and/or significance to me:

1. The date of Jacob Crosthwait's birth.

This date, 12 May 1730, places this Jacob almost certainly among the sons of that William Crosthwait who died 1743, along with Timothy, William second (who died in Culpeper 1770, with a son named Jacob, too), Abraham, and Isaac. At least, it certainly places this Jacob in that family in my judgment. Possibly Jacob was the youngest of the five brothers, but I can't prove that. At any rate, he is listed fifth in his brother Timothy's will of 1756.

2. Jacob and Mary (Brockman) Crosthwait's children.

The list found in this old family Bible (presumably started and kept by Asa Brockman Crosthwait) is substantially the same as the list to which you had access, as recorded in Nancy (Crosthwait) Taylor's Bible, and which you published in your ORANGE COUNTY (VA) FAMILIES, 1949. However, there are some differences, and altho the separate sheet I have devoted to Jacob and Mary's children contains some comments, I'd like to comment here also.

    a. The name someone interpreted as JENNINGS is plainly legible as JEMIMAH in the births, and even more legible in deaths.

    b. Aaron as a son of Jacob and Mary B. IS listed in this record. However, the circumstances are puzzling. Aaron's date of death was in the record, but the year extended out beyond the decorative margin of the page. Evidently someone cut the pages Dr. Crosthwait sent me out of the Bible containing them originally, and thereby cut off this year of Aaron's death.

Anyway, Asa B. in listing his own birth, made the fact very plain that he was "son of Aaron Crosthwait and grandson of Jacob." See typed page 152, second column.

c. "REBECCA, daughter of Jacob and Mary Crosthwait, departed this life August 21st 1836." No child named Rebecca is listed in the births of Jacob and Mary's children.

3. The name "Daniel BURRAS Crosthwait", (see deaths).

This was the child (b. 1824; d. 1825) of the second Aaron Crosthwait (b. 1799), himself the son of the first Aaron Crosthwait, son of Jacob and Mary, b. 1771. And the great-grandmother of this Daniel BURRAS Crosthwait was Elizabeth BURRUS, wife of John Brockman, these two being the parents of Eleanor Brockman who married the first Aaron Crosthwait.

4. Some of Aaron Crosthwait's (b. 1799) children's births and deaths in this record presumably kept by this Aaron's brother, Asa B. Crosthwait.

It is significant of something--I don't know what--that Asa B. Crosthwait entered into his own family's record the births and deaths of some of his brother Aaron's children, also Aaron's marriage in 1824 to Nancy McAlister. Maybe these two brothers, who lost their father when they were very little, sort of clung to each other, especially at times when and if they disliked their step-father, John Ireland.

5. More of Jacob and Mary (Brockman) Crosthwait's descendants.

Not only are William Lafayette Crosthwait, M. D., and his kin descended from Jacob and Mary B., but also all that large group of Crosthwaites in and around Morehead, Ky., and in Ashland, Ky. At least, I interpret the facts of this record that way--until documentary proof can be found to prove otherwise.

Miss Grace Crosthwait, P. O. Box 214, Morehead, Ky., a teacher in Morehead High School, wrote me in 1952 that "My great-grandfather Asa moved to Alabama, but Grandfather Aaron returned to Kentucky in 1854 and settled in Rowan County." Grace thought then, and I too considered it likely, that her family descended from Elijah Crosthwait, who (she said) "founded Crosthwaite Station near Winchester, Ky., in 1779." I didn't believe that claim, of course. I gave her the extract from Jacob's will which showed Elijah was his son.

Now I believe the evidence in this Bible record shows Grace's family descended from AARON Crosthwait, who married Eleanor Brockman. Either one-- Elijah or Aaron--these Crosthwaites still evidently descended from your Mary Brockman who married Jacob Crosthwait about 1764. Altho nothing in this record states where Asa B. Crosthwait was living during his earlier married life, it is to be assumed he was living in Kentucky where his father's and grandfather's Crosthwaits had lived. That he moved to Alabama about 1838-39 is shown by his entry of the birth of his son, Richard Henry Lee Crosthwait.

Incidentally, Grace Crosthwaite's Grandfather Aaron Crosthwait had a son named Jacob. He was Grace's "Uncle Jake", living at Farmers, Ky., wherever that is. But news received from the wife of a cousin of Grace's in Ashland, Ky., at Christmas told me that "Uncle Jake" passed away this past fall.

Also, Grace has a brother in Morehead, Ky., named Asa Brockburn or Brockman Crosthwaite. After Grace learned of the Brockman ancestry thru information I sent her a couple of years ago, she wrote that she had thought the name her brother carries was "Brockburn", but she indicated he had been named for forefathers. In view of this information, I do not know whether Grace's brother himself carries his name as Asa Brockburn or Asa Brockman Crosthwaite. Isn't it strange how these names of Asa and Brockman and Jacob, etc., have come right on down thru all the years?

                    Sincerely,

                    (Miss) Georgia Crosthwaite

(151)

CHILDREN OF JACOB AND MARY (BROCKMAN) CROSTHWAIT

As Found in the Old Family Bible Record
supplied by
WILLIAM LAFAYETTE CROSTHWAIT, M. D., Waco, Texas

LISTED IN BIRTHS:

Samuel Crosthwait, b. 19 August 1765

Nancy Crosthwait, b. 31 October 1766

Jemimah Crosthwait, b. 30 July 1768 (the name Jemimah is listed also in deaths, and the word is clearly legible as Jemimah, a dau.)

Reuben Crosthwait, b. 15 May 1771 (the figure "1" had been corrected, and the word "one" written after it. This date of 1771 conflicts with that ascribed as birth-date of AARON.)

Absolem Crosthwait, b. 1 July (or Jan.) 1774 (the figure "4" appears to have been corrected.)

Elijah Crosthwait, b. 17 May 1776 (the figure "6" looks as if it may have been changed from some other figure. This name had been almost crossed out, but was still legible.)

Mary Crosthwait, b. 22 May 1785

Aaron, "son of Jacob Crosthwait was born March 1771." (Aaron is listed also in deaths.)

The fact that Aaron is listed last, with a date conflicting with Reuben's above, is puzzling. Possibly the child was given two names, such as Reuben Aaron, and entered into the birth record as Reuben only, but was called (at least in later years) Aaron. Pure speculation, of course. Jacob Crosthwait did have a son named Aaron, as proved by the fact that Jacob mentions this deceased son when he wrote his will in 1803 (probated Dec. 28, 1807).

LISTED IN DEATHS ONLY:

Quote: "Rebecca daughter of Jacob and Mary Crosthwait departed this life August 21st 1836"

Here is another puzzle. Rebecca is not listed among the births of Jacob and Mary's children. Possibly one of the three daughters who is listed had a double name. If so, Mary is probably the one, because Jemimah's death is listed just above that of Rebecca, and Nancy's tombstone is said to read that she died in 1835 (Brockman's ORANGE VIRGINIA COUNTY FAMILIES, 1949) If Mary's name was Mary Rebecca, she could have been called Rebecca to distinguish her from her mother Mary. Note that these children's Grandmother Brockman was named Rebecca, as given in Brockman's SCRAPBOOK, 1952.

The above-quoted Bible record is presumed to have been started and kept by Asa Brockman Crosthwait until his death in 1849.

Georgia Crosthwaite
Garden Grove, California
13 January 1957

(152)

C
O
P
Y

FAMILY RECORD

Supplied by

WILLIAM LAFAYETTE CROSTHWAIT, M. D., Waco, Texas

BIRTHS

Jacob Crosthwait was born 12th of May 1730

Mary Crosthwait was born 15th of Sept. 1745

Samuel Crosthwait was born 19th of August 1765

Nancy Crosthwait was born 31st of October 1766

Jemimah Crosthwait was born 30th of July 1768

Reuben Crosthwait was born 15th of March 1771 (one) (last figure marked over and word "one" written after)

Absolem Crosthwait was born 8th of Jan. (?) 1774 (last figure had been changed from something else to "4")

Elijah Crosthwait was born 17th of May 1776 (Note that Elijah's name had been almost marked out.)

Mary Crosthwait was born 22nd of May 1785

Aaron son of Jacob Crosthwait was born March 1771

(end of first column)

Asa B. son of Aaron Crosthwait and Grandson of Jacob was born July 27, 1797

Mary Crosthwait consort of Asa B. was born 11th of Jan. (?) 1802

Aaron son of Aaron Crosthwait was born Feb. 26, 1799

Daniel Burras son of Aaron Crosthwait was born 23rd of Nov. 1824

Aaron son of Asa B. Crosthwait was born 4th of May 1823

Sarah Ann daughter of Asa B. Crosthwait was born April 2nd 1824

* (see below)

Eleanor consort of Aaron Crosthwait was born April 9, 1773

Jacob Wilson son of Asa B. Crosthwait was born August 31, 1826

(end of 2nd column and first page)

* (this entry accidentally omitted above by this copyist)
Mary Eleanor daughter of Asa B. and Mary was born March 31, 1825

Eleanor daughter of John Brockman and first consort of Aaron Crosthwait and then of John Ireland was born the 9th of April 1773 -- mother of A. B. Crosthwait

(153)

BIRTHS, cont.

Asa B. son of Asa B. Crosthwait was born the 12th of Dec. 1827

Elijah Taylor son of Aaron Crosthwait was born June 17, 1826

Jacob Wilson father of Mary Crosthwait was born January 15, 1778

James Monroe son of Asa B. and Mary Crosthwait was born Nov. 5, 1828

Elizabeth daughter of Asa B. and Mary Crosthwait was born Sept. 18, 1829 Friday evening

Shelton son of Asa B. and Mary Crosthwait was born Nov. 17, 1830

William son of Asa B. and Mary Crosthwait was born Sept. 23, 1831

(end of third column)

DEATHS

Jacob Crosthwait departed this life the 25th of Dec. 1807 or 180_
(As Jacob's will probated Dec. 28, 1807, this was 1807

Aaron son of Jacob Crosthwait departed this life the 4th Nov. ___
(This date had extended out beyond the decorative margin and had been cut off the page, but it had to be earlier than 1803, the year that Jacob Crosthwait made his will, because Eleanor Brockman Crosthwait was already the wife of John Ireland when the will was written.)

Mary Crosthwait consort of Jacob departed this life
(this entry was unfinished.)

Jemimah daughter of Mary and Jacob departed this life March 1808 or 1809

Rebecca daughter of Jacob and Mary Crosthwaite departed this life August 21, 1836
(Note that Rebecca's name does not appear in the list of Jacob and Mary (Brockman) Crosthwait's children, col. 1)

Sarah Ann daughter of _____ (illegible) and Mary Crosthwait depa ____ this life the 2nd of Sept. 18___

Daniel Burras son of Aaron Crosthwait departed this life Dec. 1825

Jacob Wilson son of_____(illegible) and Mary Crosthwait depart__ _____ life the 25th of Oct. 1826 (?)

Asa B. son of Asa B. and_____ Crosthwait departed this lif_ Dec. 31, 1829 (?)

(end of 4th column)

William son of Asa B. and Mary Crosthwait departed this life Sept. 27, 1831

Thomas Jefferson son of Asa B. Crosthwait departed this life Saturday 14th Sept. 1833

James Mallory son of Aaron Crosthwait departed this life Sept. 1, 1831

Washington Miller son of Asa B. and Mary Crosthwait died Dec. 6, 1834

Mary consort of Asa B. Crosthwait departed this life August 21, 1836

- - - - - - - - - - - - - - -

Theodore son of Asa B. and Eliza Magdaline Crosthwait departed this life Tuesday the 20 of Feb. 1838

(154)

Eliza daughter of Asa B. and Eliza Crosthwait departed this life Nov. 7, 1843

Asa B. Crosthwait departed this life August the 8th (?) 1849

(end of column)

BIRTHS (hand-written)

Isaac Owen son of Asa B. and Mary Crosthwait was born August 21, 1832

Thomas Jefferson son of Asa B. and Mary Crosthwait was born August 31, 1833

Washington Miller son of Asa B. and Mary Crosthwait was born Dec. 4, 1834

Catharine Miller daughter of Asa B. and Mary Crosthwait was born Sept. 28, 1835

Carson R___ son of Asa B. and Mary Crosthwait was born August 21, 1836 and Mary
(Left unfinished--probably started to write that Mary died same day.

- - - - - - - - - - - - - - - - -
- - - - - - - - - - - - - - - - -

Theodore son of Asa B. and Eliza Magdaline Crosthwait was born Thursday the 15th of Feb. 1838

Richard Henry Lee son of Asa B. and Eliza M. Crosthwait was born in Oakville Lawrence County Ala April 26, Friday 1839

Eliza daughter of Eliza and Asa B. Crosthwait was born August 17, 1841 in Oakville (two words illegible because written over decorative border) On Tuesday

(end of column)

(The following entries are found on the first page of the four-page fold; but are listed last in this copy.)

Page 1:

MARRIAGES

Asa B. Crosthwait was married to Mary Wilson daughter of Jacob Wilson the 11th of July 1822

Aaron Crosthwait was married to Nancy McAlister daughter of Daniel the 2nd of January 1824

Aaron son of Jacob Crosthwait was married to Eleanor daughter of John Brockman August 23, 1791

Mary Eleanor daughter of Asa B. and Mary Crosthwait was married to William Greenslade (? Grumlade? Grunslade?) in Lawrence Co. Ala August 9, 1843

- - - - - - - - - - - - - - - - -
- - - - - - - - - - - - - - - - -

Eugina (sp?) Josaphine daughter of Asa B. and Eliza Crosthwait was born April 16 18__

(end of column)

Eliza Magdaline Miller wife of A. B. Crosthwait was born January 6, 1819

David Miller son of Asa B. and Eliza M. Crosthwait
(The rest of this entry is so faint as to be illegible.)

J. M. Crosthwait was married to I. L. Enochs June 27th 1847

(In the next entry the first two lines are so faint as to be illegible, except the word "Eliza"; but 3rd line can be read.)

Eliza_____
Asa B. Crosthwait June 17, 1845

(Then a blank space of perhaps an inch.)

Isaac Owen son of J. M. and I. L. Crosthwait was Borne June the 1st 1848

(The last entry on this page is in pencil and very faint; it seems to be a repetition of the death entry of Mary (Wilson) Crosthwait, 1836)

Mary Crosth_____(cut off) Mother of J. M. Crosthwait (some words written over the decorative border; and readable below the border--) 1836 (?)

      This copy made by

                        Georgia Crosthwaite
                        Garden Grove, Calif.
                        8 January 1957

(156)

INFORMATION FOUND IN THE OLD FAMILY RECORD SUPPLIED BY

William Lafayette Crosthwait, M. D., Waco, Texas

(Arranged by Georgia Crosthwaite, 1-7-57)

Dr. Crosthwait's line of descent:

1. William Crosthwait, d. 1743, Orange County, Colonial Va., not found in this record.
2. Jacob Crosthwait, b. 12 May 1730; d. 25 Dec. 1807, Clark County, Ky.
3. Aaron Crosthwait, b. March 1771; d. 4 Nov. _____; m. 23 Aug. 1791, Ky.
4. Asa Brockman Crosthwait, d. 27 July 1797; d. 8 August 1849, Alabama (?)
5. James Monroe Crosthwait, d. 5 Nov. 1828; died in Mississippi
6.
7. William Lafayette Crosthwait, M.D., 107 So. Eighteenth St., Waco, Texas

Children of Asa Brockman Crosthwait, "son of Aaron and grandson of Jacob Crosthwait."

By first wife, Mary Wilson, b. 11 Jan. 1802; d. 21 Aug. 1836; m. 11 July 1822

1. Aaron, b. 2 May 1823
2. Sarah Ann, b. 2 April 1824; d. 2 Sept. 18____
3. Mary Eleanor, b. 31 March 1825;   m. 9 Aug. 1843
4. Jacob Wilson, b. 31 Aug. 1826; d. 25 October 1826 (2 months)
5. Asa Brockman, b. 12 Dec. 1827; d. 31 Dec. 1829 (2 yrs.)
6. James Monroe, b. 5 Nov. 1828; m. I. L. Enochs, 27 June 1847
7. Elizabeth, b. 18 Sept. 1829
8. Shelton, b. 17 Nov. 1830
9. William, b. 23 Sept. 1831; d. 27 Sept. 1831 (4 days)
10. Isaac Owen, b. 21 Aug. 1832
11. Thomas Jefferson, b. 31 Aug. 1833; d. 14 Sept. 1833 (2 weeks)
12. Washington Miller, b. 4 Dec. 1834; d. 4 Dec. 1834 (same day)
13. Catharine Miller, b. 28 Sept. 1835
14. Carson R ____, b. 21 August 1836 (same day his mother died)

MARY (WILSON) CROSTHWAIT DIED 21 August 1836.

By second wife Eliza Magdaline Miller, b. 6 Jan. 1819; m. 13 April 1837
15. Theodore, b. 15 Feb. 1838; d. 20 Feb. 1838 (5 days)
16. Richard Henry Lee, b. 26 April 1839 (born in Alabama)
17. Eliza. b. 17 August 1841; d. 7 Nov., 1843 (2 yrs. plus)
18. Eugina Josaphine (writing too faint to be legible)
19. David Miller   (writing too faint to be legible)

Children (in this record) of Aaron Crosthwait (1771-   ) and Eleanor Brockman (b. 9 Apr. 1773); m. 23 Aug. 1791:
Asa Brockman, b. 27 July 1797; d. 8 Aug. 1849
Aaron (2nd)   b. 26 Feb. 1799

Children of Aaron Crosthwait (2nd) and Nancy McAlister; m. 1824
Daniel BURRAS, b. 23 Nov. 1824; d. Dec. 1825
Elijah Taylor, b. 17 June 1826
James Mallory (sp?)

Is the Aaron Crosthwait (3rd one, but not son of 2nd one), b. 4 May 1823 (son of Asa Brockman and Mary Wilson Crosthwait) the grandfather of Grace Crosthwaite, Morehead, Ky.?

G. Crosthwaite

ASA BROCKMAN

Asa Brockman is an old settler of Ray County, Mo. and was born in Clark County, Kentucky, in the month of April 1826.

While he was yet an infant, his father, Mr. Joseph E. Brockman, immigrated to Missouri and after stopping about a year in Howard County, settled in Ray (section 22, township 51, range 28) and here has been the home of our subject ever since.

Asa Brockman received his education in the district schools of this county and remained at home working on his father's farm until he was twenty-two years of age, and then, fired by the excitement of the discovery of gold, he in 1849 went to California. He made the trip over land with an ox team.

He engaged in mining in California and remained there about eighteen months, returning at the expiration of that time to Ray County, by way of, Isthmus of Panama and New Orleans.

On his return home he took charge of his father's place and has since conducted and managed the farm.

Mr. Brockman was married in the autumn of 1852 to Miss Sarah F. Hudgens, daughter of B. A. Hudgens, Esq. of Ray County. Ten children were born as the result of this union; Joseph E., married Victoria Bellew. Their children are listed incorrectly as children of Asa and Mary Brockman on pages 98 and 99; John C.; H. M.; Nancy Jane; wife of J. Rossell; Lou Isabel, wife of Joseph Brown; James Ark; Sarah H.; and Asa B.

Mr. Brockman lived on the old homestead of his father, a fine tract of 280 acres of valuable upland.

Both himself and wife were members of the Christian Church at South Point, near Albany.

Asa Brockman was first lieutenant of Company C, 51st Regiment E.M.M. He enlisted in said company C, commanded by Captain John Sacry, in 1862. He was in the battle of Glasgow, in 1864 and taken prisoner in the fall of 1864 in said engagement. He was paroled and never afterward entered the service.

FIFTY-FIRST REGIMENT E.M.M.

Company C

Asa Brockman, first lieutenant, October 2, 1862; vacated March 12, 1865.

Anderson Elliott, second lieutenant, October 2, 1862; vacated March 12, 1865.

John Sacry, Captain, October 2, 1862; vacated March 12, 1865.

CHRISTIAN CHURCH AT SOUTH POINT

This church was organized at a school house, then situated two miles east of South Point, in Camden township, in April 1840, with the following original members, Viz: Jacob Warriner, Thomas Blair, John Riffe, Willis Warriner, George Blair, William Brockman, Joseph E. Brockman, Mary Brockman, Polly Warriner, Eliza J. Heu.

In 1854 the congregation erected a handsome frame building for divine worship at South Point.

Sarah Elliott was Mrs. Mary Balleu's sister (Sally).
Martha Ralph was the daughter of Jesse and Elizabeth Simpson.
Mahala Vaughn married Mr. Nat Pettus.

Joseph E. Brockman and Mary Brockman were among the first members when the church was organized in 1840.

Jane (Rosell) Happy was a member there in later years.

Fourteen of the family are resting in Old South Point Cemetery.

On the dedication of the church house at South Point the church was reorganized.

The following is a list of those who were members at that time: John Riffe, E. F. Withrow, Nancy Withrow, Foster Tribble, Mary Tribble, Zaza D. Ralph, Martha A. Ralph, Asa Brockman, Sarah Brockman, James Windsor, Lucinda Windsor, Thomas Blair, John Tarkey, Lydia Tarkey, Jackson Riffe, A. B. Ralph, Mary Ralph, John Chastain, William Artman, Jesse B. Simpson, Elizabeth Simpson, James Riffe, Willis Warriner, Mahala Vaughn, J. B. Elliott, Sarah Elliott, Emily Young.

Correction's

The Will of James Taylor, Albermarle County, Va., whose wife was Frances Brockman, daughter of William Brockman (died 1809) was dated December 2, 1819, and probated May 9, 1821. Witnesses were Samuel Elliott and William Brockman. In this Will James Taylor, lends to his wife Franky, for life his plantation and certain slaves. He leaves certain personal property to his son John, daughter Betsy Coper for life and then to her children; daughter Franky slaves and at her death to her children if any; son Jonathan, son Brockman, the latter gets the residue of the estate upon death of widow Frances Brockman Taylor, except dower which is to be distributed to all heirs.

Note: In previous books the spouse of Frances Brockman was given as John Taylor which was incorrect. W.E.B.

Catherine Brockman, daughter of William Brockman, Jr. of Albermarle, married Dabney Spicer, April 2, 1817. She married John Lewis January 25, 1833.

Page 89. Ambrose Madison was grandfather of President Madison, and John Madison, sheriff of King and Queen, 1703, was great grandfather.

The Will of John Mercer, Duplin County, S. C., 1781 named a daughter Nancy Brockman, and she was doubtless wife of the second Major Brockman, possibly son of John and Amelia Martin Brockman. The Mercers intermarried with the Seldens and Masons and were from Caroline Co., Va.

There is much evidence that Henry Brockman, who married Rebecca Salmon, lived in the Barbados many years and whether he was son of Thomas or of Sir William I cannot tell, but obviously he descended from the first John Brockman of Essex, England.

Page 119. William Rhodes, Will 1744 Orange Co., Va. was not the father of Hezekiah Rhodes, will 1762 Orange Co., Va. They were brothers.

"The Old Middlesex Parish Register"

William Rhodes m. Hannah Miller Sept. 13, 1722 Children:

1. Hezekiah Rhodes b. Oct. 8, 1723 (see Hezekiah Rhodes d. Dec. 10, 1723, Page 181)
2. William Rhodes b. Dec. 3, 1724
3. John Rhodes b. Nov. 4, 1727
4. Christopher Rhodes b. Nov. 25, 1730
5. James Rhodes b. Feb. 1, 1734, d. April 11, 1738
6. Hezekiah Rhodes b. June 8, 1738

Mrs. Robert M. Lester, 606 Pittsboro Rd., Chapel Hill, N. C., has data of the descendants of the children of William and Hannah Rhodes.

(160)

Kalamazoo, Michigan

September 13, 1956

Mr. W. E. Brockman
Midland National Bank
Minneapolis, Minnesota

Dear Mr. Brockman:

   A year ago last April my little daughter and I drove to Hillsboro, Illinois and other points in Montgomery County in search of information on our family. I searched records in the county court house, The Montgomery News, the library; and visited cemeteries and relatives. We were at the last moment referred to Mr. Walter R. Sanders in Litchfield. We spent several hours there searching for information on Harvey, Blackburn, Brown, Brockman, and Craig lines.

   Mr. Sanders later sent me some information on the Brown-Brockman line. He suggested that perhaps I could get some further information from you. Apparently a Mrs. Malinda T. Baird of Pasadena wrote to me asking about the Reverend Ambrose Brockman line. My great grandfather was an Ambrose Brockman, whose wife was Maria. I have never heard though that he was a minister. I had supposed they were farmers.

   Following is the information I have on our line of Brockmans:
Ambrose Brockman - married Maria___?___
They were residents in or near Warrensburg, Missouri. He died in Johnson County, Missouri about 1847, and she about 1872.

   They were the parents of the following children:

1. John W. Brockman - married Nancy R_____
2. Martha Annis - married - William LaFayette Brown
  B. Oct. 8, 1841   B. Dec. 17, 1839
  D. Jan. 20, 1883   D. May 7, 1886

  (They were my mother's parents, and were married March 7, 1861. Both died in Montgomery County, Illinois.)

3. Caroline E. - married - Henry Clay Peters
4. Hariet (or Harriet) - married - David (or Daniel) Knight

   My grandfather Brown was the son of Hiram Brown who married Elizabeth Craig. Hiram was the son of Richard who was born in Virginia (D.C. when it belonged to Maryland)? Richard married Sarah Womack, one of their children, Charlotte was the second wife of Samuel Brockman -
B. 2-26-1808, Ky. D. 1-12-1881.
Charlotte died 7-10-1866, age 55 yrs., 3 mos.
Charlotte's brother, Daniel B. 1800-10, married a Brockman and moved to Johnson County, Mo., where my great grand parents, Ambrose and Maria Brockman lived. Charlotte is buried in the Brown cemetery in Montgomery county.

In the Harvey line, my grandfather, Alexander Harvey married Mary Jane Blackburn. He had a brother John who married Martha Ellen Blackburn, Dec. 11, 1858. They had a son John W. Harvey who married Mary D. Brockman Feb. 12, 1874.

I can remember my mother saying that a little French gal got into our ancestry someway. Her name was Sally Sally. I don't know how to spell it, or whether she was on the Brockman side or the Brown.

Yours sincerely,

George A. Harvey

1120 Lakeway Avenue
Kalamazoo 28, Michigan

P.S. Mr. Sanders mentioned your reference to a Shelton Brockman. My grandmother Brown, nee Brockman, had a son "John Shelton". He lived only about 15 months. It would seem though that there must be some related ancestry in our respective lines.

- - - - - -

September 17, 1956

Mr. George A. Harvey
1120 Lakeway Avenue
Kalamazoo 28, Michigan

Dear Mr. Harvey:

So far as I am able to tell, your ancestor, Ambrose Brockman, whose wife's name is Maria, was the son of Thomas Brockman of Albermarle County, Virginia, who married in 1770 a daughter of Henry Shelton. Thomas was a revolutionary soldier and moved to Kentucky and later to Illinois. He had a son, Samuel, who married Charlotte L. Brown. He had several other children, some of which died in Kentucky and some in Illinois. I believe that Ambrose Brockman was another son who went to Missouri where he died. According to your letter he had one son, John W. Brockman, who married Nancy R., a daughter Martha who married William Lafayette Brown, a daughter Caroline Elizabeth who married Henry C. Peters, and a daughter Harriet who married David Knight. Now I do not have the proof that Ambrose was the son of Thomas but I believe him to be. Also, I believe he had a son named Shelton, which was the surname of his wife.

W. E. Brockman

THE BROCKMANS OF RANDOLPH CO., MO.

Henry Brockman, emigrated to the Barbadoes Islands thence to Maryland where there is recorded, in 1674, the sale of his title to a grant of land.

He then continued to King and Queens County, Va. There is no documentary proof of his marriage or of his heirs. The Court House with all records having been destroyed during the Civil War.

1st Generation

Samuel and Mary Brockman. Deeds recorded in Orange Co. Va., show that he sold large holdings in King and Queens Co. in 1732 and moved to Orange Co. purchasing 300 a. tracts of land there.

His will probated in 1766, lists large bequests to his wife and each of his seven children.

2nd Generation

Samuel and Rebecca Brockman. He died in 1792.

3rd Generation

John and Elizabeth Burris Brockman. His will probated in Orange Co. in 1835 lists bequests of land and slaves also lists his 11 children.

4th Generation

Elijah and Sally Tomlin Brockman. The Book states they were married in 1796 and that deeds show they sold their property in Va. in early 1800 and all trace lost to the author.

A letter from Laura Cox, a daughter of John Wash B. dated July 26, 1922, and enclosing a note signed by Uncle John Wash, to my Brother Vinson Adams, states that his grandparents were Elijah and Sally Tomlin B. They no doubt moved to Ky. No complete list of their children.

5th Generation

Jacob and Mary Kabler Brockman. He was born in 1810, d. 1873, legend is that he came from Ky.

Martha Brockman, Moberly, Mo. grand daughter of Jacob's son Elijah, gave me much data on Jacob's children from old Bible records. Many Brockmans were Millers in Va. and in Boone Co., Ky.

Jacob lived at or near Bagbyo Mill.

6th Generation

Children of Jacob and Mary.

Thos. J. Brockman	b.	d.	2-6-1854
Louis C. "	b.	d.	10-21-1853
Susan Ann "	b.	d.	7-14-1856
Wm. Allen "	b. 1831	d.	
Elijah S. "	b. 6-15-1835	d.	12-18-1876
John Wash. "	b. 7-26-1839	d.	
Nimrod W. W."	(Killed in action Dalton)	d.	5-12-1864

Battle of Resacca, Ga. (Ga. in Civil War. Bledsoes Battery)
Mary Ellen Brockman M. John Simpon Minor

E. Elizabeth "	M. 1849 b. 1833	d.	1904
John Thomas Adams	b. 1830	d.	1851

7th Generation

Jacob V. Adams   b. Dec. 1849   d. 1926 M. Sarah E. Bradley

8th Generation

Claude B. Adams   b. 1878   M. Emma Marksheffee 1904
Came from Higbee, Mo. to Colorado in 1902.

(164)

Family Chart, Prepared by George Hunter Terrett III
Who was born 1856, married Alice Gillespie,
1892 and died 1926. Mrs. Terrett
died 1916

There were two children, George H. who married
Louise Francis, and Marguerite Alice
who married W. E. Brockman
June 8, 1918.
One Child,
Elizabeth Susan who married
Robert Bruce Klaverkamp
August 24, 1957.

(See Page 165)

(165)

Terrett Family Genealogy Chart

- **Cap. W. H. Terrett, 1752-1826**
  - W. H. Terrett, 1707-1758
  - Margaret Pearson, 1720-1796
    - Simon Pearson
    - Nathaniel Chapman
    - Constance Pearson, 1712-1797
- **Amelia Hunter, 1756-1830**
  - Elizabeth Chapman, 1733-
  - Dr. John Hunter, 1700-1763

Cap. Geo. H. Terrett, 1778-1843

- **Mary Keene, 1783-1833**
  - Capt. Newton Keene
  - Sarah Butler, 1715-1772
    - Maj. Lawrene Butler
    - Sarah Burditt
- **Burdett Ashton, 1747-1814**
  - Charles Ashton, 1712-1781
    - Chas. Ashton, 1671-1731
    - Chas. Ashton

Hannah Butler Ashton, 1785-1860

- **Burdette Ashton, 1747-1814**
  - Chas. Ashton, 1712-1781
    - Sarah Burditt
    - Maj. Lawrene Butler
  - Sarah Butler, 1715-1781
- **Mary Keene, 1783-1833**
  - Capt. Newton Keene
    - Keene
    - Wray

Col. Geo. H. Terrett, 18 - 1875

Mary Ashton, 1787-

- **Helen Wray**
  - Wray
  - Frances Dade
- **Col. Charles Stuart**
  - Chas. Stuart, 1730-
    - Jane Gibbon
    - Rev. David Stuart

Jacob Wray Stuart

Margaret Stuart, 1823-1904

Geo. Hunter Terrett m. Alice Gillespie 1892, 1856-1926

Marquette Alice Terrett m. W. E. Brockman 6-8-1918, -?- 1895-

Georg. G. Terrett, Feb. 20, 1899 - May 23, 1950

GEORGE HUNTER TERRETT
1807-1875

George Hunter Terrett was born near Alexandria, Virginia in 1807, and, after a long career in the United States Marine Corps and later the Confederate States Army and Marine Corps, he died in 1875, we believe, at the old Oakland home place and was there buried, later being removed to Arlington National Cemetary. My wife, formerly Marguerite Terrett, a granddaughter and Mrs. Catherine Terrett Parsons, a grandniece visited the old burial ground last month and found gravemarkers of the family. Mrs. Parsons is a daughter of Thomas Terrett, Jr., whose father was Thomas Senior. Her husband is Arthur C. Parsons and they reside at 2706 Cathedral Avenue, Washington, D.C.

George Hunter Terrett was commissioned a second Lieut in the Marine Corps from Virginia, April 1, 1830. He served in many capacities in the waters near home and in foreign waters, and was attached to many different ships and in 1844 was Senior Marine Officer on board the Flagship Cumberland in the Mediterranean. He was commissioned Captain, March 16, 1847, and was sent to Vera Cruz, Mexico in June. On October 24, he was commissioned a Major by Brevet to rank from September 13, 1847, for gallant and meritorious conduct at the storming of the Castle of Chapultepec and his advance upon the San Cosme Gate. He later served on the Independence, the Minnesota, and accompanied Admiral Peary to open up Japan to trade in the fifties. He was in charge of the Navy Yard and Marine Barracks at Washington in April, 1861. He resigned his commission April 22, and became a Major in the Confederates States Navy. Because of the limited Naval activities of the Confederate States he was transferred to the Confederate States Army as Colonel. On April 14, 1865 he was captured at Amelia Courthouse and sent to Old Capitol Prison at Washington, D.C., and later sent to Johnsons Island, Ohio where he was released on parole July 25, 1865, upon taking the oath of allegiance to the United States.

The large Oil Painting made of Major George Hunter Terrett in Italy hangs in the home of his granddaughter, Mrs. W. E. Brockman, now of Minneapolis, Minn., and may eventually be turned over to the Department of Defense for the walls of the Pentagon. During the Civil War the home at Oakland was burned and the family went South, returning after the war to rebuild Oakland and he spent the remainder of his life in his beloved homeland.

W. E. Brockman

INDEX to
Orange County, VA FAMILIES - Vol. #2

Name	Page	Name	Page	Name	Page
ABBOT, RODGER	139	. WILLIAM	19,30,34,50	ADDAMS, THOMAS	35
ABEL, JOHN	6	ACREE, REBECCA MORRIS	28	ADDISON, JEAN	19
. JOSEPH	50	WILLIAM	28	ADDOMS, ELEY WELSH	2
. MARGARET TINDAR	6	ADAMS,	136	JAMES	2
. MARGARET TINDER	4	. ANN	48	ADKINS, JAMES	140,143
. MARY	8	. BENJAMIN	8,86	. JOHN	19
ABELL, ALEAPER	11	. BETSY	19	. NANCY	19
. ALEXANDER	35	. CATHERINE	22	. SUSANNA	19
. CABEL	29,35,40	. CLAUDE B.	163	ADKINSON, JOHN	24
. JOHN	29,64,85	. DELIA SMITH	18	MARY	24
. JOHN S.	41	. ELISHA	18	AERERBON, OBEDIAH	135
. MARGARET	85	. ELIZABETH BROCKMAN	163	AERY, AMANDA DAWSON	47
. NANCY	31	. EMMA MARKSHEFFEE	163	. ELIZABETH SHIFLET	32
. POLLY	35	. FRANKEY	12	. GEORGE	32
. POLLY ABELL	35	. JACOB V.	163	. WILLIAM	26,47
. RICHARD	11	. JAMES	8,10,12,34,85	AHART, FRANKEY	15
. RICHARD S.	41	. JOHN	65,85	. POLLY	28
. SALLY KING	29	. JOHN THOMAS	163	. RACHEL	26
. SARAH	40	. JUDITH BURNLEY	31	AHEART, CATHERINE	24
. SARAH HILMAN	41	. LUCH	42	. CHRISTIANA	6
. SUSANNA	29	. LUCY	24	. CHRISTINA	4
ABLET, EDWARD	139	. MARY	18,42,86	. JACOB	4,6
ABRAHAM, BARBARA CLARK	44	. MARY CHAMBERS	8	. JOHN	9
. BOOTON	44	. MILLY COLEMAN	8	. MARY BRUCE	4,6
. FRANCIS	28	. NANCY	33	. PEGGY PEARSON	9
. JESTIN MALLORY	28	. PATSY HARPER	34	AHRRIS, ANN	125
ACRE, BETSY	26	. ROBERT	138	AIRY, MARY STOWERS	13
. ELIZABETH	21	. SARAH BRADLEY	163	WILLIAM	13
. ELIZABETH ACRE	21	. THOMAS	18-19,24	ALAN, JAMES	126
. JAMES	21	. THOMAS B.	31	PATSY WOOLFOLK	126
. LUCY	34	. VINSON	163	ALBRIGHT, GEORGE	15
. NANCY	19	. WILLIAM	33	ALCOCK, CATY BELL	10
. SALLY	30	ADCOCK, ELLEN	102	. JOHN	68,145

INDEX to
Orange County, VA FAMILIES - Vol. #2

Name	Page	Name	Page	Name	Page
. MARY BELL	11,80	ALLBRIGHT, JOHN	36	. FRANCES PEARSON	28
. PATSY	42	ALLEE, ELIZABETH GALT	103	. FRANCIS ESTES	39
. ROBERT	11,68	. JAMES GALT	103	. HENRY	24
. WILLIAM	10,68	. JAMES WILLIAM	103	. JAMES	39
ALCOCKE, JOSEPH	33	. LAURA E.	103	. MICHAEL	41
LUCY	33	. MAUDE FRANKLIN	102-103	. NANCY BEAZLEY	24
ALDERSON, BECKROL	143	. NELL FRANKLIN	103	. NANCY WILLIAMS	41
JOHN	143	. W.L.	103	. ROBERT	28,41
ALEXANDER, ANNA BURRUS	41	. WARREN LOGAN	102	. WILLIAM	27
. BENJAMIN	84	ALLEN, BARBARY	9	ANDERSON,	139
. ELIZABETH	16	. BENJAMIN	75	. ANN	39
. FRANKEY AHART	15	. ELIZABETH WALLACE	24	. BENJAMIN	30
. FRANKEY EHART	15	. JAMES	12	. CULVERT	75
. JAMES	3,6,15-17,84	. JOHN	140	. ELIZABETH	50
. JERUSA TOWNSEND	6	. PATSY WOOLFOLK	12	. ESTHER	50
. MARTHA TOWNSEND	3	. REUBEN	75	. FRANCES	41
. SAMUEL D.	41	. WILLIAM	24	. FRANCIS	50
ALKINS, AMY PIGG	4	. ZACKARY	145	. GEORGE	50,57,76,136
. ANN BURRASS	4	ALMOND, JOHN	65	.	138,141-142,145
. FRANKEY CHILES	24	ALSOP, FANNY	31	. HANNAH	50
. GENTRY	24	ALVERSON, BACKNEL	136	. ISAAC	145
. JAMES	4	JAMES	146	. JACOB	33,39,41
. JOHN	4	ALVIS, AGNES ARMSTRONG	21	. JANE	50
. JOSEPH	3	HENRY	21	. JEFFERSON D.	113
. MILDRED	44	AMBERGER, CONRADS	50	. JOEL	29,46
. MILLY JAMES	3	AMBUGER, BARBARA	75	. JOHN	39,50,145
. WILLIAM	4,29	CORNADE	75	. LUCY HAWKINS	33
. WINIFRED BRIANT	4	AMOS, ANN MARR	21	. LUCY REDDISH	29
. WISDOM	24	JOSEPH	21	. MARGARET	50
ALKINSON, SALLY SILBY	25	AMUS, BENJAMIN	19	. MARY	33,46,50
THOMAS	25	NANCY ACRE	19	. MARY MILLER	30
ALLAN, JAMES	75	ANCEL, NANCY	27	. MILLY BELL	21
WILLIAM	75	ANCELL, ELIZABETH	41	. NANCY LOWER	39

168

INDEX to
Orange County, VA FAMILIES - Vol. #2

Name	Page	Name	Page	Name	Page
. NANNA	22	. MARGARET GOLDEN	28	. ELIZABETH POE	15
. NATHAN D.	21	. NICHOLAS	9	. FRANCES JENNINGS	11
. SARAH	38	. PEGGY SANFORD	25	. FRANKIE WISDOM	7
. SUSANNAH	76	. SALLY	27	. GENTRY	48
. THEODOSIA	24	. SARAH	9	. HEZEKIAH	13
. URIAH	72	. SUSANNA	11	. JAMES	6,14-15,24,142
. VICTORIA C. MORGAN	113	. THOMAS	25	.	146
. WILLIAM	33,39,50,57	. WILLIAM B.	33	. JOHN	7,11,18,25-26
.	141-142,145	. WILLIS	26,28,33	.	29-30,48,64,68,82,146
ANFORD, JOHN	139	ARRINGTON, WILLIE	99	. JONATHAN	36
APPLEBY, ROBERT	50	ARTMAN, WILLIAM	158	. JOSEPH	5,7,11,35,47
ARA, MELONE	35	ASHBY, THOMAS	57	. LUCY	24
ARANZY, ZANNY	20	ASHER, JOHN	139	. MARGARET	21,48
ARCHER, ANN	2	ASHTON, BURDETT	165	. MARGARET ATKINS	48
JONAS	135	. BURDETTE	165	. MILLY JAMES	5
ARHART, JACOB	2	. CHARLES	165	. MILLY QUISENBERRY	36
NANNY BALLARD	2	. HANNAH B.	165	. NANCY	23
ARMSTRONG, AGNES	21	. MARY	165	. NANCY ATKINS	23
ARNETT, JANE E.	41	. MARY KEENE	165	. PATSY	32
. LIDDIA	37	. SARAH BURDITT	165	. PEGGY	32
. WILLIAM	22,37,41	. SARAH BUTLER	165	. PEGGY CAMPBELL	30
ARNOLD, ANNA	27	ASKEW, JOHN	140	. REBECCA	26
. BENJAMIN	27	ATKINS, ALICE MALLORY	47	. RHOADA	18
. BILLY F. BROCKMAN	99	. AMEY PIGG	6	. RHODY	38
. ELIZABETH ATKINS	14	. ANN	11	. ROSANNA	29
. EUGENE	99	. ANN ATKINS	11	. SALLY	26
. IRIS	134	. ANN BURRASS	7	. SALLY ATKINS	26
. ISAAC	141-142,145	. ANN M.	43	. SALLY CHILES	13
. JAMES	14,145-146	. ANNIE	38	. SILENCE	11
. JANE	99	. DAVIS	47	. SPENCER I.	39
. JANE MARTIN	33	. DICKINSON	48	. SPENCER J.	43,45
. JOANNA	26	. EDWARD	7,23	. SUSAN WEBB	48
. JOSEPH	80	. ELIZABETH	14,39	. SUSANNA	25

INDEX to
Orange County, VA FAMILIES - Vol. #2

Name	Page	Name	Page	Name	Page
. SUSANNAH	18	BAILES, CENCY OLLIVER	31	MEDLEY	20
. THOMAS	144	JOSEPH	31	BALLARD, ANN	2,5
. WALLER	26	BAILEY, LEWIS	24	. BLAIR	135
. WILLIAM	6	. LUCY MALLORY	24	. DAVID C.	35
. WINIFRED BRYANT	6	. MARY LEE GRYMES	23	. ELIZ. HUCKSTEP	35
. WISDOM	23	. WILLIAM P.	23	. ELIZA BURT	43
AUSBUM, MILLY CUDDEN	5	BAILORS, M.	138	. ELIZABETH	23
ROBERT	5	BAILY, JAMES	29	. ELIZABETH GAINES	11
AUSBURN, MILLY CUDDEN	3	. JANE	46	. ELIZABETH SMITH	4,7
ROBERT	3	. JANE BAILY	46	. ELIZABETH THORNHILL	25
AUSTIN, DAVID	34	. NANCY MALLORY	29	. GARLAND	43
. FANNY WILLIAMS	34	. SAMUEL	46	. JAMES	43
. JANE MELONE	48	BAIN,		. JOHN	28
. JOHN	31	. ELIZABETH SHOPSHIRE	1	. LARKIN	11
. JUSTINA BURRUS	31	. JOSEPH	1	. MARTHA	23
. MARY SNOW	28	BAIRD, MALINDA T.	160	. MARY	2
. MILDRED	47	BAITTAILS, NICKLAS	138	. MARY SNOW	18
. NANCY	34	BAKER,		. MILLY	13
. RICHARD	28	. AMERICA WOOLFOLK	125	. MOREMAN	23
. WILLIS	48	. BOTT	141	. NANNY	2
AXFORD, HIGGIN	75	. ROBERT	78	. PHILIP	13
. JOHN	75	. SAMUEL	75,138	. SARAH GOODALL	40
. SUSANNAH	75	. VIRGINIA	105	. SUSANNA	24
AYHEART, FELICIA	33	BALKON, THOMAS	145	. THOMAS	4,7,140,143
AYLETT, MAJOR	136	BALL, ELIZA ANN	46	. WASHING	25
BABER, NANCY SPRADLING	9	. FAYETTE	40	. WILL	140
.	20	. FRANCES PAYNE	40	. WILLIAM	18,143
. ROBERT	9,20	. FRANCIS WILLIAMS	40	. WILSON	40
BACON, STOVIN	138	. JESSE	46	BALLEU, MARY	158
BADGER, MARGARET	47	. JESSIE	40	BALLEW, VICTORIA	98
BAGGOTT, JAMES	43	. SAMUEL	139	BALMAINE, ALEXANDER	11
JUSTINA JOHNSON	43	. WILLIAM	147	LUCY TAYLOR	11
BAGLEY, SARAH	69	BALLAD, JANE DEHONEY	20	BALYE, JOHN	26

INDEX to
Orange County, VA FAMILIES - Vol. #2

POLLY	26	. PHILIP	32,68,82	BARR,	98
BAMBRIDGE,ANN	50	. PHILIP P.	28	BARRETT,PATRICK	44
BAMGARDENER,FREDERICK	73	. RICHARD	19,58,140	. PEGGY	14
BANISTER,ARTHUR	68,82	.	143-144,146	. SALLY BRIDWELL	44
OLIVER	68,82	. SARAH	37	BARTLETT,HARRY	128
BANKER,CHRISTINE	47	. THOMAS	1,11,19,37,43	BARTLOW,SARAH	124
BANKS,ANN DAVIS	28	.	58,68-69	BARTON,	
. DOROTHY SNAYMAN	105	BARCUS,ARCHIBALD	42	. ELEANOR BROCKMAN	99
. GENARD	78	BARKER,JAMES	15	. FRED	99
. GERARD	28	. KETURAH ROBINSON	34	. JOHN	31
. J.P.	105	. LEONARD	34	. MILLY MAY	31
. WILLIAM	50	. SARAH MAZES	15	BASHAW,ELIZABETH	108
BARBAGE,BETSY	7	BARKSDALE,A.M.	47	BASKINE,WILLIAM	50
BARBER,ANN	133	. ANN DOUGLAS	5	BASKINS,WILLIAM	50
THOMAS	133	. NATHANIEL	5	BASS,LORAINE	114
BARBOUR,AMBROSE	2	BARLEY,ROBERT	50	BATCHELOR,CARL LOT	115
. CATHERINE THOMAS	2	BARNARD,		. HELEN	115
. FRANCES JOHNSON	28	. CIRRELDA HALE	103	. MALLIE CAREY	115
. GABRIEL	18	. CIRRELDIA	103	. MARY A.H.	110
. J.W.	28,33	. FRANCIS ANN	103	. NAPOLEON B.	110
. JAMES	18,68,82,135,139	. MARY	103	. REBECCA GAYDEN	110-111
. JOHN	135	. THOMAS	103	. THOMAS	110,112,116
. LUCY	21,71	BARNET,	144	. VICTORIA C.	110
. LUCY JOHNSON	18	JOHN	138	. VIOLET	111
. M. JAMES	138	BARNETT,ANN	1,11	BATLEY,ALFRED	34
. MARIA	47	. ANNE	1	MISHEL WRIGHT	34
. MARY	83	. ELIZABETH CARRELL	1,11	BATTAILE,	137
. MARY MOORE	19	. JOHN	65,85,137	. ALFRED	36,45
. MARY T.	43	. MARION	146	. ANN TALIAFERRO	14
. MARY THOMAS	1,11	. WILLIAM	1,11	. ELIZ.	45
. MORDICAI	68	BARNSTER,ARTHUR	82	. LAURENCE	14
. NELLY M.	33	OLIVER	82	. NICHOLAS	144
. PEGGY ATKINS	32	BARNUM,SALLIE	125	BATTAILES,	143,145

INDEX to
Orange County, VA FAMILIES - Vol. #2

BATTITT, LAWRENCE	140	. JAMES	42	. CATHERINE	69
BATTLE, ALFRED	48	. JANE	49	. CHARLES	16
. POLLY JONES	48	. JOHN	27,34,49,58	. ELIZABETH	7
. SARAH	147	. JUCINDA HAYNES	34	. ELIZABETH WAIT	16
BATTLES,	142	. LURINNA	41	. GUSTIN	15
BATTLEY,	141	. ROBERT M.	30-31,34	. JAMES	7-8,71
MOSES	135	. SARAH WINSLOW	30	. JOHN	15,80
BAUGHAM, BENJAMIN	141	BEAL, CHARLES	142	. MILDRED	80
BAUGHKER, BETSY	32	. RICHARD	142,144	. MILLY	8
BAUGHON, JOSEPH	22	. TAVENNER	144	. SALLY EAVES	15
POLLY	22	. TAVENOR	142	. SARAH	15
BAUGKER, CATHERINE	32	. TEVENER	143	. THEODORA	15
ELIZABETH	43	BEALE,	140	. WILLIAM	20,69
BAUKERAND, JACOB	48	. ANN	78-79	BEAVEEN, JOHN	140
POLLY DAVIS	48	. CHARLES	78	BEAZEY, BETSY	25
BAWLING, JOHN	2	. ELIZABETH	78	BEAZLEY, ANN	33,38,47
MARY BALLARD	2	. FANNY	30	. AUGUSTINE	25
BAXTER, JAMES	36	. FRANCIS	1,78	. BETTY	24
SALLY PAYNE	36	. HANNAH GORDON	11	. CATHERINE	12
BAYLE, JOHN	26	. MOLLY	79	. CHARLES	35
POLLY	26	. RICHARD	79	. ELIZABETH	32
BAYLOR, GEORGE	65	. TAVERNOR	78	. FRANKY POWELL	25-26
JOHN	58,144	. WILLIAM	11,136	. JAMES	12,33,38,68
BAYNE, HENRY	50	BEALES, M.	138	.	82-83
BEACH, DELILA TRUE	27	BEALS, CHARLES	45	. JOHN	26,47
. HENRY	27	MARY GORDON	45	. LUCY PORTER	26
. JOSEPH	27	BEASLEY, ALICE	114	. MARY	38
BEACHAM, THOMAS	142	. ALICE GAMMONS	114	. NANCY	24
BEACON, ELIZABETH	23	. ALICE O.	113	. SARAH	20
BEADLES, ANN	27	. ANN	7	. SUSANNA GRAVES	35
. CLARY	31	. AUGUSTINE	15	. VALENTINE	25-26
. DELILAH	68,83	. BENNET	50	. WILLIAM	35,68,83
. ELIZABETH WINSLOW	42	. BETSY POWELL	20	BECK, SARAH	122

INDEX to
Orange County, VA FAMILIES - Vol. #2

BECKET, JERMIMA KEA	38	. BETSY	29	. ROBERT W.	34
RICHARD	38	. BOSWELL	46	. ROGER	15,20,43,78-79
BECKETON, JOHN	146	. BROCKMAN	34	.	136-137,140,142-143
BECKETT,		. CATY	10	.	144-145
. NANCY THORNHILL	29	. ELIZA P.	26	. SALLY	3,6,43
. RICHARD	29	. ELIZABETH	8,26,46,50	. SALLY B.	32
BECKHAM, ABNER	14-15	. ELIZABETH CAVE	132	. SALLY BURNLEY	18
. BENJAMIN	35,49	. ELIZABETH JOHNSON	11	. SAMUEL	58
. ELIZABETH	19	. FANNY MINTON	28	. SARAH MILBURN	28
. FRANCES THOMAS	15	. FRANCES NEWMAN	46	. SUSANNA	5
. HENRY	19,145-146	. FRANCIS	28	. SUSANNA ADKINS	19
. JAMES	58	. HENRY	19,35,68,83	. SUSANNAH	15
. JOHN	33	. JACOB	31	. THOMAS	8,10,15,18
. MARYANN PORTER	35	. JAMES	50,58,68,80	.	21-23,28,58,68,78-79
. NANCY	22	. JAMES M.	80	.	80-81,83,86,92
. NANCY PORTER	49	. JOHN	12,26,28,50,58,81	. WILLIAM	11,18,32,57-58
. REBECCA HANCOCK	33	.	86,142-143,146	.	68,70,80-81,137
. STEPHEN	141,145	. JOSEPH	26	. WILLIAM B.	46
BECKUM, THOMAS	141	. JUDITH BURNLEY	12	. WILLIAM BROCKMAN	132
BEECON, PHILLIS	23	. LUCY REYNOLDS	22	BELLEW, VICTORIA	157
BEEDLE,		. MARGARET	8,50	BELLFIELD, ELIZABETH	132
. ELIZABETH CASSEN	6	. MARTHA TALIAFERRO	31	. MARIA PORTER	132
. JOHN	6	. MARY	8,11,58,80,96,125	. MARY MERIWETHER	132
BEEDLES,		. MAY HULDA	35	. RICHARFD	132
. ELIZABETH CASEN	4	. MILLER	68	. THOMAS WRIGHT	132
. JOHN	4	. MILLY	21	BENION, MARTIN	76
BEGEN, ROBERT	140	. NANCY	19	. SARAH	76
BEGGS, ROBERT	141-142	. PATRICK	16	. WILLIAM	76
BEGORE, ROBERT	143	. POLLY	15	BENNETT, B.	15
BELFIELD, WRIGHT	139	. POLLY QUISENBERRY	16	BARTLETT	69,79
BELK, MARGARET	140	. REBECCA	20	BENSON, CATHERINE	124
BELL, ANN	2	. REBECCA BROCKMAN	34	. CHARLES	124
. ANNE T. SCHENK	34	. RHOADA ATKINS	18	. ELEANOR	124

INDEX to
Orange County, VA FAMILIES - Vol. #2

BEORID,JACOB	136	. JOSEPH	27-28,35	. MILLY	40
BEORILL,JACOB	136	. LUCY OVERTON	47	. REBECCA	36
BERREY,MARY	3	. MATILDA	28	. REBECCA BINGHAM	36
BERRY,ANTHONY	38	. NANCE MALLORY	15	. WYATT	36
. JANE LEE	38	. NANCY	41	BINNS,THOMAS	140
. MARY	6	. NANCY LANDRUM	13	BIRD,ANDREW	58
. RACHEL ROW	30	. NICHOLAS	39	. JAMES	50
. WILLIAM S.	30	. POLLY	25	. SAMUEL	140
BERRYMAN,REUBEN	82	. PROCTOR	47	BIRDINI,RICHARD	137
BESS,SALLY	36	. ROBERT	50,77,146	BIRT,RUTHY	8
BEVERLEY,AGATHA	90	. ROSANNA ATKINS	29	BISHOP,ANN CLARK	15
. ROBERT	90	. SALLY LEATHERS	17	. JANE TERRELL	17
. WILLIAM	57	. SELENA	39	. JOSEPH	15,17
BEVERLY,AGATHA	117	. SUSAN	35	. SAMUEL	40
WILLIAM	117	. WILLIALM	80	. SARAH VIA	40
BHEECONE,STEVEN	139	. WILLIAM	17,77,146	BISWELL,JOHN	74
BIBB,CHARLES	124	BICKET,JOHN	139	BIXING,JOHN	136
. CHRISTIAN	89,125	BICOON,WILLIAM	139	BLACK,ALPHA RAINES	38
. ELIZABETH WOOLFOLK	124	BIGGERS,BETSY	32	. JACOB	35
. MOURNING GROOM	47	. HULDAH	22	. JOSHUA	38
. SARAH BROCKMAN	10	. MASON	22,32,34	. MARGARET	50
. THOMAS	10	. PHOEBE	34	. NANCY CAVE	35
. WILLIAM	47	. ROBERT	138,144	. NANCY SEBREE	40
BICCONE,SIMON	139	BIGGINS,ROBERT	143	. THOMAS	50
BICKERS,ABNER	41	BILL,FANNY BOSTON	27	. WILLIAM	40
. BENJAMIN	39	WILLIAM	27	BLACKBOURN,ARTHUR	75
. CABEL	17	BILLINGSBY,FRANCIS	50	. ESTHER	75
. ELIZABETH	27	BINGHAM,	32	. WILLIAM	75
. GEORGE	15,39	. GEORGE	16,18,21-26	BLACKBURN,	160
. JOANNA	39	.	29-30,32-33,36-37-38	. MARTHA E.	161
. JOANNA MARTIN	39	.	39	. MARY J.	161
. JOEL	29	. JOSIAH	36	BLACKERBY,	
. JOHN	13	. MARIA	39	. JANE MARSHALL	18

INDEX to
Orange County, VA FAMILIES - Vol. #2

. THADDEUS	18	. JUDITH	47	. EMMA	134
BLACKERLY,		. JUDITH BURTON	27	. IRIS ARNOLD	134
. ELIZABETH HERRING	24	. MARIA SORRILL	45	. J.M.	134
. JAMES	86	. NANCY BRANHAM	31	. JIM	134
. THOMAS	24,86	. POLLY BRANHAM	34	. JOHN JAMES	134
BLACKWELL, ANN G.	46	. POLLY STROTHER	30	. JOHN MILTON	114,134
. ANN GORDON	44	. REUBIN	30	. JOHN WILLIAM	115
. ANNY	19	. SUSANNA DAVIS	45	. KATHERINE MCGRAW	134
. ELIZABETH BURTON	41	. WILLIAM	21,34	. LOLA L.	114
. JAMES	41	. YELVERTON	27	. LULA D.	115
. JOSEPH	44	BLALOCK, G.B.	114	. MAGGIE	134
. LELAND	34	. HATTIE R. MORGAN	114	. MARIE WELCH	134
. MARY E.	46	. MAGGIE M.	114	. MARY J.	134
. NANCY BURTON	34	. MATTIE D. MORGAN	114	. MARY L. GREEN	115
. WILLIAM	44	. MOSES MARLVEN	114	. MATTIE D. MORGAN	114
BLAIR, ALEXANDER	50	. REBA JEWELL	114	. MATTIE MORGAN	134
. BARBARA G.	48	BLALUCK,	133	. MORRIS LASALLE	114
. BETSY	19	. A.B.	115	. MOSES	114
. ELIZABETH SMITH	2	. AL CHARLES	115	. MOSES MARLVEN	114,134
. GEORGE	158	. ALONZO	134	. REUBEN	134
. HELEN	48	. AMANDA	114-115,134	. WILLIAM D.	134
. HELEN SHEPHERD	15	. AMANDA D.	134	. ZULA BELL HAYES	114
. JAMES	15,50	. AMANDA J. HASTINGS	114	BLANKENBACKER, ZACHAIM	51
. JANE	50	.	134	BLANKENBAKER,	
. JOHN	2,50	. ANN BELL	134	ZACHANIAH	73
. MARY	50	. CARRIE E.	134	BLEDSOE,	131,138,163
. THOMAS	158	. CLARA WELCH	134	. AARON	10,14,19-20,68
BLAKE, CORNELIUS	140	. CORA MAE WILSON	134	.	85
BLAKEY,		. CORINE	134	. ABRAHAM	135,140
. ELIZABETH DAVIS	21	. DAISY G.	114	. ANN PERRY	4,6
. GEORGE SMITH	45	. ELIZABETH PROFF	115	. ANNE	130
. JAMES	31	. ELLA E. WELCH	134	. ELIZABETH	24
. JAMES G.	45	. ELONZA	134	. ELIZABETH STEVENS	130

INDEX to
Orange County, VA FAMILIES - Vol. #2

. GEORGE	35,140,143,145	BOEING,EPHRIAM	124	. JOSEPH	13
. HANNAH	47,130,132	BOGGINI,PATRICK	74	. LUCY WRIGHT	4,7
. HOWARD	68,79	BOGUARD,		. MALINDA	40
. ISAAC	135,138	. BERNICE BROCKMAN	104	. MARTHA	41
. JOANER PITCHER	35	. MAURICE	104	. MARY	2,5
. JOHN	13,20,33,39,58,68	BOHANAUGH,ROBERT	137	. MARY ANDERSON	33
	79,145	BOHANNAN,WILLIAM	138	. POLLY	45
. MARGARET PERRY	39	BOHANNON,	144	. REUBEN	9,11,13
. MARY	2,5,10	. LAVINIA MARQUESS	22	. REUBIN	27,33,41
. MILLY	19	. THOMAS	22	. ROBERT	4,7,78,141-142
. MOSES	4,6,11,47	BOHAON,BENJAMIN	147	.	145,147
. NANCY	14	BOHON,ANN	10	. SALLY	33
. PEACH	65	BENJAMIN	10,145	. SARA HAWKINS	9
. PEACHY	86	BOHUNNE,THOMAS	140	. SARAH	13
. POLLY DEAR	20	BOLING,JOHN	15	. SARAH MOSELEY	26
. ROBERT	143	. PHEOBE HAWKINS	13	BOSWELL,ANN	12,74
. SARAH STEVENS	132	. SUSANNAH BELL	15	. CHARLES	18,37,40,45
. SUSANNA PITCHER	33	. WILLIAM	13	. DOROTHY	74
. THOMAS	135,140	BOLLING,JOHN	65,86	. FOSTER FRANCES	74
. WILLIAM	130,135	WILLIAM	86,146	. FRANCIS	74
BLOODWORTH,JOSEPH	137	BOLTON,SARAH MOSELEY	26	. GARRETT	44
BLOWS,GEORGE	2	BOND,JOHN	139	. GATEWOOD	74
KATHERINE KEEN	2	BONNER,JOHN	76	. GEORGE	74
BLUEFORD,JOHN	135	BOOTH,		. JAMES	74
BLUNDER,ROBERT	69,76,140	MARY J. BLALUCK	134	. JOHN	74
	143	BOQUITT,	66	. LUCY	45
BLUNT,CHARLES	135,139	BORDEN,BENJAMIN	58	. LUCY THOMPSON	18
. MICHAEL	22	BOSS,OBADIAH	120	. MARTHA MIDDLEBROOK	46
. SUCKEY	22	BOSTON,ELIZABETH	16,40	. MARY SLEET	40
BNELL,JOHN	68	. ELIZABETH VAUGHN	19	. PATSY DOLIN	44
BOBOCK,JASON	129	. FANNY	27	. POLLY	37
BOBON,TYENTON	136	. GEORGE	19	. RANSOM	74
BODO,JOHN	142	. JOHN	40,45,71,78,146	. SAMUEL T.	46

176

INDEX to
Orange County, VA FAMILIES - Vol. #2

Name	Page	Name	Page	Name	Page
. WILLIAM	40	BOWLING, CHARLES	15	. ELIZABETH WELLS	27
BOTT, JOHN	25	. JOHN	79	. GEORGE	3,5,17,30
SUSANNAH SPOTSWOOD	25	. SARAH MCKENNEY	15	. JAMES	27
BOTTS, JEMIMAH	73	. WILLIAM	79	. JOHN	24
JOHN	73,137	BOWRKE, MARTIN	50	. LUCY	17,30
BOURN, ANDREW	77	BOXLEY,		. LUCY RICE	3,5
. ELIZABETH	10	. DRUCILLA GRAVES	20	. MARY B.	47
. HENRY	10,142,146	. GEORGE	20	. NANCY	13
. JANE NEWMAN	49	BOYD, SUSANNAH	108	. POLLARD	47
. JEANY	7	BOYE, WILLIAM	65	. POLLY MARSHALL	25
. JOHN	49	BOYER, MARTHA THOMPSON	24	. RICHARD	136,138,140
. ROBERT	77	THOMAS	24	.	142-144,146
BOURNE, AMBROSE	19	BOYS, ANNE BROCKMAN	88	. SALLY	25
. JANE NEWMAN	19	JOHN	88	. SALLY HANCOCK	24
. SIMON	136	BOZE, JOHN	85	. SARAH	163
BOUTWELL, JOHN	140	WILLIAM	85	. WILLIAM	25
BOUTWILLS,	143	BRABHAM, JULIA M.	114	BRADSTREET, FRANCIS	50
BOUZEY, JOHN	78	MARY A.	113	BRADY, DANIEL	50
BOWCOCK, ELVINA	47	BRACKEN, EDWARD	18	. JUDY	50
. JUDITH DOUGLAS	22	BRACKENRIDGE,		. WILLIAM	50
. TANDY	22	. ALEXANDER	75	BRAG, JENNY YORK	24
BOWEN, ANN	10	. GEORGE	75	MOORE	24
. EPHRIAM	38	. JANE	75	BRAGG, BENJAMIN	10
. FRANCIS	1	BRACKSON,	143	. POLLY PRETTYMAN	10
. FRANCIS CRISTOPHER	1	BRADBURD,	146	. POLLY TWENTYMAN	10
. HENRY	141,145	BRADBURN, ISAAC	140,142	BRAHAM, MILLIE	1
. JOHN	34	WILLIAM	142-144	BRAIDENHEART, SUSAN	43
. POLLY LEATHERS	38	BRADEN, JOSEPH	30	BRAMHAM, FANNY HUGHES	15
. SALLY SEAL	34	POLLY NEAL	30	. JOHN	146
. SARAH	145	BRADFORD, ALEXANDER	25	. MARMADUKE	15
BOWER,		. HANNAH BURTON	25	BRANBANE, JOHN	145
. MARGARET LANDRUM	13	. JOHN	140	BRANDT, PAULINE	91,118
. THOMAS	13	BRADLEY, ELIZABETH	17	BRANHAM, FRANCIS	50

INDEX to
Orange County, VA FAMILIES - Vol. #2

. JOHN	80,136,138	. EZEKIEL	36	BRIDWELL,SALLY	44
	141-142,145	. FANNY HANEY	49	BRIGHTWELL,ABSALOM	23
. LUDLOW	68	. JAMES	40	WINEFRED PINES	23
. MARMADUKE	17	. JOB	14	BRITAIN,MARY	73
. MARY	80	. MOLLY FRANKLIN	13	SAMUEL	73
. NANCY	31	. RACHAEL GIBBINS	40	BRITTAN,SAMUEL	74
. POLLY	34	. RICHARDS	14	BROADNAX,	
. POLLY SISSON	16	. SUSANNAH	14	. JULIAN BROCKMAN	89
. ROBERT	31,34,68	BREEDLOVE,BROADERS	32	. THOMAS	89
. SPENCER	142	. EDWARD	34	BROADUS,RICHARD	146
. TAVNER	16	. ELEANOR MITCHELL	33	BROCK,ABSOLOM	49
BRASBONE,GEORGE	135	. HANEY HARVEY	34	. ARCHIBALD	37
BRAWFORD,SAMUEL	50	. JUDY BUCKNER	9	. ELIZABETH BUCKNER	49
BRAXTON,	144	. MADISON	9	. JOHN	136
GEORGE	137,140	. NANCY DOVELL	32	. RICHARD	143-144
BRAY,MARY STOCKS	11	. NATHANIEL	33	. SAMUEL	136
PATRICK	11	BREEDWELL,		. SARAH MASON WEBB	49
BRAZER,JAMES	141	. ANNY BLACKWELL	19	. SARAH MOYERS	37
BREADWELL,LIDDY	25	. THOMAS	19	. WILLIAM	66,145
BRECKENRIDGE,		. WILLIAM	19	. WINGFIELD	49
. ALEXANDER	50	BREMER,JOHN F.	38	BROCKMAN,	95,97,126,137
. GEORGE	50	POLLY DEMSEY	38	.	148,160
. JAMES	50	BRENT,DANIEL	42	. WILLIAM	121
. JANE	50	ELIZABETH SAMPSON	42	. ABIGAIL PADGETT	102
. JOHN	50	BRIANT,WINIFRED	4	. AGATHA	90,122-123
. LETITIA	50	BRICE,WILLIAM	82	. AGNES MERRY	128
. ROBERT	50,58	BRIDGE,RICHARD	136	. ALFRED	88,104
. SMITH	50	BRIDGES,ANN ROW	13	. ALICE	101
BREEDING,ACQUILES	10	. HOWARD	104	. ALICE HARBISON	102,104
. BETSY HANEY	36	. LUCY FRANKLIN	104	. AMBROSE	90,102,117,129
. ELIZABETH FRANKLIN	14	. MARY ROW	18	.	160-161
. EPHRAIM	49	. MATHEW	18	. AMELIA	16
. EPHRIAM	13	. WILLIAM	13	. AMELIA BROCKMAN	16

INDEX to
Orange County, VA FAMILIES - Vol. #2

Name	Page	Name	Page	Name	Page
. AMELIA MARTIN	95-96	. CLARENCE A.	98	. FLORA RANDOLF	105
.	159	. CLARENCE AUBREY	129	. FLORENCE ST.LEGER	87
. ANDREW	16,128	. CLIFTON	97,99	.	89
. ANN	90,101	. CLINTON OLIVER	104	. FLORINE	101
. ANN E.	123	. CRISTO	12	. FLORINE DAWSON	101
. ANN FERGERSON	123	. CURTIS	35	. FRANCES	159
. ANNE	88-89	. DAISY CHOPPELL	105	. FRANCES SHISHLER	128
. ASA	43,97,157-158	. DAISY SLIFER	104	. GERTRUDE	98
. ASA B.	98-99,157	. DERWOOD	98	. GRANDVILLE	99
. ASA D.	101	. DORA HENDRICKS	104	. GUSSIE	95
. ASA DAWSON	101	. ELEANOR	99,149,152-154	. GUTHRIE	99
. ASA MICK	98	.	156	. HANNAH	77
. ASA T.	99-101	. ELIJAH	18,163	. HARMON	99
. BARNEY	96,128	. ELIJAH S.	163	. HARMON F.	97
. BASIL	104	. ELIZ.	25,34	. HARRIET	160-161
. BERLINDA	102	. ELIZA E.	104	. HARVEY M.	98-99
. BERNICE	104	. ELIZA. CATTERTON	123	. HATTIE KELLAR	99
. BERTIE COOPER	105	. ELIZABETH	10,77,87,89	. HATTIE KELLER	98
. BILLY F.	99	.	102,123,163-164	. HELEN	88,104
. BLANCHE	99	. ELIZABETH BURRIS	162	. HELEN SAWKING	88
. BLEDSOE	25	. ELIZABETH BURRUS	149	. HENRY	87-88-89,93,96
. C.A.	97	. ELIZABETH EMBRE	96-97	.	159,162
. CAROLINE	88,161	. ELIZABETH GRAVES	45	. HENRY FRANKLIN	105
. CAROLINE E.	160	. ELIZABETH LANDRUM	25	. HENRY HUGH	102,104
. CARRAL	99	. ELIZABETH MASON	89,102	. IDA SMITHEY	98-99
. CATHERINE	159	.	129	. ISRAEL	97
. CATY	90	. ELIZABETH RANDOLPH	88	. JACOB	163
. CEDRIC ALONZO	105	. ELLEN	102	. JAMES	10,12,14,30,68
. CHARLES	129	. ELLEN ADCOCK	102	.	82,88-89,129
. CHARLOTTE BROWN	160	. ETTA ANN MICK	98	. JAMES A.	98
.	161	. FANNIE	123	. JAMES ARK	157
. CHRISTIAN BIBB	125	. FLETCHER SIMMS	88	. JAMES ARTHUR	99,104
. CLARA	90	. FLORA ANNA	101	. JAMES FRANCIS	101

INDEX to
Orange County, VA FAMILIES - Vol. #2

. JAMES MASON 102	. LOU ISABELL 98	. MARY C. SPENCE 101
. JAMES W. 123	. LOUIS C. 163	. MARY COLLINS 95-96
. JAMES WESLEY 100-102	. LUCY 102	. MARY CULBERTSON 97
. JANE EVERING 88	. LUCY JANE 102	. MARY DOCKRELL 98
. JEANETTE MARSHALL 105	. LUCY LEONA 104	. MARY E. 101,129,163
. JEMIMA 3,5	. LUCY QUISENBERRY 43	. MARY F. 123
. JESSIE 129	. 100	. MARY G. 105
. JESSIE JONES 95-96	. LUCY SIMMS 102	. MARY HUDGINS 99
. JOHN 13,16,24,34,58,68	. LUCY YOUNG 88	. MARY J. 101
. 77,87,89,92-93,95-96	. MAGGIE D. 101	. MARY KABLER 163
. 102,129,136,138,140	. MAHALA E. 105	. MARY L. 99
. 142-144,146,149,154	. MAHALA WALKER 102,104	. MARY PATTERSON 7,95-96
. 159,162	. MAJOR 7,77,95-96,159	. MARY PROCTOR 101
. JOHN ALONZO 105	. MARGARET 101,129	. MARY QUISENBERRY 100
. JOHN C. 98-99,157	. MARGARET CHAPMAN 88	. 101
. JOHN CREEL 99	. MARGARET CLARK 88	. MARY RUSH 98
. JOHN H. 101	. MARGARET LEE 101	. MARY SMITH 10
. JOHN L. 128	. MARGERY 88	. MARY SPENCE 100
. JOHN N. 99	. MARGUERITE TERRETT 164	. MARY WOOLFOLK 92,124
. JOHN W. 160-161	. 165-166	. MATTIE 99
. JOHN WASH 163	. MARIA 160-161	. MAUD JONES 98-99
. JOHN WILLIS 102	. MARTHA 88,102,128,161	. MICHIE 101
. JOSEPH 77,98,128-129	. 163	. MILDRED 99,104
. JOSEPH E. 97-98	. MARTHA A. 160	. MILLY 128
. 157-158	. MARTHA MCGORDER 104	. MILLY BROCKMAN 128
. JOSIE 131	. MARY 9,77,88,91-93	. MILLY TURNER 30
. JULIAN 89	. 118-120,122-123,127	. MILTON 97
. LAURA 104,163	. 148-149,151,158,161	. MITCHELL 122
. LEWIS 69,93-94,96,129	. 162	. MOLLIE ANN 99
. LONNIE 105	. MARY A. BUSH 98	. MOSES 19
. LOU ANNA REED 104	. MARY BELL 96,125	. MYRTLE 101
. LOU I. 99	. MARY BROCKMAN 123	. NANCY 24,68,82,99,102
. LOU ISABEL 157	. MARY C. 101-102,104	. NANCY BLEDSOE 14

INDEX to
Orange County, VA FAMILIES - Vol. #2

Name	Page(s)	Name	Page(s)	Name	Page(s)
NANCY DURRETT	15		125-129,131-132,136		143,158-159
NANCY ELIZABETH	102		140,142-144,146,161	WILLIAM ALLEN	163
NANCY J.	98		162	WILLIAM HENRY	104-105
NANCY JANE	157	SARAH	10,77,98,124	WILLIAM MASON	89,129
NANCY LONG	13		128-129,158	WILLIAM S.	123
NANCY MERCER	159	SARAH A.	99	WILLIAM SIMMS	102,104
NANCY QUISENBERRY	35	SARAH H.	157	WILLIE ARRINGTON	99
NANCY R.	160-161	SARAH HUDGENS	157	ZENOBIA	99
NANCY SIMMS	102	SARAH HUDGINS	98	ZOUCH	88
NELLY	16,19	SHELTON	161	BROKEMAN,JOHN	87
NELLY BROCKMAN	19	SIMMS	102,104	BRONAUGH,CHARLES B.	34
NIMROE W.W.	163	STEPHEN	96-97	ELIZ. BROCKMAN	34
ORA MYRTLE	101	SUKEY	8	BRONSUGH,CHARLEY	28
OSWALD	128	SUSAN	11	MARY DANIEL	28
PEGGY	125	SUSAN ANN	163	BROOK,DOROTHY TAYLOR	13
POLLY	24	SUSAN HUGUELY	101	GEORGE	13-14
RACHEL	77,101-102	SUSIE	99,105	JANE	17
RACHEL ALICE	101	THEODORE J.	163	ROBERT	137
RACHEL GARTIN	102,104	THOMAS	87,129,161	SARAH	137
RACHEL H.	101	THOMAS P.	96	SUSANNAH	90
REBECCA	34,92,124,162	TOMMY	99	BROOKING,ANN THOMPSON	4
REBECCA SALMON	89,159	VICTORIA BALLEW	98		7
ROBERT	98	VICTORIA BELLEW	157	BELINDA	45
ROBERTA NIBLIK	99	VIRGIL	99	JAMES R.	49
ROGER JACOB	101	VIRGINIA	128	MARTHA	49
ROGER LEE	101	W.E.	87,96,100,130,132	MARY TAYLOR	11
ROSIA	99		160-161,164-166	MILDRED WILHOIT	46
SALLIE	99	WALTER	104	PATSY RUSSELL	12
SALLY	92,105	WALTER D.	123	ROBERT	12,45
SALLY TOMLIN	163	WILLIALM	129	ROBERT U.	46
SALLY TOMLINSON	18	WILLIAM	10,16-17,24-25	SAMUEL	11
SAMUEL	8-10-11,15,68		34,45,66,77,87-88,92	WILLIAM	4,7
	80,89-93,96,117,124		102,122-124,128-129	BROOKMAN,JOHN	77

INDEX to
Orange County, VA FAMILIES - Vol. #2

. SAMUEL	140	. JENNIE	99	. SARAH	3
. SARAH	77	. JESSE	99	. SARAH WOMACK	160
. WILLIAM	77	. JIM	122	. SMITH	99
BROOKS, GEORGE	11	. JODA	99	. TABIATHA	99
. JANE	22	. JOHN	26,45,50,58,65,72	. THOMAS	50,135,143,145
. RACHEL	22	. JOHN MELTON	134	.	147
. SUSANNA	17	. JOHN SHELTON	161	. WILLIAM	47,49-50,99
BROUGHTON, SARA KAMP	11	. JOSEPH	157	.	134,146
THOMAS	11	. JOSEPH A.	98-99	. WILLIAM LAFAYETTE	160
BROUN,	125	. JUDITH WALLER	45	.	161
BROWEL, CHRISTLEY	135	. LINNEY	3	BROWNING, THOMAS	84
CORTNEY	135	. LINNY	5	BROYLE, CHRISTOPHER	73
BROWN,	160	. LOU I. BROCKMAN	99,157	COURTNEY	140
. ALICE	3,5	. LOU ISABELL	-	BRUCE, CATHERINE	12
. ANN	50	. BROCKMAN	98	. CHARLES	58,68,78,82
. ANN BELL BLALUCK	134	. LUCY M.	118	. CHRISTIANA AHEART	6
. ANN HORD	47	. LUCY MCALLISTER	118	. CHRISTINA AHEART	4
. BERNIE	39	. MARGARET	9	. DAVID	135,140,144,146
. BEZABEL	42	. MARGRET	50	. ELIZABETH	18,68,82
. CATEY	11	. MARTHA A. BROCKMAN	160	. GEORGE	135
. CHARLES	99	. MARTHA BROCKMAN	161	. JANE	2
. CHARLOTTE	2,160-161	. MARY	50	. LOUDOWN B.	31
. CORINE BLALUCK	134	. MARY HANCOCK	49	. MARY	4,6
. DANIEL B.	160	. MARY J. BLALUCK	134	. MILLY ESTES	31
. DOROTHY	131	. NANCY BICKERS	41	. MORDECAI	4,6
. ELIZABETH	26	. NANCY BURTON	39	. WILLIAM	68
. ELIZABETH CRAIG	160	. NANCY HARROD	13	BRUDEN, SALLY	29
. ELIZABETH PRICE	42	. NAPOLEON	134	BRUDING, BERRYMAN	29
. HENRY	45,72	. POLLY BOSTON	45	BRUNER, CATY KIBLINGER	24
. HIRAM	160	. RICHARD	160	PETER	24
. HUGH	50	. ROBERT	50,141	BRUTH, KENDAL C.	32
. JAMES	11,13,65	. SANDERSON	41	POLLY W. BURTON	32
. JANE WOOD	122	. SARA	6	BRYAN,	138

INDEX to
Orange County, VA FAMILIES - Vol. #2

Name	Page	Name	Page	Name	Page
. DANIEL	43	. WILLIAM	41,58	. REUBEN	12
. DENNIS	50	BULLARD, AMBROSE	124	. RICHARD	4,68
. FRANKEY LONG	37	BETTY WOOLFOLK	124	. SALLY	18
. JEREMIAH	37	BULLOCK, RICHARD	66	. SARAH	29
. MARY T. BARBOUR	43	BUNCH, WILLIAM	137	. ZACH	77
BRYANT, CHARLES	48	BUNFARNES, FREDERICK	137	. ZACHARIAH	12
. EDWARD	16	BUNTINE, WILLIAM	50	. ZACHARY	16
. FRANKIE THORNTON	6	BURBRIDGE, ANN	2	. ZACK	58,68,87
. FRANKY THORNTON	3	THOMAS	140	. ZACKARY	77
. JEREMIAH	75	BURDITT, SARAH	165	BURNLY, GARLAND	81
. JOHN O.	16	BURGES, EDMUND	21	HARDIN	85
. MORGAN	57	SARAH	21	BURRAS, SUKEY	13
. POLLY HAMBLETON	16	BURGESS, THOMAS	136	BURRASS, ANN	4,7
. POLLY SNOW	48	BURGISS, THOMAS	146	BURRIS,	92
. THOMAS	3,6,72,82	BURK, FRANCIS	2	. CIRRELDA FRANKLIN	102
. WILLIAM	140	. LUCY DAVIS	2	.	103
. WINIFRED	6	. THOMAS	50	. ELIZABETH	162
BRYON, JOHN	143	BURKE, JOHN	50	. MARTHA ELIZABETH	103
WILLIAM	143	BURKS, ISAAC	33	. OTIS E.	102-103
BRYSON, MARY	8	JANE MILLER	33	BURROWS, JANE	4,7
BUCHAN, ROBERT	142	BURN, ELIZABETH KNIGHT	43	. MARY	1
BUCK, ANTHONY	19	JAMES	43	. SUSANNA	6
MARY SHEPHERD	19	BURNLEY, ELIZA S. JONES	4	. SUSANNAH	3
BUCKHANNON, JOHN	18	. FRANCES TAYLOR	7	BURRUS, ANN	8,44
BUCKHAUNON, JOHN	10	. FRANCIS	31	. ANN HENDERSON	124
MARY SMITH	10	. GARLAND	7,58,68	. ANNA	41
BUCKNER, BALDWIN	17	. HARDIN	58,68,81	. CATY RUCKER	13
. ELIZABETH	49	. JACK	79	. CYNTHIA MILLS	14
. FANNY BURTON	17	. JAMES	21,58	. EDMUND	13,124
. HORACE	49	. JUDITH	12,31	. EDWARD	124-125
. JANE	9,84	. MARY	16	. ELIZ.	20
. JUDY	9	. MARY BELL	68,81	. ELIZABETH	149
. PHILIP	84	. NANCY PARSONS	21	. EMILY	49

INDEX to
Orange County, VA FAMILIES - Vol. #2

. FRANCES TANDY	124	. MARTHA	40	BYRNE,THOMAS	50
. JOHN	68,80,89,124-125	. MARY	32	CAIMS,JAMES	13
. JOSEPH	48	. MARY WHITE	7	CAIR,ANDREW	140
. JUSTINA	31	. MAY	4,6,17,25,27,35,40	CALDWELL,AGNES	51
. MARY	12,68	.	45,58,72,79,82,84	. DAVID	51
. MOURNING	14	. MILLY MAY	31	. GEORGE	51
. NANCY TERRILL	48	. NANCY	34,39	. JAMES	51
. ROGER	14	. POLLY W.	32	. JANE	51
. ROSANNA	12	. SARAH	35	. JEAN	51
. SAMUEL	13	. SARAH HEAD	4	. JOHN	51
. SARAH	68	. WILLIAM	20,30,34,58	. MARY	51
. THOMAS	14,124	.	139	. SAMUEL	51
. WILLIAM T.	35,44,48-49	BURUS,GEORGE	85	. SARAH	51
BURRUSS,EDMOND	145	BUSH,ANN	86	. WILLIAM	51
BURT,ELIZA	43	. BUCHANAN	58	CALLAWAY,WILLIAM	137
BURTIS,MARY	73	. CABEL	36	CALLENDER,	
RICHARD	73	. EDMUND	21	. ELOIS M. MORGAN	114
BURTON,AMBROSE	58	. ELIZABETH WALKER	21	. GLADYS A. MORGAN	114
. ANN GOODRIDGE	30	. JOHN	58,65,86,135	. LLOYD	114
. BETSY GOODRIDGE	22	. JOSIAH	69	. PRISCELLA MORGAN	113
. CLARISSA	38	. LIDDY BREADWELL	25	. RAY	113
. ELIZABETH	22,41	. LUCINDA TAYLOR	36	. SMYLEY	114
. FANNY	17,33	. MARY A.	98	CAMBLE,ELIZABETH	51
. FRANKIE	6	. PHILLIP	58,140,143	. ESTHER	51
. FRANKY	3	. THOMAS	25	. JANE	51
. HANNAH	25	BUSHER,JOSEPH	146	. JOHN	51
. JAMES	7,22,32,39,58,65	BUTLER,JOHN	50	. MARY	51
. JOHN	31	. LAWRENCE	165	. RACHEL	51
. JOSEPH	32	. SARAH	165	CAMIKE,POLLY	31
. JUDITH	27	BUTTERY,THOMAS	137	CAMP,FRANCIS WILLIS	1
. LUCY	17	BYRD,	66-68	. JAMES	27
. MARGARET	39	GEORGE	50,137	. MARY WOOD	27
. MARIA	45	BYRN,THOMAS	139	. WILLIAM	1

INDEX to
Orange County, VA FAMILIES - Vol. #2

CAMPBELL, ALEXANDER	47	TIMOTHY	51	. CATHERINE	17
. ANDREW	59	CAROHANT, CATHERINE	51	. CHARLES	139
. ANN M. ATKINS	43	. DANIEL	51	. DOROTHY	13
. ANN MALLORY	47	. ELIZABETH	51	. EDWARD	140
. ARCHIBALD	11,69,80	. JOHN	51	. ELIZABETH DANIEL	35
.	141-142,145-146	. MARY	51	. JAMES	47
. CHARLES	51,146	CARPENTER, JOHN	57,73-74	. JANE NEWCOME	47
. DOUGALL	51	.	135	. JOHN	15
. DUNCAN	69,80	. MILDRED	47	. JOSEPH	15,59
. EDWARD	81	. PLEASANT	47	. JUDITH	13
. ELIZABETH	51	. WILLIAM	59,135	. POLLY BELL	15
. GENNET	51	CARPINTER, WILLIAM	140	. POLLY DANIEL	37
. JOHN	44-45,51,75,139	CARR, ADAM	135	. SARAH	3
. MARY	51	. BARBARA	51	CARTEY, BETSY	26
. PATRICK	51	. JANE	51	CASAY, AGNES TAYLOR	12
. PEGGY	30	. JOHN	51	WILLIAM	12
. ROBERT	43	. LUCY	51	CASELEAR, MATHIAS	140
. RUTH	105	. MARTHA	51	CASEN, ELIZABETH	4
. SUSANNA ARNOLD	11	. MARY MALLORY	1	CASH, CATY	26
. VIRGINIA	26	. SARAH	36	CASON, BENJAMIN	43
. WILLIAM	21,51,59,65,86	. WILLIAM	1,51	. EDWARD	68-69,80,83
CANADY, SAMUEL	137	CARRELL, ELIZABETH	1,11	. JOHN	69,80,145
CANTERBERRY, MARY A.	5	CARROL, JACOB	9	. MARY THOMPSON	18
CANTERBURY, MARY	2	TABITHA REYNOLDS	9	. MOLLEY	80
CAPHER, MICHAEL	140	CARROLL,		. MOLLY	69
CARD, ABRAHAM	2	. ELIZABETH CLARK	48	. NANCY GRAVES	43
ANN ARCHER	2	. FRANK	85	. WILLIAM	18,69,80
CARDER, JOHN	139	. JOHN	69,80	CASSEN, ELIZABETH	6
CAREKER, ANDREW	140	. WILLIAM	48	CASTLER, MATHIAS	135
CAREY, MALLIE	115	CARRUTH,		CATHAY, JAMES	59
CARLETON, MARTHA	20	MARGARET SCRUGGS	105	CATHEY, ANDREW	51
CARNES, MARTHA	26	CARTER, ADCOCK	35,37	. ANN	51
CARNEY, EASTER	51	. BENJAMIN	37	. ELIZABETH	51

INDEX to
Orange County, VA FAMILIES - Vol. #2

. GEORGE	51	. BETTY SIMS	25	.	135,140
. JAMES	51	. DANIEL	137	. SARAH	132
. MARGARET	51	. DAVID	78,87,131,136	. SARAH ANDERSON	38
. WILLIAM	51	.	140,142-144,146	. SARAH SNOW	34
CATTERTON,BENJAMIN W.	46	. ELIZABETH	14,27,74,132	. SINCLAIR	38
. ELIZ. PRICE	46	. ELIZABETH	-	. WILLIAM	7,9,15,26
. ELIZA.	123	.	BELLFIELD 132	.	34-35,66,108,130-131
. ELIZABETH	38	. ELIZABETH WHITE	17,132	.	132
. FRANCIS	39	. FRANCES	15,132	. WILLIAM D.	49
. NANCY	32	. FRANCES B.	49	CAVES,LEICESTER	130
. NANCY CLARKSON	39	. FRANCES CHRISTY	9,132	CAVIN,	
CAUTHORN,FANNY	40	. FRANCES SMITH	49	. AMANDA D. BLALUCK	134
CAVANAGH,PHILINUS	80	. HANNAH	7,21,132	. PEARLA ANN MORGAN	114
PHILOMON	80	. HANNAH BLEDSOE	130,132	. VAN	114,134
CAVANAUGH,ANN	130	. IRENE	131	CAZA,MARY SLAUGHTER	36
. ANNE CAVE	130	. JENNY SNOW	19,132	WILLIAM	36
. BENJAMIN	130	. JOHN	9,130,132,140	CERTAIN,ISAAC	142
. ELIZABETH	130	. JUDY JOLLET	132	CHAMBART,FANNY DAWSON	40
. PHILEMON	51,130	. JUDY JOLLETT	15	HENRY	40
CAVE,ABNER	25-26,49	. LAVINA B.	48	CHAMBER,JOSEPH	140
. ANN CAVENDER	132	. LUCY BRADLEY	30	CHAMBERLAIN,ALICE	26
. ANNA STONEHOUSE	130	. LUCY MCGEE	132	CHAMBERS,ABRAHAM	14,141
. ANNE	130	. LUCY SHELTON	30	.	145-146
. BARTLETT	19,34,132	. MARIA PORTER	29	. ARCHIBALD	142
. BELFIELD	27,59,68,72	. MARY RAMSEY	132	. CATY	10
.	83	. MILDRED CHRISTY	132	. ELIZABETH	21,51
. BELLFIELD	132	. NANCY	35	. MARY	8
. BEN	11	. PHILIP C.	46	. MARY DAWSON	14
. BENJAMIN	14,17,20,58	. PHILIP G.	49	. MILLY ROBINSON	14
.	73-74,78,86-87,130	. POLLY	49	. RACHEL	35
.	131-132,135,139,143	. REUBEN	132	. REBECCA	15,17
.	145	. RICHARD	29-30	. THOMAS	8,14,35,51,59
. BETSY SIMS	26	. ROBERT	30,48,58,74,132	CHAMPEL,FRANCIS WILLIS	5

186

INDEX to
Orange County, VA FAMILIES - Vol. #2

WILLIAM	5	. MARGARET	88	. JANE	33
CHANCELLOR, BETSY	32	. MARIA VERDIER	37	. JENNY LAND	7
. ELIZ.	35	. NATHANIEL	74,165	. JOHN	71
. JANE	32	. REYNOLDS	23	. MALACHI	136
. JOHN	32	. RICHARD M.	37	. MALACK	143
. PENELOPE	34	. SARAH	76	. MALAKI	144
CHANCY, JOSEPH	51	. THOMAS	27	. MALIKI	142,146
CHANDLER,		CHARLES I,	88	. MALLIKI	140
. ELIZABETH TERRELL	15	CHARLES II,	87	. MARY	20
. FRANCIS MCNEAL	14	CHASEAM, MILDRED	25	. POLLY	39
. JAMES	14	CHASTAIN, JOHN	158	. SALLY	13
. JANE	65	CHAVELAND, JOHN	69	. SARAH BROCKMAN	124
. JEREMIAH	39	CHEW,	137-138	. SUSANNAH	20
. JOHN	15,86	. ALICE	1,125	. THOMAS	124
. JOSEPH	8,17,143	. JOSEPH	27	CHILTON,	89
. JUSTIN	125	. LARKIN	136,140	. BLACKWELL	44
. JUSTINE	8	. M. LARKIN	138	. THOMAS	88
. NANCY HOMS	17	. MILLY	11	CHINTON, JOHN	140
. ROBERT	2,5,70	. THOMAS	58-59,144	CHISAM, BENJAMIN	19
. SUKEY EDMONSON	2	CHEWNING, ELIZA	44	. ELIZABETH BECKHAM	19
. SUKEY ROBINSON	5	. ROBERT	38,44	. THOMAS	15
. TIMOTHY	125	. SALLY	38	CHISHAM,	
CHANLOR, JOSEPH	146	CHEWS,	143	. CATHERINE RAINES	13
CHAPMAN,	98	CHILD, JAMES	45	. JAMES	13,85
. CATHERINE YANCY	41	CHILDS, HENRY	10	. SALLY	23
. CONSTANCE PEARSON	165	. JAMES	41	. WILLIAM	65,85
. ELIZABETH	165	. NANCY	41	CHISHOM, BENJAMIN	22
. ELIZABETH EARLY	27	CHILES, CATHERINE	45	. JOHN	25
. GEORGE	16	. ELIZABETH WOOLFOLK	124	. MILDRED	25
. ISAAC	76	. FRANCES	31	CHISM, ANN	5
. JINNEY	14	. FRANKEY	24	. CATHERINE	20
. JOSEPH	14,59	. HENRY	69,124	. JOHN	20
. JOSHUA	41	. JAMES	7,13,31,39,65	CHISOM, ANN	3

INDEX to
Orange County, VA FAMILIES - Vol. #2

Name	Page
CHISSAM, SALLY	25
THOMAS	25
CHISSON, MARY	145
CHISTRAM, BETSY	20
CHIZIN,	142
CHOICE, TULLY	72
TURLEY	140
CHONCHER, WILLIAM	141
CHOPPELL, DAISY	105
CHRENSHAW,	
. NANCY PARROTT	35
. THOMAS	35
CHRISTIAN, JOHN	59
CHRISTIFER, JOHN	144
CHRISTIFOR, WILLIAM	144
CHRISTLE, EEWALD	73
CHRISTOPHER,	136
. JOHN	136, 138-139
	141-142, 144-145
. NICHOLAS	51, 73, 138-139
. WILLIAM	136, 139, 146
CHRISTY, FRANCES	9, 132
. JULIUS	9
. MILDRED	132
CHRONECKER, WILLIAM	136
CHURNING,	
. JUDITH CARTER	13
. LORIMER	13
CHUVNING, ROBERT	36
CIMBRO, THOMAS	142
CLARK, ANN	15, 28
. BARBARA	44
. CATHERINE JAMERSON	37
. CATY	37
. DILLAH PAYNE	28
. ELIZABETH	23, 48
. ELIZABETH GRAVES	30
. ELIZABETH JOHNSON	29
. ELIZABETH VAWTER	25
. FRANCES	42
. GILLY	121
. HENRY	24, 29, 45
. HENRY JAMES	39
. HUMPHREY	88
. JAMES	27, 30, 82
. JANE	32
. JANE TERRILL	42
. JOHN	15, 17, 23, 28, 32, 37
. JOSEPH	24, 31, 33, 72
	81-82
. LARKIN	20
. LIZEY PETTY	24
. LUCY LEE	45
. MACY	15
. MARGARET	88
. MARTHA E.	24
. MARTHA E. CLARK	24
. MARY	17, 82
. MARY ANN	35
. MARY MANSFIELD	39
. MILDRED	37
. NANCY	31, 38-39
. NANCY HALL	27
. NANNEY GRASTY	24
. NATHANIEL	27
. OPAL	104
. PATRICK	28
. PEGGY	37
. REBECCA BELL	20
. REUBEN	24
. REUBIN	24
. ROBERT	65
. SALEY	33
. SALLY PAYNE	27
. THOMAS	35, 37
. TIBATHA	33
. VIRGINIA	49
. WALKER	25
. WILLIAM	39, 42, 44-45, 49
	72, 136-137, 139
CLARKE, BETSY COOK	16
WILLIAM	16, 48
CLARKSON, ANSELM	13
. MILLY JONES	13
. NANCY	39
CLATTERBUCK, MARY	44
WILLIAM	44
CLAY, HENRY	97, 111
NANCY	110-111
CLAYBORN, JOHN	136
NATHANIEL	136
CLAYTER, ELIZABETH	44
CLAYTON,	
. ELIZABETH -	
STUBBLEFIELD	17
. HENRY	12
. JOHN	140
. PHILIP	17, 76
. PHILLIP	59

188

INDEX to
Orange County, VA FAMILIES - Vol. #2

CLEAVE, SARAH	46	. JOELL	16	.	83,86,136-138,140,142		
CLEAVELAND, PATTY	3	. JUDAH	9	.	143-144,146		
CLEE, ELIZABETH	23	COFFEE, JAMES	140	. JOHN	17,26,31,51,65		
CLEMENTS, HENRY	23	JOHN	140,143	. MARGARET	26,51		
POLLY	23	COFFERY, AMEY	6	. MARY	1,124		
CLEVELAND, ALEXANDER	143	ANN	4	. MILDRED	30		
. EDWARD	140	COGER, ELIZA	75	. MILLY	8		
. ELX.	140	. JACOB	75	. MILLY CHEW	11		
. JOHN	69,79,140	. MICHAEL	75	. MOLLY	17		
. PATTY	5	COGWELL, RALPH	10	. NANCY	17,69,83		
. SITHE	69,79	SARAH REYNOLDS	10	. POLLY	69,83		
. WILLIAM	69,79,117,144	COKER, THOMAS	135	. ROBERT	132		
CLIFFORD,		COKRANE, PATRICK	2	. SALLY	69,83		
. FLORENCE ST.LEGER	87	WINIFRED SPENCER	2	. SARAH	45		
. JOHN	87	COLADAY, JAMES	137	. SARAH TAYLOR	7		
CLIFT, WILLIAM	139	COLE, EDWARD	51	. SPILBY	69		
CLOARE, MICHAEL	137	. RACHEL	51	. SUSANNAH HAWKINS	8		
COAL, RICHARD	147	. WILLIAM	51	. THOMAS	8,27,45,59,69		
COALING, WILLIAM	144	COLEMAN, AMBROSE	34,77-78	.	72,80-83,135		
COATES, JOHN	9	.	142-144,146	. WILSON	38,69,83		
SARAH THOMPSON	9	. BETSY	22	COLIER, MARTIN	45		
COATS, JEREMIAH	14	. BETTY	69,83	COLLIER, BETSY HAM	34		
SALLY WEBSTER	14	. BETTY DAVIS	11	. HUDSON	34		
COBBLER, FREDERICK	139	. CATHERINE	38	. POLLY	45		
COCK, DANIEL	140	. CATY	69,83	COLLINS,	126		
COCKBURN, ROBERT	6	. ELIZABETH	69,83	. AMEY	107,110		
SARA BROWN	6	. ELIZABETH BRADLEY	17	. ANN	8,33		
COCKRAN, PATRICK	10	. FANNY	27	. ANN BEAZLEY	33		
COCKRANE, PATRICK	5	. FANNY HILMAN	34	. ANN COLLINS	8		
WINIFRED SPENCER	5	. FRANCIS	11	. ANNE	51		
CODDEN, WILLIAM	141	. GARNER	69	. BEN	27,32		
COE, GINNES	138	. JAMES	7,11,17,20,22,27	. BETSEY	107,109-110		
COFER, JAMES	9	.	59,68-69,71-72,78,81	. BETTY YAGER	27,32		

INDEX to
Orange County, VA FAMILIES - Vol. #2

. CATEY	108	. LANUD	106	. WILIE	110
. CATHERINE	108-109	. LEWIS	20,106-107	. WILLIA	109
. CATY	2		109-110	. WILLIAM	3,6,19,21,32
. CHOICE	107	. LEWIS D.	16,33		37,90,106,108
.. CUPID	107,110	. LOIS	109-111	. WILLIAM W.	43
. DIANNAH CARTER	107,109	. LOUIS	107,109	. WILLIE	106
. EDWARD	8,22,32,85	. LOWIS	106	COLMAN, THOMAS	140
	106-107,109-110	. LUCY BURTON	17	COLY, MILLY MCCLARY	44
. ELIZA	46	. MARGARET	17	WILLIAM	44
. ELIZABETH	19,22,32,90	. MARGARET WILLIAMS	42	COLYER, ELIZA HAYNA	28
	107,109,111	. MARY	9,17,95-96	. LUCINDA	43
. ELIZABETH BASHAW	108	. MILDRED JOHNSON	49	. MARTIN	43
. ELIZABETH KIRTLEY	26	. PATTY	3	. PRESTON	28
	32	. PATTY SNELL	3,6	CONALLY, PATRICK	45
. ELIZABETH LEE	110	. PEG	107	POLLY HILL	45
. ELIZABETH MITCHELL	17	. PEGG	110	CONAWAY, FRANCES	147
. ELIZABETH PERRY	110	. PEGGY DAHONEY	17,32	CONNELLY, SARAH	73
. ELIZABETH WILLIAMS	16	. PETER	107,110	SILVESTER	73
. FANNY RIDDLE	31-32	. PHILLIS	107	CONNER, ANN	4
. FRANCES	21,32	. PLIMETH	107	. BETSY	15
. FRANCES B. CAVE	49	. PLIMOTH	107,110	. CHARLES	80
. FRANCES WILLIAMS	43	. REUBEN	32	. ELIZABETH	13
. FRANCIS	17,32	. REUBIN	31	. ELLEN	80
. FRANCIS T.	42	. RICHARD	16-17	. EMILY SMITH	47
. GEORGE	17	. SALLY	5	. JAMES	139
. ISOM	107	. SALLY QUISENBERRY	37	. JOHN	6,15,46,70,80,132
. JACK	107	. SARAH HARVIE	15		143,146
. JAMES	15,17,49,51	. SUSANNAH	128	. LEWIS	79
. JOHN	26-27,32,47,49	. SUSANNAH LEWIS	105-106	. LUCY DANIEL	6
	106,109,136,138,140	. TANDY	33	. MARY	3,5,80
	146	. THOMAS	106	. PHILIMON	80
. JOSEPH	89-90,105-106	. WALLER	106	. SARAH TERRILL	46
	128	. WILEY	107,109	. TIMOTHY	59

INDEX to
Orange County, VA FAMILIES - Vol. #2

Name	Page	Name	Page	Name	Page
. WILLIAM	47	. POLLY TURNER	19	PATTY	4,6
CONNERS, ANN	6	. SUSANNAH GARTON	10	COPLIN, NICHOLAS	137
CONNICO, WILLIAM	138	. THOMAS	20,80,136-137	COPPAGE, CHARLES	27,32
CONNOR, JOHN	10	. WILLIAM	10,140	. LYDIA WAIT	27
. MARY	10	COOKBURN, ROBERT	3	. LYDIA WAYT	32
. MARY LANCASTER	10	SARAH BROWN	3	CORCORAN,	
. RACHEL	10	COOKE, ANNE BROCKMAN	89	. DIANA MORGAN	117
CONWAY,	138	. JOSEPH	65,84	. MARY	117
. CATLET	20	. MILES	89	. MOE	117
. CATLETT	34,40,59,86	. THOMAS	84	CORLEY, JOHN	75
. ELIZABETH	15	. WILLIAM	145	CORNEGIS, CAMELUS	74
. GEORGE	34	COONS, JOHN P.	43,49	CORNELIUS, AUGUSTINE	14
. HARRIET TAYLOR	40	SUSAN BRAIDENHEART	43	. OYSTIN	14
. LUCY H. MACON	35	COOPER, BARBARA	74	. SARAH TERRELL	14
. NELLY	71	. BENJAMIN	28	CORRELL, MARION	103
. REUBIN	35	. BERTIE	105	CORTHONE, JOHN	35
. SUSAN F.	46	. BETSY TAYLOR	159	COTTON, JOSEPH	51
. SUSANNAH	20	. BROCKMAN	159	. JUDITH R. GRYMES	31
. VIRLINDA TALIAFERRO	34	. DOLLY	28	. PETER	31
CONYERS, JOHN	144	. HUGH W.	111	COULTON, JOSEPH	59
COOK, ABRAHAM	144	. JAMES	21	COUNELBY, JAMES	70
. BETSY	16	. JOHN	145	COURSEY, POLLY	4,7
. CHARLES GEORGE	51	. JONATHAN	159	COUSINS, RICHARD	143
. DANIEL	136,142	. MARY A.	111	COVINGTON, THOMAS	59
. ELIJAH	19	. MARY A. MCCLENDHAN	111	COWARD, BENJAMIN	135,139
. FIELDING	80	. MARY M. WEBB	35	. JAMES	137,143-144
. GEORGE	51,140	. MARY QUISENBERRY	12	. JONATHAN	142
. JAMES	51	. MILDRED SMITH	21	COWGILL, BETSY MARTIN	10
. JOHN	89,136,138	. NANCY	32	. DANIEL	10
. MARY CHILES	20	. OWEN	35	. ISAAC	17
. MICHAEL	135	. SUSANNAH LANCASTER	28	. SALLY GILLOCK	17
. MICHALE	140	. WILLIAM	12,51	COWHERD,	146
. NANCY	26	COPE, MARGARET	8	. ANN	46

INDEX to
Orange County, VA FAMILIES - Vol. #2

. COLBY	46	. MARY BRYSON	8	. JANEY	15		
. DRUCILLA	25	. MILLY OLLIVER	9	. JANEY CRAWFORD	15		
. ELIZABETH	77	. SALLY	34	. JEMIMAH	1		
. FANNY WOOLFOLK	126	. SAMUEL	125	. JEREMIAH	15		
. FRANCES	12	. SARAH	22	. JOHN	51		
. FRANCES WOOLFOLK	17	. TABITHA	30	. MARGARET	51		
. FRANCIS	43,48,65,85	. THOMAS	9,12,28,30	. MARTIN	24		
. FRANCIS K.	39	. WILLIAM	14,34,135,141	. MARY	51		
. HARRIET	48	.	143	. PATRICK	51		
. JAMES	66,77	. WILLIAM D.	37	. SUSANNA LAMB	24		
. JOHN	69,83,126	COYLER,POLLY	45	. WILLIAM	51,75,135,139		
. JONATHAN	72,80	COZER,JAMES	146	. ZACHARIAH	43		
. LUCY SCOTT	12	CRADDOCK,	89	CRAWLEY,VALENTINE	141		
. REUBEN	17,69,83,126	CRAFTON,C.M.	126,128	CREEL,SAMUEL	135		
. SARA HENSHAW	39	CRAIG,	160	CREGLER,CHRISTOPHER	43		
. SARAH	43	. ELIJAH	10	CRENSHAW,SPOTSWOOD	40		
. YELVERTON	69	. ELIZABETH	160	WINIFRED GRAVES	40		
COWHILL,GEORGE	16	. FRANCES THOMAS	45	CREW,JACOB	14		
PHOEBE WAIT	16	. HELEN	105	. MARTHA DOLLINS	14		
COX,ANN	12	. LIDIA	10	. TABITHA	21		
. BERRYMAN	41	. SAMUEL	45	CRIGLER,FANNY PRATT	44		
. BETSY ESTES	14	. TALIAFERRO	70,78	PETER	44		
. FANNY WHITE	37	. TOLIVER	59	CRIMBS,BRAD	140		
. FRANKEY	12	CRANDAM,JOHN	143	CRISE,LARENCE	140		
. GEORGE	135	CRASK,JAMES	19	CRISHER,DAYWAT	135		
. JACOB	26	JANE HOLLINS	19	CRISTER,DOGWALL	135		
. JAMES	138,141	CRATES,EDWARD	9	CRISTLEY,DAYWAT	135		
. JOAN	22	CRAVEN,ROBERT	59	CRISTOPHER,FRANCIS	1		
. JOHN	8	CRAWFORD,ABBIE RAINS	43	CROCKET,JANE	51		
. LAURA BROCKMAN	163	. ANN	51	. JOHN	51		
. LUCY ESTES	26	. ARCHELAN	15	. MARGARET	51		
. MARTHY	143	. GEORGE	51	. MARSHALL	51		
. MARY	125	. JAMES	51	. ROBERT	51		

INDEX to
Orange County, VA FAMILIES - Vol. #2

. SAMUEL	51	. DANIEL BURRUS	153,156	. NANCY	148,151-152
CRODEWAIT,WILLIAM	137	. DAVID MILLER	156	. NANCY MCALISTER	149
CROMWELL,	88,130	. ELEANOR	152	.	154,156
OLIVER	87	. ELEANOR BROCKMAN	149	. NELLY BROCKMAN	16
CRONCHON,WILLIAM	138	.	152-154,156	. REBECCA	149,151,153
CROOKS,JOSEPH B.	38	. ELIJAH	149,151-152	. REUBEN	151-152
KITTY HENNESEY	38	. ELIJAH TAYLOR	153,156	. RICHARD H.L.	149,154
CROSBY,VALENTINE	142	. ELIZA	154-156	.	156
CROSS,ELIZABETH	102	. ELIZA M.	153-154	. SAMUEL	151-152
. ELLEANER	51	. ELIZA MILLER	154,156	. SARAH ANN	152-153,156
. JOSHUA	43	. ELIZABETH	153,156	. SHELTON	153,156
. MARY DANIEL	43	. EUGINA J.	154	. THEODORE	153-154,156
. RICHARD	51	. EUGINA JOSEPHINE	156	. THOMAS JEFFERSON	153
CROSSTHWAIT,ELIJAH	92	. GEORGIA	150-151	.	154,156
. MARY BROCKMAN	93	.	155-156	. TIMOTHY	148
. WILLIAM	138	. GRACE	149-150,156	. WASHINGTON MILLER	153
CROSSTHWAITE,		. I.L.	155	.	154,156
MARY BROCKMAN	92	. I.L. ENOCHS	154	. WILLIAM	148,153,156
CROSSWHITE,JOHN	40	. ISAAC	148	. WILLIAM LAFAYETTE	149
MILLY	40	. ISAAC OWEN	154-156	.	152,156
CROSTHWAIT,AARON	16,149	. J.M.	154-155	CROSTHWAITE,	148
.	151-152,154,156	. JACOB	148-153,156	. ELIZ.	39
. ABRAHAM	148	. JACOB WILSON	152-153	. ISAAC	67
. ABSOLEM	151-152	.	156	. JACOB	67
. ASA B.	152-155	. JAMES MALLORY	153,156	CROSWAIT,TIMOTHY	144
. ASA BROCKBURN	150	. JAMES MONROE	153,156	CROSWAITH,JOHN	39
. ASA BROCKMAN	148-151	. JEMIMAH	151-153	CROSWHITE,ABRAHAM	146
.	156	. MARY	149,151-153	CROTHWAIT,TIMOTHY	76,84
. CARSON R.	154,156	. MARY BROCKMAN	148-149	WILLIAM	146
. CATHARINE	154	.	151	CROTHWAITE,ABRAHAM	74
. CATHARINE MILLER	156	. MARY E.	154	. TIMOTHY	74,76
. DANIEL BURRAS	149	. MARY ELEANOR	152,156	. WILLIAM	74,76
. DANIEL BURRES	152	. MARY WILSON	154-156	CROUCHER,WILLIAM	145-146

INDEX to
Orange County, VA FAMILIES - Vol. #2

CROW, ELIZABETH	28	. AVERILLA	90	. POLLY	83
CROWDER, HENRY	135	. CHARLES	59,136,138,141	. SARAH	16
WILLIAM	142	.	143	. SARAH DADE	16
CROWLEY, JEFFRY	137	. CHICHLEY	90	. SARAH TALIAFERRO	8
CROXTON, DELPHY TURNER	25	. ELIJAH	23	. TOWNSHAND	82
. JOHN	80	. ELIZABETH BROCKMAN	89	. TOWNSHEAD	16
. JOSEPH	25	. ELIZABETH VAUS	90	. WILLIAM	16,71
. RICHARD	80	. JAMES	90	DAHONEY,	
CRUMP, BENJAMIN	1	. JOHN	89-90,138	. JINNEY CHAPMAN	14
. JOHN	46	. MARGARET	27	. PEGGY	17,32
. MARY	46	. MARY	75	. RHODES	14
. MARY B. PRICE	1	. NANCY DANIEL	23	. THOMAS	17,32
CRUTCHFIELD,		. ROBERT	89	DALEY, JAMES	52
. ANN TAYLOR	22	. THOMAS	75	DALLUCK, MARTIN	137
. THOMAS	22	CURTUS, JOHN	139	DALTON, JOHN	23
CRUTHER, WILLIAM	79	CUSHINGBERRY, JAMES	4	POLLY EARLES	23
CUBBON, STEPHEN	136	JANE BURROWS	4	DANGERFIELD, WILLIAM	79
CUDDEN, MILLY	3,5	CUSSINE, RICHARD	51	DANIEL,	86,126
CUDDING, PAGE	6	CUTHBERT,		. ALEXANDER MOORE	145
PEGGY	3	. ELLEN FRANKLIN	102	. ALSE FINNELL	20
CULBERTSON, MARY	97	. JEANNE	102	. ANN	8
CULLEY, JOHN	8	. THOMAS	102	. BEVERLY	11
MARY LAND	8	CYMON, WILLIAM	145	. CORNELIUS O.	16
CUMMINGS, ALEXANDER	56	DABNEY, ALEXANDER	6,68	. ELIJAH	138
CUMMINS, ALEXANDER	51	SALLY BELL	6	. ELIZABETH	35,126
CUNBROW, BRADLEY	144	DADE, FRANCES	165	. ELIZABETH MERRY	1,84
CURGIO, THOMAS	143	. FRANCIS	8,15,69,72	.	126-127
CURNETT, JAMES	105	.	82-83	. ELIZABETH REYNOLDS	28
. LORETTA	105	. HARRIET	44	. FRANCES HUMPHREYS	2
. MARY G. BROCKMAN	105	. LAWRENCE	69,82	. FRANCIS HUMPHRIES	5
CURRER, NICHOLAS	68	. LAWRENCE T.	44	. FRANKEY	20
CURRIE, JAMES	73	. MARY I.	82	. JAMES	4,20,142-144
CURTIS, ANN	90	. MARY J.	69	. JAMES B.	43

INDEX to
Orange County, VA FAMILIES - Vol. #2

. JANE	9	CATHERINE SHEPHERD	19	. BARTLETT	22
. JANE HIATT	11	DARNEL, HANNER	2	. BENJAMIN	29,145
. JANE MCCULLY	31	DARNELL, ANNA	5	. BEREMAN	79,141,147
. JOHN	3,6,59,141,145	. CYNTHIA MALLORY	33	. BERRYMAN	76,142
. LEWIS	128	. ELIZABETH	45	. BETTY	11
. LUCY	6	. ELIZABETH EHART	17	. CHARLES	111,138
. LUCY DAVIS	4	. FRANCIS	32	. CUDDEN	37
. LUCY MARSHALL	3,6	. LUCY	26	. DASHIA HAM	38
. MARIA	45	. MARY	42	. DIANA GAYDEN	111
. MARTHA	37	. MARY ANN	26,32	. EDNA	25
. MARY	28,43	. NELSON	33	. ELIJAH	30
. MARY GAINES	10	. POLLY AHART	28	. ELIZABETH	11,16,21,41
. MINERVA	49	. POLLY EHART	28	. ELIZABETH EARLY	9
. NANCY	23	. RICE	28,42,45	. ELIZABETH HARVEY	40
. NANCY R.	48	. THOMAS	17	. ELIZABETH JONES	30
. PEGGY PLUNKETT	16	DARNOLD, ABRAHAM	25	. ELIZABETH MALLORY	46
. POLLY	37	SUSANNA	25	. ELIZABETH PANNILL	13
. REUBEN	1,59,77,84	DAUGHAUNEY,		. EVAN	41
.	126-128,140,142,144	HANNAH RHODES	119	. FRANCES	8
.	146	DAVIDSON, D.N.	131	. FREDRICK D.	47
. REUBIN	45	. GEORGE	52	. HARRIET GOODRIDGE	43
. REUBIN R.	28	. JANE	52	. HENRY	52
. ROBERT	2,5,59,69-70,82	. JOHN	52	. ISAAC	17,30,38,45
.	127	. SAMUEL	52	. ISUM	111
. SAMUEL	142	. THOMAS	52	. JACK	143
. THOMAS	28	. WILLIAM	52	. JAMES	7,10,52,146
. VIVIAN	59,143-145	DAVIS, ABSOLEM	20	. JANE	37
. VIVION	9,142	. AGGY	7	. JANE JONES	29
. WILLIAIM	31	. ANN	28	. JERUSHA	20,36
. WILLIAM	10,86	. ANN MODISET	10	. JERUSHA DAVIS	20
DANIELS, JOHN	51	. ASA	43	. JINKENIAS	18
DANSLEY, THOMAS	142	. AULEY ROGERS	43	. JOHN	4,13,42-43,52,59
DARBY, ADAM	19	. BABBY LOWRY	18	.	65,76,139

INDEX to Orange County, VA FAMILIES - Vol. #2

Name	Page
. JONATHAN	10,15,69,81
. JOSEPH	7,10-11,16,143
. JULIA	42
. LENARD	3
. LEONARD	6
. LEWIS	38
. LUCH GRADY	40
. LUCY	2,4,10
. MARY	3-4,7,14,32,38,52
.	76,79
. MARY EASTIN	13
. MARY JOHNSON	7
. MARY JONES	4
. MARY SNOW	43
. MATHEW	78
. MATTHEW	70
. MILDRED EDDINS	47
. MILLY	15
. MITCHEL	46
. MITCHELL	40
. NANCY	32
. NANCY EASTON	13
. OWEN	111
. PHELLEMON	34
. PHILIMON	8
. POLLY	48
. POLLY HILMAN	41
. RACHEL	3,6
. REUBEN	143
. REUBIN	40
. RHODA	36
. SALLY	28
. SALLY BOSTON	33
. SALLY LOWRY	22
. SAMUEL	52
. SARAH	2,30
. SUCKEY	10
. SUSA	79
. SUSANNA	19,45
. SUSANNA BURROWS	6
. SUSANNAH	22
. SUSANNAH BURROWS	3
. THOMAS	9,59,84-85
. WILLIAM	13,33,42-43,52
.	136,138-139
. ZACHARIA	144
DAVISON, JOHN	138
DAWLER, WINIFRED	3
DAWSON, AMANDA	47
. ANN CHISM	5
. ANN CHISOM	3
. BENJAMIN	69
. FANNY	40
. FLORINE	101
. FRANCES	45
. JAMES	27,69,79
. JOHN	3,5,10,14,18,45
.	59-60
. LINWOOD H.	102
. LYNWOOD H.	101
. MARY	14
. MARY WAUGH	1
. MILLEY	69
. MILLY	79
. MUSGRAVE	1
. NANCY HUGHES	27
. NANCY POLLARD	18
. NATHANIEL	101-102
. POLLY S.	14
. RACHEL BROCKMAN	101
.	102
. ROBERT	69,146
. SALLY	17
. THOMAS	136
. WILLIAM	20,23
. WILLIAM H.	47
DAY, ELIZABETH	24
. FRANCIS	33
. HENRY	82
. SARAH	82
. SUSANNA	26
DEAL, PHILIP	73
DEALMORE, JOHN	51
DEALWOOD, JOHN	142,146
DEAN, CHARLES	40
. ELIZA	42
. ELIZABETH	41
. ELIZABETH BOSTON	40
. NANCY	48
. REBECCA	12
DEANE, GEORGE	35
. JOHN	46-47
. MARY	40
. MARY DEANE	40
. MARY KINDLE	35
. SARAH BOSTON	13
. WILLIAM	13,35,40-41
DEAR, BETTY	3
. CATHERINE	11,23

INDEX to
Orange County, VA FAMILIES - Vol. #2

. CATHERINE SMITH	5	. JANE	20	. ANN QUISENBERRY	39
. EDMUND	70	. THOMAS	20	. JANE RHODES	119
. ELIZABETH	11	DELANEY, DISE	21	. JOHN	119
. FRANKEY	10	. LISSA	8	. NANCY WOOD	34
. JEREMIAH	136	. MARY	11	. RALPH	39
. JOHN	2,5,8,10	DELANY, JOHN	2	. ROBERT	11
. KATHERINE SMITH	2	SUSANNAH WATTS	2	. RUTH PARISH	11
. LUCY	8	DEMPSEY, DANIEL	47	. THOMAS	34
. LUCY FENNELL	4,7	. PHOEBE	47	DIER, JAMES	137
. POLLY	20	. THOMAS	34	JEREMIAH	51
. ROBERT	137	DEMSEY, ALLEN	38	DIGMAN,	
. THOMAS	4,7,15,20	. LEWIS	48	. MARY G. BROCKMAN	105
DEARING, EDWARD	78,140	. POLLY	38	. THLEWOMAS	105
.	144	. POLLY MCCLARNEY	48	DILLY, MARY DEVENNEY	44
. ROBERT	144,146	DENNISON, JAMES	46	RICHARD	44
DEBORD, LUCY	32	NANCY LUCAS	46	DIX,	95
DEDMAN, FRANCES	34	DENTON, JOHN	59	DIXON, CHARLOTTE BROWN	2
. JOHN	29	DESRM, ROBERT	137	. JOHN	37
. MARY	16	DEVENNEY, C.	44	. LUCY RUMSEY	37
. NANCY	29	. CORNELIUS	30	. SAMUEL	2
DEELWOOD, MARY	73	. MARY	44	DIZEN, JOHN	136
DEER, BETTY	5	DEWALL, CLAIBORNE	36	DOANE, ELIZABETH MAYS	14
JOHN	145	POLLY FAULCONER	36	JOHN	14
. DEERING, EDWARD	143,146	DEWIT, CHARLES	75	DOBBIN, JOHN	59
. JAMES	9,59	. MARTIN	75-76	DOCKRELL, MARY	98
. MARY	14	. MERCY	75	DOD, WILLIAM	16
. MARY RUMSY	9	DEWITT, CHARLES	59	DODD, ANNA	12-13
. ROBERT	11,14,17,139	DICKENSON,		. JAMES	26,37,70
.	143	. ANN QUISENBERRY	38	. JOHN	16,27,141
. SARAH	11	. BENNETT	47	. MARGARET	37
. SUSANNAH	17	. MILDRED CARPENTER	47	. NANCY COOK	26
. THOMAS	9	. RALPH	38	. SALLY JOHNSON	27
DEHONEY, HANNAH	20	DICKINSON,	92	. SUSANNAH LEE	16

INDEX to
Orange County, VA FAMILIES - Vol. #2

Name	Pages
. WILLIAM	16,27,36
DODSON, THOMAS	137
DOGGETT, GEORGE	59
DOHONEY, ELIZABETH	29
HANNAH	29
DOHONY, JAMES	5
. R.H.	14
. WINIFRED VAWTER	5
DOLEWOOD, JOHN	141
DOLIN, ELIZABETH	46
. JOHN	44,46
. PATSY	44
DOLLENS, JOHN	69
PRESLEY	69,143
DOLLINGS, JOHN	79
PRESLEY	79
DOLLINS,	
. ELIZABETH HENSLEY	14
. MARTHA	14
. REUBEN	14
. SUKY	33
. WILLIAM	14,19
DOLWOOD, JOHN	136,139
MARY	138
DOMRON, AUSTIN	121
. LESLIE	121
. NANNIE RHODES	121
DONELY, JOHN	139
DONOHONY, JAMES	3
WINIFRED DAWLER	3
DONOVER, JOHN	14
SALLY GAER	14
DOOLEY,	
. ELIZABETH BROCKMAN	102
. URIAH	102
DOOLING,	
. ELIZABETH FINNELL	15
. THOMAS	15,52
DORSON, ROBERT	145
DOTSON, JOHN	137
DOUGLAS, ANN	5
. CHARLES	19,70
. DORCAS	2
. ELIZABETH	52
. GEORGE	87
. JOHN	12,22,69,71,140
.	143
. JUDITH	22
. MARGARET	65,87
. MARY PAYNE	19
. THOMAS	77
DOUGLASS, DORCAS	5
. GEORGE	137
. MILDRED	8
. WILLIALM	30
DOVELL, NANCY	32
DOWELL, ELIZABETH	47
. ELIZABETH GARITSON	43
. JANE	45
. JOHN	43
. LUCY VAUGHN	44
. NATHAN	44
. RICHARD	44
DOWLING, FRANCIS LUCAS	40
JOHN	40
DOWNER, THOMAS	135,140
DOWNEY, ALEXANDER	3,72
.	80-81-82
. SALLY BELL	3
DOWNS,	140
HENRY	59,76,135,143
DRAKE,	
. CAROLINE BROCKMAN	88
. HANNAH	52,73
. RALPH	88
. SAMUEL	51,73,137-138
DRAPER, MARTHA BOSTON	41
RICHARD	41
DRESSER,	
. MARTHA BROCKMAN	102
. SAMUEL	102
DRUMRIGHT, CHRISTIANE	122
DUCK, AMANDA E.	112-113
. BEATRICE MORGAN	113
. JAMES	112
. JIMMY	113
. MARY PEOPLES	112
DUDLEY,	86
DUDSON, THOMAS	137
DUFF, ARTHUR	52
MARY	52
DUKE, LINE GIBBS	26
WILLIAM	23,26
DULLING, JOHN	52
DUNAWAY, GEORGE	38
. JOHN	38,40
. PEGGY HAINEY	38
. POLLY SUTHERLAND	38,40
DUNBROW, BRADLEY	144

INDEX to
Orange County, VA FAMILIES - Vol. #2

DUNCAN, JOSEPH	4	. ELIZABETH DAVIS	41	. GEORGE	70,78,137,140
. NANCY STEPHENS	4	. ISAAC	41	. ROBERT	60,76
. WILLIAM	59	DUVALL, SALLY	11	EASTIN, CHARLES	69
DUNCOME, ELIZABETH	1	DYER, JAMES	51,139	. ELIZABETH	8
DUNGAN, MARGARET	52	DYLLEN,	143	. ELIZABETH HENDERSON	8
DUNIVEN, ELIZABETH	36	EARLAY, JAMES	12	. JOHN	10,69,80
DUNLAP, ALEXANDER	59,76	EARLES, POLLY	23	. MARY	13,69,80
ANN	76	RODHAM	23	. NANCY	69,80
DUNN, AUTHUR	51	EARLEY, FRANCIS	12,80	. PHILIP	8,80
. FOUNTAIN D.	44	. JOHN	80	. PHILL	140
. JOHN	37	. THEODON	12	. PHILLIP	69
. MARY BLEDSOE	2,5	. THEODORE	80	. REUBEN	13,69,80
. NANCY CRAIG VIA	44	EARLY, ELIZABETH	9,27	. SARAH GRIFFITH	10
. SUSANNA MAUPIN	37	. ELIZABETH THOMPSON	37	EASTING, STEPHEN	2
. WILLIAM	2,5	. GARNER	69	SUSANNA JOHNSON	2
DUNNING, ELIZABETH	52	. JACOB	37	EASTON, NANCY	13
DUREN, JESSE	108	. JAMES	27,36,43,60	EATON, ELIZABETH	21
SARAH GAYDEN	108	.	70-71	. ELIZABETH DUNIVEN	36
DURETT, JOHN	137	. JOEL	4	. WILLIAM	36
DURHAM, JOHN	52	. JOHN	48	EAVE, JOSEPH	144
THOMAS	75	. JOSEPH	60	EAVENS, THOMAS	141
DURRENT, JOEL	28	. LUCY SMITH	4	EAVES,	
DURRETT, ACHILLES	29	. LUCY T.	43	. NANCY HIGHLANDER	21
. BETSY	16	. MARGARET TIMBERLAKE	48	. SALLY	15
. DEANA	28	. SARAH CARR	36	. WILLIAM	15,21
. ELIZABETH THOMPSON	25	. SARAH GRAVES	36	EDDINS, ABRAHAM	36
. JOEL	15-16,23,29	. THEODOSIA	9	. ABRAM	85
. KILLAM	25	. THEODOSIA WHITE	120	. AMELIA SIMS	48
. LYDIA QUISENBERRY	29	. WILLIAM	36	. ELIJAH	21
. NANCY	15	EASTEN, PHILIP	146	. FRANCES	35
. RICHARD	137,140,143	PHILOMEN	144	. FRANCES COLLINS	21,32
. WILLIAM	137	EASTHAM, ANN THORNTON	21	. JOHN	138
DURRITT, DAVIS	41	. EDWARD	21	. JOSEPH	32

INDEX to
Orange County, VA FAMILIES - Vol. #2

Name	Page
. MARIA BURTON	45
. MILDRED	35,47
. NANCY DAVIS	32
. NANCY OSBORN	21
. POLLY	36
. SARAH MANSFIELD	41
. SMITH	45
. TANDY	48
. THOMAS	21,32,42,47
. WILLIAM	41,135
EDINGS, THEOFULUS	139
WILLIAM	138
EDINGTON, EDMUND	21
PRISCILLA GORDON	21
EDINS, JOHN	135
SELINA	42
EDMISTON, DAVID	52
. ISABELLA	52
. JESSE	52
. JOHN	52
. MOSES	52
. RACHELL	52
. WILLIAM	52
EDMONDSON, JOSEPH	65
THOMAS	135
EDMONSON, JOSEPH	146
. SUKEY	1-2,84
. THOMAS	138,144,146
EDMUNDSON, JOHN	91
EDWARD, FRANCIS	27
. MARY MITCHELL	121
. ROBERT	142
. SAMUEL	121
EDWARDS,	
. AGATHA BROCKMAN	122
.	123
. BRICE	122
. BRICE W.	123
. CHRISTIAN	122
. ELISHA	21
. ELIZABETH EATON	21
. JOHN	39,85,136,139
. JOSEPH	27,47
. JOSEPH L.	33
. JULIA	122
. LEONARD	123
. MARY A. RHODES	123
. MARY ANN RHODES	122
. OLIVIA OLIVER	41
. RACHEL	14
. ROBERT A.	123
. SALLY	33
. SELENA BICKERS	39
. THOMAS	122-123
. WILLIAM	41
EHART, ABRAM	16
. ADAM	38
. CATHERINE	12,24
. ELIZABETH	17
. FRANKEY	15
. JUDITH KIRK	16
. MICHAEL	38
. POLLY	28
. RACHEL	26
. SARA	38
. SARA EHART	38
EHEART, LAVINA B. CAVE	48
MICHAEL L.	48
ELETT, JAMES	140
ELLEN, JAMES	78
ELLES, JAMES	40
MARY C. WOOLFOLK	40
ELLIOT, ALBIN	26,30
. ANN HALL	40
. GEORGE	40
. JAMES	136
. MARY KNIGHT HALL	46
. URCILLA GAINES	26
. WILLIAM	46
ELLIOTT,	143
. ANDERSON	157
. J.B.	158
. SAMUEL	159
. SARAH	158
ELLIS, BARBARA	2
. CLARISSA	41
. JAMES H.	41
. JOHN	45
. MARIA	45
. MARY A.	50
. REBECCA	29
. SALLY	36
. THOMAS	29,36,86
. THOMAS H.	50
. WILLIAM	41
ELUCK, POLLY	26
EMBRE, ELIZABETH	96-97
. JOHN	142-143
. JUDITH PAYNE	10

200

INDEX to
Orange County, VA FAMILIES - Vol. #2

Name	Page	Name	Page	Name	Page
. RICHARD	10	. SUSAN	35	EWE, JOSEPH	52
EMBREE, RICHARD	125	. WILLIAM	20,26,28-29,31	EWER, MARJORIE	105
EMBREY, ANN	77	.	33,35	FAIRFAX, CATHERINE	133
. ELIZABETH	77	. WINIFRED HOLLADAY	6	FANT, FANNY JAMES	29
. JOHN	140,145	. WINIFRED HOLLIDAY	3	JOHN T.	29
. WILLIAM	77	ESTIS, EDMUND	39	FARGISON, THOMAS	137
EMBRY, JUDY	1	. JOHN	22	FARGUSON, ANN	78
EMGRAM, WILLIAM	60	. SARAH COX	22	. JOHN	85
EMMERSON, JAMES	42	EUBANK, JOHN	140	. JOSHUA	78,85
JEMIMAH TINDER	42	EUBANKS, JOHN	143	. MARY A. MILLS	27
ENNIS, JOHN	137	EVANS, ARCHIBALD	111	. SAM	75
ENOCHS, I.L.	154	. CHARLOTTE	111	. SAMUEL	60
EPHRIAM, GEORGE	137	. JOHN	33,36,52	. VIVAN	27
ESTES, ABRAHAM	34	. NANCY KING	33	FARISH, MARY S.	36
. BETSY	14	. SALLY	111	THOMAS	36,68,82
. ELISHA	25,39	. THOMAS	142	FARNEYHOUGH, ELIZ.	30
. FANNY	33	. WILLIAM	60	. JOHN	37
. FRANCES HARVEY	43	EVE, JOSEPH	22,138	. SALLY	36
. FRANCIS	39	.	143-144,146	FARRISH, THOMAS	82
. JANE OGG	43	. MARY	11	FARROW, JOHN	135
. JENNY	25	. POLLY SMITH	22	FAULCONER, ANN	42
. JOHN	39,45	EVENS, JOHN	136	. BETSY CHISTRAM	20
. LITTLETON	43	. JOSEPH	143	. CARTER B.	38
. LUCY	4,7,26	. NANCY	18	. CATY	24
. MARIA BINGHAM	39	EVERING, JANE	88	. DAVID	17,36
. MARIA DANIEL	45	EVERT, GEORGE	76	. EDWARD S.	43
. MARY S.	20	MARGARET	76	. ELIAS	25
. MILLY	31	EVES, FANNY JENKINS	29	. ELIZABETH	19,40,42
. NANCY	39	THOMAS	29	. ELIZABETH FAULCONER	40
. POLLY HARVY	28	EVINS, JOHN	140	. ELIZABETH JACOB	43
. SALLY	29	EWALL, AGATHA	75	. ELIZABETH JONES	35
. SALLY COX	34	. JOHN	75	. ELIZABETH PERRY	44
. SAMUEL	3,6,43	. THOMAS	75	. FRANCIS	28

INDEX to
Orange County, VA FAMILIES - Vol. #2

. FRANCIS FAULCONER	28	. SAMUEL	21	FERRELL,EDWARD	140
. GEORGE	17	. SARAH BURGES	21	. GEORGE	18
. HUGH	40	. SARAH GRADY	17	. POLLY WOLF	18
. HUGH M.	44	. THOMAS	19,35	FIELD,HENRY	60,75-76,139
. JAMES	17	. WILLIAM	20,42-43,49	FIELDS,HENRY	136
. JENNY	19	FAULCOWR,DAVID	14	MARY	52
. JENNY FAULCONER	19	. LUCY	14	FILLINGER,	
. JOHN	2,5,24,28,42,46	. WILLIAM	14	. BETSY FERREL	22
. KEMP	44	FEARNEY,AGY LUCAS	3,6	. HENRY	22
. LUCH	46	. SALLY MORTON	6	FINDELL,HENRY	137
. LUCY	33	. SARAH NORTON	3	FINELL,	
. MARG.	39	. THOMAS	3,6,30	. ELIZABETH CHAMBERS	21
. MARG. MORRISON	5	. WILLIAM	3,6	. JOHN	21
. MARGARET	44	FEARNEYHOUGH,ANN	4	FINK,MARK	140
. MARGARET MORRISON	2	. ELIZABETH JONES	44	TIMOTHY	139
. MARIA NEWMAN	38	. JOHN	44	FINKS,MARK	135
. MELINDA HORD	43	. NANCY	37	FINLASON,JOHN	52,60,139
. MILDRED	49	FELIX,ELIZABETH	23	FINLASSON,SLEET	65
. MILLY	37	WILLIAM	23	FINLEY,PATRICK	52
. MILLY SISSON	17	FENELL,JOHN	139	FINNEL,ELIZABETH	3
. NANCY	38	FENNEL,CHARLES	5	. JAMES	15
. NANCY COLEMAN	17	NANCY SAUNDERS	5	. JOHN	146
. NANCY FAULCONER	38	FENNELL,JEANY BOURN	7	. LUCY	23
. NANCY SANDERS	15	. LUCY	4,7	. REBECCA CHAMBERS	15
. NEWMAN	34,38	. WILLIAM	7	. SIMON	23
. NICHOLAS	28,33	FERGERSON,ANN	123	. WILLIAM	146
. PETER	74	FERGUSON,ELIZ.	33	FINNELL,ALSE	20
. POLLY	36	JOSHUA	65	. ANNA R.	20
. POLLY NEWMAN	25	FERNEYHOUGH,AGNES	42	. BENJAMIN	3,5,22,72
. REUBEN	19	. ESTER	49	. CATY SURRY	20
. REUBIN	28	. JOHN	42	. CHARLES	3,14
. RICHARD	15,37	. THOMAS	49	. ELIZ. ROBINSON	22
. SALLY	28	FERREL,BETSY	22	. ELIZABETH	15

INDEX to
Orange County, VA FAMILIES - Vol. #2

. ELIZABETH BOURN	10	FITZHIGH, HENRY	142	. WILLIAM		31
. GEORGE	17	FITZHUGH,	141	FLICK,		
. JAMES	17,20-21	. ALICE	25	. BARBARY KIBLINGER		19
. JOHN	20	. ANN TALIAFERRO	9	. CATHERINE LOWER		21
. JONATHAN	146	. ELIZABETH CONWAY	15	. JOHN		19
. NANCY	15,49	. HENRY	15,25,147	. WILLIAM		21
. NANCY SAUNDERS	3	. JOHN B.	15	FLINN, SAMUEL		47
. REBECCA CHAMBERS	17	. WILLIAM	9	FLOYD, ANNIE		22
. REUBEN	10	FITZHUGHS,	145	. CHARLES		52
. SALLY DAWSON	17	FITZPATRICK, JOHN D.	65	. JANE HERRING		22
. SARAH C. SLEET	5	FLANAGIN, WILLIAM	144	. JOHN		52,138
. SARAH CARTER	3	FLANDERS, WILLIAM	52	. SAMUEL		22
. WILLIAM	20,31	FLANNAGEN, REUBEN	143	FORD, ABSOLEM		15
FINNEY, FANNY	17	FLEAK, ANDREW	18,120	. ANN		2,36
JOHN	72,144	. FRANKEY RHOADS	18	. ANN MOORE		11
FISHER, FANNY MASON	29	. FRANKY RHODES	120	. BENJAMIN		38
. JAMES	29	FLECK, ANDREW	19	. CATHERINE		41
. JOHN	38	. BETSY SMATTS	20	. DANIEL		39
. LUDWICH	135	. ELIZABETH	19	. DAVID		135
. MARG. FAULCONER	39	. HENRY	20	. HARLIN		45
. PATRICK	67	FLEEK, ANDREW	17	. LUCY		31
. WILLIAM	39	. JOHN	22	. MARGARET GRADY		45
FITZ, BATTAILE	27	. POLLY	22	. MOLLY RANSDELL		15
ELIZ. TALIAFERRO	27	. RACHEL LOWER	17	. PATSY		15
FITZGARRELL,		FLEET,	143	. RHODY ATKINS		38
. CATHERINE BRUCE	12	. MADISON	138	. SUSANNA STUBBLING		29
. SARAH	14	. MARY	140	. WILLIAM	11,29,31,36,41
. STEPHEN	12	FLESHMAN, PETER	73,137	FORESTER, JOHN		52
. WILLIAM	12	ZACHARIAH	136	FORRESTER, JOHN		135
FITZGARRETT, THOMAS	67	FLETCHER,		FORTSON, BENJAMIN		14
FITZGERALD, EASOM	25	. DELILA SULLIVAN	31	. SALLY HEAD		14
MARY SELF	25	. ELIZABETH PAYNE	30	. THOMAS		60
FITZGERRALL, JAMES	143	. WASHINGTON	30	FOSTER, ANTHONY		3,6,69

INDEX to
Orange County, VA FAMILIES - Vol. #2

. CATEY	23	FRANKLIN,BERNARD	69	. JONATHAN	14
. CATY SNELL	17	. CHARLES PERRY	104	. LAWRENCE	143
. ELIZABETH	2,5,21	. CIRRELDA	102	. SUSANNAH BREEDING	14
. ELIZABETH PRICE	3,6	. EDWARD	13-14,78,140	FRASER,WILLIAM S.	48
. FRANCES JONES	4	. ELIZABETH	14	FRAYS,LAWRENCE	73
. FRANCIS JONES	6	. ELIZABETH CROSS	102	FRAZER,ANN BURRUS	44
. GEORGE	92	. ELLEN	102	. JAMES	145
. HASKEW	17	. EULAH	103	. JOHN	52
. JOHN	13,17,143	. HARRY JOHN	104	. WILLIAM S.	42,44
. LUCY	21	. HOWARD KINSER	104	FRAZIER,ALEXANDER	52
. MARY	6	. JAMES SIMMS	102	. POLLY MORRIS	31
. MARY SAWYER	2,5	. JANE	104	. SHADRACK	31
. MARY SINGLETON	92	. JEANNINE LESLIE	104	FREDRICK,	
. MILLY	13	. JESSE	102	. BETSY BAUGHKER	32
. NANCY	18	. JOHN	10	. PHILIP	32
. RACHAEL	2	. JOHN BYRON	103	FREEMAN,RHODA	113
. SUSANNAH DEERING	17	. KATHERINE LESHER	104	SALLY	25
. TABITHA HAWKINS	16	. LOU	140	FRIETT,JOHN	137
. THOMAS	2,4-6,146	. LUCY	104	FROGMORTH,	142
. WILLIAM	16,23	. LUCY BROCKMAN	102	FROGMORTON,	144
FOUSHEE,CHARLES	141-142	. MARY C.	103	FRY,PHILIP	49
	145	. MARY E.	103	TRUEMAN	137
. JOHN	145,147	. MARY LESLIE	104	FRYAR,JOHN	87
. JOSEPH	145	. MARY PEARSON	10	FRYE,	
. NANCY GRAVES	15	. MAUDE	102-103	. CATHERINE BAUGKER	32
. THORNTON	15	. MOLLY	13	. JOHN	32
FOX,ELIZABETH HERNDON	19	. NANCY M.	103	FRYS,	136
. STEPHEN	19	. REUBEN	140	FUGATE,RANDALL	73
. THOMAS	136,138	. WILLIAM EDWARD	104	FULCHER,JOHN	76
FRANCIS,LOUISE	164	. WILLIAM T.	102	FUNK,JOHN	60
FRANK,SAM	83	. WILLIAM THOMAS	103	FURGUSON,JOHN	24
SARAH	83	FRANKLYN,BERNARD	79	FURNACE,	
FRANKLEY,EDWARD	78	. EDWARD	143	. ELIZABETH DUNCOME	1

INDEX to
Orange County, VA FAMILIES - Vol. #2

Name	Page	Name	Page	Name	Page
. JOHN	1	. MELINDA SANDERS	43	. ZACHARIAH	41
FURNEY, FANNY	17	. MILLY ROW	23	GARITSON, ELIZABETH	43
FURNIS, JACOB	9	. POLLY WHITE	28	GARLON, REUBEN	20
MARY PAGE	9	. REUBEN	60	GARMAN, THOMAS	140
FURNISH, ELIZABETH	86	. RICHARD	8,43,60	GARNER, FRANCIS	70
. JACOB	86	. ROBERT	26	JINNETTE	24
. JAMES	65,86	. SALLY	11	GARNET,	141
. JANE	86	. THOMAS	23	JAMES	142
. JOHN	86	. URCILLA	26	GARNETT, ANDREW	32
. MARY	86	. WILLIAIM	141	. ANN	4,6
. SAMUEL	86	. WILLIAM	69,80	. ANTHONY	60
. WILLIAM	86	GALAGAN, THOMAS	52	. ELIZABETH BELL	26
FURRILL, BENJAMIN	79	GALASBY,		. FRANCES CHILES	31
GABLE, LAURA	115	. BETSY GOODRIDGE	18	. JAMES	30-31
GAER, NATHANIEL	14	. JOHN	18	. LARKIN	26
. SALLY	14	GALT, ELIZABETH	103	. RACHEL HAWKINS	1
. SALLY HAM	16	GAMBLE, MATHEW	19	. SALLY	13
. WILLIAM	16	NANCY BELL	19	. SALLY B. BELL	32
GAHAGON, THOMAS	141	GAMBOE,		. SARAH	32
GAIDEN,	108,133	. CATHERINE CHISM	20	. SUKEY BROCKMAN	8
GAINES, AUGUSTINE	28	. SAMUEL	20,25	. THOMAS	1,8
. BETSY LEWIS	3,6	GAMBRET, BETSY LEE	24	. URSULA	19
. CATY	2,26	WALTER	24	GARR, ANDREW	73
. DISNEY	18	GAMMONS, ALICE	114	. JOHN ADAM	73
. ELIZABETH	11	. CORNELIUS	114	. LAWRENCE	73
. ELIZABETH EASTIN	8	. DELILA J. WOODALL	114	. LEWIS	10
. FRANCIS	3,6	GARDE, MARY YATES	18	. MARGARET	10
. JAMES	65,67	WILLIAM	17-18	GARREL, JAMES	20
. JANE	69,80	GARDENER, SARAH	2	SARAH TAYLOR	20
. JENNY	16	GARDNER, DANIEL	35	GARRELL, DEMEY	13
. JOANNA SANDERS	23	. LUCINDA MARTIN	41	SALLY STANTON	13
. JOHN	16,23	. MALINDA HARRIS	35	GARRETT, MATTHEW	147
. MARY	8,10	. THOMAS	79	SOLOMON	65

INDEX to
Orange County, VA FAMILIES - Vol. #2

Name	Page	Name	Page	Name	Page
GARRISON, LIVINIA	46	. BETSY	106	. MARTHA	111
GARTH, AMANDA HEAD	49	. C.	106	. MARY	108
. D.C.	49	. CADESBEY	111-112	. MARY A. COOPER	111
. JOHN	135,140	. CATEY COLLINS	108	. MERIDAY	111
GARTIN, RACHEL	102,104	. CATHERINE	109	. NANNY	108-110
GARTON, ANTHONY	69,83	. CATHERINE COLLINS	108	. NASH	111
. MARTHA	44	. CATY COLLINS	2	. PATSEY	111
. MILLIE SULLING	1	. CHARLES	108	. PETER	111
. POLLY HANCOCK	21	. CLARICY	106,109	. POLLY	110
. SPENCER	21	. DIANA	111	. REBECCA	110-111
. SUSANNAH	10	. DORCAS WADE	111	. REBECCAH	110
. URIAH	10,69,83	. ELIJAH	108	. REUBEN	108
. ZACHARIAH	1	. ELIZABETH	108,111-112	. SALLY EVANS	111
GARY, MICHAEL	135	. FRANCES RUTLEDGE	108	. SARAH	108
GATES,	86	. FREDERICK	111	. SARAH GLADDEN	108
GATEWOOD,		. GADESBEY	110	. SEREFINA	111
. AMY QUISENBERRY	29	. GEORGE	106-112,133	. SERESINA	111-112
. HENRY	29	. GEORGE L.	111-112	. SIMON	111
. WILLILAM	74	. GRIFFEN	111,116	. SOLOMON	111
GATON,	108,133	. HANNAH	108,111	. SPENCER	108
. GEORG	133	. HANNAH HOWARD	111	. SUSANNA	108
. LOIS COLLINS	109	. IVESON GREENE	110	. SUSANNAH BOYD	108
. LOUIS COLLINS	107,109	. JANE HEARN	108	. TEMPEY T. PIPKIN	108
. VIOLET	107	. JOHANNA WEBSTER	133	. TOM	111
GAVELY, THOMAS	137	. JOHN	2,108-109,133	. URIAH C.	108
GAY, JOHN	52	. LOIS COLLINS	109,111	. WILLIAM	108
. MARGARET	52,74	. LOWIS COLLINS	106	. WINNEY	133
. SAMUEL	52	. LYPHEX	111	. WINNY	108
. THOMAS	52	. MALINDA	108	GAYDON,	108
. WILLIAM	74	. MARGARET LEA	110	GAYTON,	133
GAYDEN,	133	. MARGARET MCWATERS	108	. ELIZABETH	133
. ABNER	108	. MARGARET MUSE LEA	110	. GEORGE	133
. AGRIPPA	109-112	. MARIAH	111	. HANNAH	133

INDEX to
Orange County, VA FAMILIES - Vol. #2

Name	Page	Name	Page	Name	Page
. RICHARD G.	133	. WINTIFRED	14	. BETSY CARTEY	26
GEAR, JANE WATSON	23	GER, SPOTSWOOD	146	. ELIZA COLLINS	46
. JOSHUA	23	GERMAN, THOMAS	143	. ELIZABETH HARVEY	21
. MARY	21	GERRELL, SUSANNA	16	. ELIZABETH MORRIS	42
. POLLY ROGERS	21	GETTYS, WILLIAM R.	106	. ELIZABETH STONE	46
. WILLIAM	21	GHOLSON,	105	. FANNY ESTES	33
GEARHARDT, LYNN	102	JOHN	143-144	. JOHN	21,46,60,86
GEDON, ANN	133	GIBBINS, JOHN	144,146	. JONATHAN	76,78,135
GEER, BETSY MCDANIEL	48	. LUCY DEBORD	32	. JOSHUA	46
. ELIZABETH	25	. RACHAEL	40	. M.	141
. JOHN	48	. THOMAS	32	. MARGARET	52,76,78
. JONATHAN	25	. WILLIAM	52	. NELLY	40
. POLLY LAMB	25	GIBBON, JANE	165	. PEGGY	44
. RANSOM	25	GIBBONS, ANN	36	. PETER	33,44
. SARAH THACWEL	25	THOMAS	36	. SUSANNAH	18
GENTRY, AARON	24	GIBBS, AGGY DAVIS	7	. WILLIAM	26,42
. JAMES	40,48	. ANN JOHNSON	1	GILASBY, AGNES	52
. NELLY GIBSON	40	. CHURCHILL	71	. JAMES	52
. PEACHY LANGFORD	48	. FRANCIS	67	. JENNET	52
. POLLY OGG	24	. JACK	146	. JESSE	52
GEORGE, ANN	124-125	. JAMES	1,79	. WILLIAM	52
. ANNE	76	. JOHN H.	26	GILBERT,	
. CATHERINE	38,69,81	. JULIUS	7	. AGNES FERNEYHOUGH	42
. EDWARD	69,81	. KISSY WAYT	43	. ANN FEARNEYHOUGH	4
. ISAAC	69,81	. LINE	26	. AQUILA	33
. JOHN	76	. LUCY WAYT	29	. FANNY NEWMAN	33
. JOSEPH	69,81	. MARY ANN WAYT	39	. JOSEPH	42
. LUCY HAWKINS	16	. WILLIAM	39	. THOMAS	4,7
. RANNILL	136	. WILLIAM C.	43	GILL, JAMES	60
. SAMUEL	139	. ZAC	138	GILLASBY, DAVID	69
. WILLIAM	16,81	. ZACHARIAS	29	GILLESPIE, ALICE	164-165
. WINIFRED	81	. ZACHARY	60,137,139,144	GILLESPY, ANN WHITE	19
. WINNEFRED	69	GIBSON, ABEL	52	JOHN	19

INDEX to
Orange County, VA FAMILIES - Vol. #2

GILLETT, SALLY PANNILL	14	MATTHEW	52	GOODALL, BETSY	33
SAMUEL	14	GLASS,	142	. CHARLES	39-40,69,82
GILLISON, JOHN	66	JEHEW	145	. DAVID	16,33,38,69,82
GILLOCK,		GLASSCOCK, RHODA	113	. ELEANOR	38
. BETSY TWENTYMAN	12	GLASSELL, ANDREW	4,6	. ELIZABETH DAVIS	16
. ELIZABETH	17	. ELIZABETH TAYLOR	4,6	. FONTAINE	42
. ELIZABETH MORGAN	9	. JOHN	81	. FRANKEY COX	12
. HANNAH WOLFENBURGER	4	GLAYTON, PHILIP	76	. ISAAC	31,69,82
. HANNAH WOLFENGERGER	7	GLOVER, EDWARD	75	. JAMES	8,33,38-39
. JOHN	4,7	WILLIAM	75	. JOHN	10,16,28,60,69,82
. LAURENCE	12	GODDEN, WILLIAM	138	.	137
. LAWRENCE	17	GOFORTH, MILLY FOSTER	13	. JONATHAN	21
. SALLY	17	THOMAS	13	. LUCY DAVIS	10
. THOMAS	9	GOHAGON, THOMAS	143	. LUCY RIDDLE	39
GILLUM, MARTHA	77	GOLDEN, ANN WALTON	21	. MARY	38
RICHARD	77	. MARGARET	28	. MILLY HUCKSTEP	31
GILMER, JOHN	32	. NANCY	11	. PARK	40,49
SARAH MINOR	32	. RICHARD	21	. PARKS	12
GIPPS, HELEN BROCKMAN	88	. WILLIAM	144	. PATSY RUSSELL	21
ROGER	88	GOLDER, JOHN	52	. PEGGY TEAL	42
GIVENS,	125	GOLDING, NANCY	45	. POLLY	49
MARY	95	. POLLY PRICE	28	. RICHARD	65
GIVINS, ELIZABETH	52	. REUBEN	28	. SALLY	16
. JAMES	52	. RICHARD	32,45	. SALLY DAVIS	28
. JANE	52	. W.M.	21	. SALLY HARVEY	8
. JOHN	52	. WILLIAM	11	. SARAH	40
. MARGARET	52	GOLDSON, JOHN	136,142	. TIBATHA CLARK	33
. MARTHA	52	GOLEMAN, THOMAS	16	. WILLIAM	10
. SAMUEL	52	GOLLOSTHEN, JOHN	74	GOODIN, MARY	53
. SARAH	52	MARGARET RICE	74	GOODLET, ADAM	71
. WILLIAM	52	GOLSON, JOHN	141	GOODMAN, GEORGE	113
GLADDEN, SARAH	108	GON, GRACEY GRACE	17	. RHODA GLASSCOCK	113
GLASBY, MARGARET	52	JOHN	17	. SARAH E.	113

INDEX to
Orange County, VA FAMILIES - Vol. #2

Name	Page	Name	Page	Name	Page
GOODRICH, BETSY	13	. JAMES	34	. ALEXANDER	52
. BETTY DEAR	3	. JOHN	21,138	. JESSE	28
. BETTY DEER	5	. MARTHA MAJOR	21	. JOHN	52
. JOHN	3,5	GOTELLUS, REBA M.	115	. LIDIA CRAIG	10
GOODRIDGE, ANN	30	GOUCH, JOHN	143	. SALLY FAULCONER	28
. BETSY	18,22	GRACE, ANN	53	. SAMUEL	10
. FANNY BURTON	33	. ANN MCNEAL	5	GRASTY, ANN	13
. GEORGE C.	33	. ANN MICHEAL	2	. ELIZA	48
. HARRIET	43	. GEORGE	2,5,17	. ELIZABETH MORTON	27
. MARY	42	. GRACEY	17	. ELIZABETH PAYNE	33
. RICHARD	18	GRADY, ANNA	12	. G.S.	24,45
GOODWIN, ELIZA STEVENS	49	. BENJAMIN	22	. G.T.	93
JOHN M.	49	. CATHERINE ADAMS	22	. GEORGE	33
GORDON,	138	. CATY MONTAGUE	24	. GOODRICH	27
. ANN	44	. FANNY	31	. GOODRICH S.	36
. ELIZA GRASTY	48	. FRANKEY	18	. NANNEY	24
. HANNAH	11	. HANNAH MONTAGUE	24	. SARAH GREENWAY	93
. JAMES	10-11,72,81	. JOHN	31	. SUSAN	45
. JOHN	11	. LUCH	40	. SUSANNA	13
. JOHN C.	48	. MARGARET	45	. THOMAS	29
. JOHN H.	48	. MARY	52	GRAVES,	86
. LUCY	20	. RICHARD	24	. ABSOLEM	14
. MARY	11,45,48	. SAMUEL	18,24	. ANN R. WEBB	46
. MARY GORDON	11	. SARAH	17	. ANNA GRADY	12
. NAT.	20	. SARAH PROCTOR	31	. BENJAMIN	19,32
. NATHANIEL	11,45	. WILLIAM	12,17,31,40,45	. BETSY HILMAN	20
. PRISCILLA	21	GRAEYDON, RALPH	133	. CHARLES TANDY	46
. SAM	21	GRAMBRIEL,		. CLAIBOURN	45
. SARAH	10	. MARTHA HUTCHERSON	46	. DRUCILLA	20
GOSNEY,		. WALTER	46	. ELIJAH	21
. ELIZABETH MCKENNEY	29	GRANES, POLLY RUCKER	29	. ELIZABETH	30,45
. REUBEN	29	WALKER	29	. ELIZABETH COLLINS	19
GOSS, HAMILTON	21-22,25	GRANT,	65	.	32

INDEX to
Orange County, VA FAMILIES - Vol. #2

. ELIZABETH PLUNKETT	46	. GABRIEL	37	. MASSA	80	
. FANNY WHITE	23,44	. MARGRET	139	. SALLY	7	
. FELICIA WHITE	14	. SARAH BARBOUR	37	. THOMAS	137	
. FRANCIS	36	. THOMAS	47	. WILLIAM	143	
. ISAAC	18,20,40,46	. WILLIAM	52	GRESSOM,BETSY	21	
. JACOB	23	GRAYDON,	108	GRIDDIN,WILLIAM	135	
. JOANNA	31	. JOANNA	133	GRIFFEY,ABELL	17	
. JOEL	18	. RALPH	133	. CATHERINE SUTTON	17	
. JOHN	47,141-144	GRAYHDON,	133	. FANNY WISDOM	13	
. JONATHAN	43	GRAYSON,JOHN	77	. JOSEPH	13	
. JOSEPH	143-144	. MARTHA	77	GRIFFIN,DAVID	15,136	
. LEWIS	44,131	. ROBERT	74	. JAMES	146	
. LYDIA	28	. THOMAS	74	. JOHN	78,138	
. MARIAN MARQUESS	23	GREEN,	130	. JOSEPH	13	
. MOURNING BURRUS	14	. EDWARD	52	GRIFFITH,DAVID	10,143	
. NANCY	15,43	. ELIZABETH PRICE	1	. MARY	15	
. PETTY WHITE	27	. MARY E. BROCKMAN	101	. SARAH	10	
. REBECCA	92	. MARY L.	115	GRIGRY,ANN	28	
. RICHARD	15,18,60	. NICHOLAS	1	JOHN	28	
. RODA	23	. ROBERT	52,60,74	GRIGSBY,	146	
. ROSA LEE	131	. SAMUEL	139	. BERLINDA PORTER	41	
. SALLY	20	. WILLIS	101	. ELISHA	19	
. SAMUEL	136	GREENE,R.A.	94	. ELIZABETH PORTER	19	
. SARAH	18,36	GREENSLADE,		. REUBEN	41	
. SARAH GRAVES	18	. MARY E. CROSTHWAIT	154	GRINNAN,A.G.	118	
. SUSANNA	35	. WILLIAM	154	GRINNILS,REBECCA	14	
. SUSANNAH	18	GREENWAY,SARAH	93	SARAH	14	
. THOMAS	12,14,20,28,31	GREER,	133	GRINNON,MARY SHEPHERD	41	
	35,141-145	GREGORY,ISAAC	38	WILLIAM S.	41	
. WILLIAM	20,27	. LUCY SAMPSON	38	GRITT,MARY	9	
. WINIFRED	40	. NANCY LANCASTER	36	SALLY	9	
GRAY,ELIZABETH	117	. OBEDIAH	36	GROOM,DISE DELANEY	21	
. FRANCIS	117	GRESHAM,JOHN	80,85	. ELIZABETH HARRIS	48	

INDEX to
Orange County, VA FAMILIES - Vol. #2

Name	Page	Name	Page	Name	Page
. JOHN	21,65,84,86	GUNN, JAMES	66	. DUCIA MAIDEN	26
.	142-144	GUPTON, STEPHEN	141-144	. ELIZABETH MARR	31
. MAJOR	40	GUSHAM, AMBROSE	79	. ELIZABETH PICKET	44
. MOURNING	47	GUSUM, WILLIAM	140	. ELIZABETH SHEPHERD	24
. SALLY	39-40	GUTRIDGE, JOHN	140	. ELLIS R.	129
. SOLOMON	48	GUY, HENRY	60	. MARY E. BROCKMAN	129
. SOLOMON R.	47	SAMUEL	60	. MARY KNIGHT	46
GROVE, JOHN	145	HACKET, CHESLEY	77	. NANCY	27
GRUNTER, JEMIMA	3,6	MARTIN	77	. SUSANNAH DAVIS	22
GRYAN, MARY GIVENS	95	HACKETT, GARRETT	125	. THOMAS	44
GRYMES, ANDREW B.	85	MARY	125	. WILLIAM	22
. BENJAMIN	144	HACKLEY, ELIZABETH	17	. WILLIAM J.	24
. BETTY J.	8	FRANCIS	67	HALLOWAY, JAMES	76
. HANNAH	15	HADON, JOHN	139	HALSONN, RICHARD	140
. HARRIET DADE	44	HAGGARD, ARCHIE	99	HALY, JOSEPH	143
. JOHN	118,135,139	MARY L. BROCKMAN	99	HAM, BENNETT	45
. JOHN D.	69,83	HAILEY, FRANCIS	5	. BETSY	34
. JUDITH R.	31	HAINEY, JAMES	38	. CLARY WISDON	1
. LUDWELL	8,15,60,69,83	PEGGY	38	. DASHIA	38
. MARY LEE	23	HAKINS, WILLIAM	136	. FRANKEY	44
. PETER	85	HALE, CIRRELDA	103	. JOSEPH	9,34
. PEYTON	44,47	. ELMER	103	. JUDITH	29
. REBECCA WORMLEY	47	. FLMER	103	. LUCINNA	45
. SIMON	118	. OPAL HARVEY	103	. LUCINNA HAM	45
. THOMAS N.	47	HALES, JOHN	46	. MARY	30
. WILLIAM	71	MARY E. BLACKWELL	46	. MILLY	38
GULBY, THOMAS	52	HALEY, EDWARD	135,138	. SALLY	16
GULLEY, ENOCH	70,82	. JAMES	90,135,138	. SAM	16
. JOHN	8	. THOMAS	146	. SAMUEL	1,18,30,38,45
. MARY LAND	8	. WILLIAM	146	. SARAH HEAREN	9
. RICHARD	70	HALL, AMBROSE	31	HAMBLETON, EDWARD	16-17
GULLY, ENOCH	70	. ANN	40	.	70
THOMAS	144	. BAZEL	26	. ELIGE	26

INDEX to
Orange County, VA FAMILIES - Vol. #2

. ELIZA. RIPPITO	17	. ELENDER HANCOCK	29	HANSON,	138
. ELLIS	70	. JAMES	29	HAPPY,JANE ROSELL	158
. JOHN	19	. JEMIMA BROCKMAN	3,5	HARBISON,ALICE	102,104
. LEROY	22	. MARY	49	HARDIMAN,	
. MARG.	31	. MUNROE B.	43	. ELIZABETH KINSER	45
. MARGARET COLEMAN	26	. NANCY	41	. JAMES E.	45
. MATHEW	70	. POLLY	21	HARDIN,GEORGE	135
. NUTTY POWELL	19	. REBECCA	33	HARDWICK,JOHN	140
. POLLY	16	. SALLY	24	ROBERT	124
. POLLY BALYE	26	. SIDNEY OVERTON	43	HARDY,CHARLES	103
. SARAH	14	. SUSAN	33	. EULAH FRANKLIN	103
. SUCKEY BLUNT	22	. WILLIAM	3,5,11,21,24	. MARY	103
. THEOPHILUS	19	.	29,33,41	HAREGRIPE,JOHN	135
. THOMAS	26,70	HANES,SARAH	20	HARPER,PATSY	34
HAMILTON,ALICE	80	HANEY,BAZLE	41	. SAMUEL	78
. AUGUSTA	112	. BETSY	36	. THOMAS	78
. EDWARD	24	. DARBY	53	HARRAL,THOMAS	140
. ELLIS	70,80-81	. ELIZABETH DEAN	41	HARRELL,EDWARD	53
. FRANCIS RICHARD	13	. ELIZABETH WATSON	47	. JOHN	53
. JENNY OLIVE	22	. FANNY	49	. MARGARET	53
. JOHN	13,24,70	. JAMES	10,48,65	. MARY	53
. MARTHA	80	. JOHN	47	HARRIS,	124
. MARY	70,80,84	. MARY M. RUNKLE	35	. ALICE	122
. MATHEW	70,84	. MAY	35	. CATY	18
. SARA W. RIPPATO	24	. NANCE PETROS	10	. ELIZABETH	48-49
. THOMAS	70,81	. NANCY	48	. ELVINA BOWCOCK	47
. WILLIAM	22	HANSBORGOW,JOHN	135	. FRANCES ROWZEE	2
HAMM,JOSEPH	27	HANSFORD,BEN	9,60	. FRANCIS	35
NANCY SMOOT	27	. BENJAMIN	60,86	. FRANCIS ROWZEE	5
HAMMACK,JOHN	145	. BENONI	60	. JAMES	29
HAMMER,HENRY	69	. JOHN	36	. JANE	22
HAMMOCK,JOHN	141-142	. LUCINDA	30	. JOHN	2,5,23
HANCOCK,ELENDER	29	. SARAH KING	36	. JOSEPH	53

INDEX to
Orange County, VA FAMILIES - Vol. #2

. LEWIS	32,41	. NANCY HARRISON	30	. JOEL	147
. LINDSAY	22	. POLLY SIMS	41	. JOHN	7,23,141-142,145
. LUCY	35	. WILLIAM	41	.	161
. MALINDA	35	HARROD,BENJAMIN	19	. JOHN W.	161
. MARTHA SMITH	41	. BETSY BLAIR	19	. LAYTON	47
. MARY	125	. JOANNA ARNOLD	26	. LUCY ESTES	7
. MARY S. ESTES	20	. JOHN	13	. MARION CORRELL	103
. MILLY PRICE	23	. NANCY	13	. MARJORY HAYDEN	103
. MOSES	136,141	. RICHARD	26	. MARTHA E.	-
. MOSES T.	47	HARSNAP,JOHN	140	. BLACKBURN	161
. OLLY	36	HART,HENRY PHILIP	53	. MARY	14
. OVERTON	48	. JOHN	75	. MARY BROCKMAN	161
. PEGGY GIBSON	44	. SILAS	75	. MARY C. FRANKLIN	103
. PETER	20	HARTSOOK,ELIZABETH	50	. MARY E.	103
. REUBEN	141-144	HARVEY,	160	. MARY J. BLACKBURN	161
. SABINA	49	. ALEXANDER	161	. NANCY	23
. SALLY ESTES	29	. ALLEY WOOD	23	. NANCY M. FRANKLIN	103
. THOMAS	49	. ANTHONY	28,32	. NANNY	3,6
. WILLIAM	44	. ANTOINETTE WEBBER	103	. NATHANIEL	103
HARRISON,ANDREW	76	. BENJAMIN	3,5	. NORAH M. PENN	103
. ANTHONY	141	. BERNICE	103	. OPAL	103
. BATTELL	146	. BERTRAM T.	103	. RALPH S.	103
. BATTLE	143	. ELEANOR GOODALL	38	. ROBERT S.	103
. CHARLES	145	. ELIZABETH	21,40	. SALLY	8
. DANIEL	60	. ELIZABETH DOWELL	47	. SARAH HOBBS	7
. ELIZABETH TAYLOR	44	. ELIZABETH FELIX	23	. SUSAN	103
. FRANCES	91	. FRANCES	43	. SUSANNA	5
. GEORGE	91	. FRANCIS	3	. SUSANNA HARVEY	5
. JABEZ	44	. HANEY	34	. SUSANNAH	3
. JOHN	60	. HARRY FRANKLIN	103	. SUSANNAH HARVEY	3
. LAWRENCE	143	. HENRY	67	. THOMAS	7,34,38
. LEWIS	30	. HERBERT EDWARD	103	. WALTER LOGAN	103
. NANCY	30	. JEANETTE	103	. WILLIAM	23

INDEX to
Orange County, VA FAMILIES - Vol. #2

. WILLIAM FRANKLIN	103	. ANN FORD	36	. SUSAN STROTHER	1,11
HARVIE, JOHN	15	. ANNA SCOTT	31	. SUSANNA STROTHER	1
. SARAH	15	. AURELIUS	18	. SUSANNAH	8
. SARAH HOBBS	4	. BENJAMIN	18,22,25	. TABITHA	16
. THOMAS	4	.	141-142,145-146	. THOMAS	41,147
HARVY, ELIZABETH	25	. BETSY COLEMAN	22	. WILLIAM	1,53,136,138
. JENNY	29	. ELIJAH	30	.	141-142,145,147
. JONATHAN	25	. ELIZABETH	53	. WM. STROTHER	80,84
. MARGARET ROSS	25	. ELIZABETH JONES	41	HAWLEY, BENJAMIN	27
. POLLY	28,37	. ELIZABETH RECTOR	22	FRANCIS EDWARD	27
. SALLY	34	. ELIZABETH SCOTT	30	HAWS, HENRY	135,140
. WILLIAM	25	. ELLICK	34	HAY, ANN BROCKMAN	90
HARWOOD,		. JAMES	22,60	JOHN	90
. ELIZABETH SUTTON	14	. JOHN	69,80,136	HAYDEN, MARJORY	103
. MOSES	14	. JOHN B.	36	HAYES, MOSES	8
HASAY,		. JOICE QUISENBERRY	27	. SARAH PETTY	8
. ELIZABETH LEATHERS	48	. JOSEPH	8	. ZULA BELL	114
. MICHAEL	48	. LUCH	36	HAYNA, ELIZA	28
HASKEW, JOHN	143	. LUCY	1,16,33,69,80	HAYNES,	
HASTINGS, AMANDA J.	114	. MARY GAINES	8	. ELIZA E. BROCKMAN	104
.	134	. MARY PERRY	41	. FRANK	104
. ANDREW	134	. MOSES	1,11,27,65,69,80	. JUCINDA	34
. MARY J. MCGRAW	134	.	84	HAYS, ANDREW	53,60
HATCH, ALMA H. MORGAN	114	. PHEOBE	13	. BARBARA	53
CORNELIUS	114	. POLLY BICKERS	25	. CATHERINE	53
HATER, CONRAD	136	. RACHEL	1	. CHARLES	53
HATON, MARY	69	. REUBEN	73	. FRANCIS	53
HAUSE, CONRAD	19	. REUBIN	26,33	. JOAN	53
. JOHN	17	. RODDY	26,41	. JOHN	53
. SUSANNAH THOMPSON	19	. SALLY SCOTT	22	. MARGARET	53
HAWKINS, ALEXANDER	31	. SARA	9	. PATRICK	53
. ALICE CHAMBERLAIN	26	. SARAH BOYLE	80	. REBECKA	53
. ANN	15	. SEBREE	8	. ROBERT	53

214

INDEX to
Orange County, VA FAMILIES - Vol. #2

. RUTH	53	THOMAS	141,143	HENLEY,FRANCIS	77
. WILLIAM	53	HEAREN,FRANCIS	9	. MARTHA WINSLOW	28
HAYTON,MARY	76	SARAH	9	. OSBORNE	28
HEAD,AMANDA	49	HEARN,JANE	108	HENNESEY,KITTY	38
. ANTHONY	135,139	HEIGHT,JOHN	141	HENNESSY,PETER	17
. BENJAMIN	10,60,65,72	HELM,		WINNEY ROUTT	17
	83	. MATILDA TALIAFERRO	10	HENRY,BENFIELD	25
. ELIZA HUCKSTEP	39	. WILLIAM	10	. BENJAMIN	15
. ELIZABETH FINNEL	3	HENDERSON,ALEXANDER	8,53	. BENSON	48
. ELIZABETH KIRTLEY	6	.	70	. DULLEY	15
. FANNY	27	. AMBROSE	34	. ELIZABETH KIRTLEY	25
. FANNY HUCKSTEP	48	. ANN	124	. ELIZABETH WARREN	16
. GEORGE	140,143	. DEREAS	53	. FRANCES	14
. GEORGE MARSHALL	13	. ELIZABETH	8	. HILL	7
. HADLEY	72	. FRANKEY DANIEL	20	. JEREMIAH	36
. HARRIETT	47	. FRANKY MERRY	127	. LUCY KIRTLEY	24
. JAMES	3,6,14,60,69-70	. JOHN 20,24,37,43,85,89		. NANCY ROBERTS	15
.	83	. 91,124-125,127,129		. SUSANNA JONES	7
. JENNY PLUNKETT	21	. 136,138,142-144,146		. WILLIAM	14-16
. JOHN	12,27,47,49	. JOSEPH	144	. ZACHARY	24
. JULIA RHODES	122	. JOSEPH MILES	89	HENSHAW,EDMUND	39,69
. MARGARET GARR	10	. LUCY ACRE	34	. EDWARD	42
. MARSHALL	48	. MARGARET BROCKMAN	129	. ELIZABETH	42
. MILLY RUCKER	13	. NANCY	13	. ELIZABETH NEWMAN	16
. NANCY SANFORD	12	. PEGGY BROCKMAN	125	. JOHN	8,16,21,39,42-43
. SALLY	14	. RICHARD	125	. MARY N.	39
. SAM	140	. RICHARD I.	129	. PATTY NEWMAN	8
. SARA	6	. SARAH BROCKMAN	129	. PHILIP T.	49
. SARAH	4,33	. THOMAS	53	. SARA	39
. TAVENAH	21	. WILLIAM	135	. SARAH ANN SCOTT	49
. VALENTINE	39	HENDLEY,	99	. SARAH COWHERD	43
. WILTON	48	HENDRICKS,DORA	104	. VIRGINIA	42
HEALY,	11	HENING,DAVID	11	HENSLEY,CYPRESS	33

INDEX to
Orange County, VA FAMILIES - Vol. #2

Name	Page	Name	Page	Name	Page
. ELIZABETH	14	. LUCY	31	. SALLY HOLBERT	39
. ELIZABETH MAIDEN	26	. LUCY LUCAS	38	. THOMAS	22,24
. ELIZABETH OLIVER	34	. MAHALO LANDRAM	46	. WILLIAM	12,35
. FRANCIS	145	. MARY B. BRADLEY	47	. WILLIAM R.	32
. HANNAH	33	. MARY PENCE	39	HESTAND, ABRAHAM	22
. JAMES	26	. MARY SCOTT	1	. JOHN	22
. JANE	65	. MARY STEVENS	29	. TANLIPY HOWELL	22
. JOHN	34-35	. MILDRED MONTAGUE	47	HEU, ELIZA J.	158
. POLLY	35	. NANCY	44	HIAETT, JOHN	143
. SEDER	31	. NANCY ADAMS	33	HIATT, BARBARY ALLEN	9
. WILLIAM	14	. POLLY	21,32	. BENJAMIN	11
. WINNEY THOMPSON	31	. SALLY	18,26,45	. ELIZABETH	6
HERMAN, FREDRICK	34	. SARAH JONES	45	. JANE	11
MARY JAMERSON	34	. SARAH TEALE	30	. JOHN	9,70,80,136,138
HERNDON, ANN	16	. SUKEY PERRY	11	.	146
. BENJAMIN	12,29,38,40	. THOMAS	13	. LEWIS	9-10
.	45,47	. WILLIAM	11	. MARY CONNOR	10
. CATHERINE EHART	12	. ZACH	60	. SARAH	70,80
. EDWARD	47	. ZACHARIAH	1,19	. SARAH ARNOLD	9
. ELIZ. QUISENBERRY	39	HERREN, WILLIAM	137	. WILLIAM	146
. ELIZABETH	19	HERRENDEN, JOHN	53	HICKS, ANN	21
. ELIZABETH WRIGHT	8	HERRIN, MILLY	39	. CHARLES	32
. ESTER FERNEYHOUGH	49	HERRING, ELIZABETH	24,28	. EMMA	122
. EZEKIEL	45	. FRANKY	44	. JOHN	45
. FIELDING	44,47	. GEORGE	39	. JUDITH WATSON	32
. GEORGE	30,34,37	. JAMES	9	. LUCINDA SLEET	45
. HANNAH BLEDSOE	47	. JANE	22	. RACHEL	18
. HENRY	26,43	. JOICE	35	HIGDON, JOHN	19
. JAMES	16,26,39,49	. JONATHAN	38	MARY ROSS	19
. JOHN	8,30-31,33,39,46	. JUDAH COFER	9	HIGHLANDER,	
. JOHNNY	83	. MOLLY SHIFLETT	12	. FANNY PITTIS	30
. L.	83	. POLLY HILL	38	. GEORGE	21
. LUCINDA WOOD	26	. SALLY	32	. JACOB	30

INDEX to
Orange County, VA FAMILIES - Vol. #2

. NANCY	21	. URIEL	20,24,41,43,49	HOFFMAN,JOHN	135
HILL,	138	HINDERSON,JOHN	141	HOGANS,DELLA	113
. ANNIE LAURIE	93-94	HINS,LAURA E. ALLEE	103	HOGGS,	67-68
. ELIZABETH GRAY	117	ROBERT	103	HOLADAY,EDWIN	44
. FRANCES LATHAN	44	HINSHAW,EDMUND	10	HOLBERT,	
. HENRY	4,40,44-45	MACY NEWMAN	10	. CATHERINE KINSER	48
. JANE	129	HINSLEY,HANNAH	16	. ELIJAH	38-39
. JOHN	44,91,129	JOHN	16	. RICHARD	48
. LENARD	71	HIPKINS,ANDREW	70,78	. SALLY	39
. M.	138	LEWIS	70,78	HOLCOMB,RICHARD	135
. MARTHA	45	HITE,ANN T. MAURY	27	HOLDEN,JOSEPH	141
. MATILDA PAYNE	40	. ISAAC	9,27	HOLLADAY,EDWARD	31
. NANCY TATE	13	. JACOB	60	. JOSEPH	78
. POLLY	38,45	. JOHN	60	. MARY	75
. RICHARD	45,142,145,147	. JOST	75	. SAMUEL	75
. SAMUEL	13	. NELLY MADISON	9	. WILLIAM	75
. SUSANNAH JONES	4	HOARD,SUSAN VERDIER/	34	. WINIFRED	6
. THOMAS	117,136	WASHINGTON	34	HOLLAND,GEORGE	1
HILMAN,BETSY	20	HOBBS,SARAH	4,7	MARY COLEMAN	1
. DEADEMA	43	WILLIAM	75	HOLLEY,BENJAMIN	26
. FANNY	34	HOBDAY,EDWARD	80-82	HOLLIDAY,JOHN	126-127
. FRANCES PITCHER	39	. JOHN	14,81	. WILLIAM	75
. JOANNA	24	. MARTHA	81-82	. WINIFRED	3
. JOANNAH	49	. MARY DAVIS	14	HOLLINGSWORTH,JOSEPH	74
. JOSEPH	18,24,29,34,39	. SARAH	81-82	HOLLINS,EDWARD	19
	41	HOBDEY,EDWARD	70	JANE	19
. LUCY	24	. JOHN	70	HOLMES,ARMISTEAD	37
. POLLY	41	. MARTHA	70	. DAVID	19
. SALLY	18	. SARAH	70	. LUCY WILLIS	37
. SALLY GRAVES	20	HOBSON,GEORGE	60	HOLSAPPLE,GEORGE	26
. SARAH	41	JOHN	75	PHOEBE HUBBERT	26
. SUSAN	41	HOCKING,JOHN	139	HOLT,JOHN	137
. SUSANNA ABELL	29	HODGKIN,WILLIAM	133	. MICHAEL	75,135

INDEX to Orange County, VA FAMILIES - Vol. #2

Name	Page	Name	Page	Name	Page
. MICHALE	140	HORNSEY, MACK	25	. LUCINDA	43
. PETER	60	HORSLEY, JAMES	33	. MARY BEAZLEY	38
HOMDON, MARY ANN	26	JANE CHILES	33	. MILLY	31
HOME, CATHERINE	90	HOSKINS, ANNE	74	. WILLIS	38
. GEORGE	53	WILLIAM	74	HUDGENS, B.A.	157
. THEODORE	90	HOUCK, HENRY	41	SARAH	157
HOMES, JAMES	18	MILDRED LUCAS	41	HUDGINS, BALLARD	98
SALLY HILMAN	18	HOUK, HENRY	49	. MARY	99
HOMS, NANCY	17	HOUSE, EDWARD	55	. NANCY JACKSON	98
HONEY, JOHN	53	HOUSEWORTH,		. SARAH	98
HONSON, THOMAS	53	. MARTHA BROOKING	49	HUDSON, JOHN	16
HOOK, JANE	53	. VALENTINE	49	. JOSHUA	146
. ROBERT	53	HOWARD, CHARLES P.	16	. MALINDA VAWTER	44
. WILLIAM	53	. HANNAH	111	. MARY DEDMAN	16
HOOMES, JOSEPH	3	. JANE TAYLOR	16	. NANCY CHILDS	41
RACHEL DAVIS	3	. JOHN	60,135	. RUSH	60,77,147
HOPES, ARTHUR	147	. MARG. SULLIVAN	14	. WILLIAM	41,44,143
HOPKINS, JAMES	53	. RICHARD	14,16	HUFFMAN, ANNA	40
. JOSEPH	146	. WILLIAM	144,146	. ELIJAH	40
. THOMAS	142,145	HOWARTH, JAMES	86	. HENRY	75
. WILLIAM	139	HOWELL, TANLIPY	22	. JOHN	75
HORD, ANN	47	HUBBARD, BENJAMIN	144	HUFMON, JOHN	140
. DANIEL	39	. BETSY DURRETT	16	HUGESON,	
. ELIZA	45	. CARTER	16	. MARGERY BROCKMAN	88
. ELIZA HORD	45	. DEANA DURRETT	28	. WILLIAM	88
. ELIZABETH PERRY	39	. JOSEPH	28	HUGH, THOMAS	142
. JESSE	43,45,47	HUBBERT, PHOEBE	26	HUGHES, ALEXANDER	27
. JESSIE	49	HUBERT, PETER	26	. ANN G. BLACKWELL	46
. KILLIS	39	HUCKSTEP, ELIZ.	35	. ARMSTEAD	23
. MELINDA	43	. ELIZA	39	. ELIZ. MITCHELL	27
. PETER	45	. FANNY	48	. FANNY	15
. SARAH	49	. JOHN	31,35,39,48	. FRANCIS	13,15,27
HORN, BENJAMIN	136	. JOSIAH	43	. GEORGE W.	37

INDEX to
Orange County, VA FAMILIES - Vol. #2

Name	Page	Name	Page	Name	Page
. NANCY	27	. JOSHUA	21	. MARGARET	53
. POLLY HARVY	37	. NANCY LOYD	17	. MARY	53
. SALLY CHISHAM	23	. NEHAMIAH	17	. ROBERT	137
. THOMAS	141-142,145,147	. NEHEMIAH	14,132	. WILLIAM	53
. WILLIAM	46	HUNLEY,JAMES	20	HYDE,BENJAMIN	72
HUGHS,FRANCIS	29	SUSANNAH CHILES	20	HYTE,FRANCIS BEALE	1
. MARY DAVIS	3	HUNT,ANNE	75	JACOB	1
. SALLY	29	. FRANCIS DARNELL	32	IMGRAM,JOHN	139
. THOMAS	3,146	. HARRY	75	INGRAM,JOHN	136
HUGUELY,SUSAN	101	. JAMES	25	IRELAND,	
HUMBLE,MARY OVERTON	32	. JOHN	137	. ELEANOR BROCKMAN	152
WILLILAM	32	. ROBERT	32	. JAMES	137
HUME,	96	. SARY	14	. JOHN	149,152-153
. BENJAMIN	24	. SUSANNA DARNOLD	25	. MARY CROSTHWAIT	153
. ELIZABETH	32	HUNTER,AMELIA	165	IRWIN,ANTHONY	53
. ELIZABTH TALIAFERRO	24	. CARRIE	93	ISAAC,CAROLINE SPENCER	1
. FRANCIS	45	. ELIZABETH CHAPMAN	165	GEORGE	1
. JAMES	37	. JANE HARRIS	22	ISBELL,HENRY	135
. JOHN	48	. JOHN	165	JAMES	140
. LUCY JONES	45	. PLEASANT	22	JACKSON,ANN MILLER	50
. MARGARET DODD	37	. WILLIAM	80	. DRURY	35
. NANCY JONES	48	HUSSEE,EASTER	53	. ELIZABETH	35
HUMES,ELIZABETH PAYNE	23	HUTCHEN,		. JOHN	32
FRANCIS	23	. SILER ROBINSON	18	. JOHN M.	48
HUMPHREYS,FRANCES	2	. WILLIAM	18	. MARGARET	34
HUMPHRIES,FRANCIS	5	HUTCHERSON,		. NANCY	98
. GEORGE	53	. CATHERINE DEAR	23	. NANCY R. DANIEL	48
. SUSANNAH WEBB	2,5	. ELIZ. LANCASTER	41	. POLLY HERNDON	32
. WILLIAM	2,5	. JAMES	23	. THOMAS	76,135,140
HUNDLEY,BETSY GRESSOM	21	. MARTHA	46	. WILLIAM	50,74,135,140
. ELIZABETH CAVE	14,132	. WASHINGTON	41,46	JACOB,BENJAMIN	43
. JAMES	21	HUTCHINSON,WILLIAM	20	. ELIZABETH	43
. JOHN	17	HUTCHISON,JOHN	53	. FRANCES	49

INDEX to
Orange County, VA FAMILIES - Vol. #2

. POLLY MARTIN	25	. MILLY	3,5	. EDWARD	53
. WILLIAM	25	. NANNIE	26	. FRANCES	11
JACOBS, ANN FAULCONER	42	. POLLY	20	. JOHN	11,42,141
. BENJAMIN	22,42,49	. SPENCER	8	. KELLY	77
. CATHERINE SMITH	49	JAMESON, JAMES	61	. LUKE	10
. DAVID	121	. POLLY SAMUEL	16	. MARY E. WILLIS	42
. FLORENCE RHODES	121	. THOMAS	60,70,78	JERMAN, THOMAS	53
. GEORGE	49	.	141-142,145-146	JOHNSON,	
. JOEL	42	. THOMAS R.	16	. ALICE FITZHUGH	25
. MARY TAYLOR	42	. WILLIAM	60-61,70,78	. ANN	1
. NANCY	36	JANELL, WILLIAM	65	. ANN BARNETT	1,11
. NANCY STRAGHN	30	JARRALD, JEREMIAH	41	. ANNE BARNETT	1
. NATHAN	30	LUCRETIA SIMS	41	. ARCHIBALD	53
. ROBERT	36	JARRELL, FRANCES SIRUS	16	. BENJAMIN	61,68,72,79
. SARAH MARTIN	22	. JAMES	9,16	.	82
. THOMAS	42	. JEREMIAH	42	. COLIN	50
JAMERSON, CATHERINE	37	. MARY	9	. DIANNAH RICHARDS	20
. DOLLY	39	JEFFRYS, RICHARD	76	. ELIPHALET	42
. MARY	34	JENKINS, DAVID	45	. ELIZABETH	11,29
. REBECCA MAUPIN	38	. ELIZABETH DARNELL	45	. ELIZABETH CAVE	27,132
. WILLIAM	38	. ELIZABETH TAYLOR	23	. ELIZABETH SMITH	24
JAMES,	144	. FANNY	29	. ELIZABETH TERRILL	18
. ANNEY	23	. JOHN	34	. FRANCES	28,70
. CATLETT	65,86	. LUCH HAWKINS	36	. FRANCIS	78
. DANIEL	2	. LUCY	47	. GRACE	78-79
. DAVID	83	. QUIRE	36	. ISAAC	18,39,41
. FANNY	29	. SALLY PETTIS	32	. JAMES	23-24,31
. FRANCES DAVIS	8	. SARAH	45	. JANNIE MORGAN	114
. GEORGE	22,83	. SARAH TERRY	34	. JOHN	65,70,78-79
. JOSEPH	29	. THOMAS	23	. JOHN B.	48
. LUCY	22,29,83	. WILLIAM	32	. JOHN MARSHALL	79
. LUCY DAVIS	2	JENNINGS, ANN	40	. JUSTINA	43
. MILDRED	146	. AUGUSTINE	42	. LUCY	18

INDEX to
Orange County, VA FAMILIES - Vol. #2

- LUCY ALCOCKE 33
- MARTIN 20,61,65,79
- MARY 7,41,48,70,78
- MARY A. ELLIS 50
- MILDRED 49
- MONROE 114
- NANCY 15
- NANCY QUISENBERRY 31
- PATSY ALCOCK 42
- PEGGY 106
- PETER 53
- PETER R. 42
- RICHARD 33
- ROBERT 61,78-79
- SALLY 15,27
- SARAH 15
- SUSAN 47
- SUSANNA 2
- SUSANNAH 19
- THOMAS 20
- VALENTINE 20,27,49,72
- WILLIAM 1,11,25,53,76
  79-80,84,132,139,145
- WILLIAM R. 79
- WILLIAM W. 37

JOHNSTON, ANN 53
- ELIZABETH 53
- JOHN 53
- WILLIAM 53,143

JOLLET, JAMES 15
- JUDY 132
- SALLY 32
- SOPHIA 15

JOLLETT, CLARISA 37
- DRADA 43
- ELIZABETH 47
- FIELDING 43
- JAMES 30,47
- JUDY 15
- LUCY W. 30
- MARY 15
- SIMEON 46
- SIMSON 46

JONATHAN, JOHN 26
  POLLY ELUCK 26

JONES, 145
- ABBE 80
- AMBROSE 138
- ANN 18,23
- BENJAMIN 2,5
- BENJAMIN H. 39
- BETSY 31
- BURKETT 43
- CATY 46
- CATY ROBINSON 10
- CATY SHECLER 48
- CATY SHELAR 48
- EDMUND 48
- ELIJAH 12
- ELIZA S. 4
- ELIZABETH 9,23,30,35
  41,44
- ELIZABETH FOSTER 2,5
- ELIZABETH MASON 43
- ELIZABETH PARISH 47
- ELIZABETH SWAN 87

- ELIZABETH TRAWIN 77
- ELIZABETH WHITELAW 39
- ELLIOT 45
- FANNY 12,30
- FIELDING 41-42,48
- FRANCES 4
- FRANCIS 6,28,38,41
- FRANCIS SLAYOR 43
- GABRIEL 75,84
- GRACE LEONARD 1
- HANNAH 35
- HUGH 72,80,84,141
-   145-146
- JAMES 23,46,65,126
- JANE 29
- JANE E. ARNETT 41
- JESSIE 95-96
- JOHN 9-10,12,35,37,43
  60,75,77,87,142,147
- JOSEPH 65,84
- JOSIAH 74
- JUDAH 13
- LUCY 38,45
- M. THOMAS 138
- MARGARET 9
- MARY 4,84
- MARY JOHNSON 41
- MATON 12
- MAUD 98-99
- MECAJAH 42
- MILLY 13
- MILLY FAULCONER 37
- MOSIAS 43

221

INDEX to
Orange County, VA FAMILIES - Vol. #2

Name	Page	Name	Page	Name	Page
. NANCY	28,48	KAVANAUGH,ANN	5	KENDAL,	
. NICH	80	. ELIZABETH	9	. ELIZABETH MERIDETH	48
. PATTY STOWERS	13	. HANNAH	5	. THOMAS G.	48
. PEGGY OVERTON	35	. PHILEMON	132	KENDALL,BETSY	40
. POLLY	48	. PHILIMAN	70	. EDY	19
. POLLY WRIGHT	43	KAVENAUGH,ANN	3	. HENRY	19,53
. REBECCA DEAN	12	KAVINNER,HANNAH	2	. JOSHUA	44
. REUBEN	13	KEA,JERMIMA	38	. MARY L.	44
. RICH	80	KEATON,EDNA DAVIS	25	. ROBERT	19
. RICHARD	1,30	NELSON	25	. RUTH	19
. ROBERT	25,33,35,60	KEATTON,JAMES	137	. SALLY	21
. SALLY FREEMAN	25	JOSEPH	137	. URSULA GARNETT	19
. SARAH	45,74	KEEN,KATHERINE	2	KENDEL,JOHN	27
. SIVAN	87	KEENE,MARY	165	POLLY	27
. SUSAN	77	KEETON,		KENNADY,	
. SUSAN BICKERS	35	. ELIZ. CHANCELLOR	35	MADGE PROCTOR	100
. SUSAN WRIGHT	42	. JOHN	35	KENNEDY,	96
. SUSANNA	7	KEITH,PEYTON	26	. JAMES	65
. SUSANNAH	4	SALLY PETTY	26	. LITTLETON	45
. THOMAS	9,13,35,37,53	KELEY,WILLIAM	75	. MARTHA HILL	45
.	60,69,135-137,146	KELLAR,HATTIE	99	. MELL D.	100
. WALTER	25	KELLER,HATTIE	98	. REUBEN	45
. WILLIAM	136,138,142	KELLEY,JAMES	145	KENNER,ELIZABETH	126
.	145-146	KELLY,CATHERINE	53	KENNEY,FANNY BEALE	30
. WILLIAM L.	41	. JAMES	141,147	WILLIAM	30
. WILLIAM W.	47	. JOHN	135	KENNON,PHILIP	49
. ZACHARIAH	12	. LIANNA RUMSEY	29	SARAH HORD	49
JOSEPH,JONATHAN	11	. MICHAEL	53	KENTLEY,FRANCIS	79
SARAH DEERING	11	. SPENCER	29,31	JOHN	79
KABLER,MARY	163	. WILLIAM	53,139	KER,JAMES	70
KAMP,SARA	11	KEMBROW,BRADLEY	143	KERCHER,ANDREW	74
KARR,JOHN	61	KEMP,RICHARD	53,137	KERCHLER,MATHIAS	53
KATHER,CONRAD	136	KENBERRY,THOMAS	141	KERCHNALL,JOHN	145

INDEX to
Orange County, VA FAMILIES - Vol. #2

Name	Page	Name	Page	Name	Page
KERR, JAMES	79	. GABRIEL	22	. JOSEPH	34
KERSEY, AGNES TAYLOR	12	. HOLCOMBE R.	49	. LUCY	24
WILLIAM	12	. HULDAH BIGGERS	22	. MARY PRESLEY	26
KEY, MARTHA DANIEL	37	. JANE	53	. ST. CLAIR	23
. NANCY	30	. JOHN	27,31,53	. THEODOSIA ANDERSON	24
. WALTER	37,45	. JULIAN	28,33	. WILLIS	26
KEYES,		. JULIEN	31	KITCHEN, CHARLES	83
. MABEL E. -		. JULIUS	65	KITE, ROSA LEE GRAVES	131
. THORNSBERRY	104	. MARGARET	53	KLAVERKAMP,	
. STANLEY	104	. MARY ABEL	8	. ELIZABETH BROCKMAN	164
KIBLINGER, BARBARY	19	. MARY ANN PEACHER	49	. ROBERT BRUCE	164
. CATY	24	. MARY WAYT	11	KLU, CATHERINE PRICE	35
. DANIEL	24	. NANCY	33	JOHN	35
. JACOB	19,73	. REUBIN	47	KLUG, GEORGE SAMUEL	73
KIEFFER, MICHAEL	135	. RHODA	49	KNIGHT, AGNES	18
KIMBRO, THOMAS	143	. ROBERT	53	. DANIEL	160
KIMBROM, BRADLEY	146	. SADRUT	11	. DAVID	160-161
KIMBROUGH, THOMAS	146	. SALLY	29	. ELIZABETH	21,43
KINDAL, HENRY	53	. SARAH	36,53	. ELIZABETH ROGERS	22
KINDELL, JOHN	138	. WILLIAM	53	. EPHRIAM	18
KINDLE, MARY	35	KINSER, CATHERINE	48	. FRANCES CAVE	15,132
THOMAS	53	. ELIZABETH	45	. HARRIET BROCKMAN	160
KINES, JOHN	53	. LUCY	48	.	161
KING EDWARD IV,	89	KIRK, BETTY	74	. LUCY	43,45
KING WILLIAM,	89	. ELIZABETH	139	. MARY	18
KING,	90	. JAMES	74	. MATHEW	18,48-49
. AZARIAH	8	. JUDITH	16	. MOLLY	14
. CATHERINE	53	KIRKHEAD, DAVID	75	. NANCY HANEY	48
. CYNTHIA ROW	27	KIRTLEY, ANN PANILL	23	. THOMAS	89,139
. ELIZABETH	53	. ELIZABETH	6,25-26,32	. WILLIAM	15,22,43,45
. ELIZABETH JOLLETT	47	. ELIZABETH SIMS	34	.	132
. FANNY	33	. FRANCIS	78-79	. WILLIAM B.	31,38,43
. FRANCIS YATES	31	. JONATHAN	24	KNIGHTTON, WILLIAM	65

INDEX to
Orange County, VA FAMILIES - Vol. #2

KRAUS, HARRY	102	. PEGGY LAMB	20	. ROBERT	8,146
. JESSE FRANKLIN	102	. POLLY	25	. SALLY HERNDON	45
. LYNN GEARHARDT	102	. POLLY WATSON	32	. SARAH	42
KUCHNALL, SAMUEL	146	. REBECCA SLAUGHTER	31	. SUSANNA	44
KYNER, JOHN	137	. RICHARD	49,54,67,136	. SUSANNAH	28,30
LACEY, WILLIAM	139	. SALLY	22	. THOMAS	3,5,41
LACY, ALLEN R.	41	. SUSANNA	24	LAND, JENNY	7
ELIZABETH ANCELL	41	. WILLIAM	21,28,31,67	. JOHN	8
LAHONEY, DANIEL	17	. WILLIS	31	. MARY	8
. FANNY FINNEY	17	LAMLOTTE, EDWARD	54	. RICHARD	70,82
. FANNY FURNEY	17	LAMPART, EDWARD	54	LANDFORD, JAMES	39
LAMB, ANN	49	LANCASTER, BENJAMIN	36,44	JAMES MARTIN	39
. ANN JONES	23	. BETSY CONNER	15	LANDRAM, LEWIS	46
. ANN WATSON	15	. DOLLY COOPER	28	MAHALO	46
. BENJAMIN	20	. EDMUND	28,42	LANDRUM, ELIZABETH	25
. BETSY	15	. ELIZ.	38,41	. JAMES	17
. CATEY	23	. FRANCES NAILLEY	3	. JOHN	17
. ELIZABETH HERRING	28	. FRANCIS HAILEY	5	. JOSIAH	65
. FANNY	38	. HENRY	17	. LEWIS	26
. FRANCIS	143	. JAMES	40	. MARGARET	13,85
. FRANKEY	16	. JOANNA SINGLETON	4	. MARY COLLINS	17
. JAMES	15,67	. JOHANNA SINGLETON	6	. NANCY	13
. JEREMIAH	23,67	. JOHN	28,30,38	. REBECCA ATKINS	26
. JOHN	10,16,20,32,43,45	. JONATHAN	45	. REUBIN	25
	67,70,82	. LUCY DEAR	8	. SUSANNA ATKINS	25
. LITTLEBERRY	67	. MARTHA	30	. THOMAS	17,25,85
. LUCY KNIGHT	43,45	. MARY	10	LANDUM, JOSIAH	85
. MARTHA	47	. MARY WRIGHT	17	THOMAS	85
. MARY GEAR	21	. NANCY	36,40	LANE, JOHN	21
. MATHEW	44	. NANCY LANCASTER	40	. LYDIA	130
. NELLY	10,70,82	. POLLY	30	. MARY	32
. NELLY LAMB	10	. REUBEN	15	. POLLY WHITELAW	26
. PEGGY	20	. RICHARD	4,6	. ROBERT G.	26

INDEX to
Orange County, VA FAMILIES - Vol. #2

Name	Page	Name	Page	Name	Page
. TABITHA CREW	21	. MARGARET	110	LECKIE, ANN V. REDDIS	41
LANGFORD, PEACHY	48	. MARGARET MUSE	110	WILLIAM S.	41
LANSLEY,		. NANCY CLAY	110-111	LEDGERWOOD, AGNES	54
. CATHERINE PITCHER	35	. WILLIAM	142	. ELEANOR	54
.	37	LEACH, ANDREW	86	. JAMES	54
. JOHN	35,37	LEAK, ROBERT	10	. JANE	54
LANTHON, PATRICK	142	. SUSANNA	10	. MARTHA	54
LANTHORN, PETER	145	. SUSANNA LEAK	10	. WILLIAM	54
LANTON, JAMES	29	LEATHERER, JOHN	4	LEE, ABNER	31
. MARY WALKER	9	SARAH WHITE	4	. AMBROSE	45
. PETER	79	LEATHERES,		. ANNA DODD	12-13
. SARAH	79	. DOLLY MALLORY	41	. BETSY	24
. THOMAS	9	. JAMES	41	. CATEY FOSTER	23
LANTOR, HANNAH WEBB	12	LEATHERS, ALEXANDER	46	. CHARLES	70,141-142
. JACOB	14	. ELIZA ANN	49	.	145-146
. MILDRED	14	. ELIZABETH	48	. ELIZABETH	110
. PETER	12,146	. JAMES F.	47	. ELIZABETH BELL	8
. THOMAS	71	. JAMES T.	48	. ELIZABETH TERRILL	45
LARNEY, THOMAS	145,147	. JOHN	10	. FANNY LAMB	38
LATHAM, JOHN	54	. JONATHAN	49	. FRANCIS	39
LATHAN, FRANCES	44	. LUCY JENKINS	47	. GEORGE	23
LAVIT, SIDNEY	17	. LUCY MITCHELL	46	. HENRY	38
LAWSON, GEORGE	47	. NANCY FINNELL	15	. JAMES	70
M.	137	. POLLY	38	. JANE	38
LAY, ELIZABETH SEBREE	37	. SALLY	17	. JOHN	8
JOHN	37	. SARAH	10,46	. KENDALL	10
LAYN, JOHN	143	. SARAH WHITE	120	. LUCY	45
LAYTON, JOHN	136	. WILLIAM	14-15	. MOSES	45
MARY	75	LEAVEL, WILLIAM	69	. NATHANIEL	38
LEA, AMEY COFFERY	6	LEAVELL, FRANCIS BELL	28	. POLLY LIMECO	22
. ANN COFFERY	4	LEWIS	28	. RICHARD	12-13
. DAVID	110	LEBO, GUSSIE BROCKMAN	95	. SALLY	31
. GIDEON	4,6	M.B.	96	. SALLY LEE	31

INDEX to
Orange County, VA FAMILIES - Vol. #2

. SALLY TERRILL	36	LESHER, KATHERINE	104	. LOYOLA MORGAN	113
. SAMUEL	31	LESLIE, MARY	104	. SARAH M. MORGAN	114
. SARA MANSFIELD	14	LESTER, ROBERT M.	159	. SEAMORE	113
. SARAH GORDON	10	LEVAUNE, MAJOR	135	. VELMA A.	114
. SUSANNAH	16	LEWIS, BETSY	3,6	LIMECO, POLLY	22
. WILLIAM 22,24,36,39,70		. CATHERINE BROCKMAN	159	LIMMANDS, ELIJAH	19
. ZACHARIACH	14	. CHARLES	70,81	LUCY SANDAGE	19
LEECH, ANDREW	65	. EDWARD	70,81	LINDS, LANDON	48
LEEK, MILLA	128	. EMALINE TWYMAN	45	LINDSAY,	86,93
LEFORE, JUDITH	35	. HOPKINS	70,81	. ADAM	17,19
LEGER, FLORENCE ST	87,89	. JAMES	17	. BETSY	13
LEITH, PARTHENIA	110	. JOHN	61,106,159	. CABEL	10,20,28
REBECCA GAYDEN	110	. MARY WALLER	105	. CALEB	61,68
LELAND, JOHN	12	. MARY WRIGHT	17	. CELEY MILLS	35
LENARD, CATHERINE	78	. RICHARD	143-144	. FANNY MILLS	32
. PHOEBE	70	. SUSANNAH	105-106	. JAMES	137
. WALTER 70,78,135,140		. THOMAS	74	. LANDON	35
LENOX, MARY	3	. THOMAS M.	45	. LARKIN	44
LEONARD, GRACE	1	. WALLER	105	. MARY	22
. LAUGHLY	70	. ZACHARY	105-106	. MINERVA DANIEL	49
. PATRICK 54,77,142,145		LIGHTFOOT, GOODRICH	61	. MOSES	145
. PHOEBE	70	.	73-74,76,139	. NANCY	44
. WALTER	70	. MARY	73-74	. NANCY SHEPHERD	8
LEPPOR, ANDREW	54	. WILLIAM	74,76	. REBECCA	44
. GERINS	54	LILBORNE, ANN	75	. REUBEN	70,79
. ISBELL	54	LILBOURNE, JOHN	75	. REUBIN	24,32
. JAMES	54	LILEY, JAMES	137	. ROBERT	49
. JANE	54	LILLARD, JOHN	139	. SALLY	24
. MARGARET	54	LILLY,		. SALLY STEVENS	10
. MARY	54	. CARRIE E. BLALUCK	134	. SARAH	44
. NICHOLAS	54	. EDGAR	114	. SUCKY	17
. SARAH	54	. FANNIE L.O. MORGAN	114	. WILLIAM	8,31
LERNEY, THOMAS	54	. FRANK	114	LINNEY, ANN BELL	2

INDEX to
Orange County, VA FAMILIES - Vol. #2

. ANN BURRUS	8	. FRANKEY	37	LOWELL,		
. WILLIAM	2,8	. GEORGE	135,140	. ELIZABETH HARVY	25	
LINTER, JAMES	65	. HENRY	11	. JAMES	25	
LINTON, JAMES	85	. JAMES	10	LOWER, CATHERINE	21	
. MOSES	23	. JOHN	23,54	. ELIZABETH	20,23	
. NANCY PEED	23	. JOHN D.	23	. JUDITH HAM	29	
. NANCY REED	23	. JOSHUA	45,85	. MICAL	20	
. PEGGY	9	. LUCY	8	. MICHAEL	21,39	
LLOYD, HENRY	48	. LUCY A.	47	. NANCY	39	
. LUCY	44	. LUCY MANSPOILE	11	. PETER	23,29	
. MARY	48	. MARY S. FARISH	36	. RACHEL	17	
. ROBERT	44-45	. MARY S. PARISH	36	LOWERY, JOHN	109	
. SARAH	45	. NANCY	13,23	. JOHN L.	101	
. SARAH MOUBRAY	33	. NANCY STEVINSON	20	. MYRTLE BROCKMAN	101	
. THOMPSON	33	. RICHARD	20	LOWINS, FRANCIS	2	
LOGAN, DAVID	54	. ROBERT B.	47	SARAH DAVIS	2	
. JANE	54	. SABINA HARRIS	49	LOWRY, ABNER	25	
. MARY	54	. SPOTSWOOD	49	. BABBY	18	
. WILLIAM	54	. WEIR	3,6	. NANCY	25	
LOGGINS, WILLIAM	135	. WILLIAM 27,36,42,44,54		. NANCY DEDMAN	29	
LONG, ALEXANDER	54	.	70,81,141,144	. NANCY LOWRY	25	
. ANN	1	LONGAN, EDMUND	33	. NANCY REDMAN	29	
. ANN SINALT	3	SALLY EDWARDS	33	. SALLY	22	
. ANN SMITH	6	LONGAR, EDMUND D.	47	. TABITHA	19	
. ARMISTAD	37,40	LONGWORTH, WILLIAM	73	. THOMAS	29	
. BELINDA	44	LOOK, WILLIAM	146	LOYD, BETSY	34	
. BETSY KENDALL	40	LORING, MARY VAWTER	37	. BETSY BELL	29	
. BROWN	70	THOMAS	37	. ESTHER	43	
. ELIZABETH	12,42,54,70	LORRILL,		. FELICIA AYHEART	33	
.	81	. ELIZABETH CLEE	23	. GEORGE	29	
. ELIZABETH BICKERS	27	. THOMAS	23	. JOHN	17	
. ELIZABETH REYNOLDS	10	LOVE, ROBERT	108	. NANCY	17	
. FRANCES DAWSON	45	LOW, THOMAS	61	. NANCY MONTAGUE	17	

INDEX to
Orange County, VA FAMILIES - Vol. #2

. ROBERT	43	LUMPKIN,WILSON	94	. WILLIAM	71
. SALLY GRESHAM	7	LYND,JOHN	54	. WINNEY ROUTT	31
. SARAH	27	LYON,MICHAEL	54	MAGGARD,BETSY LAMB	15
. THOMAS	7	LYRIAL,JOHN	77	HENRY	15
. WILLIAM	12,27,34	MACCALL,JOHN	140	MAHANES,	
. WILLIS	33	MACON,JAMES M.	39	. ELIZ. BROCKMAN	25
LUCAS,AGY	3,6	. LUCETTA NEWMAN	39	. SAMUEL	25
. ANN BURBRIDGE	2	. LUCY H.	35	MAHONEY,JENNY	122
. BETTY	77	. SARAH MADISON	14	. JIMMEY CHAPMAN	14
. CATHERINE AHEART	24	. THOMAS	14,35	. RHODES	14
. CATHERINE EHART	24	MADEN,JACOB	42	MAIDEN,DUCIA	26
. ELIJAH	24	JULIA DAVIS	42	ELIZABETH	26
. ELIZABETH	18,77	MADISON,	89,137	MAION,RICHARD	133
. EZEKIEL	24	. AMBROSE	9,44,62,70-71	MAJOR,MARTHA	21
. FRANCIS	40	.	80-82	MARY	92
. JOHN	33,41,67,77,137	. ANDREW	159	MAKES,JOHN	146
. LUCY	38	. CARLETT	31	MALLORY,	131
. MILDRED	41	. DOLLY PAYNE	92	. AGGY E.	40
. MOLLY	17	. FRANCES	23,144,146	. ALICE	47
. MOSES	78	. FRANCIS	5,68,71-72,75	. ANN	21,47
. NANCY	46	. JAMES	14,61-62,71-72	. ANN JONES	18
. NANCY BROCKMAN	24	.	76,141-142,144,146	. BETSY	34
. NANCY WOOD	22	. JANE WILLIS	44	. BETTY	77
. RACHEL	17	. JOHN	89,159	. CYNTHIA	33
. SALLY GARNETT	13	. MARY	82,89	. DOLLY	41
. THOMAS	13,77	. MARY WILLIS	71,83	. DOROTHY CARTER	13
. WILLIAM	2,12,17,77,143	. NELLY	9,33	. ELIJAH	27-28
. ZACHARIAH	22	. NELLY C.	28	. ELIZ.	39
LUCK,GEORGE A.	44	. NELLY CONWAY	71,83	. ELIZ. THOMPSON	46
MARY L. KENDALL	44	. NELLY WILLIS	71	. ELIZABETH	28,46
LUCUS,JAMES	13	. SARAH	14	. FRANCES	26
NANCY HENDERSON	13	. SUSANNA BELL	5	. HANNAH CAVE	21
LUGGETT,ELIZABETH	1	. THOMAS	89	. HENRY	8,18,26,33,40,70

INDEX to
Orange County, VA FAMILIES - Vol. #2

.	78,81	. JOHN	29,45	MARK,JOHN	136
. HENRY HICK	77	. NANCY GOLDING	45	MARKS,JOHN	138-139
. ICHABOD	40	. REBECCA	29	MARKSHEFFEE,EMMA	163
. JAMES	24	MAN,JOHN	54	MARKSPILE,ANN LONG	1
. JESTIN	28	MANDEN,JAMES	79	MICHAEL	1
. JOHN	4,7,48,61,143,145	LUCY MARY	79	MARQI,PETER	78
. JUDITH	39	MANNAN,ROBERT	36	MARQUESS,JOHN	22-23
. JUDITH PAYNE	27	MANNEN,ANDREW	55	. LAVINIA	22
. LUCH	35	MANNER,ANDREW	77,141,143	. MARIAN	23
. LUCINDA MARTIN	40		145	MARR,ALEXANDER	1,21,71
. LUCY	24	MANNING,ANDREW	81	.	83
. LUCY LONG	8	ELIZABETH	9	. ANN	21
. MARY	1,36,77	MANOWELL,JOHN	136	. BETSY MILLER	34
. MARY P.	48	MANPIN,DAVID	36	. ELIZABETH	31
. MARY PAYNE	20	JERUSHA DAVIS	36	. FRANCIS RUCKER	45
. NANCE	15	MANSFIELD,ADAM	14	. HENRY	45
. NANCY	21,29	. ELIZ. C.	30	. JOEL	34
. NANCY MALLORY	21	. GEORGE	66	. JOHN	71,83
. NATHAN	46	. JAMES W.	37	. SALLY HARVY	34
. PHILIP	36	. MARY	14,39	. SARAH RUCKER	1
. POLLY BROCKMAN	24	. MILDRED CLARK	37	. THOMAS	34
. REUBEN	13	. MOURING	30	MARSH,LUCY W. JOLLETT	30
. ROBERT	21,34	. ROBERT	30,37,39	. PETER	30,37,43
. ROGER	20,77	. SARA	14	. THOMAS	46,66
. SALLY MORTON	36	. SARAH	41	MARSHALL,	143,146
. SARAH SAWYER	4,7	. SELINA EDINS	42	. ADELE	121
. SUSANNAH	13	. WILLIAM	41	. ANN BOSWELL	12
. THOMAS	39	. WILLIAM H.	42	. CHARLOTTE	29
. URIAL	77	MANSPITE,JACOB	73	. COLEMAN	39
. URIEL	21,34,41,62,130	MANSPOILE,ADAM	19	. DAVID	121
. WILLIAM	13,36,43,78	. JOHNNY	19	. ELLEN WOOD	28
MALONE,ELIZABETH	47	. LUCY	11	. GEORGE	12
. ELY	47	. SALLY WOOD	19	. HENRY	28

229

INDEX to
Orange County, VA FAMILIES - Vol. #2

Name	Page	Name	Page	Name	Page
. JAMES	78	. BETSY	10	. WILLIAM JOSEPH	114
. JANE	18	. BRICE	17	. ZACHARY	137
. JEANETTE	105	. CATHERINE	23	MARYE, PETER	78
. JOANNA BICKERS	39	. ELIZABETH	16	MASON,	159
. LUCY	3,6,78-79	. ELIZABETH JONES	9	. ANNA TANDY	33
. LUCY MARY	77-78	. FANNY SISSON	28	. BAILY	38
. MERRINEAU	18	. FRANCIS	37	. BAYLOR	37
. MILDRED	123	. GEORGE	9,28,70	. BETSY	13
. MILDRED MILLER	121	. HENRY	22,25,28	. CATY CLARK	37
. MILDRED RHODES	119	. JAMES	39	. CATY JONES	46
. MINGO	78	. JANE	33	. CHARLES	13-14,18,45,71
. MUNGO	79,144	. JOANNA	39	.	81
. MURGO	144	. JOHN	23,145-146	. ELIZABETH	43,71,81,89
. NANCY ANCEL	27	. JOSEPH	78	.	102,129
. POLLY	25	. LOLA L. BLALUCK	114	. ELIZABETH FAULCONER	19
. RICHARD	120	. LUCINDA	40-41	. FANNY	29
. ROY MUNGO	78	. MALLORY	39-40	. GEORGE	23,45-46,71,81
. SALLY RHODES	120	. MARGARET SNELL	34	. ISAM B.	20
. SARAH	20	. MARY KNIGHT	18	. JAMES	18,71,81
. SARAH WHITELAW	45	. NANCY	3	. JOHN	18-19
. SUSAN RHODES	120	. NANCY FEARNEYHOUGH	37	. JOSEPH	33,71,81
. SUSANNAH	78-79	. NANNEY	6	. LUCY JONES	45
. THOMAS	20,25,27,120	. PATSY ATKINS	32	. LUCY SALBREE	18
. W.G.	119	. POLLY	25	. LUCY SEBREE	20
. WILLIAM	78	. R.M.	70	. LYDIA GRAVES	28
. WILLIS	45	. RACHEL LUCAS	17	. MARGARET	55
. WINGO	77	. RICHARD	145	. MICAJAH	81
. WOODIE G.	121	. ROBERT	16,61,70,80,143	. NANCY	50,71,81
MART, MARY	120	.	146	. NANCY CLARK	38
MARTAIN, JOHN	145	. SARAH	22	. NANCY OAKS	18
ROBERT	138,144	. THOMAS	47,145	. PETER	29,71,81
MARTIN, AMELIA	95-96,159	. WILLIAM	32,34,37	. REBECCA	71,81
. BENJAMIN	18,78	. WILLIAM H.	33	. SAMUEL	28,81

INDEX to
Orange County, VA FAMILIES - Vol. #2

. SANDERS	46,50	. LEONARD H.	27	MCALAGANT, JAMES	54
. SARAH	14	. LEONARD HILL	81	MCALESTER, ALEXANDER	70
. THOMAS	38	. MARY	70,81,83	ELIZABETH	70
. WILLIAM	38	. MATHEW LUDWELL	81	MCALISTER, ALEXANDER	70
MASSEY, ALLAN	71	. MATTHEW	70	. CARY TURNER	21
. CHARLES	71	. PENELOPE	71,81,83	. CLARY TURNER	21
. EDMUND	26	. VIRGINIA CAMPBELL	26	. ELIZABETH	70
. MARY	26	. WALKER	70-71,81,83	. JOHN	21
MASTIN, MORDICAI	13	. WILLIAM GRYMES	81,83	. LOUISA	49
MATHERSHED, MARY MINOR	1	MAXWELL, ALEXANDER	54	. NANCY	149,154,156
NATHANIEL	1	. DULLEY HENRY	15	. NATHANIEL	80
MATLOCK, MOURNING	107	. JOHN	54	MCALLISTER, LUCY	118
MATTHEWS, JOHN	61	. MARGERET	54	MCCADDAN, PATRICK	54
WILLIAM	136,138	. MARY	54	MCCANLESS, ELIZABETH	54
MATTISON,	138	. THOMAS	15,54	. MARKHAM	54
MATTISONS,	138	MAY, JOEL	31	. WILLIAM	54
MATTOX, WILLIAM	71,77	. JOHN	137	MCCARTIES, DANIEL	138
MAUNER, ANDREW	142	. MARION	122	MCCAULEY, POLLY	19
MAUPIN, DAVID	36	. MILLY	31	MCCLAMOCK, JENNY ESTES	25
. JANE BEADLES	49	. THOMAS	89	JOHN	25
. JENNINGS	20	. VIRGIE RHODES	121	MCCLANAHAN,	
. JERUSHA DAVIS	36	MAYFIELD, ABRAHAM	132,136	HELEN BROCKMAN	104
. REBECCA	38		143-144	MCCLARNEY, FRANCIS	66
. SALLY MILLER	20	MAYHUGH, POLLY	20	. POLLY	48
. SUSANNA	37	MAYO, HOWARD CARLYLE	118	. ROGER	18
. TYREE	49	. LETTISA	46	. SARAH MORRIS	18
MAURY, ABRAHAM	70,83	. NORMA M. RAMSEY	118	. USLEY	66
. AMBROSE	71	. ROBERT A.	44	MCCLARY, CATY PICKER	24
. ANN	81,83	. SARAH TALIAFERRO	44	. DAVID	24
. ANN T.	27	. WILLIAM	44	. MILLY	44
. JOHN	81	MAYS, ELIZABETH	14	. PHOEBE DEMPSEY	47
. LENARD H.	26	WILLIAM	89	. WILLIAM F.	47
. LENOARD HILL	83	MAZES, SARAH	15	MCCLASKEY, DONALD	104

INDEX to
Orange County, VA FAMILIES - Vol. #2

LULA THORNSBERRY	104	. BETSY	48	. SAMUEL	54
MCCLAYLAND, DANIEL	67	. DERENSEY	17	. WILLIAM	54
HANNAH	76	. ELIZABETH MILLER	16	MCDRAUGH, WILLIAM	84
MCCLEALAND, DANIEL	84	. ELIZABETH TAYLOR	86	MCFARLAN, FANNY ALSOP	31
MCCLEAN, MARGARET	54	. GEORGE	16	. JOHN	31
WILLIAM	54	. JANE	75	. WILLIAM	31
MCCLENDHAN, MARY A.	111	. JEREMIAH	22	MCFARLAND, SALLY	36
MCCLURE, AGNES	54	. JOHN	135	MCFARLING,	
. ANDREW	54	. LIZA	28	. FRANCES DEDMAN	34
. ELEANER	54	. PATRICK	16	. JOHN	31,34
. JAMES	54	. RACHEL BROOKS	22	MCFIELD, JOHN	55
. JEAN	54	. RANDOLPH	75	MCGEE, JOHN S.	35
. JOHN	54	. SALLY LAMB	22	. LUCY	132
MCCOUGHEY, LORAINE	103	. SIMEON	48	. LUCY HARRIS	35
MCCOY,		. STACY	22	MCGINNIS, JAMES	55
. ELIZABETH NICKINGS	12	. SUSANNA BROOKS	17	MCGORDER, MARTHA	104
. GEORGE	12	. WILLIAM	54	MCGRAW, KATHERINE	134
. HENRY	135	MCDONALD, ALEXANDER	147	. MAGGIE BLALUCK	134
. JOHN	54,137	. ELIZABETH MILLER	16	. MARY J.	134
MCCOYLE, MICHALL	33	. JOHN	55	. MARY J. BLALUCK	134
NANCY MCKINNEY	33	. PATRICK	16	. SYLAUNS	134
MCCRACKIN, JAMES	61	MCDONO, WILLIAM	143	. WILLIE	134
MCCULLAN, JAMES	40	MCDONOLD, WILLIAM	144	MCHENRY, BARNET	75
. JOHN	15	MCDONOUGH, WILLIAM	75	MCHOLT, GEORGE	136
. PATRICK	15	MCDOWELL, EPHRAIM	54	MCHONEY, JAMES	25
. SARAH	15	. JAMES	54,75	PATSY SLEET	25
. SARAH WALKER	15	. JANE	54	MCKELAMY, SUSANNAH	20
. THEODORA BEASLEY	15	. JOHN	54,61,75	MCKENNEY, ELIZABETH	29
MCCULLEY, JAMES	54	. MAGDALE	75	. JOHN	55
MCCULLOCK, ANN	55	. MAGDALENE	54	. SARAH	15
MCCULLOUGH, JAMES	74	. MARGARET	54	. WILLIAM	15,29
MCCULLY, JANE	31	. MARTHA	54	MCKEY, ELLA	113
MCDANIEL, ALEXANDER	28,86	. ROBERT	54	MCKINLEY,	

INDEX to
Orange County, VA FAMILIES - Vol. #2

Name	Page	Name	Page	Name	Page
. ANNA R. FINNELL	20	. MARTHA	14	MEGRIGRL, DANIEL	145
. HUGH	20	. PATRICK	61	MELBURN, SARAH TAYLOR	24
MCKINNEY,		MCNIEL, MARTHA	28	WILLIAM	24
. BETSY POLLARD	23	PATRICK	55	MELONE, JAMES	48
. JAMES	137	MCPHEARSON, ALEXANDER	136	. JANE	48
. JOHN	54	MCPHERSON, ALEXANDER	54	. JOHN	42
. NANCY	33	. MARGARET	54	. REBECCA	42
. TRAVIS	23	. ROBERT	54	. SUSAN	42
. WILLIAM	33	. SUSANNAH	54	MELONS, MARY WAYLAND	32
MCKOY, AGNES	54	MCQUIDDY, MARY	11	WILLIAM	32
. JAMES	54	MCSHAMROCK, MARTHA	18	MELORE, JOHN	68
. JANE	54	MCSWAIN, NEIL	74	MERCER, JOHN	159
. MARGARET	54	MCWATERS,	108	NANCY	159
. MARTHA	54	MARGARET	108	MEREDITH, JAMES	137
. WILLIAM	54	MEACRY, THOMAS	141	MERIDETH, ELIZABETH	48
MCMEANS,		MEAD, W.T.	104	MERIWETHER,	
. BERNICE HARVEY	103	MEADOW, JACOBS	39	. ANN ANDERSON	39
. RAY	103	NANCY ROACH	39	. CHARLES H.	39
MCMILLAN, EDY KENDALL	19	MECARTIES, DANIEL	138	. MARY	132
. JAMES	19	MEDLEY, AMBROSE	3,6	MERRIWEATHER, GARRETT	44
. JOHN	19	. FANNY HEAD	27	MARY A. MINOR	44
. LUCY	19	. FRANKIE BURTON	6	MERRIWETHER, ANN MINOR	23
MCMILLEN, JOHN	19	. FRANKY BURTON	3	CHARLES	23
MCMULLIN, JAMES	42	. JACOB	27	MERRY,	126,143
. JOHN	42	. JOHN	84	. AGNES	128
. PEACHY WALKER	42	MEEK, GUY	135	. AGNES THOMAS	126-127
MCMURE, DANIEL	61	MEEKS, DONALD	105	. ANN	127-128
MCMURRIN, DAVID	54	. FRYE	140	. ANN A. PRETTYMAN	126
MARGARET	54	. SUSAN M.	-	. ANN PRETTYMAN	128
MCNEAL, ANN	5	. THORNSBERRY	105	. ELIZABETH	1,84,126-128
. ELIZABETH	2	MEEZINGS, JOSEPH	23	. ELIZABETH DANIEL	126
. FRANCIS	14	POLLY CLEMENTS	23	. ELIZABETH STEPHENS	126
. JANE	18	MEGINEE, JAMES	146	. FRANKY	127

INDEX to
Orange County, VA FAMILIES - Vol. #2

. JAMES	127	. ANN	10,48,50	. NANCY E. BROCKMAN	102
. JOHN	126-127	. ANN JENNINGS	40	. ROBERT	10,15,25,33,40
. KATHERINE SUGGETT	127	. ANN MILLER	48	.	61,66
	128	. ANN STEVENS	19	. SALLY	20
. MARY	13,126-128	. BENJAMIN	85	. SARAH LLOYD	45
. PRETTYMAN	62,69-70,72	. BETSY	34	. SARAH PLUNKETT	18
. 77,81-82,87,126-127		. CATY	17	. SIM	139
	128	. CHRISTIAN	32	. THOMAS	18,20,38,41,48
. SAMUEL	127	. DANIEL	48	. WILLIAM	141
. THOMAS	61,70,77,84,87	. DAVID	121	MILLERS,WILLIAM	141
.	126-128,142,144	. ELIZA	154,156	MILLIGAN,WILLIAM	10
. WILLIAM	126-127	. ELIZABETH	15-16	MILLIKIN,WILLIAM	70
MERRYMAN,		. ELIZABETH BEAZLEY	32	MILLS,ANN	12,42
. ELIZ. STEVENS	28	. ELIZABETH SORRELLE	48	. CELEY	35
. WILLIAM	28	. FRANCES	48	. CHARLIE	131
MESSER,JOHN WILLARD	134	. HANNAH	159	. CYNTHIA	14
MAGGIE BLALUCK	134	. HANNER	119	. FANNY	32
MICHAEL,FRANCIS	61	. HENRY	4,7	. JAMES	54
MICHEAL,ANN	2	. ISAAC	77	. MARGARET	24
MICHELL,FRANCIS	136	. JACOB	73,139	. MARY A.	27
MICHI,FRANCIS EARLEY	12	. JAMES	45	. NATHANIEL	14,24,27
JOHN	12	. JANE	33	.	32-33,35,61
MICK,ETTA ANN	98	. JESSE	19	. SARA	33
MIDDLEBROOK,ARCHIBALD	45	. JOHN	30,41,48,62,66,71	. SOPHIA	48
. ELIZABETH	4,6	.	81,86	MILTON,JAMES C.	25
. LUCY BOSWELL	45	. JOHN M.T.	102	MARY TAYLOR	25
. MARTHA	46	. JUDITH	16,86	MINER,JEREMIAH	62
. NATHANIEL	25,36,46	. MARGARET	85	MINOR,ANN	23
. SUSAN	36	. MARGARET PIGLEN	4,7	. DABNEY	23,32,44
MILBURN,SARAH	28	. MARY	25,30	. JERE	84
MILIKIN,MARY	84	. MARY LLOYD	48	. JOHN SIMPON	163
WILLIAM	80	. META RHODES	119,121	. MADISON	138
MILLER,	143	. MILDRED	121	. MARY	1

INDEX to
Orange County, VA FAMILIES - Vol. #2

Name	Page(s)
. MARY A.	44
. MARY DAVIS	76
. MARY E. BROCKMAN	163
. SARAH	32
. SUSANNAH	8
. WILLIAM	76,136,138, 141-142,145,147
MINTON, FANNY	28
JOHN	28
MITCHEL, DAVID	54
. ELIZA	54
. JAMES	54
. JOHN	55
. MARTHA	54
. REBECCA GRINNILS	14
. SARAH	54
. WILLIAM	14
MITCHELL,	84,125
. ANDREW JACKSON	123
. CLARISSA	123
. CLARISSA JANE	124
. ELEANOR	33
. ELIZ.	27
. ELIZABETH	17
. GEORGE	79
. GEORGE WESTON	118
. HENRY	17,46
. JAMES	54,140-141,143
. JOHN	37,123
. LUCY	46
. LUCY M. BROWN	118
. MARY	121
. MOLLY LUCAS	17
. NANCY PARROTT	47
. NANCY RUMSEY	29
. NELLY WOOD	37,123
. POLLY	47
. ROBERT	47
. THOMAS	29,50
. VIRGINIA BAKER	105
. WEST	27
. WILLIAM	17,33,37,47
MITCHUM, MARIAH	125
MODISET, ANN	10
MOFFETT, JOHN	61
MOLLEN, JOSEPH	137
MOLTON, JOSEPH	144
MONGAGUE, DAVID	44
. JOHN	22
. NANCY HERNDON	44
MONROE, WILLIAM	55
MONTAGUE, ANDREW	17
. ANTOINET	76
. CATY	24
. ELIZABETH	77,84
. HANNAH	24
. JOHN	22-24
. MILDRED	47
. NANCY	17
. PETER	66,76-77,84,145
. POLLY	22
. SARAH	84
. THOMAS	77,142-144
MONTAUGE, SUKEY PERRY	36
WILLIAM	36
MOODY, BETSY STOWERS	32
JOHN	32
MOONEY, MARYAN	4,6
MOOORE, FRANCES	18
MOORE, ALEXANDER	31,70,81
.	145
. ANN	1,11
. AUG.	136
. BERLINDA BROCKMAN	102
. BERNARD	1,70-71,80-81
. BETTY J. GRYMES	8
. CATEY PRICE	1
. COINE	137
. DAVID	141,146
. ELIZABETH BROWN	26
. ELIZABETH CROW	28
. ELIZABETH THOMAS	8
. FRAN	80
. FRANCIS	1,61,70,72,77, 80-81,84,141-142,145
.	146
. GEORGE	102
. JAMES	26
. JOHN	4,32
. LUCY	84
. LUCY BARBOUR	71,80
. LUCY ESTES	4
. LUCY FORD	31
. LUCY HAWKINS	1
. MARY	19
. MARY WRIGHT	41
. NANNIE JAMES	26
. REBECCA	9
. REBECCA H. SMITH	27

INDEX to Orange County, VA FAMILIES - Vol. #2

Name	Page(s)
. REUBEN	61,70-71,80-81
. ROBERT	38,81
. ROBERT F.	28
. SUSANNA DAY	26
. THOMAS	141-142
. THOMAS R.	28
. WILLIAM	8,26-27,54,61
.	68,70,139
. WILLIAM A.	41
. YELLY	26
MORAN, JOHN	138
WILLIAM	141
MORECOOK,	91
MORGAN, ALFORD	117
. ALICE A. NEYLAND	113
. ALICE BEASLEY	114
. ALICE O. BEASLEY	113
. ALMA H.	114
. AMANDA	113
. AMANDA E. DUCK	112-113
. AMELIA	117
. ARON	116
. ASKER	117
. AUGUSTA HAMILTON	112
. BEATRICE	113
. BENJAMIN	112,116
. BENJAMIN F.	113
. BETSY	111
. BETSY GAYDEN	109
. BETTY	116
. BOB	116
. BRADFORD	113
. CLARENCE	114
. CLARISA	116
. CLAUDE UDEAVE	113-114
. CLORINDA TORRANCE	112
. CYNTHIA E.	113
. CYNTHIA E. MORGAN	113
. CYNTHIA ELIZABETH	112
. DELLA HOGANS	113
. DIANA	116-117
. DONNIE	114
. DREW	114
. ELIZA	43
. ELIZABETH	9,116-117
. ELIZABETH GAYDEN	111
.	112
. ELLA MCKEY	113
. ELMIRA	116
. ELOIS M.	114
. EULALIA	113
. EVA EDNA TARVER	114
. FANNIE L.O.	114
. FIELDEN	116
. FIELDING	116
. FIELDING BRADFORD	112
.	113-114
. FRANK EUGENE	114
. GAYDEN WRENN	113
. GLADYS A.	114
. HATTIE R.	114
. HINDS HARTSTEIN	113
. HIRAM	112-113,116-117
. HOWARD THOMAS	114
. JAMES	112,116,137
. JANNIE	114
. JOHN	55,113,116-117
.	141,145,147
. JOHN G.	112-113
. JOHN GAYDEN	112
. JULIA M. BRABHAM	114
. LEONARD FIELDING	113
. LORAINE BASS	114
. LOYOLA	113
. MAGGIE M. BLALOCK	114
. MARGARET WILSON	113
. MARSHALL	113
. MARY	55
. MARY A. BRABHAM	113
. MATTIE	134
. MATTIE D.	114
. MAY	113
. MEREDAY	116
. MITTIE	113
. MORGAN	61
. MYRTICE	114
. PEARLA ANN	114
. PHOEBE	112,116-117
. PRISCELLA	113
. REBA JEWELL	-
. BLALOCK	114
. RHODA FREEMAN	113
. RICHARD	61
. ROBERT H.	113
. RUFUS	114
. SARAH	116
. SARAH A.E. SITES	112
.	113
. SARAH E. GOODMAN	113

INDEX to
Orange County, VA FAMILIES - Vol. #2

. SARAH M.	114	. JOHN 3,5,21,28,33,49		. FENLASON	78
. SOLOMON	117	. JOSIAH	25	. FENLEY	78
. THELMA J. WELCH	114	. LINNEY BROWN	3	. HANNAH	71,81
. THOMAS	55,135,142	. LINNY BROWN	5	. HUGH	78
. VELMA A. LILLY	114	. MARY SIMMONS	35,37	. JOHN	70,78
. VICTORIA C.	113	. MOLLY COLEMAN	17	. LUCY	78
. WILEY	113	. MOLLY KNIGHT	14	. MARG.	5
. WILIE	116	. MOLLY ROACH	37	. MARGARET	2
. WILLIAM	109,111-112	. MORRIS PETTY	40	. MARGRET	78
	115-116	. NANCY	29,42	. SARAH	3,5,78
. WILLIAM AUGHTY	114	. NANCY FINNELL	49	. THOMAS	70-71,81
. WILLIAM HAMILTON	113	. PATSY O.	21	. WILLIAM	78
. WILLIE	114	. PATSY SHIFFLETT	37	MORSE,FRANCIS	12
MORGIN,CHARLES	139	. PEGGY REYNOLDS	4,7	LUCY WARD	12
VALLENTINE	136	. POLLY	31,37	MORTAGUE,PETER	146
MORPHET,CATHERINE	54	. RAEFF	141	MORTON,ANN	74,84
. GEORGE	54	. REBECCA	28	. ANN T.	37
. JOHN	54	. REUBEN	62	. ELIJAH	9,36-37,70,77
. MARY	54	. REUBIN	17,30	.	141-143,146
MORPHUS,JOHN	139	. SALLY ACRE	30	. ELIZABETH	27
MORRIS,ADEN C.	49	. SALLY WRIGHT	31	. ELIZABETH WILLIAMS	48
. BETSY ACRE	26	. SAMUEL	61	. EVELINA TAYLOR	49
DABNEY	40	. SARAH	18	. GEORGE	48,61,68,70,75
. DAVID	3,6,37	. SUKEY SHIFLET	25	.	141-142,146
. ELIJAH	25	. SUKY DOLLINS	33	. GEORGE W.	49
. ELIZABETH	42	. SUSANNA	43	. JAMES	27,32,76
. ELIZABETH GEER	25	. SUSANNAH GRAVES	18	. JANE	9,16,74
. FANNY SHIFFLETT	49	. THOMAS	4,7,26,31,67	. JEREMIAH	61,74-76-77
. FENLY	147	. WILLIAM	37,42,55,146	.	84,141-142,145
. GEORGE	18,21,35,37	. WINIFRED	-	. JOHN	12,16,141-142,145
. GILSON	14	. QUISENBERRY	25	.	147
. JANE	55	. WM. ANDERSON	25	. JOSEPH	137-138
. JEMIMA GRUNTER	3,6	MORRISON,BOSWELL	70	. MARGARET CURTIS	27

INDEX to
Orange County, VA FAMILIES - Vol. #2

Name	Page	Name	Page	Name	Page
. MARY G. WEBB	36	MILDRED COLEMAN	30	NAILOR, BENJAMIN	120
. MARY TANDY	12	MULHOLLAND, OWEN	55	MARY RHODES	120
. MILLY TAYLOR	2,5	MULLALAN, JOHN	54	NALLE, MARTIN	33
. RICHARD	147	MULLICAN, MARY	34	. NELLY M. BARBOUR	33
. ROBERT	27	MUNDAY,		. NELLY MADISON	33
. SALLY	6,36	. MILLY CROSSWHITE	40	NASH, THOMAS W.	49
. SARAH	147	. NANCY OLIVER	40	VIRGINIA CLARK	49
. SUSANNA	29	. SAMUEL	40	NAYLOR, JANE WATTON	38
. WILLIAM	2,5,29,36,69	. WILSON	40	THOMAS	38
	74,136,138-139	MUNDY, BURRUS	39	NEAL, ANN MILLER	10
MOSELEY, SARAH	26	ELIZ. CROSTHWAITE	39	. CATHERINE BEAZLEY	12
MOSELY, LEONARD	25	MURPHY, CHARLES	66	. CHARLES	10,13
MOSLEY, FANNY	25	. ELIZABETH	75	. FIELDING	12,30
MOSSELL, NEHEMIAH	3	. LUCY ATKINS	24	. MILLY BEASLEY	8
PATTY COLLINS	3	. MILES	75	. MISCAJAH	8
MOTHERSHEAD, JOHN	13	. SUSANNA	25	. POLLY	30
SUKEY BURRAS	13	. ZACHARIAS	24	NEALE, CATEY	17
MOTHERSHED, NATHANIEL	8	MURRAY, JOHN	21	. CATY	82
RUTHY BIRT	8	MURRELL, JOHN	76	. CHARLES	70,76,78
MOTLEY, NORMA	118	MURRY, PRETTYMAN	11	. FIELDING	71,82
MOUBRAY,		MUSGROVE, ALEXANDER	37	. JOHN	78
. MARY CLATTERBUCK	44	POLLY MORRIS	37	. POLLEY	71
. SARAH	33	MUSIC, JOHN	3	. POLLY	82
. ZACHARIAH	44	MARY BERREY	3	. WILLIAM	76
MOULDIN, RICHARD	135	MUSICK, JOHN	6	NEALL, JOHN	141
MOYER, LURINNA BEADLES	41	MARY BERRY	6	NEAPPOILLE, JACOB	137
WILLIAM H.	41	MYERS, GEORGE	140	NEIL, LEWIS	62
MOYERS, CHRISTOPHER	137	. HORACE	116	NEILSON, CHARITY	55
. GEORGE	135	. PENDER	116	. DAVID	55
. LURINA	45	. PHOEBE MORGAN	116-117	. JAMES	55
. MICHAEL	37,45	MYRES, DANIEL	112	NELSON, AGNES	22
. SARAH	37	PHOEBE MORGAN	112	. ANN	104
MOZING, JAMES	30	NAILLEY, FRANCES	3	. ANN ADAMS	48

INDEX to
Orange County, VA FAMILIES - Vol. #2

Name	Page
. BARBARA	104
. ELIZ. QUISENBERRY	35
. ELIZABETH	27
. JAMES	26-27,35,48
. MILDRED BROCKMAN	104
. SARA SMITH	26
. THOMAS	35
. WALTER	104
. WILLIAM	26
NETHERLAND,JOHN	72
NETHERTON,JOHNH	81
NEWCOME,JANE	47
NEWMAN,ALEXANDER	26,62
.	141-142,145
. ANDREW	24,37,46
. CATHERINE CHILES	45
. CHARLES	45
. ELEANOR WRIGHT	37
. ELIZABETH	16
. ELIZABETH TUTMAN	43
. FANNY	33
. FRANCES	19,46
. GEORGE	43,66,69
. JAMES	8,10-11,16,72
. JANE	19,49
. JINNETTE GARNER	24
. JOHN	27,44
. LUCETTA	39
. LUCY BARBOUR	21
. LUCY FAULCONER	33
. LUCY SLEET	26
. MACY	10
. MALINDA	32
. MARIA	38
. MILDRED ALKINS	44
. PATSY	26
. PATSY O. MORRIS	21
. PATTY	8
. POLLY	25
. REUBEN	85
. SARA	38
. SIDNAH QUISENBERRY	27
. THOMAS	21,38,43,49
.	145-146
. VIRANDY	43
. WILLIAM	25-26,32-33,38
. WILLIAM E.	39
NEWPORT,JOHN	55,76,87
	139
NEYLAND,ALICE A.	113
NIBLIK,ROBERTA	99
NICHOL,P.	139
THOMAS	138
NICHOLLS,ELIZABETH	119
WILLIAM	55
NICHOLS,JOHN	46
SARAH PRITCHETT	46
NICKING,NATHANIEL	12
NICKINGS,ELIZABETH	12
NIGHT,THOMAS	136
THOMAS K.	138
NIPPER,	
. ELIZABETH FLECK	19
. JACOB	19
NIX,GEORGE	141
NIXON,	
. ELIZABETH GAYDEN	108
. HENRY	141-142,145
. JOHN	108
. NANCY	4,6
NOCH,JOHN	143
NOEL,JOHN	142,146
NOELAND,ANNIE	121
FANNIE	121
NOOMES,JOSEPH	6
RACHEL DAVIS	6
NORIN,JOHN	136
NORMAN,BETSY WARKIN	43
. CUTHBERT	15
. DANIEL	42-43
. SOPHIA JOLLET	15
NORRIS,CABEL	36
. MARGARET WATSON	43
. OLLY HARRIS	36
. WILLIAM	43
NORTHAN,JAMES	55
NORTON,JOHN	146
SARAH	3
NORWELL,ESTEN	6
ESTIN	3
NOVEL,JOHN	144
NUTLY,ELIZABETH	14
OAKES,CHARLES	138
. JOHN	125
. MAINYARD	30
. POLLY LANCASTER	30
. REUBIN	34
OAKS,JOANNA GRAVES	31
. JOHN	31

INDEX to
Orange County, VA FAMILIES - Vol. #2

Name	Page	Name	Page	Name	Page
. LUCY	18	. ELIZABETH	34	OVERTON,	68
. MAJOR	38,40	. FRANCIS	34,40-41	. BEVERLY	13
. MARTHA	38	. JAMES	49	. CLADISH	28
. MARTHA OAKS	38	. KILLIS	13,20	. ELIZABETH CONNER	13
. MOURNING	40	. LUCRETIA SIMS	49	. FANNY	42
. NANCY	18	. NANCY	11,40,80	. FRANCIS PALMER	21
. REUBIN	38	. NANCY WHITE	16	. JOHN	13,20
OBERT, AGATHA	90	. OLIVIA	41	. JOSHUA	21
BERTRAM	90	. TABETHA	79	. LUCY	47
OFFIELD, RANSOM	140	. TABITHA	11,80	. MARTHA CARLETON	20
OFFILL, WILLIAM	135,140	. WINNEY RIDDELL	20	. MARY	32,55
OFFRAIL, CATHERINE	55	OLLIVER, CATY	9	. NANCY BRADLEY	13
MORRIS	55	. CENCY	31	. OBEDIAH	42
OGG, ALEXANDER	31,71,83	. FRANCES	31	. PEGGY	35
. FRANKEY LAMB	16	. MILLY	9	. POLLY RICHARDS	13
. JAMES	43	. TABATHA	9	. SIDNEY	43
. JANE	43	ONEALL, MICHAEL	137	. WILLIS	13,20-21,30,32
. JOHN	16,55,71,83	ORANT, JOHN	9	.	35
. MARTHA	31	PEGGY LINTON	9	OWELL, CHRISTOPHER Y.	137
. MARY	55	ORENT, JOHN	12	OWEN, CHESCHESTER	42
. POLLY	24	OSBORN, NANCY	21	FRANCES CLARK	42
. SALLY GOODALL	16	WILLIAM	21	OWENS, CATY HARRIS	18
. WILLIAM	16	OSBORNE, ANN TALIFERRO	37	. JOHN	14
OLIVE, ELIZABETH	22	. BRAXTON	37,39	. SARAH HAMBLETON	14
. JAMES	8	. FIELDING	26	. STURD	18
. JENNY	22	. HOLLAND	36,44	PADGETT, ABIGAIL	102
. SUSANNAH MINOR	8	. MARY MASSEY	26	. JOHN	22
OLIVER, ARCHIBALD	80	. ROBERT	36	. NANCY BECKHAM	22
. CABEL	16	. SALLY FARNEYHOUGH	36	PAGE, BELINDA LONG	44
. CALEB	80	OTT, CATHERINE PENCE	21	. ELIJAH	23,71
. CATY	80	MICHAEL	21	. ELIZABETH	9
. DURET	80	OVERPACK, GEORGE	26	. ELIZABETH ALEXANDER	16
. DURRETT	79-80	MARTHA CARNES	26	. ELIZABETH LONG	42

INDEX to
Orange County, VA FAMILIES - Vol. #2

. ELIZABETH		. SALLY	14	PARSONS,ARTHUR C.	166
. MIDDLEBROOK	6	. WILLIAM	23,68,81	. CATHERINE TERRETT	166
. JAMES	13,44	PARISH,ELIZABETH	47	. DAVID	23
. JOHN	6,9,55,71,140,143	. JOHN	11	. ELIZABETH CLARK	23
. JUDITH SNOW	39	. JOSEPH	62	. GEORGE	55
. MARY	9	. MARY S.	36	. MARY	55
. MARY COLLINS	9	. RUTH	11	. NANCY	21
. NANCY	71,83	. THOMAS	18,36,68	. RICHARD	55,74
. NELLY SISK	23	PARKER,ALEXANDER	66	PATTERSON,ELIZABETH	55
. SINCLAIR	42	. HANNAH CAVE	7,132	. FRANCES	55
. TANDY	39	. MARY	132	. JOHN	3,6
. WILLIAM	16	. MARY THOMAS	2,5	. MARY	7,95-96
. WINNY SHEFFLET	13	. RICHARD	7,132	. NANCY	28
PAGETT,EDWARD	16	. WINSLOW	2,5	. PAGE CUDDING	6
PAGGETT,ANN	28	PARKS,CLARISSA BURTON	38	. PEGGY CUDDING	3
. ANN CLARK	28	. JOHN	55	. ROBERT	55
. JAMES	23	. RICHARD H.	38	. SUSANNA	7
. PHILLIS BEECON	23	. THOMAS	55,139	. TURNER	7
. WILLIAM	28	PARRISH,THOMAS	82	PATTEY,JOHN	138,141
PALLIS,POLLY JAMES	20	PARROT,FANNY SIMMONS	35	. THOMAS	138
THOMAS	20	. JOHN	35	. WILLIAM	138
PALMER,BENJAMIN	35	. JUDITH	27	PATTON,JAMES	62
. FRANCIS	21	. JUDITH WAYLAND	34	PATTY,JENNINE	141
. JOHN	133	. WILLIAM	27,34	PAUL,CATEY NEALE	17
. JUDITH LEFORE	35	PARROTT,		. ELIZA ANN LEATHERS	49
. WILLIAM	66,86	. ELIZABETH CATTERTON	38	. JACOB	17
PANEL,WILLIAM	13	. ELIZABETH HARTSOOK	50	. JOHN	49
PANILL,ANN	23	. ELIZABETH WILLIAMS	44	. RACHEL EDWARDS	14
PANNELL,JONATHAN	139	. GEORGE	38,50	. ROBERT	14
WILLIAM	138	. NANCY	35,47	PAYNE,ANN COLLINS	33
PANNILL,ELIZABETH	13	. WILLIAM	35,66	. CHARLES	38
. GEORGE	48	. WOODSON	44	. DILLAH	28
. JOHN	62	PARSON,HAMILTON GOSS	18	. DOLLY	92

241

INDEX to
Orange County, VA FAMILIES - Vol. #2

. ELIZABETH	23,30,33	. MARY ANN	49	. ELIZABETH	31
. ELIZABETH BLEDSOE	24	. WILLIAM	44,49	. ELIZABETH LUCAS	18
. ELIZABETH MALLORY	28	PEACHES,REUBEN	15	. JOHN	18,31,39
. FRANCES	40	SARAH JOHNSON	15	. MARY	39
. GABRIEL	27	PEACOCK,THOMAS	55	PENDLETON,BENJAMIN	19
. GEORGE	10,80	PEARCE,JEREMIAH	62	. ELIZ. BURRUS	20
. JESSIE	40	WILLIAM	77	. ELIZ. QUISENBERRY	13
. JOHN	17,19,24-25,27-28	PEARCEY,CHARLES	67,71,82	. ELIZABETH	-
.	33,40	. ELIZABETH	71,82	. QUISENBERRY	19
. JUDITH	10,27	. FRANKEY	71,82	. ELIZABETH TAYLOR	11
. LUCY	41	PEARCY,MARTHA	81	. FANNY THOMPSON	30
. LUCY JONES	38	PEARSON,		. JOHN	11,30
. MARY	19-20	. BETSY GOODRICH	13	. JOHN S.	49
. MARY MAJOR	92	. CONSTANCE	165	. LUCY WILLIAMS	49
. MATILDA	40	. ELIZABETH	18	. RICE	13
. MILDRED CHASEAM	25	. FRANCES	28	. ROBERT	20
. MILLY	17	. HENRY	62	PENN,NORAH M.	103
. MILTON	35	. JOHN	13	PENNILL,ANN MORTON	84
. NANCY FOSTER	18	. MARGARET	165	WILLIAM	69,84
. REUBEN	23	. MARY	10	PENNINGTON,ISAAC	62
. REUBIN	36	. MICHAEL	135	PEOPLES,MARY	112
. RICHARD	18,62	. PEGGY	9	PERCY,CHARLES	20
. ROBERT	33,39	. ROBERT	9	ELIZABETH LOWER	20
. SALLY	27,36	. SIMON	165	PEREGORY,MOSES	44
. SARAH BURTON	35	. TABATHA	16	PEREGOY,MOSES	38
. SUCKY LINDSAY	17	PEARY,	166	SARA NEWMAN	38
. THOMAS	17,20	PECK,JACOB	4,7	PERKINS,FERRIBY	111
. WILLIAM	18	. LEONA	103	. ISAAC	74
PEACH,BAILEY	16	. POLLY COURSEY	4,7	. LEWIS	111
NANCY VAUGHN	16	PEED,NANCY	23	. MARTHA GAYDEN	111
PEACHER,EDMUND	24	PEGO,NANCY	30	. PATSEY GAYDEN	111
. LUCH	44	PEMICK,ROBERT	76	PERRY,	84
. LUCY HILMAN	24	PENCE,CATHERINE	21	. ABRAHAM	20

INDEX to
Orange County, VA FAMILIES - Vol. #2

. ANN	4,6,71,82	. ELLEN	103	.	71-72
. ANN RIPPETO	47	. HENRY	103	. JOHN	41
. ANN WEBB	20	. HENRY HARVEY	103	. LIZEY	24
. BENJAMIN	71,80	. MARY E. HARVEY	103	. MORRIS	40
. ELIJAH	20	PETERS,		. PATRICK	40
. ELIZABETH	39,44,110	. CAROLINE BROCKMAN	161	. PATSY	22
. HENRY	71,80	. CAROLINE E.	-	. POLLY KENDEL	27
. JACKEY	106	. BROCKMAN	160	. REBECCA	28
. JAMES	14	. HENRY C.	161	. SALLY	26
. JAMES LEWIS	38	. HENRY CLAY	160	. SARAH	8
. JANE	38	PETLEY,JOHN	147	. THOMAS	139
. JANE PERRY	38	PETROS,NANCE	10	. WILLIAM	139
. JOHN	71,82	PETTEY,CATHERINE	78	. ZACHARY	27
. LANUD COLLINS	106	. GEORGE	78	PEYTON,ANNA HUFFMAN	40
. LEWIS	1	. JOHN	136,146	. GARNETT	23
. LUCY FAULCOWR	14	. THOMAS	136	. JAMES	40
. MARGARET	39	PETTIE,	89	. WILLIAM	62,73
. MARY	41	. REBECCA	89	PHILIPS,CONYERS	30
. MARY BURROWS	1	. ROBERT	89	. DAVID	7
. MARY WOOD	50	PETTIES,	89	. ELIZ. FARNEYHOUGH	30
. MILLEY	106	PETTIS,JOHN	32	. MARY DAVIS	7
. MOLLY	122	SALLY	32	. MILLY DAVIS	15
. MOSES	11	PETTRI,JERMINA	142	. THOMAS	15
. NANCY	39,106	JOHN	142	PHILLIPS,DAVID	4,135,140
. NANCY TANDY	14	PETTUS,MAHALA VAUGHN	158	. EDMUND	55
. PETER	14,38-39,41,44	. NAT	158	. FRANCIS WHITE	120
. POLLY WHARTON	20	. THOMAS	139	. JOHN	135
. RACHEL	12	PETTY,	89	. JOSEPH	55,137,140,143
. SUKEY	11,36	. ANN	41	. LEONARD	135
. SUSAN BROCKMAN	11	. BETSY	41	. LUTHER	98-99
. WILLIAM	50	. CATHERINE	71	. MARY DAVIS	4
. WILLIAM W.	47	. ELIZABETH MCNEAL	2	. RICHARD	138
PERSONS,ANTOINETTE	103	. GEORGE	2,22,24,26,28	. SARAH A. BROCKMAN	99

INDEX to
Orange County, VA FAMILIES - Vol. #2

Name	Page	Name	Page	Name	Page
. SARAH BROCKMAN	98	PIPKIN, TEMPEY T.	108	. GEORGE	55
. T.	141	PIRCE, WILLIAM	135,140	. JOHN	55
. WILLIAM	16,74,135,140	PITCHER, BETSY MASON	13	. MARGARET	55
PHILPOT, THOMAS	141	. CATHERINE	35,37	. MARTHA	55
PHITS, POLLY MONTAGUE	22	. FANNY COLEMAN	27	. MARY	55
THOMAS	22	. FRANCES	39	. ROBERT	55,74
PIAM, WILLIAM	140	. JOANER	35	. SARAH	55
PICHER, REUBEN	72	. JONATHAN	13	. SETH	74
PICHETT, MACE	82	. SUSANNA	33	. WILLIAM	55
PICKER, CATY	24	. THOMAS	55	POATE, LEWIS L.	50
PICKETT, CHARLES	45	. WILLIAM	27,33,35	POE, BENJAMIN	143
. ESTER	16	PITTIS, FANNY	30	. ELIZABETH	15
. FRANCIS	135	JOHN	30	. LUCY	19
. JAMES	135	PITTS, ELIZABETH	74	POINDEXTER,	
. JANE DOWELL	45	JOHN	74	. CLARISSA MITCHELL	123
. MACE	16,71	PITTY, CATHERINE	78	. CLASSISA	121
PICKINS, GABRIEL	55	PLANTAGNET, ANNE	89	. ISAAC NEWTON	123
. JOHN	55,62	PLATT, MARY	106	. JANE P.	123
. MARGARET	55	PLUNKABEAMER,		. JOHN ANDREW	123
PIDGEON, WILLIAM	76	. MATTHIAS	136	. JOSEPH	121
PIERCE, JEREMIAH	47	. NICHOLAS	136	. JOSEPH D.	123-124
. JULIA	33	PLUNKETT, BENJAMIN	77	. MARTHA A.	123
. SARAH	19	. EDWARD	55	. MARY M.	123
. WILLIAM	135	. ELIZABETH	46	. MILDRED	121,123
. ZACHARIAH	66	. FRANCES	41	. SARAH	123-124
PIGG, AMEY	6	. JENNY	21	. SUSAN	124
AMY	4	. JESSY	21	. WILLIAM S.	123
PIGLEN, MARGARET	4,7	. JOHN	77	POLLARD, BETSY	23
PINE, LEWIS	142	. MARY	38	. EDMUND	18,23
PINER, THOMAS	55	. PEGGY	16	. JAMES	139
PINES, WINEFRED	23	. SARAH	18,77	. NANCY	18
PIPER, ELIZABETH WHITE	27	. THOMAS	18	. SALLY HERNDON	18
WILLIAM	27	POAGE, ELIZABETH	55	POLLOCK, ELIZ.	17

INDEX to
Orange County, VA FAMILIES - Vol. #2

WILLIAM	17,32	. REBECCA	16	. FRANKY	25-26
POMDEXTER,		. SARAH	16,108	. HONORIAS	15,78
PHOEBE HAWKINS	13	. WILLIAM	19,39,41	. HONOROS	137
PONDGRASS, JOHN	139	POTH, JOHN	139	. JAMES	16,41,69,71
POOR, MICHAEL	55	POTTER,	89	.	79-80
PORTER, ABNER	19,26,29,62	. AGATHA OBERT	90	. JANE SMITH	47
.	71	. CHRISTOPHER	90	. JOHN	11
. ANN	17	. ELIZABETH	90	. JOHN W.	28
. B.	139	. HARRIET	92,117	. JOHN WEST	26
. BENJAMIN	26,72,136,144	. HARRIETT	90	. JOICE	26,38
.	146	. LETTY	90,92,117-118	. LEWIS	19,80
. BENJAMIN F.	49	POULTER, JOHN	11	. LEWIS G.	16,38,40,43
. BERLINDA	41	PATTY RANSDELL	11	.	46-47
. BETSY PROCTOR	9	POUND, JOHN	141-142,145	. LEWIS GORDON	71,81
. CAMP	17,22,68,71	. PATSY	35	. LUCRETIA	18
. CATHERINE CARTER	17	. SAM	136	. LUCY MCMILLAN	19
. CHAMP	83	. SAMUEL	138-139	. MARY	49
. CHARLES	9,71	. WILLIAM	146	. MISINIAH	9
. ELIZABETH	19	POWELL, AMBROSE	9,67,132	. NANCY SHELAR	41
. FRANCES	11,38	.	137	. NUTTY	19
. JOHN	17,35,62,71,138	. ANN	86	. PTOLAMY	69
. JOHN A.	46	. BENJAMIN	16,20,67	. PTOLEMY	17,82
. LUCY	26	. BETSY	20	. REUBEN	23
. MARIA	29,132	. ELIJAH	24	. RICHARD	139
. MARY	1,71,83	. ELISHA	9	. ROBERT	132
. MARY C.	22	. ELIZ. JENNETT	79	. SALLEY	79
. MARY CRUMP	46	. ELIZA P. BELL	26	. SALLY	15-16,46
. MARY N. HENSHAW	39	. ELIZABETH	43	. SALLY GRITT	9
. MARYANN	35	. ELIZABETH BALLARD	23	. SALLY POWELL	16
. NANCY	49	. ESTER PICKETT	16	. SIDNEY LAVIT	17
. NICHOLAS	108	. FIELDING	24	. SIMON	67,78-79
. PATSY NEWMAN	26	. FRANCIS	18	. SUSANNA BALLARD	24
. POLLY MCCAULEY	19	. FRANKEY	11	. THOMAS	67

INDEX to
Orange County, VA FAMILIES - Vol. #2

. WILLIAM LEWIS	18	. SYLVIA	79	. WILLIAM	4,6
. WINNEY	15	. THOMAS	29	PROFF, ELIZABETH	115
POWER, ROBERT	87	. WILLIAM	146	PROSIE, JACOB	74
PRATT, FANNY	44	. ZACKARY	143	PULLIAM, ABSOLEM C.	49
. JONATHAN	44	PRITCHETT, BENJAMIN	21	. JAMES	31
. JOSEPH	145	. POLLY HERNDON	21	. RHODA KING	49
. NANCY WHITE	46	. ROBERT	46	. WILLIAM	29
. WILLIAM	46,136,141	. SARAH	46	PURIM, THOMAS	144
PRESLEY, MARY	26	PROCTOR, BETSY	9	PURTON, MAY	6
PRETTYMAN, ANN	128	. ELIZABETH HIATT	6	SARA HEAD	6
. ANN A.	126	. ELIZABETH WIATT	4	PUTNAM, ZACHARIAH	139
. MERRY	14	. FANNY GRADY	31	PYLER, KATE	121
. MURRY	11	. G.V.	99	QUAR, ROSE	147
. POLLY	10	. GEORGE	9,31,79	QUARLES, ANN	21
PRICE, AJALON	71	. GRAHAM V.	101	. FRANCES VIVION	7
. ANGELON	147	. GRAHAM W.	100	. WILLIAM	7
. ARCHIBALD	141,145	. HEZEKIAH	9	QUELL, DAVID	137
. CATEY	1	. JAMES EMMETT	100	QUICK, GEORGE	33
. CATHERINE	35	. JOHN	31,62	MILDRED RAINES	33
. ED	138	. KAREN ELIZABETH	100	QUIN, JOHN	62
. EDWARD	55,136,142	. MADGE	100	QUINN, ANN WOOD	9
. ELIZ.	46	. MARGARET BROCKMAN	101	. DEALEM SMITH	33
. ELIZABETH	1,3,6,42	. MARGARET L.	100	. GARLAND	33
. ELIZABETH DOHONEY	29	. MARTHA SINGLETON	3,6	. JOHN	15
. ELIZABETH SIMS	36	. MARY	101	. RICHARD	9
. GEORGE	28,42,69	. MARY C. SMITH	100	QUINSENBERRY, JAMES	4
. JOHN	36,71	. MARY ELLEN	100	JANE BURROWS	4
. MARY B.	1	. MICHAEL SPENCE	100	QUISENBERRY, AARON	25,29
. MILLY	23	. NANCY YOUNG	9	.	72,83
. MUNGO	146	. ROGER LEE	100	. AMY	29
. POLLY	28	. SARAH	31	. ANN	38-39
. RICHARD	71,79	. THOMAS	28	. BENJAMIN	39-40
. RICHARD MOORE	62	. URIAH	3,6	. DANIEL	36

INDEX to
Orange County, VA FAMILIES - Vol. #2

Name	Page	Name	Page	Name	Page
. DOLLY	34	RAINES, ALPHA	38	RANDEL, NANCY	31
. ELIZ.	13,35,39	. ANNIE FLOYD	22	WILLIAM	31
. ELIZA	46	. CATHERINE	13	RANDELL, PATTY	11
. ELIZABETH	19	. FRANCES EDDINS	35	SANFORD	11
. EMILY BURRUS	49	. MERRY	22	RANDOLF, FLORA	105
. GEORGE	9,26-27,29,35	. MILDRED	33	RANDOLPH,	89
.	39,46,72	. POLLY	36	. ELIZABETH	88
. HENRIETTA REYNOLDS	29	. REUBIN	33	. JOHN	143
. HENRY	34	. WILLIAM	35	RANEY, JOHN	56
. HEZEKIAH	49	RAINS, ABBIE	43	RANFIELD, JOHN	136
. JAMES	7	. ELIZABETH WILLIAMS	44	RANSDAL, JOHN	145
. JANE	26	. FIELDING	44	RANSDALE, JOHN	142
. JANE BURROWS	7	. JOHN	145	RANSDEL, JOHN	147
. JANE DANIEL	9	RAKESBRAW, JOHN	141	RANSDELL, BETSY	12
. JOICE	23,27,33	RAKESTRAW, JOHN	56,142	. JESSEE	82
. LUCY	43,100	RAKSTRAW, JOHN	143	. MOLLY	15
. LYDIA	29	RALLS, MARY ANN CLARK	35	. PATTY	11
. MARY	12,31,38-39	ROBINSON	35	. SANFORD	15,72,82
.	100-101	RALPH, A.B.	158	RAWLINS,	131
. MARY RHOADES	36	. MARTHA A.	158	RAWSON, ARCHIBALD	73
. MILLY	36	. MARTHA SIMPSON	158	SARAH	10
. MOSES	12,27,29,72,83	. MARY	158	RAY, JOSEPH	55
. NANCY	31,35	. ZAZA D.	158	. LARNE	143
. POLLY	16	RALSON, MARTHA	56	. WILLIAM	139
. SALLY	33,37	ROBERT	56	READ, ANN	56
. SALLY GROOM	39-40	RAMDEL, JOHN	141	. CARVEL H.	49
. SALLY WRIGHT	35	RAMSEY, MARY	132	. DYSA RUMSEY	25
. SARAH BURNLEY	29	. NORMA M.	118	. ELIZABETH	56
. SIDNAH	27	. NORMA MOTLEY	118	. JOHN	55
. VIVIAN	35	. ROBERT	56	. JOSEPH	56
. WILLIAM	19,23,72	RANDAL, JOHN	136	. MILDRED FAULCONER	49
. WINIFRED	25	RANDALL, ELIZABETH	3,5	. WILLIAM	25
RAINE, SIMON	74	JOHN	138,140	RECTOR, ELIZABETH	22

INDEX to
Orange County, VA FAMILIES - Vol. #2

RED,THOMAS	137	. LUCY	22	. ASHLY	121
REDDIS,ANN V.	41	. LUCY FINNEL	23	. BENJAMIN	119
REDDISH,LUCY	29	. MARY	37	. CATHERINE	121
REDDY,ANN WALLER	125	. MAY	27	. CHARLIE	121-122
REDMAN,JOHN	29	. NANCY NIXON	4,6	. CHRISTIANE	-
NANCY	29	. PEGGY	4,7	. DRUMRIGHT	122
REED,BLANCH	104	. RACHEL	9,146	. CHRISTOPHER	119,159
. DICY	37	. RICHARD	5,23,145	. CLYDE	121
. JAMES	56	. SARAH	10	. DANIEL	121,123
. LOU ANNA	104	. SUSANNA WRIGHT	5	. ELAINE	121
. NANCY	23	. SUSANNAH WRIGHT	2	. ELIZABETH	119
REID,ANN	19	. TABITHA	9	. ELIZABETH NICHOLLS	119
REMBOUGH,JACOB	46	. WASHINGTON	29	. EMMA HICKS	122
REYNOLDS,AARON	10	. WILLIAM	4,6,26-27	. EPOPHRODITIES	122
. ANNA DARNELL	5	.	33-35,49	. EPPHRODITES	120
. BENJAMIN	2,79	. WILLIAM W.	29	. EPPRODITIES	120
. CATHERINE	5,34,78	RHOADES,CLIFTON	38	. EPRPHRODITES	119
. CATHERINE REYNOLDS	5	. ELIZABETH	36	. ERVIN	122
. CATHERINE SWAN	29	. GEORGE	36	. EUGENE	122
. CATY CHAMBERS	10	. JOHN	44	. EZECKIAS	119
. CORNELIUS	77,145	. MARGARET FAULCONER	44	. EZEHIAS	119
. ELIZABETH	2,10,22,28	. MARY	36	. FANNIE NOELAND	121
.	79	. MILLY HAM	38	. FLORENCE	121
. ELIZABETH REYNOLDS	2	. RICHARD	26	. FRANKY	120
. FENNETTA	17	RHOADS,EPAPHRODITUS	18	. GEORGE	15
. HANNAH JONES	35	FRANKEY	18	. GILLY CLARK	121
. HANNER DARNEL	2	RHODES,ALEX	122	. HANNAH	76,84,119
. HENRIETTA	29	. ALICE	119	. HANNAH MILLER	159
. JANE QUISENBERRY	26	. ALICE HARRIS	122	. HANNER MILLER	119
. JOHN	2,5,142	. AMY	121	. HERBERT	122
. JOICE QUISENBERRY	33	. ANN	119	. HEZEKIAH	119-120,137
. JOSEPH	2,5,17,37,141	. ANN WHITE	119-120	.	159
.	146	. ANNIE NOELAND	121	. HORACE	121-122

INDEX to
Orange County, VA FAMILIES - Vol. #2

. HUGH	122	. RAYMOND	122	. MILLEY	76
. JAMES	119,121-122,159	. REGIONALD	121	. MILLY	74
. JANE	119	. REUBEN	120	. MILLY BINGHAM	40
. JOHN	16,119-120,122	. RICHARD	16	. SAMUEL	74,76
	159	. ROBERT	8,122	. SARAH	74,76
. JULIA	122	. ROBERT ROBERTS	121	. WILLIAM	74,135,140
. JULIA EDWARDS	122	. ROY	121	RICHARD I,	87
. KATE PYLER	121	. SALLY	120,122	RICHARD II,	87
. LAWRENCE	121	. SAMUEL E.	121	RICHARD, FRANCIS	13
. LISSA DELANEY	8	. SARAH	123	. JOHN	3
. LOSSIE	121	. SARAH BECK	122	. MILLY WATTS	3
. LUCY WRIGHT	16	. SARAH J. SPICER	121	. WILLIAM	13
. MAGGIE	121	. SETH	119	RICHARDS, AMBROSE	24
. MARTHA JANE	121,123	. SUSAN	120	. DIANNAH	20
. MARY	119-121	. TABATHA PEARSON	16	. ELIZ. LANCASTER	38
. MARY A.	123	. TABITHA	120	. EZEKIAH	42
. MARY ANN	122-123	. THEODOSIA	13,120	. FOUNTAIN	48
. MARY BROCKMAN	118-120	. THOMAS	118,120-123	. HEZEKIAH	38
.	122-123	. VIRGIE	121	. IKE	48
. MARY MART	120	. VIRGINIA	121	. J.K.	22
. MARY WATTS	120	. WILLIAM	84,119,121-122	. JOHN	6,34,45
. MARY WRIGHT	15	.	159	. MARY ADAMS	42
. META	119,121	RIADER, ISAAC	20	. MILLY WATTS	6
. MILDRED	119	SUSANNAH MCKELAMY	20	. PHILEMON	4,7,66
. MILDRED POINDEXTER	121	RICE, ANNE	74	. POLLY	13
.	123	. ARMON BOHANAN	74	. RICHARD	40,42,47-48
. MILLY	120	. FISHER	74,76	. ROBERT	146
. MOLLY PERRY	122	. HARRY	76	. SOPHIA MILLS	48
. NANCY	120	. HENRY	40,74,76,136,138	. SUSANNA WOODS	7
. NANNIE	121	. LUCY	3,5	. SUSANNAH WOOD	4
. OLIVIA	122	. MARGARET	74	. WILLIAM	14,20,140,143
. OSCAR LEE	122	. MICH.	67	RICHARDSON, JOSIAH	40
. PEYTON	122	. MICHAEL	74,76	SARAH ABELL	40

249

INDEX to
Orange County, VA FAMILIES - Vol. #2

Name	Page	Name	Page	Name	Page
RICHE, PATRICK	56	. JOHN	158	ROAD, JOHN	79
RICHERSON, HARRY	85	RIGBY, JOHN	55	ROADES, EZEKIAH	138
RIDDELL, JAMES	13,20	RIGHT, JAMES	10	ROBB, JAMES	80
. SALLEY	72	SARAH RAWSON	10	ROBBARDS, SUSANNA	22
. THEODOSIA RHODES	13	RIKEDON, JOHN	87	ROBBINS, MARY FOSTER	6
. WINNEY	20	RION, SOLOMAN	139	. MARY LENOX	3
RIDDLE, BETSY GOODALL	33	RIPBERGER, THEODORE	121	. THOMAS	3,6,79
. CHARLES	42	VIRGINIA RHODES	121	. WILLIAM	79
. ELIZABETH SEAL	28	RIPPATO, SARA W.	24	ROBERSON,	
. FANNY	31-32	RIPPETO, ANN	47	. ELIZ. MALLORY	39
. FIELDING	18	. MARTHA TAYLOR	24	. JAMES	56
. JAMES	31-32,67,69,120	. PETER	24	. WILLIAMS	39
. JOHN	28,42	RIPPITO, BETSY STOW	20	ROBERT, FRANCES HENRY	14
. JOYCE	9	. ELIZA.	17	THOMAS	14
. JOYCE RIDDLE	9	. JOHN	17	ROBERTS, AGNES KNIGHT	18
. LEWIS	9,62,72	. LOUISA MCALISTER	49	. BENJAMIN	62
. LUCRETIA SIMS	42	. THOMAS P.	49	. CATHERINE WHITEHEAD	47
. LUCY	39	. WILLIAM	20	. CURTIS	38
. MARY GOODALL	38	RIPPON,	137	. ELIZABETH SILK	22
. MARY POWELL	49	RIXEY,		. GEORGE	16
. MILLY WAITS	18	. BETSY SUTHERLAND	16	. HUGH	15,22
. SALLY POWELL	46	. JOHN	16	. JAMES	47,67
. TAVERNOR	38	ROACH, ABSOLON	66	. JOHN	17-18,62
. TAVNEY	46	. BETSY LINDSAY	13	. LAVINIA TIPPETT	16
. THEODOSIA RHODES	120	. DAVID	55	. MARY WHITE	17
. THOMAS	49	. JAMES	13,37,72,81	. NANCY	15
. THOMPSON	49	.	145-146	. ROBERT	121
. VALENTINE	33	. JOHN	72,81	. SALLY CHEWNING	38
. WILLIAM	9,72,79	. MOLLY	37	. THOMAS	16,22
RIENER, FANNY OVERTON	42	. NANCY	37,39	ROBERTSON,	89
JOHN	42	. SARAH LEATHERS	46	. AMANDA BLALUCK	114-115
RIFFE, JACKSON	158	. TINCEY ROW	45	.	134
. JAMES	158	. WILLIAM	45-46	. ARTHUR PAUL	115

INDEX to
Orange County, VA FAMILIES - Vol. #2

. BENJAMIN	107	.	109-110	. SILER	18
. BENJAMIN O.	115	. CATY	10	. SUKEY	5
. BENJAMIN OTIS	114-115	. CHARLES	55	. SUSAN JOHNSON	47
. BOOKER JEFFERSON	115	. CHRISTOPHER	90	. SUSAN MELONE	42
. CAROL JEAN	115	. ELIZ.	22	. SUSANNAH BROOK	90
. ELIZABETH COLLINS	22	. ELIZABETH POTTER	90	. THOMAS	4,6,37,42
	32	. FANNY JONES	30	. WILLIAM	1,12,17,26,90
. ELIZABETH DOLIN	46	. FEEDY	107	.	110,117
. FANCES CAMILLE	115	. FRANCES	33-34	ROBISON,	146
. FRANCES PORTER	11	. FRANCIS	33	OHN	73
. GINGER ILEEN	115	. FRANKEY ADAMS	12	ROBUKS,ELIZABETH SISK	21
. HELEN BATCHELOR	115	. GEORGE	56,62	. HUGH	21
. INEX HELEN	115	. HUGH	47	. THOMAS	21
. JOHN	11	. JAMES	1,56,90	ROCHESTER,	87
. JOYCE M.	115	. JEAN	56	ROCK,DAVID	137
. LAURA GABLE	115	. JOHN	1,11,18,42,62,90	RODES,	119
. RICHARD	22,32	. JOSEPH	25	ROEBUCK,GEORGE	143
. SUSAN VALLI	115	. JUDY EMBRY	1	ROGERES,	
. WILLIAM	28	. KETURAH	34	. ELIZABETH KNIGHT	21
. WILLIS	46	. LUCY	4,6	. JOHN	21
ROBESON,JOHN	10	. LUCY ROBINSON	4,6	ROGERS,AARON	12
ROBINSON,	89,141-142	. M.	145	. AMY	27
. ACHILLES D.	43	. MARGARET COLLINS	17	. AULEY	43
. AGATHA	90,117	. MICHAEL	22	. BARBARA ELLIS	2
. AGATHA BEVERLEY	90	. MILLY	14	. BENJAMIN	32
. AGATHA BEVERLY	117	. MOSES	30	. ELIZ. FERGUSON	33
. AGNES	20	. NANCY ROACH	37	. ELIZABETH	22
. AGNES SMITH	1	. PHILADELPHIA SNELL	25	. ELIZABETH JACKSON	35
. ANN CURTIS	90	. PHOEBE	22	. FRANCES TWYMAN	38
. ARTEMEUS	14	. POLLY WILLIAMS	22	. JAMES	35,44
. ARTEMUS	22	. RICHARD	90	. JERMENIUS	33
. BENJAMIN	90	. SALLY BELL	43	. JOHN	2,21,25-27,45,135
. BETSEY COLLINS	107	. SARAH LANCASTER	42	.	140

251

INDEX to
Orange County, VA FAMILIES - Vol. #2

. JONATHAN	38	ROSELL, JAMES W.	98	ROW, ANN	13
. JOSEPH	32	. JANE	158	. CYNTHIA	27
. KELLER	30	. NANCY J. BROCKMAN	98	. EDMUND	18,27
. LUCY DARNELL	26	ROSELLE, ARTHUR	99	. ELHANAN	43
. MALINDA NEWMAN	32	. FRANCIS	99	. ELIZABETH	42
. MARGARET WOOD	44	. HARVEY	99	. HETTY	38
. MARY HAM	30	. JAMES W.	99	. MARY	18
. MARY LANE	32	. LOUELLA	99	. MARY D. SANDERS	43
. MILDRED CHISHOM	25	. MAY	99	. MILLY	23
. NANCY	12	. MINA	99	. RACHEL	30
. PENELOPE CHANCELLOR	34	. NANCY BROCKMAN	99	. RICHARD	13
. POLLY	21	. VESTA	99	. THOMAS	23,30,38,42,45
. POLLY COLLIER	45	ROSENCRANTS, ALEXANDER	66	.	49,62,71,86,144
. POLLY COYLER	45	ROSS, DAVID	56	. TINCEY	45
. SALLY	18	. MARGARET	25	ROWLAND, EDMUND	73
. SARAH	12	. MARY	19	. EDWARD	56,76
. THOMAS	34	ROSSE, ALEXANDER	56	. MARY	76
. WILLIAM	45,67	ROSSELL, J.	157	ROWSEE, JOYN	135
ROGS, DOC	142	NANCY J. BROCKMAN	157	ROWZEE, FRANCES	2
ROHR, ALICE	123	ROSSON, ARCHELAUS	21	FRANCIS	5
. JOE	123	. ARCHILAUS	19	ROY,	141
. MARTHA POINDEXTER	123	. HANEY R. WARREN	21	. M.	145
. ROBERT	123	. THOMAS	85	. MUNGO	62
ROLLINS, LUCY HERNDON	31	. WILLIAM	66,139	ROYS, MONGO	147
RICHARD	31	ROSZELL, DELPHIA	16	RUCHER,	137,144
ROOTS, PHILLIP	135,140	ROTH,	119	RUCKER,	138
ROSE,	141-142	ROTHROCK,		. BELFIELD	33
. EDWARD	115	. ELIZ. POLLOCK	17	. BETTY TINSLEY	7
. FRANCES MADISON	23	. GEORGE	17	. CATY	13
. INEX HELEN	-	ROUSE,	117	. CATY TALIAFERRO	18
. ROBERTSON	115	FRANCES	56	. COLEBY	81
. ROBERT H.	23,42	ROUTT, WILLIAM P.	38	. ELIZABETH RANDALL	3,5
. WILLIAM	138	WINNEY	17,31	. ELLAY	32

INDEX to
Orange County, VA FAMILIES - Vol. #2

. ELLIOT	13	NANCY SOUTHERLAND	48	. WILLIAM	13,62,74,128	
. EPHRIAM	5	RUMSEY, DYSA	25	.	139	
. EPHRIM	3	. ELIJAH	29	RUTHERFORD, ANNE	75	
. FRANCIS	45	. ELIZABETH	4,7	. REUBEN	75	
. HARRIETT HEAD	47	. LIANNA	29	. THOMAS	62	
. ISAAC	77	. LUCY	37	RUTLEDGE, FRANCES	108	
. JEMIMAH CRAWFORD	1	. NANCY	29	RUTTER, JOHN	56	
. JOEL	11,33	. PATTY COPE	4,6	RYAN, JOHN	55	
. JOHN	7,13,62	. POLLY CAMIKE	31	. SOLEMAN	56	
. LUCY	49	. SALLY HUGHS	29	. SOLMAN	146	
. M.	146	. THOMAS	4,6,29	. SOLOMON	136	
. MARGARET	46	. WALKER	31	RYLEY, MICAL	56	
. MARY	10,13	. WILLIAM	37,139	SACRY, JOHN	157	
. MARY BURTON	32	RUMSY, JOHN	14	SALBREE, LUCY	18	
. MARY TURTON	32	. MARY	9	SALE,		
. MILLY	13	. MARY DEERING	14	. CATHERINE COLEMAN	38	
. MINOR	47	. PEGGY BARRETT	14	. JOHN W.	38	
. NANCY OLIVER	11	. WILLIAM	14-15	SALLY, GEORGE A.	161	
. NANCY SMITH	13	RUNKLE, JACOB	35	SALLY	161	
. NANCY WHITE	33	MARY M.	35	SALMON, REBECCA	89,92,159	
. PATSY SNYDER	44	RUSH, MARY	74,98	THOMAS	88-89,93	
. PETER	1,81,135,140,144	WILLIAM	74	SAMPSON, AMY ROGERS	27	
.	146	RUSSEL, PETER	139	. ANNEY JAMES	23	
. POLLY	29	RUSSELL,	76,142	. CLARISA JOLLETT	37	
. REUBEN	81	. JAMES D.	108	. DRADA JOLLETT	43	
. ROSANNA BURRUS	12	. MARY MERRY	13,128	. ELIJAH	27	
. SARAH	1	. NEHEMIAH	5	. ELIZABETH	42	
. THOMAS	77,135	. PATSY	12,21	. GEORGE	43	
. THORNTON	44	. PETER	62,76,136	. JAMES	23	
. WILLIAM	18,21,29-30	. SALLY COLLINS	5	. JOHN	37-38	
	45-46,49,135	. SARAH	76	. LUCY	38	
. WISDOM	12	. SUSANNA GAYDEN	108	. MARGARET	48	
RUMBOUGH, JACOB	44,48	. THOMAS	136,138-139	. MARY	46	

INDEX to
Orange County, VA FAMILIES - Vol. #2

. SALLY	34	SANFORD, ANNA ARNOLD	27	. ELIZABETH WRIGHT	2,5
. SALLY JOLLET	32	. BETSY RANSDELL	12	. MARY	2,5
. SALLY SAMPSON	34	. BETTY SCOTT	27	. SARAH	4,7
. THOMAS	15	. CATHERINE FORD	41	. WILLIAM	2,5,86,144-145
. WILLIAM	32,34	. DURRETT	81	SCALES, RICHARD	56
. WINNEY POWELL	15	. FRANCIS WEBB	13	SCHENK, ANNE T.	34
SAMS, JOHN	10,24	. HAMLET	34,39	SCHOOLER,	
. MARY BLEDSOE	10	. HANNAH GRYMES	15	. DOLLY QUISENBERRY	34
. NANCY	24	. JOHN	12	. JOSEPH H.	34
SAMUEL, ANDREW	39	. LAWRENCE	41	SCOTT, ANN	56
. HENRY	16	. MIMA	28	. ANN COWHERD	46
. JOHN	18	. MUSE	27	. ANNA	31
. PHILEMON	37	. NANCY	12	. BETTY	27
. POLLY	16	. NANCY CLARK	39	. CHARLES	48
SAMUELS, A.L.	100	. NANCY WALLACE	23	. ELIZABETH	30
SANDAGE, LUCY	19	. PEGGY	25	. ELIZABETH FAULCONER	42
SANDERS,	119-120,161	. PHOEBE BIGGERS	34	. ESTHER	56
. BENJAMIN	28	. PIERCE	16-17,22,24-26	. GEORGE	12,17,27,30-31
. BETSY	12	. REUBEN	13,23,81	.	56,63
. JOANNA	23	. ROBERT	15,81	. HARRIET COWHERD	48
. JOHN	43	. SALLY	22	. JAMES	56
. MARY	9	. STEWART	27-28,31	. JANE	56
. MARY D.	43	SARGEANT, JOHN	74	. JANE T.	42
. MELINDA	43	SARGENTS, WILLIAM	73	. JOANNAH HILMAN	49
. NANCY	15	SARTAN, ISAAC	141	. JOHN	12,42,46,49,56
. NANCY JONES	28	SAUNDERS,		.	137,140,143
. NATHANIEL	9,15,18,26	. BARBARA G. BLAIR	48	. JOHNNY	12,63,69-70,72
.	28-30,85	. ELIZABETH	13	.	80,83,86,144
. ROBERT	48	. JAMES W.	48	. LARKIN	42
. SARAH	18	. NANCY	3,5	. LUCY	12
. WALTER R.	160	SAWKING, HELEN	88	. MARGARET COPE	8
SANDRIGE, ANN HALL	40	. NICHOLAS	88	. MARY	1,56,72,82
AUSTIN	40	SAWYER,		. NANCY ABELL	31

INDEX to
Orange County, VA FAMILIES - Vol. #2

Name	Page	Name	Page	Name	Page
. NANCY WOOD	12	. SALLY JOHNSON	15	. EDMUND	63
. NELLY SHADRICK	14	. WILLIAM	2-3,5	. EDWARD	63
. REUBEN	8,22	SEKLE,PETER	20	. HENRY	67
. ROBERT	56,63	SELDEN,	159	. JOHN	141
. SALLY	22	SELF,		. MARY WHITE	120
. SAMUEL	56,63	. BROCKMAN CAMPBELL	105	. SARAH CLEAVE	46
. SARAH	49	. FRANCES SHEFLETT	12	. URIEL	43
. SARAH ANN	49	. HELEN CRAIG	105	. ZACHARIAH	46
. THOMAS	42,138	. HELEN EWER	105	. ZACHARY	63
. VIRGINIA HENSHAW	42	. JAMES HOWARD	105	SHADRACK,	
. WILLIAM	12,14,78,141	. JOHN PERRY	105	. BETSY SANDERS	12
SCOTTS,JOHN	135	. KENNETH BROCKMAN	105	. ELIZABETH	44
SCRIVENER,SAMUEL	45	. MAHALA E. BROCKMAN	105	. FRANCES	48
SCRIVNER,SUSAN	45	. MARJORIE EWER	105	. JOHN	12
SCRUGGS,MARGARET	105	. MARY	25	. SARAH	44
SCULTHROP,ANTHONY	75	. PAMELAI JEANNE	105	SHADRICK,	
HANNAH	75	. SAMUEL	12	. ELIZABETH SAUNDERS	13
SEAL,ELIZABETH	28	. VIRGINIA LORRAINE	105	. JOBE	10
. ELIZABETH POWELL	43	SEMS,ISAAC	32	. JOHN	13-14
. MARY	34	NANCY CATTERTON	32	. MOLLY	10
. PHILIP	34,42	SERIVINER,SAMUEL	14	. NELLY	14
. SALLY	34	SERTAIN,JOSEPH	147	. SARAH SANDERS	18
. THOMAS	43	SERTANI,ISAAC	147	. THOMAS	18
SEARCEY,REUBEN	107	. JOEL	147	SHAMBOLS,THOMAS	139
SEBREE,ELIZABETH	20,37	. JOHN	147	SHANDREW,	
.	72,82	SETTLE,FRANCIS	133	. DAISY G. BLALUCK	114
. HANNAH KAVANAUGH	5	SEVIER,VALENTINE	56	. EARL	114
. HANNAH KAVINNER	2	SEWERS,CHRISTOPHER	19	SHARMARARD,ELISHA	9
. JOHN	15,72,80,82-83	SARAH PIERCE	19	ELISHA POWELL	9
. LUCY	20	SHACKELFORD,MARGARET	74	SHARP,THOMAS	141,145
. MARY STROTHER	3	THOMAS	74	SHAVERS,POLLY	24
. NANCY	40	SHACKLEFORD,		SHEA,DENNIS	19
. RICHARD	15,76,143	. DEADEMA HILMAN	43	SHEAMAN,GEORGE	66

INDEX to
Orange County, VA FAMILIES - Vol. #2

Name	Page	Name	Page	Name	Page
SHEARS, JOSEPH	136	. ROBERT W.	46	. SUSANNA DAVIS	19
SHECLER, CATY	48	. SUSAN F. CONWAY	46	. TRICE	48
SHEETS, JOHN	56	. WILLIAM	18,34	SHIFFLETT, ARCHIBALD	43
SHEFFLET, ELIZABETH	13	SHEPPARD, MICHA	74	. BELINDA VAUGHN	43
WINNY	13	SHER, JEAN ADDISON	19	. BENNETT	40
SHEFLETT, ELIZABETH	12	ROBERT	19	. FANNY	49
FRANCES	12	SHERALD,		. FRANCIS MARTIN	37
SHELAR, CATY	48	CARRIE E. BLALUCK	134	. JAMES	39
. JOHN	41,48	SHERICK, MARTHA GARTON	44	. JOHN	37,41
. NANCY	41	PHILIP B.	44	. LUCRETIA POWELL	18
SHELLER, ANN COX	12	SHERMAN, JESSIE	29	. LUCY SNOW	37
JOHN	12	. JOHN H.	46	. MERRY	37
SHELTON,	89	. MARGARET RUCKER	46	. MILLY HERRIN	39
. CLARY BEADLES	31	. SALLY BRUDEN	29	. NANCY MORRIS	42
. HENRY	161	SHIFFLET, EDMUND	47	. PATSY	37
. JOHN	83,135	. ELIZABETH	12	. PICKETT	18
. LUCY	30	. FELIX	47	. POLLY	40
. THOMAS	31,88	. JOHN	19,21,36,49	. POLLY SHIFFLETT	40
SHEPHERD, ALEXANDER	15-16	. JOICE	12	. RICHARD	42
.	68	. MILLY WIAN	47	. SLATEN	43
. ANDREW	19,21,77-78,144	. MORDICAI	49	. SUSANNA MORRIS	43
.	146	. OVERTON	32	. VINA	41
. ANN PORTER	17	. PHOEBE	47	. VINA SHIFFLETT	41
. CATHERINE	19	. PHOEBE SHIFFLET	47	. WILLIAM	37,49
. ELIZABETH	24	. POLLY	49	SHIFLET, ANN HICKS	21
. GEORGE	17,41,63	. POLLY RAINES	36	. ELIZABETH	32
. HELEN	15	. POLLY SHIFFLET	49	. JOHN	21
. JAMES	49	. RACHEL HICKS	18	. SUKEY	25
. LUCINDA TAYLOR	49	. RANEY SNOW	48	SHIFLETT, EDWARD	35
. MARY	19,41	. RHODA	21	. JOHN	80,138
. MARY BURNLEY	16	. RHODA SHIFFLET	21	. JOICE HERRING	35
. N.J.	102	. SALLY HERRING	32	. MOLLY	12
. NANCY	8	. STEPHENS	18	. STEPHEN	79

INDEX to
Orange County, VA FAMILIES - Vol. #2

. WILLIAM	12	. MARY	35,37	. ELIZABETH	34,36,48
SHIP, MARTHA BURTON	40	. MARY DARNELL	42	. FRANCIS GRAVES	36
ROBERT M.	40	SIMMS, LUCY	102	. JAMES	43,46
SHIRLEY, GEORGE	136	. MARY TOWLES	129	. JAMES P.	47
SHISHLER, FRANCES	128	. NANCY	102	. JEREMIAH	13,18,34
SHISLER, LEWIS	33	. RICHARD	129	. JOANA	76
SALEY CLARK	33	SIMPSON, AARON	34	. JOANAH	87
SHITER, HENRY	137	. ANN THOMPSON	21	. JOANNA	56
SHOPSHIRE, ELIZABETH	1	. DANIEL	23	. JOHN	24,48,50
WINDFIELD	145	. ELIZABETH	158	. LUCRETIA	41-42,49
SHOST, JOHN	74	. ELIZABETH JONES	23	. LUCY T. EARLY	43
SHROPSHIRE, ANNE	76	. GEORGE	42	. MARGARET	49
. JOHN	1,76	. JAMES	70	. MARGARET TAYLOR	13
. MARY PORTER	1	. JESSE	158	. MARY WOOD	43
. WALTER	76	. JESSE B.	158	. NANCY WALKER	50
SIDNOR, JAMES	144	. JOHN	135	. NANCY WATTS	12
SILBY, SALLY	25	. MARTHA	158	. NATHANIEL	19
SARAH	25	. MARY GOODRIDGE	42	. POLLY	18,41
SILK, ELIZABETH	22	. MARY MULLICAN	34	. POLLY BOSWELL	37
SILVEY, FRANKEY DEAR	10	. WILLIAM	21	. REUBEN	36
. LUCY	20	SIMS,	89	. RICHARD	43,76,87,89-90
. MARY ADKINSON	24	. AGATHA BROCKMAN	90	.	92,118,136
. STEPHEN	10	. AGATHA ROBINSON	90,117	. RICHARD L.	36
. WILLIAM	24	. AMELIA	48	. SUSANNAH JOHNSON	19
SIMECO, JOHN	22	. ANESTER	117	. TANNIE WALKER	19
POLLY	22	. ANESTER STAP	117	. THOMAS	136
SIMES, THOMAS	139	. ANESTER STEP	117	. VIRGINIA SORRILLE	48
SIMMONDS, EPHRAIM	20	. ANN BEAZLEY	47	. WILLIAM	12,18-19,24,26
SARAH HANES	20	. BETSY	26	.	41,43,48,56,67,90,117
SIMMONS, BAZZELL	35	. BETTY	25	.	143-144
. FANNY	35	. BETTY BEAZLEY	24	. WILLIAM H.	50
. GEORGE	42,135	. BROOKS	37	SIMSON, JOHN	14,147
. JOHN	35	. ELIZA MORGAN	43	. POLLY S. DAWSON	14

INDEX to
Orange County, VA FAMILIES - Vol. #2

. WILLIAM	147	SISSON,ABNER	35	SLEEPER,CLORINDA	112
SINALT,ANN	3	. BRIENT	136	SLEET,ANN FORD	2
SINER,JAMES	141	. BRYAN	62,141-142,145	. ANN PETTY	41
SINGLETON,AMBROSE	91	.	147	. FINLASON	70
. ANNE	91	. C.	1	. FRANCES MALLORY	26
. AVERILLA	92	. CALEB	63	. FRANCES WRIGHT	23
. DANIEL	135,141,144-145	. FANNY	28	. JAMES	2,22,24,26,28,56
. ELIZABETH	92	. MILLIE BRAHAM	1	.	63,72,142,145,147
. FRANCES	91	. MILLY	17	. JOHN	23,29,40,45,72
. HENRY	92	. POLLY	16	. LUCINDA	45
. ISAAC	92	. RACHEL CHAMBERS	35	. LUCY	26,79
. JAMES	91	. SARAH	16-17,28	. MARY	40
. JOANNA	4	. WILLIAM	72,81	. NANCY	47
. JOHANNA	6	SITES,CYNTHIA	112	. PATEY	72
. JOHN	92	. LEONARD	112	. PATSY	25,72,79
. JOSHUA	91-92	. SARAH A.E.	112-113	. PATSY PETTY	22
. MANOAH	63	SKILLIRN,ELIZABETH	56	. PHILIP	41
. MARTHA	3,6	. GEORGE	56	. REBECCA PETTY	28
. MARY BROCKMAN	91	. ISABELL	56	. REUBIN	26
. PHILIP	146	. SARAH	56	. SARAH	22
. PHILLIP	141,144	. WILLIAM	56	. SARAH C.	5
. RACHEL	91	SKILTON,JOHN	140	. SUSIE	79
. RICHARD HUNT	91-92	SKIPWORTH,HENRY	110	. WEDEN	72
. ROBERT	91-92	SLATE,JAMES	141	. WEEDEN	41,79
. SAMUEL	91-92	SLATER,MARTHA LAMB	47	. WEEDMAN MCCAWLEY	72
. SUSANNAH	92	THOMAS M.	47	. WEEDON	22
SINKER,BROOKS	29	SLAUGHTER,MARY	36	SLEMON,CHRISTIAN	137
CATEY	29	. REBECCA	31	SLETT,JAMES	25
SIRUS,FRANCES	16	. ROBERT	62,74,139	JOHN	47
SISK,ELIZABETH	21	. ROGER	48	SLIFER,DAISY	104
. MARTIN	23	. THOMAS	63	SMALL,OLIVER	56
. NELLY	23	SLAYOR,FRANCIS	43	SMATTS,BETSY	20
SISON,BRIANT	139	SLAYTER,ROBERT	142-143	SMILEY,ESTEN NORWELL	6

INDEX to
Orange County, VA FAMILIES - Vol. #2

Name	Page	Name	Page	Name	Page
. ESTIN NORWELL	3	. ELIZABETH LUGGETT	1	. LUCY	4
. WILLIAM	3,6	. ELIZABETH WARREN	10	. LYDIA LANE	130
SMITH, ABRAHAM	56	. EMILY	47	. MARGARET	56
. ABSALOM	63,86	. FRANCES	19,49	. MARTHA	41
. ABSOLEM	8,28	. FRANCES	-	. MARTHA MCNIEL	28
. ABSOLOM	24	. STUBBLEFIELD	43	. MARY	10,56,74
. AGNES	1,38	. FRANCES WINSLOW	41	. MARY C.	100
. AMBROSE	145	. GEORGE	1,10,26,31,49	. MARY C. PORTER	22
. ANN	6	.	63,79,136,138,141,144	. MATHEW	135
. ANN CONNER	4	.	145-146	. MATHIAS	28
. ANN CONNERS	6	. HENRY	10,56	. MATHUAS	140
. AUGUSTINE	74	. ISAAC	75,135	. MATILDA BICKERS	28
. BENJAMIN	39	. J.W.R.	120	. MAY HULDA BELL	35
. BLESSING STEVENS	2	. JAMES	3,5,18,21,26,31	. MICHAEL	135
. BRADFORD	36	.	35,79	. MICHALE	140
. CATHERINE	5,49,79	. JANE	3,5,47,74	. MILDRED	21
. CATY	31	. JANE MORTON	9	. NANCY	13,29
. CATY SMITH	31	. JANE SMITH	3,5	. NANCY JACOBS	36
. CHARLES	9,79,144,146	. JEAN	56	. NANCY MORRIS	29
. CHARLES I.K.	146	. JEREMIAH	19,63	. NANCY SUTTON	21
. COLBY	21	. JOHN	3,5,10,15,19,21	. OSWALD	23
. DANIEL	56	.	27,29,56,62,66,70,74	. OWEN	39,141-142,147
. DANIEL M.	43	.	136,138,145	. PATSY	20
. DEALEM	33	. JOICE QUISENBERRY	23	. PATTY	22
. DELIA	18	. JOSEPH	9,17,56,63,72	. PATTY CLEAVELAND	3
. DOLLY JAMERSON	39	.	74,79-80,130	. PATTY CLEVELAND	5
. DORCAS DOUGLAS	2	. JOSTPHONICA	136	. PHILIP	28
. DORCAS DOUGLASS	5	. JUSTINE CHANDLER	8	. POLLY	17,22
. DUDLEY	44	. JUSTPHONICA	63	. POLLY CAVE	49
. EDWARD	11,36,142-144	. KATHERINE	2	. PRESLEY	41
. ELIAS	135	. LUCH MALLORY	35	. RAIF	22
. ELIZABETH	2,4,7,19,24	. LUCINDA	9	. RAIFE	19
.	56	. LUCINDA SMITH	9	. REBECCA H.	27

INDEX to
Orange County, VA FAMILIES - Vol. #2

. REES	74	. MARTHA McSHAMROCK	18	. MARY	18,28,43
. REUBEN	79	. NANCY	27	. MARY P. MALLORY	48
. ROBERT	4,6	. REBECCA MALONE	29	. POLLY	48
. ROSE WARREN	11	SNAYMAN,DOROTHY	105	. POLLY MAYHUGH	20
. SALLY BESS	36	SNELL,ANNIE WHITE	45	. RANEY	48
. SALLY KENDALL	21	. CATY	17	. SARAH	34
. SALLY TAYLOR	130	. CATY A.	22	SNYDER,PATSY	44
. SAMUEL	2,5,13,136,138	. EASTHAM	13	. SARAH JENKINS	45
. SARA	26	. ELIZ. C. MANSFIELD	30	. WILLIAM	45
. STEPHEN	2,141,144,146	. ELIZABETH MILLER	15	SOLESTER,TENBY	137
. STEPHEN I.K.	144	. JOHN	34,81,140,143	SOMMERVILLE,HARRISON	47
. SUKEY	19	. JOSEPH	15,30,45	NANCY SLEET	47
. SUKEY SMITH	19	. MARGARET	34	SONG,JOHN	11
. SUSANNA LANCASTER	44	. PATTY	3,6	SORREL,THOMAS	138
. SUSANNAH	34	. PHILADELPHIA	25	SORRELLE,ELIZABETH	48
. TARTAN	35	. PHILMON	78	SORRILL,MARIA	45
. TEMPLE	130	. ROBERT	22,25	THOMAS	45
. THOMAS	49,123	SNIDER,HENRY	135	SORRILLE,THOMAS	35,47-48
. USILLA	13	SNOW,AGGY E. MALLORY	40	VIRGINIA	48
. WILLIAM	9,22,29,56,63	. AGNES	31	SORRILLS,JOHN N.	47
	67,126-127,136-137	. AUGUSTINE	40	SARAH A. STANARD	47
	139,141	. BERD	20	SOUTHERLAND,	125
SMITHE,ROBERT	146	. BYRD	43	. JOHN	48
SMITHERS,		. EARLY	48	. MARY JOHNSON	48
SUSANNAH SINGLETON	92	. ELIZABETH LOWER	23	. NANCY	48
SMITHEY,IDA	98	. HOLLAND	39	. WILLIAM	48
SMONTS,JOHN	22	. JAMES	29,37	SOWELL,THOMAS	124-125
POLLY FLEEK	22	. JENNY	19,132	SOYELL,	124
SMOOT,CABEL	18,21,27	. JENNY HARVY	29	SPALDING,BESSIE	103
. JAMES	18	. JOHN	23,48,66	. CHARLES	103
. JENIFER	29	. JUDITH	39	. ELMA	104
. JOHN	30	. JUDITH MALLORY	39	. FANNY JONES	12
. LUCY THORNTON	30	. LUCY	37	. LEONA PECK	103

260

INDEX to
Orange County, VA FAMILIES - Vol. #2

. LORAINE MCCOUGHEY	103	. SARAH	78	. WILLIAM H.	21
. MARY C. BROCKMAN	104	. SARAH J.	121	STANTON, ANN	12
. MARY E. FRANKLIN	103	SPINCER, ANN THORNTON	14	. BETTY	11
. RICHARD G.	103	SETH	14	. CHRISTY	13
. ROBERTSON	12	SPINKS, WILLIAM	116	. DELILAH	3
. ROSCOE H.	103	SPOTSWOOD,	145-146	. ELIZABETH	23,56,75
SPARKS, HENRY	135	. ALEXANDER	139	. JANE	75
ZACKARIAS	136	. JOHN	85-86	. JEMIMAH	11
SPEAR, WILLIAM	142,144	. MARY	17	. MARY	75
SPEERS, ELIZABETH	22	. ROBERT	25	. MATHEW	56,136
SPENCE, MARY	100	. SUSANNAH	25	. SALLY	13
MARY C.	101	. T.	17	. SALLY POWELL	15
SPENCER,	142,145	SPOTTSWOOD,	145	. SARAH	75
. ANN	12	SPRADLIN,		. SPENCER	15
. CAROLINE	1	. ELIZABETH FOSTER	21	. THOMAS	75,135,139-140
. EDWARD	12,62-63,74,76	. JOHN	21	. WILLIAM	75-76
	77,139,141,143	SPRADLING, DAVID	9	STAP, ANESTER	117
. ELEANOR WOOLFOLK	12	NANCY	9,20	STAPP, ACHILLES	9
. FRANCES	14	SPRIGGS, EBENEZER	28	. BETSY BARBAGE	7
. JOSEPH	12,70-71,80,132	MIMA SANFORD	28	. MARGARET VAWTER	9
. WINIFRED	2,5	ST. LEGER,	89	. MARGARET WAWTER	9
. WINTIFRED GEORGE	14	. ANNE PLANTAGNET	89	. THOMAS	7
SPENSER,	136	. JOHN	87	STAUNTON, BEVERLY	11
SPICER, BENJAMIN	22,78	. THOMAS	89	. DELIAH	6
. CATHERINE BROCKMAN	159	STAGE, DAVID HARREL	4	. JEMIMAH STANTON	11
. CATY A. SNELL	22	. DAVID R.	6	. MARY	75
. DABNEY	159	. MARYAN MOONEY	4,6	. SARAH	75
. EDWARD	146	STANARD, JAMES	136	. THOMAS	75
. JOSEPH	78	. SARAH A.	47	STEELE, MARY MCQUIDDY	11
. LUCY ELLEN	78	. WILLIAM H.	47	SAMUEL	11
. NANCY WOOD	16	STANIS,	66	STEELEY, PAULINE	104
. RAWSEN	78	STANNARD, MADAM	137	STEP, ABRAHAM	117
. RAWSER	16	. MARY	126	. ANESTER	117

INDEX to Orange County, VA FAMILIES - Vol. #2

Name	Page(s)
. DOROTHY	117
. JOSEPH	74
. JOSHUA	77,117
STEPHENS, AGNES NELSON	22
. AGNES ROBINSON	20
. ANN S.	30
. BENJAMIN	22
. CHARLES	136
. EDMUND	20,22
. ELIZABETH	126
. ELIZABETH NELSON	27
. JAMES	136
. JOHN	30,136,142
. JOSEPH	19,85,144
. LUCY	49
. NANCY	4
. NEWTON	45
. SUSANNA WHITE	45
. WILLIAM	27,136,144
STEPHENSON, CHARLES	33
. SUSAN HANCOCK	33
. WILLIAM	56
STEPP, JAMES	146
JOSHAWAY	145
STETT, JAMES	15
STEVENS,	66,86
. ANN	19
. ANN GRIGRY	28
. ANN S. STEPHENS	30
. BENJAMIN	29
. BETSY PETTY	41
. BLESSING	2
. CHARLES	130,137
. DISNEY GAINES	18
. EDWARD	41
. ELIZ.	28
. ELIZA	49
. ELIZA ANN BALL	46
. ELIZABETH	130,132
. GEORGE	46
. JAMES	18,63
. JOHN	10,30,63,84,135, 143-144,146
. LUCY ADAMS	24
. MARGARET MILLS	24
. MARY	29
. MERRYMAN	28
. SALLY	10
. SARAH	132
. SARAH MONTAGUE	84
. WALLER	24
. WILLIAM	24,132,139
. WILLIAMS	138
STEVENSON, DAVID	56
. JAMES	56
. JANE	56
. JOHN	17,56
. MARY	56
. MILLY PAYNE	17
. SARAH	56
. THOMAS	56,72
. WILLIAM	56
STEVINSON, NANCY	20
STEWARD,	
. CATHERINE REYNOLDS	34
. GEORGE	136
. JOHN	34
STEWART, GEORGE	56
JOHN	77
STOCKDELL, AMY	4
. ANN	4
. DELPHIA ROSZELL	16
. JOHN	11,56,78
. SALLY DUVALL	11
. WILLIAM	16
STOCKS, MARY	11
THOMAS	11
STODGHILL, ANN	76
JAMES	76
STODGILL, JOEL	81
STOGDALL, ROBERT	85
STOGDHILL, JAMES	137
STOGDILL, ANN	135
STOKES, ELIZABETH	56
. LUCY SILVEY	20
. WILLIAM	20
STONE, ELIZABETH	46
. ELIZABETH BURTON	22
. HENRY	11,47
. JOHN	22,27,135
. JUDITH PARROT	27
. NANCY GOLDEN	11
. POLLY MITCHELL	47
. WILLIAM	135,140
STONEHOUSE, ANNA	130
WALTER	130
STORY, JOHN	76
THOMAS	76
STOVER, JACOB	75

INDEX to
Orange County, VA FAMILIES - Vol. #2

Name	Page	Name	Page	Name	Page
MARGARET	75	. SARAH	83	SUGGETT, JAMES	63
STOW, BETSY	20	. SARAH WILLIAMS	31	KATHERINE	127-128
STOWERS, BETSY	32	. SUSAN	1,11	SULLING, MILLIE	1
. JOHN	26	. SUSANNA	1	SULLIVAN, DAWSON	41
. JOICE SHIFFLET	12	. WILLIAM	3,5,69,146	. DELILA	31
. LEWIS	12-13	. WILLIAM D.	72,82	. EVERET	48
. MACK	26	STROW,		. LUCY PAYNE	41
. MARGARET JACKSON	34	. CATHERINE WALTERS	24	. MARG.	14
. MARK	32,34,135	. JOHN	24	. NANCY DEAN	48
. MARY	13	STUART, ALEXANDER	19	. WILLIAM	31
. PATTY	13	. ANN REID	19	SURRY, CATY	20
. REBECCA LINDSAY	44	. CHARLES	165	SUTHERLAND, ALEXANDER	40
. REUBIN	34	. DAVID	165	. BETSY	16
. SALLY HERNDON	26	. FRANCES DADE	165	. JOSEPH	16
. WINSTON	44	. HELEN WRAY	165	. KENNETH	13,66
STRAGHAM, MARY SANDERS	9	. JACOB WRAY	165	. POLLY	38,40
STRAGHN, NANCY	30	. JANE GIBBON	165	. RUTH WEBSTER	13
STRINGFELLOW,		. MARGARET	165	. WILLIAM	56
. MARY PLUNKETT	38	. MARY ASHTON	165	SUTTON, ALICE BROWN	3,5
. ROBERT	38	. ROBERT	19	. CATHERINE	17
STROMSON, JOSEPH	20	STUBBLEFIELD,		. ELIZABETH	14
STROTHER,		. ANN HAWKINS	15	. JAMES	66,84
. ANN CAVANAUGH	130	. ELIZABETH	17	. JOHN	66,84,137
. ANN KAVANAUGH	5	. FRANCES	43	. NANCY	21
. ANN KAVENAUGH	3	. GEORGE	3,5,15,17,37,43	. SAMUEL	72,80,143-144
. ANTHONY	75,83,135,140	.	63	.	146
. ELIZABETH	76	. MARY	37	. WILLIAM	3,5,14,21,72
. GEORGE F.	31	. ROBERT	63,86	.	80,84
. JEREMIAH	84	. SARAH MORRISON	3,5	SWAN, CATHERINE	29
. M.	139	STUBBLING, SUSANNA	29	SWARTSWELDER,	
. MARY	3	STUBBS,	119-120	. NANCY SEBREE	40
. POLLY	30	STYERS, ELIZABETH WOLF	23	. WILLIAM	40
. SAM FRANK	83	LEONARD	23	SWEARINHAM, THOMAS	63

INDEX to
Orange County, VA FAMILIES - Vol. #2

SWEENEY,	133	. LAURENCE	8-9	. MARY ADAMS	18
SWENEY, DANIEL	15	. LAW.	69	. NANCY	14
MARY GRIFFITH	15	. LAWRENCE	44,64,69,73	. ROGER	14
SWINDELL, JOEL S.	46	.	80,82,146	. ROGERS	18
. JOSEPH	46	. LEWIS	27	. SARA MILLS	33
. MARY ANDERSON	46	. LUCY	2,4	TANER, CHRISTOPHER	140
SWISER,		. LUCY THURSTON	15	TARKEY, JOHN	158
. CHRISTINE BANKER	47	. MARIA BARBOUR	47	LYDIA	158
. DAVID	47	. MARTHA	31	TARVER, EVA EDNA	114
SYKES, FRAN	78	. MARY	73	TATE, JOSHUA	26
SYLVA, GEORGE	19	. MATILDA	10	. NANCY	13
LUCY POE	19	. NICHOLAS	8	. URIAH	13
TABATHA, ROBERT	16	. RAY	64	TATUM, NANCY EVENS	18
TALBIRD, JOHN	145	. RICHARD	47	. THOMAS	18
JOSEPH	145	. SAM	135	. WILLIAM	30
TALIAFERRO,	141,145-146	. SARAH	8,44	TAYLOR,	144,146
. AMY STOCKDELL	4	. SUSANNAH CONWAY	20	. AARON	148
. ANN	8-9,14,31	. VIRLINDA	34	. ABSOLEM	19
. ANN STOCKDELL	4	. WILLIAM	24,63,73,84	. AGNES	12
. ANN TALIAFERRO	8	.	141-142,144-145,147	. ALICE	80
. BALDWIN	40	TALIFERRO, ANN	37	. ALICE CHEW	1,125
. CATY	18	TALIVER, M.	138	. ANN	22
. CRAIG	5	TALLIFEAVERS, JOHN	138	. ANN STANTON	12
. ELIZ.	27	TAMKERSLEY, CHARLES	145	. BETSY	159
. ELIZA CHEWNING	44	TANDIE,	117	. CHAPMAN	11,72,80
. ELIZABTH	24	TANDY,	92	. CHARLES	12,23-24,30,40
. FRANCES	73	. ANN MILLS	12	.	66
. FRANCIS	8,10,73	. ANNA	33	. DELIAH STAUNTON	6
.	144-145	. BETSY ADAMS	19	. DELILAH STANTON	3
. HAY	15,20,31,44,69	. FRANCES	124	. DILLA WALKER	18
. JOHN	4,37,73,138	. HENRY	12,19,33	. DOROTHEA	86
.	141-142	. JACKSON	30,33	. DOROTHY	13
. JOHN S.	47	. MARY	12	. EARCEY	137

INDEX to
Orange County, VA FAMILIES - Vol. #2

. EDMUND	144	. JOHN	9,18,29,77,107	. ZACHARIAH	1,13,16,66
. ELIJAH	18	.	130,159	. ZACHARY	125,138
. ELIZABETH	4,6,11,23,44	. JONATHAN	28,64	. ZACKARY	64,75,78,144
	74,86,139	. LARKIN	32	TEAL, EDWARD	139
. ELIZABETH	-	. LIZA MCDANIEL	28	PEGGY	42
	CAVANAUGH 130	. LUCINDA	36,49	TEALE, HENRY	30
. ELIZABETH HUME	32	. LUCY	11	SARAH	30
. ELIZABETH KAVANAUGH	9	. M.	138	TEARNEHAUGH, THOMAS	7
. ELIZABETH PEARSON	18	. MARGARET	13	TEATER, GEORGE	75
. ELIZABETH STANTON	23	. MARTHA	24,146	MARY	75
. ELIZABETH THOMPSON	12	. MARY	11,25,42,72,77,80	TEEL, DICY REED	37
. ELIZABETH WALKER	13	. MARY C.	30	HENRY	25,37
. ERAMUS	144	. MARY C. TAYLOR	30	TELL, JOHN	42
. ERASMER	75	. MARY JARRELL	9	NANCY WAUGH	42
. ERASMUS	11,146	. MILLY	2,5	TEMPLE, JOHN	2,5
. EVELINA	49	. NANCY CROSTHWAIT	148	. MARY A. CANTERBERRY	5
. FANNY KING	33	. NANNA ANDERSON	22	. MARY CANTERBURY	2
. FRANCES	7	. PHILIP	80	TEMPLEMAN, BRYCE O.	132
. FRANCES BROCKMAN	159	. REBECCA MOORE	9	TENNER, GEORGE	135
. FRANCES MOOORE	18	. REUBEN	9,64,86	ROBERT	135
. FRANCES SMITH	19	. RICHARD	72,80	TERMAN, WILLY	16
. FRANCIS	12,16,65-66	. ROBERT	7,30,33,49	TERRELL, CATY MILLER	17
. FRANKY	159	. SALLY	130	. CATY THOMPSON	33
. GEORGE	12,63,84,87	. SALLY WOOD	24	. EDMUND	34
	137-138,144	. SARAH	7,20,24,125	. EDWARD	17
. HARRIET	40	. SARAH BURNLEY	29	. ELIZABETH	15
. JAMES	3,6,11,14,17-18	. SARY HUNT	14	. HANNER	57
.	22,24-25,42,63-64,70	. ST. CLAIR	36	. HENRY C.	33
.	77,86-87,133,138,144	. STANTON	23	. JANE	17
.	146,159	. SUSANNA GERRELL	16	. JANE MORTON	16
. JANE	16	. SUSANNAH GIBSON	18	. JOHN	17
. JEMIMAH	148	. WILLIAM	13,18,24,29,44	. JONATHAN	136
. JENNINGS	148	.	74,76,86,136	. MILLIE WALKER	1

INDEX to
Orange County, VA FAMILIES - Vol. #2

. OLIVER	34	. EDWARD	72	THACWEL, SARAH	25
. PEGGY	14	. ELIZABETH	18,45	THAFOLUS, EDDINA	136
. REUBEN	1	. FANNY	72,81-82	THARP, THOMAS	142
. REUBIN	29	. FRANCES	36	THEATON, JAMES	138
. ROBERT	136,139	. JAMES	36,72,82	THOMAS,	141
. SARAH	14	. JANE	42,81	. AGATHA	127
. SUSANNA MORTON	29	. JOHN	21,36,45,48,85	. AGNES	126-127
. SUSANNAH SMITH	34	. LUCY	72,81-82	. ANN MOORE	1
. WILLIAM	15-16	. MILLIE WALKER	1	. ANN SPENCER	12
TERRET, NATHANIEL	57	. NANCY	26,48,72,81-82	. BARBOUR	11
TERRETT,		. OLIVER	13	. BETSY BEAZEY	25
. ALICE GILLESPIE	164	. PEGGY WILLIS	1	. CATHERINE	2,77
.	165	. REUBEN	26	. CHARLES	64
. AMELIA HUNTER	165	. REUBIN	26,36	. EDWARD	42,71,77,84
. CATHERINE	166	. ROBERT	21,46,72,81-82	. ELIZABETH	8,15,126,141
. GEORGE H.	164	.	146	. ELIZABETH KENNER	126
. GEORGE HUNTER	164-166	. SALLY	36	. ELIZABETH WOOLFOLK	4,7
. HANNAH B. ASHTON	165	. SARAH	46,81	. FRANCES	15,45
. LOUISE FRANCIS	164	. SUSAN GRASTY	45	. FRANKIE	6
. MARGARET PEARSON	165	. SUSAN MIDDLEBROOK	36	. FRANKY	4
. MARGARET STUART	165	. SUSANNAH MALLORY	13	. GEORGE	139
. MARGUERITE	164,166	. WILLIAM	8,28,84,135	. HENRY	42
. MARGUERITE TERRETT	165	. ZACHARIAH	1	. HENRY WOOD	42
. THOMAS	166	TERRY, CHAMP	69	. JAMES	45,126-127
. W.H.	165	. JOHN	18	. JANE THRUSTON	1
TERRILL, ANN DANIEL	8	. LUCY OAKS	18	. JOHN	36,73,76,80
. ANN MALLORY	21	. OVERTON	32	.	136-137,143
. ANN QUARLES	21	. SARAH	34	. JOSEPH	8-9,11,25,64,66
. ANN T. MORTON	37	. SARAH GARNETT	32	.	84,144-147
. ARCHIBALD	18	TETER, GEORGE	135	. JOSHUA	56
. CATY GAINES	26	THACKER,		. M. RICHARD	138
. E.	81	. FRANCES TERRILL	36	. MARTIN	32,34
. EDMUND	1,37,72,81-82	. HENRY	36	. MARY	1-2,5,11

266

INDEX to
Orange County, VA FAMILIES - Vol. #2

. MARY TAYLOR	11	. FRANCES	126	. HUGH	63
. MILDRED	127	. FRANCES ROBINSON	33	. ISABELLE	57
. OWEN	77,126-127,147	. GEORGE	21,31,57,135	. JAMES	146
. POLLY SMITH	17	. ISAAC	57	. JOHN	56,73
. REUBEN	12	. JANE	57	. RHODES	7
. RICHARD	63,70,73,77,84	. JANE MCNEAL	18	. ROBERT	57
	87,137-138,144	. JOEL	12,20	. SALLY VIVION	7
. ROBERT	1,17,63-64,84	. JOHN	18,23,33,57	. WILLIAM	57,75
	86,143-144,146	.	123-124	THORNE, BRYAN	139
. ROLAND	1	. JULIA PIERCE	33	THORNELL, JOSEPH	136
. ROWLAND	63-64,77-78,84	. LUCY	18	THORNHILL, ELIZABETH	25
.	146	. MARIA ELLIS	45	NANCY	29
. SALLY	4	. MARTHA	24	THORNSBERRY,	
. SALLY ELLIS	36	. MARY	18,57	. BLANCH REED	104
. SARAH	76	. MOSES	57	. HARRY ELMO	104
. SARAH KENNER	126-127	. OMY	57	. HENRY RAY	104
. WILLIAM	4,7,64	. REBECCA ELLIS	29	. JAMES CLINTON	105
THOMPSON,		. ROBERT	57	. LAURA BROCKMAN	104
. ACQUILES BREEDING	10	. SALLY	23	. LULA	104
. ALEXANDER	57	. SALLY LINDSAY	24	. MABEL E.	104
. ANN	4,7,21	. SAMUEL	24,72,82,147	. OPAL CLARK	104
. BENJAMIN	139	. SARAH	9,20	. PAULINE STEELEY	104
. CATEY SINKER	29	. SARAH POINDEXTER	123	. PERRY	105
. CATHERINE	18	.	124	. RALPH F.	104
. CATY	33	. SARAH THOMPSON	20	. ROBERT E.	104
. DALE M.	130	. SUSAN POINDEXTER	124	. RUTH CAMPBELL	105
. DANE M.	131	. SUSANNAH	19	. SUSAN M.	105
. DAVID	10,45,67	. THOMAS	33,57	THORNTON, ANN	14,21
. DOROTHY BROWN	131	. WILLIAM	10,29,57,63	.	141-142
. ELIZ.	46	.	135	. ANN BOHON	10
. ELIZABETH	12,20,25,37	. WILLIAM T.	18	. ANTHONY	41
. ELIZABETH BROCKMAN	10	. WINNEY	31	. CABEL	15
. FANNY	30	THOMSON, BENJAMIN	135	. CHARLES	31

INDEX to
Orange County, VA FAMILIES - Vol. #2

. DANIEL	84,145-146	.	145-146	TIMBERLAKE,MARGARET	48
. ELIZABETH WRIGHT	32	THORP,THOMAS	146	TIMMINS,ALEXANDER	56
. FRANCIS	139	THORPE,PEGGY	11	TIMMONS,ALEXANDER	51
. FRANKIE	6	THRIFT,		TINDAR,JAMES	10
. FRANKY	3	. MARGARET BURTON	39	. MARGARET	6
. GEORGE	23,26,30,83	. ROBERT	39	. MOLLY SHADRICK	10
. HENRY	74	THRUSTON,ANN	72	TINDER,ALEAPER ABELL	11
. JAMES	72,82,136,138	. JANE	1	. ANTHONY	44
.	146	. LUCY TALIAFERRO	2	. BENJAMIN	26
. JANEY	72	. WM. PLUMER	2	. ELIZABETH SHADRACK	44
. JEMIMA	73	THURMAN,NATHAN	19	. EPHRIAM	42
. JENNY	82	TABITHA LOWRY	19	. FRANCES SHADRACK	48
. JEREMIAH	82	THURNSTON,		. JAMES	14,44
. JESSE	10,66	. LUCY TALIAFERRO	4	. JEMIMAH	42
. JOHN	73	. WILLIAM P.	4	. JESSE	11
. LUCY	30	THURSION,JAMES	138	. JESSIE	42
. LUKE	22,73,136,138-139	THURSTEIN,ANN	81	. JOHN	48
.	141-142,145,147	THURSTON,JAMES	75,138	. MARGARET	4
. MARK	137	. LUCY	15	. NANCY MASON	50
. MARTHA OGG	31	. SARAH	57	. NANCY TERRILL	26
. MARY MILLER	25	TIBBIT,MATTHEW	57	. THOMAS	50
. MILICENT	73	TIEDT,JAMES CLIFFORD	115	TINSLEY,BETTY	7
. NANCY	82	. JOHN EDWARD	115	. CHARLES	142
. NANCY TWYMAN	41	. JOYCE M. ROBERTSON	115	. EDWARD	138,144,146
. NANCY WEBB	23	. REBA M. GOTELLUS	115	. ISAAC	135
. PATSY FORD	15	TILLEY,JOHN	143	. JOHN	7
. PETER	25	. LAZARUS	137	. WILLIAM	31,38
. PRESLEY	147	. MARGARET	142,144	TIPPETT,LAVINIA	16
. ROSA	72,82	. SAG.	136	SAMUEL	16
. SARAH	72,82	TILLY,LAZARRIS	146	TIRRILL,JONATHAN	139
. SARAH SLEET	22	. LAZARUS	75	TODD,	138
. THOMAS	32,40	. MARGARET	75,143	. CATHERINE WINSLOW	27
. WILLIAM	66,72,80,84	. MARGRET	141	. RICHARD	144,146

INDEX to
Orange County, VA FAMILIES - Vol. #2

Name	Page	Name	Page	Name	Page
. WILLIAM	27	TRIBBLE, FOSTER	158	. CARY	21
TOLD,	137	MARY	158	. CATEY BROWN	11
TOLES, JOHN	136	TRICE, JESSE	37	. CLARY	21
TOMLIN, SALLY	163	LIDDIA ARNETT	37	. DELPHY	25
TOMLINSON,		TRIMBLE, ANN	57	. ELISHA	34, 49
. ELIZABETH WHITE	11	. JOHN	57	. EZEKIAL	25
. GEORGE	11	. MARGARET	57	. FLEMING	32
. JOHN	7	. MARY	57	. HENRY	140
. MILDRED WHITE	7	TRIPLET, WILLIAM	73	. JAMES	27
. SALLY	18	TROWER, NANCY SMITH	29	. JANE CLARK	32
. WILLIAM	18	SOLOMON	29	. JOHN	14, 67
TOMSON, WILLIAM	139	TRUE, DELILA	27	. MARY SEAL	34
TOONE, LEWIS	146	. SUSANNA MURPHY	25	. MILLY	30
TORRANCE, CLORINDA	112	. THOMAS	25	. NANCY	21
. CLORINDA SLEEPER	112	TRUEMAN, GEORGE	79	. NATHAN	136, 138
. ROBERT L.	112	IGNATIUS	72, 79	. POLLY	19
TOWER, ANN GIBBONS	36	TUBUFIELD, EDWARD	76	. POLLY GOODALL	49
MITCHEL	36	SARAH	76	. ROBERT	75
TOWLES, JANE WHARTON	76	TUCKER, BETSY BIGGERS	32	. SALLY CHISSAM	25
. JOSEPH	144, 146	. MARY MERRY	126-127	. SARAH FITZGARRELL	14
. MARY	129	. THORNTON	32	. SARAH LOYD	27
. STOKELEY	76	TULLOCH,		. THOMAS	11, 141
TOWNSEN, JAMES	143	. NANCY WHITELAW	30	. ZEPH	47
TOWNSEND, ELIZABETH	11	. WILLIAM	30	TURNLEY, FRANCES	14
. JERUSA	6	TUNLEY, JOHN	38	. JOHN	35
. MARTHA	3	TURK, ANN	57	. PATSY POUND	35
TOWSEND, JAMES	140	. JANE	57	. SUSANNA WATTS	14
TRACEY, JOHN	84	. JOHN	57	TURTON, MARY	32
MARY	84	. MARGARET	57	TUTMAN, ELIZABETH	43
TRASEY, JOHN	66	. ROBERT	57	JOHN	43
TRAVERS, WILLIAM	133	. THOMAS	57	TWENTYMAN, BENONE	82
TREASLEY, MARY	9	. WILLIAM	57	. BERYMAN	83
TREPP, MARTIN	135	TURNER, ANN	19, 21	. BETSY	12

INDEX to
Orange County, VA FAMILIES - Vol. #2

. BONONIA	14	MARY	57	. HERMAN	66
. ELIZABETH NUTLY	14	VALLICK, MARTIN	73	. MALINDA	44
. POLLY	10	VANCE, DAVID	64	. MARGARET	9
TWYMAN, ANTHONY	25,30	VASE, FRANCIS LEE	39	. MARY	9,37
. DRUCILLA COWHERD	25	WALKER	39	. MARY RUCKER	10
. ELIZABETH MALONE	47	VASS, ELIZABETH MANNING	9	. WILLIAM	2,5,10,25,67
. EMALINE	45	. MARY SPOTSWOOD	17	.	80
. FRANCES	38	. NICHOLAS	17	. WILLILAM	67
. JOHN	33	. VINCENT	9	. WINIFRED	5
. JONATHAN	49	VATTERTON, MARY	44	VEACH, LANDER	11
. JUDITH	37	VAUGHAN, JOSEPH	21	PEGGY THORPE	11
. LUCY RUCKER	49	. NANCY TURNER	21	VEALCH, JOHN	32
. NANCY	41	. WALTER	135	NANCY COOPER	32
. PASCAL	47	VAUGHN, BELINDA	43	VERDIER, MARIA	37
. PEGGY WAYT	33	. CHARLES	44	PAUL	37
. REUBIN	25,34	. ELIZA DEAN	42	VERNON, ISAAC	28
. SARAH COLEMAN	45	. ELIZABETH	19	. NANCY PATTERSON	28
. SARAH DAVIS	30	. ELIZABETH CLAYTER	44	. RICHARD	144
. THORNEL	45	. JAMES	16	VIA, JONATHAN	46
TYLER, ABSALOM	19	. JOSEPH	19,42-44	. LIVINIA GARRISON	46
. JANE T. SCOTT	42	. LUCY	44	. MARY ELIZABETH	46
. MARY ANN HOMDON	26	. MAHALA	158	. MARY ELIZABETH VIA	46
. RICHARD	42	. NANCY	16	. NANCY CRAIG	44
. WILLIAM	26	. WALTER	135	. REUBIN	46
TYREE, JOHN	44	VAUS, ELIZABETH	90	. SARAH	40
NANCY LINDSAY	44	JOHN	90	VICKORY, HEZEKIAH	74
TYRRELL,	130	VAUTER, DAVID	80	MERCIO	74
UNDERWOOD, DANIEL	138	WILLIAM	80	VIDIER, PAUL	28
. GEORGE	139	VAWTER, ANN BALLARD	2,5	VINEYARD, JOHN	57
. GIDION	14	. BENJAMIN	37,44,46	VINNIARD, ALEXANDER	35
. JOHN	136,139,141	. DAVID	80	POLLY HENSLEY	35
URQUART, CHARLES	19	. ELIZABETH	25	VIRDIER, JAMES	43
UXTON, HENRY	57	. ELIZABETH BELL	46	VIVIAN, JOHN	81,143,145

INDEX to
Orange County, VA FAMILIES - Vol. #2

Name	Page	Name	Page	Name	Page
VIVION, FRANCES	7	. ELIZABETH	13,19,21,73	. NANCY	23
. JANE	13	.	82	. RICHARD	104
. JOHN	7,138,144	. ELIZABETH HENSHAW	42	WALLER, ANN	125
. SALLY	7	. ETTA BELLE	93	. ELIZABETH	46
VOSS, MARY SPOTSWOOD	17	. FRANCES ANDERSON	41	. ELIZABETH ATKINS	39
NICHOLAS	17	. FRANCES PORTER	38	. JAMES	39,46
VOUGHT,		. JAMES	38,64,71,79,90	. JUDITH	45
. CATHERINE MARGARET	57	.	144	. MARY	105
. JOHN ANDREW	57	. JOHN	38,42,57,70	WALLIS, GEORGE	41
. JOHN CASPER	57	.	127-128,138	. JOHN	31
. JOHN PAUL	57	. JOICE POWELL	38	. MARGARET	57
. MARY CATHERINE	57	. JOSEPH	146	. NANCY RANDEL	31
WADDELL, JAMES GORDON	20	. MAHALA	102,104	. SUSAN HILMAN	41
LUCY GORDON	20	. MARY	9	WALSH, JOSEPH	57
WADE, DORCAS	111	. MARY MERRY	127-128	. PATRICK	135
WAGGONER, CATY GAINES	2	. MILLIE	1	. THOMAS	145
. LUCINDA HANSFORD	30	. MISINIAH POWELL	9	WALTER, EDWARD	64
. RICHARD	2	. NANCY	50	WILLIAM	77
. WILLIAM G.	30	. PEACHY	42	WALTERS, CATHERINE	24
WAGONER,	67	. POLLY SIMS	18	. CHRISTOPHER	139
JAMES	144	. SANDERS	73	. ELIZABETH PENCE	31
WAIT, EDWARD	16	. SARAH	15	. GEORGE	23-24,26
. ELIZABETH	16	. TANNIE	19	. ISAAC	31
. LYDIA	27	. THOMAS	9,15,41,57,67	. JOHN	31
. PHOEBE	16	. 73,82,86,128,136,146		. MARG. HAMBLETON	31
WAITS, MILLY	18	. WILLIAM	87,127-128,145	. MITCHAEL	36
WALKER, ANN	3,5	WALLACE,		. NANCY HARVEY	23
. ANN MERRY	127-128	. BERNICE BROCKMAN	104	. SALLY MCFARLAND	36
. BENJAMIN	18,42	. ELIZABETH	24	WALTON, AGNES SNOW	31
. CHARLES	68	. ELIZABETH DAY	24	. ANN	21
. CLARA BROCKMAN	90	. HUMPHREY	57	. EDMUND P.	40
. DILLA	18	. JAMES	23-24,40	. ELIZABETH SPEERS	22
. EDWARD	137-138,144,146	. MOURNING OAKS	40	. FRANCIS	22

INDEX to
Orange County, VA FAMILIES - Vol. #2

. JOHN	36	WILLIAM	139	. JACOB	102,120
. LETICE WATSON	40	WATSON,ABNER	11,23	. JOHN	10,64
. RHODA DAVIS	36	. ANN	15	. JOHNSON	85
. SNOW	31	. BENJAMIN	49	. JOSEPH W.	2
WALTS,ED	138	. CATEY LAMB	23	. JULIUS	11
WARD,LUCY	12,72,81	. ELIZABETH	47	. MARGARET SAMPSON	48
PEGGY	72,81	. ELIZABETH DEAR	11	. MARY	120
WARDELL,CHARLES	16	. FRANCES JACOB	49	. MARY EVE	11
WARE,HENRY	135	. ISAAC	15,22-23	. MILLY	3,6
WARFIN,RICHARD	57	. JAMES	23	. NANCY	12
WARIN,WILLIAM	142	. JAMES B.	120	. NOAH	40
WARKIN,BETSY	43	. JANE	23	. RACHAEL FOSTER	2
WARNER,ANN WALKER	3,5	. JESSE	13	. ROBERT	66,85
. DANIEL	57	. JUDITH	32	. SARAH HEAD	33
. JOHN	3,5	. LETICE	40	. SUCKEY DAVIS	10
WARREN,ELIZABETH	10,16	. MAGGIE RHODES	121	. SUSANNA	14
.	21	. MARGARET	43	. SUSANNAH	2
. HANEY R.	21	. MILLY BALLARD	13	. THOMAS	33,135,139
. JOHN	10,68	. MILLY RHODES	120	. WILLIAM	7
. ROSE	11	. NANCY LONG	23	WAUGH,ALEXANDER	71,136
. THOMAS	143	. POLLY	20,32	.	138-139,141-142,145
WARRIN,WILLIAM	144	. SUSANNA ROBBARDS	22	.	146-147
WARRINER,JACOB	158	. WILLIAM	68,144	. ELIZABETH	42
. POLLY	158	WATTERS,		. ELIZABETH BOSTON	16
. WILLIS	158	. BELINDA BROOKING	45	. GEORGE	39,64,66,71,84
WASHINGTON	67	. JACOB	45	. GOREE	37
WASHINGTON,	66	WATTON,JANE	38	. GORIE	85
WATER,SHARLEY	136	WATTS,BENJAMIN	85	. MARGARET BROWN	9
WATKINS,FANNY MOSLEY	25	. CHARLES	68	. MARY	1
. ISHAM	17	. DAVID	68,143	. NANCY	42
. THOMAS	25	. EDWARD	135,146	. RICHARD	9
WATLEY,SHIRLEY	138	. ELIJAH D.	48	. SARA	39
WATS,THOMAS	139	. ELIZABETH BEASLEY	7	. SUSAN WRIGHT	37

INDEX to
Orange County, VA FAMILIES - Vol. #2

Name	Page
. WAUGH	16
WAWTER, MARGARET	9
MARY	9
WAYALDN, THOMAS	135
WAYLAND,	
. FRANCES MILLER	48
. HENRY	32,35
. JOSHUA	34
. JUDITH	34
. MARY	32
. MELONE ARA	35
. WILLIAM	48
WAYT, AMEY	34
. JOHN	29
. KISSY	43
. LUCY	29
. LYDIA	32
. MARY	11
. MARY ANN	39
. NANCY	36
. PEGGY	33
. WILLIAM	27,32-34,36,39
WEALCH, JOHN	32
NANCY COOPER	32
WEATHERALL, FRANCIS	14
WEATHERSPOON, JOHN	79,146
MARY	7
WEAVER, ANN LAMB	49
. PETER	57,137
. SAMUEL L.	49
WEBB, ANN	20
. ANN R.	46
. AUGUSTINE	46,71
. BENJAMIN	72,83
. CABEL	21
. CHARLES	81,91
. CUTHBERT	91
. ELIZABETH WALLER	46
. ELLIS	47
. FRANCES	91
. FRANCIS	13
. GARLAND	81
. HANNAH	12
. ISAAC	91
. JAMES	31
. JANE BUCKNER	9
. JANE VIVION	13
. JESSE B.	35,49,71,81
. JESSE BENNET	14
. JOHN	13-14,47
. JOHN C.	72,83
. JOSEPH	81
. JUDAH JONES	13
. JUDITH BLAKEY	47
. LEWIS	46
. LUCY WOODWARD	14
. MARGARET ATKINS	21
. MARGARET BADGER	47
. MARTHA LANCASTER	30
. MARY G.	36
. MARY M.	35
. MARY SAMPSON	46
. MAURICE	49
. MILDRED LANTOR	14
. NANCY	23
. NANCY CLARK	31
. PATSY SMITH	20
. PRISCILLA	91
. REBECCA	81
. REUBEN	23
. RICHARD	64
. RICHARD C.	20,64,71
. SARAH LEATHERS	10
. SARAH MASON	14,49
. SUSAN	48
. SUSANNAH	2,5
. VIVIAN	81
. VIVION JOHN	14
. WIATT	81
. WILLIAM	10,20-21,46,81
.	146
. WILLIAM B.	49
. WILLIAM BENNETT	30
. WILLIAM C.	9,13,20,69
.	72,81,83
. WINNY	91
WEBBER, ANTOINETTE	103
WEBSTER, ANDREW	13
. CHARITY	133
. CHARITY M.	133
. DANIEL	13
. HENRY	133
. HENRY H.	133
. JOHANNA	133
. RUTH	13
. SALLY	14
. USILLA SMITH	13
WELCH, ARCHIE	134
. CARRIE E. BLALUCK	134

INDEX to
Orange County, VA FAMILIES - Vol. #2

. CLARA	134	WHARTON,		. ELIZABETH TOWNSEND	11
. ELLA E.	134	. CATHERINE GEORGE	38	. FANNY	23,37,44
. JOHN	57	. JANE	72,76	. FELICIA	14
. MARIE	134	. JOSEPH	38	. FRANCES PLUNKETT	41
. PATRICK	57	. POLLY	20	. FRANCIS	120
. THELMA J.	114	. SALLY YOUNG	14	. FRANKEY	3
. THOMAS	147	. SAMUEL	39	. FRANKIE	6
WELL,WILLIAM C.	69	. SARA WAUGH	39	. HENRY	11,85
WELLS,		. THOMAS	72,76,136	. JAMES	37,41,45-46
. CHARLOTTE MARSHALL	29	.	138-139	. JEREMIAH	7,30,66,72-73
. ELIZABETH	27	. ZACHEUS	14	.	83
. FENNETTA REYNOLDS	17	WHATSON,JEREMIAH	141	. JERMIAH	72
. GEORGE	27	WHEATLEY,GEORGE	75	. JESSE	16
. JAMES	17	WHEELER,CATY CASH	26	. JOHN	14,17,19,23,27-28
. JOHN	136	. JESSE	26	.	37,42,57,69,72-73,83
. LEVI	29	. JOHN	57	.	120,129,137
. MARTIN	20	WHITE,AMBROSE	66,85	. JONATHAN	3,6,11
. MARY CLARK	17	. AMEY WAYT	34	. JOSEPH	73,79
. MARY HARVEY	14	. ANDERSON	43	. JUDITH TWYMAN	37
. NANCY SAMS	24	. ANN	19,119-120	. LUCH ADAMS	42
. RICHARD C.	68	. ANN WIDSOM	120	. LUCINDA HUCKSTEP	43
. SARAH MARSHALL	20	. ANNIE	45	. MARY	7,17,120
. THOMAS	17,145	. BENJAMIN	37,64	. MARY BROCKMAN	9
. WILLIAM	14,24	. CATY OLLIVER	9	. MILDRED	7
WELSH,BETSY MALLORY	34	. CONYEARS	120	. NANCY	16,33,46
. ELEY	2	. CONYERS	73	. NANCY MARTIN	3
. JAMES	64	. DANIEL	136	. NANCY WAYT	36
. JANE BRUCE	2	. EDWARD	145	. NANNEY MARTIN	6
. MARY MALLORY	36	. ELIZABETH	11,17,27,72	. NED	141
. NATHANIEL	34,36,43	.	83,132	. PETTY	27
. OLIVER	34	. ELIZABETH HARRIS	49	. POLLY	28
. SAMUEL	2	. ELIZABETH LONG	12	. RICHARD	9,11,33-34,36
. VIRANDY NEWMAN	43	. ELIZABETH MARTIN	16	.	44,64,70,72,83,89

INDEX to
Orange County, VA FAMILIES - Vol. #2

. SARAH	4,30,120	. SUKEY EDMONSON	84	. JACOB	11,16,21,42-43		
. SUSAN SCRIVNER	45	. THOMAS	84	.	67		
. SUSANNA	45	WIDSOM,ANN	120	. JAMES	18,23-24,31,40		
. THEODOSIA	120	WIGGLESWORTH,ELIZ.	124	. JOHN	4,7,17,20,34,38		
. THOMAS	12,16,70,73,79	. JOSEPH	37	.	44,66-67,141-142,145		
	83,120,144	. MARY REYNOLDS	37	.	146		
. WILLIAM	7,9,17,45-46	. WILLIAM	37	. JOSEPH	41,142,145-146		
.	49,72-73,83,85,135	WILBOR,	86	. LEN.	143		
. WILLIE	27	WILEY,DAVID	76	. LUCINDA COLYER	43		
. WILLIS	36,41	JANE	76	. LUCY	49		
. WINSTON	49	WILHITE,JOHN	57,73,137	. MARGARET	42		
WHITEHEAD,CATHERINE	47	. MICHAEL	57,137	. MARY DELANEY	11		
WHITELAW,ALEXANDER	36,39	. TOBIAS	57,73,137	. MARY STUBBLEFIELD	37		
.	45	WILHOIT,EZEKIEL	46	. MILDRED	20		
. DAVID	38	MILDRED	46	. NANCY	41		
. DOUGLAS	30	WILKINSON,DANIEL	112	. NANCY ROGERS	12		
. ELIZABETH	26,39	WILLARD,CRYSTAL	91	. NANNY HARVEY	6		
. MARY DAVIS	38	WILLETT,DAVID	22	. POLLY	22		
. NANCY	30	POLLY BAUGHON	22	. RICHARD	12,20,24		
. POLLY	26	WILLIALMS,JOSEPH	44	. ROBERT	141-142,145		
. SARAH	45	MARY VATTERTON	44	. SALLY ROGERS	18		
. THOMAS	26	WILLIAM,ROBERT	77	. SALLY THOMPSON	23		
WHITEMAN,WILLIAM	57	WILLIAMS,DAVID	42	. SARAH	31		
WHITMAN,JOHN	145	. ELIZABETH	16,44,48	. SARAH BEAZLEY	20		
. WILLIAM	57,78,141	. ELIZABETH BRUCE	18	. SINCLAIR	43		
.	145-146	. ELIZABETH ROW	42	. THOMAS	57		
WHITNEY,GEORGE	139	. ELIZABETH RUMSEY	4,7	. WILLIAM	37,138,142		
WHITUN,JAMES	136	. FANNY	34	WILLIAMSON,JAMES C.	91		
WHLE,CHRISTOPHER	73	. FELIX	44	. MILLY BLEDSOE	19		
WHORTON,GEORGE	136,138	. FRANCES	43	. T.	141		
WHOTUN,GEORGE	139	. FRANCIS	6,18,40,137	. THOMAS	19		
WIAN,MILLY	47	. FRANKEY HAM	44	. WILLIAM	135		
WIATT,ELIZABETH	4	. HETTY ROW	38	WILLIBY,POLLY CHILES	39		

INDEX to
Orange County, VA FAMILIES - Vol. #2

Name	Page	Name	Page	Name	Page
TANDY	39	THOMAS	141	. RICHARD	64,79,138
WILLIS,	102,137-138,143	WILLSON, MARY	57	.	143-144
. ANN GARNETT	4,6	WILSON, ARCHIBALD	70,86	. SARAH	30
. CARRIE HUNTER	93	. CORA MAE	134	. VALENTINE	27
. COL.	135	. DANIEL	113	WISDOM, FANNY	13
. COLL	136	. ELIZABETH	57	. FRANCES	143
. CORNELIUS	138	. JACOB	154	. FRANCIS	78,140,145
. ELIZABETH	76	. JAMES	139	. FRANKIE	7
. ELIZABETH THOMAS	8	. JOHN	57,64	. JOHN	135,139,141,143
. FRANCIS	1,5	. MARGARET	113	.	145
. HENRY	64	. MARTHA	57	. JOSEPH	2
. JANE	44	. MARY	113,154-156	. LUCY	78
. JOHN	4,28,69,76	. MATHEW	57	. SARAH GARDENER	2
.	141-142,145-146	. RICHARD	57,143	WISDON, CLARY	1
. LARKIN	48	. ROBERT	26,86	WISE, JOHN	140
. LEWIS	10,64,146	. SARAH	57	WITHERALL, GEORGE	40
. LUCY	37	. WILLIAM	57	WITHERSPOON, JOHN	2,5
. MACERLEY	138	WIN, MINOR	139	MARY BOSTON	2,5
. MARY	71,76,83	WINDSOR, JAMES	158	WITHIS, WILLIAM	141
. MARY E.	42	LUCINDA	158	WITHROW, E.F.	158
. MARY GORDON	48	WINSLOW, ANN BEADLES	27	NANCY	158
. MOSES	8,64	. BENJAMIN	28,68,139,146	WOIRHAYE, FRANCIS	41
. NELLY	71	. BEVERLY	79,144	NANCY HANCOCK	41
. NELLY C. MADISON	28	. CATHERINE	27	WOLF, ELIZABETH	23
. PEGGY	1	. EDWARD	42	. L.	23
. REUBEN	4,6	. ELIZABETH	42	. LEONARD	18
. SALLY THOMAS	4	. FERTUNATUN	30	. POLLY	18
. WILLIAM	142	. FORTUNATUS	41	WOLFENBURGER, HANNAH	4
. WILLIAM C.	37,44	. FRANCES	41	WOLFENGERGER, HANNAH	7
WILLOUGHBY,		. KENWOOD	137	WOLLS, STOVEN	138
. LUCY STEPHENS	49	. LUCY A. LONG	47	WOLS, GEORGE	138-139
. WILLIAM	49	. MARTHA	28	JOHN	139
WILLS, GEORGE	136	. MOSES	47	WOMACK, SARAH	160

INDEX to
Orange County, VA FAMILIES - Vol. #2

Name	Pages	Name	Pages	Name	Pages
WONNELL, MARK	135	. MARY WEATHERSPOON	7	. SUSANNA	7
WOOD, ALLEY	23	. MILDRED AUSTIN	47	. TABITHA COX	30
. ANN	9	. NANCY	12,16,22,34	WOODWARD, LUCY	14
. ANN MILLS	42	. NANCY ESTES	39	WOOFNOL, LENARD	139
. ELLEN	28	. NANCY KEY	30	WOOLFOLK, AMERICA	125
. ELLIOT	3,5	. NANCY PEGO	30	. ANN AHRRIS	125
. GEORGE	137	. NELLY	37,123	. ANN GEORGE	124-125
. HARRY	143	. NICHOLAS L.	30	. ANNE	126
. HENRY	7,18,25,42,142	. PEGGY CLARK	37	. AUGUSTINE	4,6,125
.	145	. REBECCA PORTER	16	. BETTY	124
. HERR.	141	. RICHARD	24	. CATHERINE BENSON	124
. HEZEKIAH	25	. SALLY	19,24	. CHRISTIAN	124
. HOPEFUL	23	. SALLY BRADLEY	25	. CHRISTIAN BIBB	89,125
. HOPEWELL	16	. SALLY RHODES	122	. CLARISSA ELLIS	41
. JAMES	26,30,42,57,64	. SARAH WHITE	30	. ELEANOR	12
.	81	. SUSAN ESTES	35	. ELIZ. WIGGLESWORTH	124
. JANE	122	. SUSANNAH	4	. ELIZABETH	4,7,124
. JENNY MAHONEY	122	. THOMAS	16,57,122,137	. ELLIS	126
. JESSE	30	.	140	. FANNY	126
. JIM	122	. WILLIAM	47,122,136	. FENDALL	126
. JOHN	141-142,145-146	.	138-139	. FRANCES	17,124
. JOHN SCOTT	72,82	. WILLIAM BELL	72,82	. FRANCES THOMPSON	126
. JOHN WESLY	122	. WILLY TERMAN	16	. FRANKIE THOMAS	6
. JOSEPH	8,64,72,82,86	. ZACHARIAH	16,37	. FRANKY THOMAS	4
. KATIE	19	. ZACHARIAS	39	. JOHN	125-126
. LEVI	35	WOODALL, DELILA J.	114	. JOHN H.	125
. LUCINDA	26	WOODFORD, CATHERINE	73	. JOSEPH	7,89,124-126
. MARGARET	44,72,82	. DANIEL	73,83	.	136,142-144,146
. MARGARET BELL	8	. FREDERICH	83	. JOSEPH HARRIS	125
. MARION MAY	122	. FREDERICK	73,83	. JUSTINE	125
. MARY	27,43,50	WOODHEAD, LETTISA MAYO	46	. LUCY	126
. MARY CONNER	3,5	WILLIAM	46	. MARGARET	125
. MARY MILLER	72,82	WOODS, RICHARD	30	. MARIAH MITCHUM	125

INDEX to
Orange County, VA FAMILIES - Vol. #2

. MARY	92,124-125	. MARY BURTIS	73	. ISAAC	38
. MARY C.	40	. ROBERT	73-74	. JAMES	73,75,83
. MARY COLEMAN	124	. SAMUEL	73-74	. JOHN	8-9,13,20,24,30
. MARY HACKETT	125	. SARAH	74	.	64,83,86,143-146
. MARY HARRIS	125	WRAY,HELEN	165	. JOHN J.	30
. MARY STANNARD	126	WREN,EDWARD	44	. LARKIN	22
. NANCY	69,83,126	. ELIZABETH	110	. LUCH FAULCONER	46
. PATSY	12,126	. ESTHER LOYD	43	. LUCH PEACHER	44
. RICHARD	89,124-125,142	. FRANCIS	110,112	. LUCY	4,7,16
.	144,146	. GEORGE GAYDEN	110,112	. LUCY JAMES	22
. ROBERT	124-125,141	. JOHN	43,110	. MALINDA BOSTON	40
. SALLIE BARNUM	125	. LUCY LLOYD	44	. MARGARET JONES	9
. SARAH BARTLOW	124	. REBECCA GAYDEN	110	. MARY	15,17,41
. SARAH TAYLOR	125	WRENN,		. MARY LINDSAY	22
. SOWEL	125	REBECCAH GAYDEN	110	. MISHEL	34
. SOWELL	124	WRIGHT,AGNES SMITH	38	. NANCY	30,43
. SOYELL	124	. ALEXANDER	31,40,44	. NANCY WRIGHT	30
. SUKEY	124	. ANN HERNDON	16	. POLLY	43
. SUSAN	36	. AUGUSTINE	22	. POLLY SHAVERS	24
. SUSAN WOOLFOLK	36	. BENJAMIN	16,18,35,46	. RACHEL PERRY	12
. THOMAS	12,17,36,40	. BETSY JONES	31	. RICHARD	139
.	125-126	. BLEDSOE	15	. ROBERT	46
. THOMAS WALLER	125	. CATY FAULCONER	24	. SALLY	31,35
. WILLIAM	36,41,125-126	. DABNEY	34	. SALLY BELL/	34
WOOLFRAY,		. EDWARD	11	. SAMUEL	139
. ELIZ. BATTAILE	45	. ELEANOR	37	. SARAH	73,83
. RICHARD	45	. ELIJAH	31	. SARAH BEASLEY	15
WORMLEY,		. ELIZA QUISENBERRY	46	. SUSAN	37,42
. JOHN	143	. ELIZABETH	2,5,8,32	. SUSANNA	5
. REBECCA	141	. ELIZABETH SEBREE	20	. SUSANNA GRASTY	13
WORTHINGTON,JACOB	47	. FRANCES	11,23	. SUSANNAH	2
. MARTHA	73	. FRANKEY POWELL	11	. THOMAS	139,146
. MARY	73-74	. GEORGE B.	16	. WILLIAM	12,23,32,37,41
	73				

278

INDEX to
Orange County, VA FAMILIES - Vol. #2

Name	Page
.	47,64,79
WYATT,	
. ELIZABETH BAUGKER	43
. JOHN	43
. SUKEY EDMONSON	1
. THOMAS	1
WYNE, JOHN	26
. RACHEL AHART	26
. RACHEL EHART	26
YAGER, ADAM	135
. BETTY	27,32
. FANNY CAUTHORN	40
. JANE CHANCELLOR	32
. RICHARD	135
. THOMAS	40
. WILLIAM	32
YANCY, BETSY LOYD	34
. CATHERINE	41
. CHARLES	34
. LATON	45
. LURINA MOYERS	45
. STEPHEN	41
YARBOROUGH, JOSHUA	136
YARBROUGH, JOSHUA	135
RICHARD	64,135
YATES, BETSY LOYD	34
. CHARLES	34,78
. FRANCIS	31
. JAMES	22
. MARY	18
. SALLY SANFORD	22
YEAGER, ADAM	140
NICHOLAS	140
YEATS, THOMAS	139
YORK, ARMISTEAD	24
. ARMSTEAD	24
. JENNY	24
. JOANNA HILMAN	24
YOUNG, AGNES	57
. BERNICE HARVEY	103
. CATHERINE MARTIN	23
. DANIEL	36
. EDWIN	11
. ELIZABETH RHOADES	36
. EMILY	158
. FRANCES WRIGHT	11
. FRANKEY GRADY	18
. JAMES	57
. JOHN	12,18,27,57
. LAWRENCE	23,125
.	144-145
. LUCY	88
. MAY REYNOLDS	27
. MILDRED DOUGLASS	8
. NANCY	9
. ROBERT	57
. SALLY	14
. SAMUEL	57
. SARAH ROGERS	12
. VERNON	103
. WILLIAM	8
YOWELL, EPHRAIM	36
. JANE DAVIS	37
. JOHN	37,136
. JONATHAN	136
. POLLY EDDINS	36
ZACHARY, BEN	3
. BENJAMIN	6
. DAVID	135
. FRANKEY WHITE	3
. FRANKIE WHITE	6
. THOMAS	135
ZACKARY, JOHN	135
ZACKRY, JOHN	140
THOMAS	140
ZIMERMAN, JOHN	73
ZIMMERMAN, CHRISTOPHER	64
.	76,87,139
. JOHN	57,73,137
. REUBEN	81
ZIMMIMAN, REUBEN	72
ZIMMINAN, CHRISTOPHER	87
ZINNERMAN, JOHN	57

www.ingramcontent.com/pod-product-compliance
Lightning Source LLC
Chambersburg PA
CBHW031410290426
44110CB00011B/326